THE INTERFACE BETWEEN COMPETITION AND THE INTERNAL MARKET

This book explores the interface between competition law and market integration in the application of Article 102 of the Treaty on the Functioning of the European Union (TFEU), focusing on the notion of 'market separation'—namely conduct that may hinder cross-border trade. The discussion reviews, among other things, the treatment of geographic price discrimination and exclusionary abuse, by which out-of-state competitors are affected.

'Market separation' cases are treated in the book as a case study for appraising the interface between competition and the Internal Market. On this basis, the book provides a comparative analysis of the Treaty requirements under Article 102 TFEU when applied in 'market separation' cases and the Treaty requirements under the free movement provisions. In addition, it utilises 'market separation' cases as a springboard for advancing an informed reformulation of the application of Article 102 TFEU when state action comes into play.

All in all, the analysis presented in the book deconstructs the elements for establishing 'market separation' as an abuse of the dominant position. It shows that there is nothing that would justify a distinctive treatment of 'market separation' under Article 102 TFEU, other than a principled understanding of Internal Market law as a whole: whatever understanding one reaches about the proper shape of the Internal Market, interrogation of the proper application of competition law comes after that and thus should be informed by this understanding.

Volume 9 in the series Hart Studies in Competition Law

Hart Studies in Competition Law

Volume 1: *Intellectual Property, Antitrust and Cumulative Innovation in the EU and the US*
Thorsten Käseberg

Volume 2: *State Aid and the European Economic Constitution*
Francesco de Cecco

Volume 3: *The Private Enforcement of Competition Law in Ireland*
David McFadden

Volume 4: *Cross-Border EU Competition Law Actions*
Edited by Mihail Danov, Florian Becker and Paul Beaumont

Volume 5: *European Merger Remedies: Law and Policy*
Dorte Hoeg

Volume 6: *Sanctions in EU Competition Law: Principles and Practice*
Michael Frese

Volume 7: *Fairness in Antitrust: Protecting the Strong from the Weak*
Adi Ayal

Volume 8: *Media Ownership and Control: Law, Economics and Policy in an Indian and International Context*
Suzanne Rab and Alison Sprague

The Interface between Competition and the Internal Market

Market Separation under Article 102 TFEU

Vasiliki Brisimi

•HART•
PUBLISHING
OXFORD AND PORTLAND, OREGON
2016

Published in the United Kingdom by Hart Publishing Ltd
16C Worcester Place, Oxford, OX1 2JW
Telephone: +44 (0)1865 517530
Fax: +44 (0)1865 510710
E-mail: mail@hartpub.co.uk
Website: http://www.hartpub.co.uk

Published in North America (US and Canada) by
Hart Publishing
c/o International Specialized Book Services
920 NE 58th Avenue, Suite 300
Portland, OR 97213-3786
USA
Tel: +1 503 287 3093 or toll-free: (1) 800 944 6190
Fax: +1 503 280 8832
E-mail: orders@isbs.com
Website: http://www.isbs.com

First published in hardback 2014
Paperback edition, 2016

Hart Publishing is an imprint of Bloomsbury Publishing plc.

British Library Cataloguing in Publication Data
Data Available

ISBN: HB: 978-1-84946-569-4
PB: 978-1-50990-927-8

Typeset by Hope Services, Abingdon
Printed and bound in Great Britain by
Lightning Source UK Ltd

Acknowledgments

This book is based on research conducted at the University of Oxford from 2008 to 2012, culminating in my DPhil thesis which was defended in November 2012. There are several people to whom I owe gratitude and without whose support this work would have never taken shape.

First and foremost, I would like to thank my two supervisors, Ariel Ezrachi and Katja Ziegler, for their continuous support and guidance, for trusting me and giving me the space to develop my ideas and analytical skills, while at the same time opening up my perspective on methodology, enhancing the academic and presentation skills which I was lacking and providing me with inspiration and valuable suggestions to further develop, build academic confidence, and progress. Working and cooperating with them has been a great pleasure and a source of valuable influence that is considerably adding to my post-DPhil life.

I am grateful to Stephen Weatherill, who has read and examined the thesis at all stages, from the Qualifying Test when the material presented was only potentially yielding the desired outcome, to the greater academic maturity of the Confirmation of DPhil Status and the final Viva examination. His genuine academic interest, his ability to appreciate academic diversity and his constructive criticism have all notably influenced my work presented in this book.

I am also deeply thankful to Angus Johnston and Alison Jones, who have, together with Stephen Weatherill, examined the thesis at the Confirmation of DPhil Status and the final Viva examination, respectively. Their suggestions and feedback have been a valuable source of inspiration, reflected in this book. During the process of developing the ideas presented in this book, many people have also contributed with constructive discussion in their area of expertise or provided me with the opportunity to present my ideas in public and discuss them, especially Graeme Dinwoodie, Dorota Leczykiewicz, Jukka Snell, Barry Rodger, Oke Odudu and Ioannis Lianos, to all of whom I am grateful.

I have no words to thank the three people who, as well as being excellent competition law colleagues at Oxford and the Centre for Competition Law and Policy, have been the closest of friends and shared all my good and bad DPhil moments: Maria Ioannidou, my office mate at the legendary Carrel XXI of the Bodleian Law Library, Julian Nowag and Pablo Marquez. Their intellectual encouragement, patience and support during our 'fun times' at the Bodleian Law Library, the 'monokatikia', in Oxford and overseas, will always be remembered with gratitude and love.

This research could not have been concluded without the financial support of the Leventis Foundation and the Hellenic State Scholarships Foundation, without the help of all the staff at the Bodleian Law Library, as well as the support of Geraldine Malloy from the Law Faculty of the University of Oxford, Dr Nakamura, Dionysia Makrynori and Maureen Freed, at times when my determination for embarking on this research project was challenged. The keen editing and proofreading skills of Natalia Wise, Anne Hinton and Alison Morley at all stages in the publication of this book are very much appreciated, as well as the help of the people at Hart Publishing, and in particular Rachel Turner. Special thanks go to Richard Hart, who has given me the opportunity to publish my work and thus make it accessible to a wide audience. The support of my new colleagues at Koutalidis Law Firm has also been very important in the final months of preparing this book for publication—in particular Stamatis Drakakakis and Katia Protopapa, who have warmly welcomed my intellectual aspirations.

The encouragement and support of my friends has been tremendous throughout the DPhil years. I would like to mention in particular the Oxford Greek gang: Vanessa T, Antonis K, Michalis R, Katerina V, Pantelis A and Eliza K; the Oxford DPhil gang: Ghada F, Eric S, Sanja B, Daniela S and Lema U; my friends from home: Zoe T, Evdokia P, Anastasia S, Athina T and Ellianna N; as well as the 2007–2008 MJur crew and the Hilda 'beasts' for providing me with a reason to travel around the world during these years. A special mention is owed to the memory of Sebastien Grifnie, a great competition law colleague at Oxford in my MJur year and a special friend, who left us too soon and who will always be remembered.

My deepest gratitude goes to my family. To my younger sister, Theodora, for her unconditional support, care and love and to my parents, Sophocles and Dimitra Brissimis, for their lifelong commitment to education, for setting an exceptional example for me to follow and conveying all the critical values that shaped my personality, for their unconditional trust and support throughout these years. To them this book is dedicated.

Contents

Table of Cases

Commission Decisions

Court of Justice of the European Union (formerly European Court of Justice)

Alphabetical

Numerical

General Court (EU) (formerly Court of First Instance (CFI)

Alphabetical

Numerical

Greece

United Kingdom

Competition Appeal Tribunal

United States of America

Table of Legislation

European Union

Directives

Regulations

France

Italy

United Kingdom

Statutory Instruments

Table of Conventions

Introduction

I. THE INTERFACE BETWEEN COMPETITION AND THE INTERNAL MARKET: MARKET SEPARATION UNDER ARTICLE 102 TFEU

It is widely assumed in the academic literature that the distinctive characteristic of European Union (EU) competition law is the correlation between competition and market integration.[1] This has been fuelled, since the inception of what is now the EU, by the clause on 'a system ensuring that competition in the Internal Market is not distorted',[2] as well as by the enforcement of the competition law provisions against conduct that has essentially the same effect as *inter*-state trade barriers, prohibited under the free movement provisions.[3]

While one may have expected that the progressive achievement of the Internal Market might render competition law enforcement more independent and less motivated by market integration considerations,[4] recent case law and the changes introduced by the Lisbon Treaty show a revival of market integration considerations under the competition law provisions, in particular Article 102 of the Treaty on the Functioning of the European Union (TFEU).[5] These trends are interesting and raise questions as to whether there still is a legitimate role for market integration under the application of EU competition law provisions and, conversely, whether these provisions are used legitimately as an instrument for

[1] Virtually all EU competition law textbooks consider market integration as an additional, stand-alone objective of EU competition law, which may conflict with other objectives under certain circumstances.

[2] Article 3(1)(g) of the Treaty establishing the European Community (TEC). The Article has been repealed by virtue of the Lisbon Treaty and replaced by Protocol No 27 TFEU.

[3] This was particularly the case in regard to Article 101 TFEU enforcement against the exercise of vertical market power, as in the distribution agreements providing for absolute territorial protection across national lines; see, eg, the seminal Joined Cases 56 and 58/64 *Établissements Consten SàRL. and Grundig-Verkaufs-GmbH v Commission* [1966] ECR 299.

[4] A Albors-Llorens, 'Competition Policy and the Shaping of the Single Market' in C Barnard and J Scott (eds), *The Law of the Single European Market: Unpacking the Premises* (Hart Publishing, 2002) 328–31.

[5] See, eg, L Parret, 'The Multiple Personalities of EU Competition Law: Time for a Comprehensive Debate on its Objectives' in D Zimmer (ed), *The Goals of Competition Law* (Edward Elgar, 2010) 82 on the objectives of EU competition law *post*-Lisbon. In addition, conduct that hinders *inter*-state trade has been added as a 'new' category of abuse of the dominant position in the latest (2011) edition of a leading EU competition law textbook; see A Jones and B Sufrin, *EU Competition Law: Texts, Cases and Materials* (4th edn, Oxford University Press, 2011) 550.

the building and the proper functioning of the Internal Market. The present book seeks to explore and analyse these fundamental questions, which define the very identity of the system of EU competition law.

In so doing, the emphasis of the research is placed on the enforcement of Article 102 TFEU against 'market separation',[6] namely conduct which has the intent or effect of hindering *inter*-Member State trade, either in the form of geographic price discrimination or in the form of exclusionary abuses, by which out-of-state competitors are affected. Therefore, this book forms part of the academic literature on Article 102 TFEU, which has grown since the Commission launched the process of reforming Article 102 TFEU at a policy level.[7] Over the past four years, five monographs have been published on Article 102 TFEU, each focusing on a different aspect of the application of Article 102 TFEU; however, none of these monographs singles out the interface between competition and the Internal Market.[8] By addressing the fundamental question of the role of market integration in the application of Article 102 TFEU, this book also seeks to make a contribution to the debate surrounding the EU regulation of unilateral anti-competitive conduct.

II. METHODOLOGICAL REMARKS ON THE ANALYSIS OF 'MARKET SEPARATION UNDER ARTICLE 102 TFEU'

The purpose of this book is to discern and rationalise the principles governing the interface between Article 102 TFEU and the allegedly distinctive objective of EU competition law, ie, market integration. A viable methodology and structure for conducting this research was identified as a result of three preliminary steps. First, the factual scenarios within the compass of market separation cases under Article 102

[6] See Case C-145/88 *Torfaen Borough Council v B & Q plc* [1989] ECR 3851, Opinion of AG Van Gerven [22] (in comparing the free movement and the competition law provisions of the TFEU): 'For that purpose they prohibit (inter alia) [conducts] which are responsible in trade between Member States for partitioning the [European] market into separate national markets.'

[7] The Commission initiative culminated in Commission (EC), 'Guidance on Commission's Enforcement Priorities in Applying Article 82 of the EC Treaty to Abusive Exclusionary Conduct by Dominant Undertaking' [2009] OJ C45/7.

[8] E Rousseva, *Rethinking Exclusionary Abuses in EU Competition Law: Rethinking Article 82 of the EC Treaty* (Hart Publishing, 2010) focuses on the distinction between agreements and unilateral conduct; E Østerud, *Identifying Exclusionary Abuses by Dominant Undertakings under EU Competition Law: The Spectrum of Tests* (Kluwer Law International, 2010) singles out the categorisation of the conduct as the basis for a spectrum of conduct-specific tests for exclusionary abuses; L Gormsen, *A Principled Approach to Abuse of Dominance in European Competition Law* (Cambridge University Press, 2010) focuses on the distinction between economic freedom and economic efficiency in regard to the aims of Article 102 TFEU; R Nazzini, *The Foundations of European Union Competition Law: The Objective and Principle of Article 102* (Oxford University Press, 2011) argues in favour of long-term social welfare, and not consumer welfare, as the objective of Article 102 TFEU; P Akman, *The Concept of Abuse in EU Competition Law: Law and Economic Approaches* (Hart Publishing, 2012) argues against the distinction between exclusionary and exploitative abuses.

TFEU were identified. Second, a comparative method for evaluating market separation cases under Article 102 TFEU was adopted, based on the definition of the Internal Market by reference to the Treaty free movement provisions in Article 26(2) TFEU. Third, it has been explored whether the type of competition law enforcement proceedings, public or private, is significant for the evaluation of market separation cases under Article 102 TFEU. These three elements shaped the structure and influenced the arguments presented in the book.

A. Factual Scenarios within the Compass of Market Separation Cases under Article 102 TFEU

This work is inspired by new factual scenarios, which reflect the economic reality at the Member State level in relation to state intervention in the market and which led to two specific market separation cases under Article 102 TFEU: *Deutsche Telekom* and *Sotirios Lelos*.[9] In both cases there is prior state regulation in the public interest, which is alleged to have contributed to the anti-competitive effect. However, this is the first time that the factual scenarios involved do not fit into the traditionally used formula for addressing state intervention in the context of Article 102 TFEU enforcement proceedings, that is, Article 106(1) TFEU. Both Deutsche Telekom and Glaxo, the incumbents involved, are unequivocally 'undertakings', which are not 'granted special or exclusive rights' by the state. In *Deutsche Telekom* the incumbent undertaking was a former state-owned monopoly, but at the material time the sector was fully liberalised. In *Sotirios Lelos*, the market power of Glaxo had not been granted by the state, but was achieved in the market. In addition, the prior state conduct was, technically, distinct from the undertaking's conduct, even though they both had an effect on the profit margins of the undertaking. For example, in *Sotirios Lelos*, the relevant state conduct was price regulation, whereas Article 102 TFEU enforcement proceedings were initiated for quantity restrictions on the part of Glaxo.

These factual scenarios have a twofold effect in regard to the interface between competition and the Internal Market. First, state intervention cannot be assessed under the typical formula of Article 106(1) TFEU in conjunction with Article 102 TFEU, precisely because there are no 'undertakings granted special or exclusive rights'. Therefore, these factual instances form a new category of 'gap' cases, which require recourse to the indirect construction of the state action doctrine (Article 4(3) Treaty on European Union-Lisbon (TEU-L)) in regard to Article 102 TFEU for the first time (see chapter five, section III). Second, it becomes apparent, for the first time, that the dominant undertakings cannot, procedurally, bring the

[9] Case C-280/08 P *Deutsche Telekom v Commission* [2010] ECR I-09555; Joined Cases C-468/06–C-478/06 *Sot Lélos kai Sia EE and others v GlaxoSmithKline AEVE Farmakeftikon Proïonton, formerly Glaxowellcome AEVE* [2008] ECR I-7139.

question of state responsibility before the European courts once Article 102 TFEU enforcement proceedings are initiated. Neither the concept of 'undertaking' nor the 'state action defence' as currently construed is an adequate and operable filter to accommodate assessment of the state action in the factual scenarios mentioned above. This is because the state conduct is a reason, but not the only reason, for the private 'autonomous conduct' of the type prohibited under Article 102 TFEU (see chapter five, sections II.A and IV).

It is important to note that market separation cases under Article 102 TFEU not only comprise cases in which non-economic values and therefore state action come into play. The majority of market separation cases merely involve conduct by dominant undertakings, which has the intent or effect of hindering *inter*-Member State trade, namely geographic price discrimination or exclusionary abuses that affect out-of-state competitors (see chapter two, section II and chapter three, section IV). Nevertheless, conduct which, by its very nature, has a cross-border element is not treated as a market separation case in this work. For example, the provision of roaming services or the provision of clearing and settlement services to an International Central Securities Depository are acts which inherently involve a cross-border movement.[10] In these factual scenarios, the cross-border element stems from the very nature of the service involved rather than the undertaking's conduct and, for that reason, they are not treated as market separation cases.[11]

B. Definition of the Internal Market

The methodology employed in this work is based on a comparative analysis of the Treaty requirements under Article 102 TFEU in market separation cases with the Treaty requirements under the free movement provisions. The comparison takes place as between the objectives (see chapter one), the addressees (see chapter two) and the material scope of the prohibitions contained in the two sets of provisions (see chapters three, four, five and six).

The definition of 'Internal Market' provided for in Article 26(2) TFEU is the reason for adopting this method of evaluation of the market separation cases under Article 102 TFEU. According to Article 26(2) TFEU, the Internal Market

[10] See, eg, Case C-58/08 *Vodafone Ltd and others v Secretary of State for Business, Enterprise and Regulatory Reform* [2010] ECR I-4999; Case T-301/04 *Clearstream Banking AG and Clearstream International SA v Commission* [2009] ECR II-3155.

[11] In these cases, the 'effect on trade requirement' should always be established. However, this is all, in terms of the application of the competition law provisions. Under the free movement provisions, precisely because the test for 'internal situations' and the substantive test for finding a restriction are conflated (see ch 1, section IV.B), it could be argued that these acts fall within the scope of the prohibitions. For example, this seems to be the premise of the Opinion of AG Maduro in relation to the Roaming Regulation (see ch 2, text to n 86).

is defined by reference to the provisions of the free movement. Therefore, it is legitimate to compare and draw analogies between the tests under the free movement provisions and the tests under Article 102 TFEU if the purpose is to rationalise the weight that is being applied to market integration for establishing an abuse of the dominant position.

In addition, convergence between the free movement provisions is assumed, in particular in regard to the conceptual foundations of finding a prohibition (see chapter three, section III) and a justification (see chapter IV, section II.A). Article 26 TFEU incorporates the four freedoms in the definition of the Internal Market and therefore reflects convergence from the perspective of their common aim, namely the construction of the Internal Market. In the detailed analysis presented in this work, emphasis is nevertheless put on the free movement of goods out of all the free movement provisions.

Goods and services are the most relevant economic factors for the present research because the market separation cases under Article 102 TFEU have exclusively been about either goods or services.[12] However, priority is given to the case law under the free movement of goods, specifically in the examination of the test which governs the finding of a trade barrier, namely a discrimination or a market access test, based on judgments concerning the rules on the use of goods (see chapter three, section III.B). The reason for this is that the case law on goods has always lagged behind in terms of shifting from a discrimination analysis to a unified market access test, which may be explained pragmatically by the nature of the contested measures. Measures affecting the provision of services almost always have a direct impact on consumers. In other words, they are equivalent to rules regulating the use of goods, which only recently reached the Court of Justice because there were many more rules concerning prior-to-use stages, such as production and marketing, to be litigated.

C. The Significance of the Type of Enforcement Proceedings: Public and Private Enforcement of Article 102 TFEU

The type of the Article 102 TFEU enforcement proceedings—public or private—is significant for the purpose of conducting the comparative analysis between the case law under Article 102 TFEU and under the free movement provisions, for two reasons.

[12] Indeed, goods and services are also close to each other, viewed from the perspective of the economic function which they perform. See, eg, Case C-390/99 *Canal Satélite Digital SL v Adminstración General del Estado, and Distribuidora de Televisión Digital SA (DTS)* [2002] ECR I-607 [29]–[33], in which the Court decided the case simultaneously in light of both freedoms. See also Joined Cases C-403/08 and C-429/08 *Football Association Premier League and others v QC Leisure and others and Karen Murphy v Media Protection Services Ltd* [2011] ECR I-09083, Opinion of AG Kokott [168]–[170].

First, the type of competition law enforcement proceedings affects the substantive standard of legality under the relevant competition law provisions, for example, the test for an abuse of the dominant position, because of the wide discretion in regard to case selection and prioritisation, which is involved in the public enforcement of competition law. In particular, the broad discretion of the Commission and the National Competition Authorities (NCAs) in regard to the cases which they decide to investigate is associated with the non-enforcement of competition prohibitions which could be over-inclusive.[13] Conversely, private litigation requires the substantive test under the competition law provisions to be clearly circumscribed in order to avoid sham litigation or over-deterrence. This is why the decentralisation of the enforcement regime and the introduction of private enforcement of competition law in Europe were launched hand in hand with the reorientation of the application of competition law towards a more economics-based approach.[14]

The link between the type of enforcement proceedings and the substantive standard under Article 102 TFEU presents a limitation to the appraisal of the existing case law under Article 102 TFEU, which is the main primary material for the present research. The majority of the existing cases originate in public enforcement proceedings, and it is expected that the Commission should only pursue cases of outright abuse. However, the very few existing preliminary references, which originate in private litigation at the national level, are useful comparators in regard to economic justifications or public policy considerations under Article 102 TFEU (see chapter three, text to nn 20–21, and chapter four, text to nn 68–69), for example. At the same time, this link between the type of enforcement proceedings and the substantive standard under Article 102 TFEU also legitimises the present work, which seeks to provide clarity and consistency by advancing a unitary framework for taking into consideration market integration under Article 102 TFEU. The possibility of private enforcement of Article 102 TFEU at the national level highlights the need for such analytical clarity.

Second, the decentralised and private enforcement of the competition law provisions before national courts means that there is no longer any asymmetry in the type of enforcement between the competition law and the free movement provisions. The free movement provisions have always been considered to grant individual rights enforceable before national courts. There is now a 'market' for law enforcement in regard to competition law, in addition to the free movement provisions, open to be tested by often ingenious private litigants. In light of this, the present

[13] See W Wils, 'Discretion and Prioritisation in Public Antitrust Enforcement, in Particular EU Antitrust Enforcement' (2011) 34 *World Competition Law and Economics Review* 353–82.

[14] Also, it is noteworthy that the Commission Guidance Paper on the reorientation of the application of Article 102 TFEU to a more economics-based approach is entitled Commission (EC), 'Guidance on Commission's *Enforcement Priorities* in Applying Article 82 of the EC Treaty to Abusive Exclusionary Conduct by Dominant Undertaking' [2009] OJ C45/7 (emphasis added).

research associates the two questions of private and state responsibility under the two sets of provisions, once the market players themselves have decided, in terms of procedure, that they are willing to bear the costs of litigating competition law. Furthermore, the proposed interface between private and state responsibility would eliminate artificial obstacles to the process of case selection suitable for public enforcement of Article 102 TFEU inasmuch as it involves the obligation of the Commission or the NCA to disapply Article 102 TFEU under certain circumstances (see chapter six, section II.C). This feeds back to the link between the type of enforcement and the substantive standard under Article 102 TFEU, because the Commission would not take up a case which has a viable defence. The present work establishes that such a defence can, in effect, be a defence based on state responsibility under the free movement provisions.

III. SUMMARY OF THE CHAPTERS OF THIS BOOK

The book is presented in six chapters. In chapter one it is argued that, historically, market integration was not a stand-alone objective of Article 102 TFEU, but, rather, that it served as the interpretative lens through which the objectives of Article 102 TFEU were viewed. This historical link between the objectives of Article 102 TFEU and market integration is legitimately echoed in the current interpretation of the jurisdictional requirement of 'effect on trade' under Article 102 TFEU. Once it is established that the conduct of the dominant undertaking 'affects trade between Member States', the assessment of its effects on competition is placed under the European rather than the national market regulatory framework. Research in the following chapters focuses on the scope of 'abuse of a dominant position', and an attempt is made to explain the extent to which market integration should affect the substantive analysis for finding an 'abuse of a dominant position'.

Chapter two suggests that Article 102 TFEU, with its distinct conditions of application and, in particular, the requirement that the undertakings possess significant market power, is the outer limit to any expansive view of the horizontal application of the freedoms. This assumes the functional definition of the notion of 'undertaking'. Accordingly, it is argued that alleged market separation by dominant undertakings should only be subjected to Article 102 TFEU rather than to both Article 102 TFEU and the free movement provisions. The analysis progresses to examine how this assessment is to be conducted under Article 102 TFEU and what weight is to be applied to economic and non-economic values, which underpin the Internal Market, for substantiating an abuse of the dominant position.

In chapter three it is argued that, in the vast majority of cases, there is no conflict between competition, as reflected in the notion of market separation as an abuse of the dominant position, and market integration, as reflected in the notion of trade barriers. A fortiori, the relocation of the clause on a 'system of undistorted competition within the Internal Market' to Protocol No 27 TFEU would permit the inherent limitations of economic integration to be taken into account under Article 102 TFEU.

When non-economic values underpinning the notion of 'justified trade barriers' come into play under Article 102 TFEU enforcement proceedings, there is always the potential for state involvement to occur, triggered in part by conduct by the dominant undertakings as part of the democratic processes. This is explained in chapter four. On this basis, it is argued that public policy considerations should be excluded from the scope of Article 102 TFEU at the outset. Therefore, the interface between market separation, as an 'abuse of a dominant position', and non-economic values, as reflected in the notion of justified trade barriers, is better understood as a question of shared responsibility of, or as a question of attribution to, the undertaking and/or the state. The subsequent chapters address this question by seeking to identify criteria for a principled attribution of the market-distorting effect to the undertaking and/or the state in cases of shared responsibility for market separation.

In effect, the state action defence is presented in chapter five, because it is the closest concept for articulating attribution criteria used by the European courts. However, it is argued that there is a structural imbalance between state responsibility under the competition law provisions ('state action doctrine'—Article 4(3) TEU-L in conjunction with Article 102 TFEU) and the dominant undertaking's responsibility for market separation. This is why the state action defence has never succeeded. The state action defence requires compulsion by the undertaking, regardless of the legality of the state action, whereas the state action doctrine requires that private responsibility under Article 102 TFEU ('autonomous conduct that constitutes an abuse of the dominant position') is a reason for the anti-competitive effect of the state action. This leads to biased outcomes against the dominant undertaking, because the undertaking has, procedurally, no other legal route to bring the question of state action legality before the European courts.

In chapter six, a revision of the state action defence is proposed in order to incorporate the assessment of the legality of state action in cases of shared responsibility for market separation between the dominant undertaking and the state, in the context of Article 102 TFEU enforcement proceedings against the undertaking. In practice, the proposed revision would lead to an assessment of the state action under the free movement provisions as a subordinate issue, at the stage of geographic market definition and, in particular, of regulatory entry barriers. Article 102 TFEU would be applied against the dominant undertaking only if the regulatory framework were in conformity with the free movement provisions, by extending the geographic market involved beyond national lines. At the constitutional level, the proposed revision is reflected in the relocation of the clause on a 'system of undistorted competition within the Internal Market' to Protocol No 27 TFEU.

1

Objectives of Article 102 TFEU and Market Integration: From a Historical Analysis to the Current Jurisdictional Approach

I. INTRODUCTION

This chapter explores, from a historical perspective, the spectrum of values underlying Article 102 TFEU as well as their relationship to market integration. It aims to identify the patterns of correlation between competition and integration. On that basis, it provides arguments as to why these patterns cannot be ignored in a future attempt to redefine the hierarchy of values promoted and protected under Article 102 TFEU, whether or not it is desirable to change them at a policy and normative level.

In section II, the two objectives of EU regulation of anti-competitive unilateral conduct (Article 102 TFEU), namely efficiency and economic freedom, are presented, both of which involve trade-offs between the various categories of protected consumers. In section III, these two objectives are linked to EU trade liberalisation by exploring the prevailing assumptions at the initial stage of the European integration project as to the relationship between competition and the Single (or Internal) Market. Therefore, the historical inquiry in this section covers, chronologically, the developments up until the enactment of the Single European Act (SEA) in 1987,[1] in light of the 1992 project to 'create an area without internal

[1] Single European Act (SEA) [1987] OJ L169/1. Weiler's three-period evolution of EU law, which involves the foundational period (1958–73), the 'Eurosclerosis' period (1973–85) and the period of the completion of the Internal Market (1985 and beyond), is well established in the literature. See J Weiler, 'The Transformation of Europe' (1990–91) 100 *Yale Law Journal* 2403; D Gerber, *Law and Competition in the Twentieth Century Europe: Protecting Prometheus* (Oxford University Press, 2001) 346 et seq; R Wesseling, *The Modernisation of EC Antitrust Law* (Hart Publishing, 2000) 9; I Maher, 'Competition Law Modernization: An Evolutionary Tale?' in P Craig and G De Búrca (eds), *The Evolution of EU Law* (2nd edn, Oxford University Press, 2011) 725–27.

frontiers'.[2] The vehicle through which the link between the objectives of Article 102 TFEU and market integration has been achieved is the teleological interpretation of the notion of 'abuse of a dominant position'. In section IV, it is argued that the historical link between competition and market integration cannot be conclusive as regards the use of Article 102 TFEU as an instrument to foster market integration almost 50 years after the original Treaty. However, the link still influences the interpretation of Article 102 TFEU because it is expressly echoed in the requirement of 'effect on trade'. The function of this requirement is a jurisdictional one and, as such, it represents the minimum legitimate role for market integration in the analysis carried out under Article 102 TFEU. The question remains as to the role of market integration under the substantive analysis of an 'abuse of the dominant position'. In section V, it is concluded that market integration has never been a stand-alone objective of Article 102 TFEU, but, rather, the lens through which the objectives of Article 102 TFEU have been interpreted.

II. OBJECTIVES OF EU REGULATION OF UNILATERAL ANTI-COMPETITIVE CONDUCT (ARTICLE 102 TFEU)

In this section the spectrum of values underlying Article 102 TFEU is addressed. The research focuses on two conflicting views as to the objectives of regulating the unilateral exercise of market power, ie, economic efficiency and economic freedom. Varying degrees of protection are afforded to different categories of consumers in the EU under each standard of objectives, but for different reasons. This enquiry represents the first step in assessing whether market integration is a distinct aim of Article 102 TFEU on the spectrum of values, alongside economic efficiency and economic freedom, or whether it is an independent variable, external to the spectrum of values behind EU competition law.

A. Competition and Economic Efficiency: A Trade-Off between Present and Future Consumers

One rationale behind Article 102 TFEU is to prevent the exercise of monopoly power, which harms society and consumers. The underlying assumption is that the profitable exercise of monopoly power is harmful to both the efficient allocation of resources and efficient production. Allocative inefficiency occurs because

[2] As defined in the original Article 8a EEC, which was inserted by the SEA and was eventually renumbered as ex-Article 14 TEC. The goal was set in Commission of the European Communities, 'Completing the Internal Market' (White Paper) COM(85) 310, June 1985, while at the same time the SEA introduced qualified majority voting in relation to the '1992 measures' (Article 100a EEC inserted by the SEA).

society has fewer desirable goods (artificial scarcity) and pays too much for those goods (wealth transfers from consumers, who continue to purchase at the monopolistic price, to producers).[3] The consumer demand that goes unsatisfied when producers restrict output and increase prices represents the 'deadweight loss of monopoly'.[4] Productive inefficiency occurs because producers who can profitably increase prices by restricting output do not have incentives or they are unable to minimise costs of production (X-inefficiency),[5] or they waste resources to achieve or protect their market power (rent-seeking).[6]

However, undertakings that can profitably increase prices by restricting output may be able to generate productive efficiency gains, for example, to exploit economies of scope and scale[7] or network effects,[8] or to use monopoly profits as resources allocated to the development of new processes and products (often termed dynamic efficiency).[9] These two sources of efficiencies directly benefit either the producers, in the case of economies of scale and scope, or future consumers, in the case of dynamic efficiencies, but not present consumers, who contribute to financing those efficiencies by either forgoing consumption or paying higher prices, at least not in the short run—hence the debate as to the standard of assessing efficiency as the objective of competition law.

[3] There is debate as to whether the wealth transfer from consumers to producers is relevant for assessing the pro- or anti-competitive effects of any conduct. The debate originates in the Chicago School of thought. Chicagoans believe that redistribution of wealth, if it is a concern at all, is not a matter for antitrust law. See R Bork, *The Antitrust Paradox: A Policy at War with Itself* (Free Press, 1993) 110–15; R Posner, *Antitrust Law* (2nd edn, University of Chicago Press, 2001) 9–32; O Williamson, 'Economies as an Antitrust Defense: The Welfare Tradeoffs' [1968] *American Economic Review* 27–28. At the EU level, see R Nazzini, *The Foundations of European Union Competition Law: The Objective and Principle of Article 102* (Oxford University Press, 2011) 32–49, who argues for the superiority of the total (social) welfare objective, but acknowledges that consumer welfare may be a better test, under certain circumstances, to achieve the intended outcome of prohibiting conduct which reduces total welfare in the long run.

[4] S Bishop and M Walker, *The Economics of EC Competition Law: Concepts, Application and Measurement* (3rd edn, Sweet & Maxwell, 2010) 25; M Motta, *Competition Policy: Theory and Practice* (Cambridge University Press, 2004) 41–44; C Veljanovski, *The Economics of Law* (2nd edn, Institute of Economic Affairs, 2006) 115.

[5] H Leibstein, 'Allocative Efficiency vs "X-Efficiency"' [1966] *American Economic Review* 392 introduced the term to convey the idea that monopoly power, and 'the "quiet life" that comes with it', bring about managerial inefficiency.

[6] R Posner, 'The Social Costs of Monopoly and Regulation' (1975) 83 *Journal of Political Economy* 807; *cf* F Fisher, 'The Social Costs of Monopoly and Regulation: Posner Revisited' (1985) 93 *Journal of Political Economy* 410. After all, the actual amount of losses is an empirical issue: Motta (n 4) 44–45.

[7] In the context of merger analysis, see, eg, the so-called 'Williamson trade-off', which shows that productive efficiency gains from small cost reductions usually offset the allocative efficiency losses from increasing prices above cost; Williamson (n 3); O Williamson, 'Economies as an Antitrust Defence Revisited' (1977) 125 *University of Pennsylvania Law Review* 699.

[8] Motta (n 4) 82–85; N Economides, 'The Economics of Networks' (1996) 14 *International Journal of Industrial Organization* 682–83; H Hovenkamp, *The Antitrust Enterprise: Principles and Execution* (Harvard University Press, 2005) 278–85.

[9] This hypothesis is often attributed to J Schumpeter, *Capitalism, Socialism and Democracy* (6th edn, Unwin Paperbacks, 1987), who was among the first to state that perfect competition is incompatible with innovation.

There is not much economic evidence that market structure (either monopoly or competition) has a significant impact on innovation with regard to the trade-off between static (price) and dynamic efficiency.[10] However, it is firmly established in economic theory that innovation is critical to economic growth, because it brings about new commodities, new processes, new sources of supply and new business models.[11] It is critical because it transforms the Darwinian selection process within an industry of individual firms which compete through innovation for temporary market dominance, from which they may be displaced by the next wave of product advancements, a process described as 'creative destruction'.[12] For that reason, it is argued, and supported by empirical evidence in the case of industries such as the communications and media industries as well as pharmaceuticals,[13] that the interests of future consumers should as a policy choice trump the interests of present consumers when in opposition to one another, thereby also changing the cost-error minimising analysis of the application of competition law.[14]

[10] G Sidak and D Teece, 'Dynamic Competition in Antitrust Law' (2009) 5 *Journal of Competition Law and Economics* 586–99; G Manne and J Wright, 'Innovation and the Limits of Antitrust' (2010) 6 *Journal of Competition Law and Economics* 166–67. See also A Schmutzler, 'The Relation between Competition and Innovation: Why is it Such a Mess?' (2010) Centre for Economic Policy Research Discussion Paper No 7640; see also C Velu and S Iyer, 'Dominance and Innovation' (2010) Cambridge Working Papers in Economics 1009 for a review of the economic literature and for examples of the inability to expect a priori one relationship between market concentration and innovation. According to W Kerber, 'Should Competition Law Promote Efficiency? Some Reflections of an Economist on the Normative Foundations of Competition Law' in J Drexl, L Idot and J Moneger (eds), *Economic Theory and Competition Law* (Edward Elgar, 2009) 98–101, this is the reason why the innovation dimension remains to a large extent outside mainstream neoclassical equilibrium theory and its normative role is not clear.

[11] In Schumpeter's own words, 'this kind of competition ... is so much more important that it becomes a matter of comparative indifference whether competition in the ordinary sense functions more or less promptly; the powerful lever that in the longrun expands output and brings down prices is in any case made of other stuff': Schumpeter (n 9) 84–85. See M Carrier, *Innovation for the 21st Century: Harnessing the Power of Intellectual Property and Antitrust Law* (Oxford University Press, 2009) 31–33 for examples of studies that measure the portion of economic growth attributable to innovation, which is considerable.

[12] The terms are used by Schumpeter (n 9) 81–86. See also R Posner, 'Antitrust in the New Economy' (2001) 68 *Antitrust Law Journal* 925–43; and Sidak and Teece (n 10) 603–10 with further references to the literature of evolutionary theory in economics.

[13] H Shelanski and G Sidak, 'Antitrust Divestiture in Network Industries' (2001) 68 *University of Chicago Law Review* 1; R Schmalensee, 'Antitrust Issues in Schumpeterian Industries' [2000] *American Economic Review* 192; N Petit, 'The Economics of Parallel Trade: Iconoclast Views on a Dogma of EU Competition Law' (2010) SSRN Papers; G Tsouloufas, 'Limiting Pharmaceutical Parallel Trade in the European Union: Regulatory and Economic Justifications' (2011) 36 *European Law Review* 389–90. *Cf* A Fatur, *EU Competition Law and the Information and Communication Technology Network Industries: Economic versus Legal Concepts in Pursuit of (Consumer) Welfare* (Hart Publishing, 2012) 7–98; and M Carrier, 'Two Puzzles Resolved: Of the Schumpeter-Arrow Stalemate and Pharmaceutical Innovation Markets' (2007–08) 93 *Iowa Law Review* 403–14 for a slightly more nuanced approach to the industry-specific empirical evidence.

[14] S Singham, 'Competition and Innovation: A Non-Zero Sum Approach to Economic Growth' (2010) 2 *Competition Policy International Antitrust Journal* 3, 7; Manne and Wright (n 10) 166–67; G Immordino and M Polo, 'Optimal Legal Standards in Antitrust: Traditional v Innovative Industries' (2011) Innocenzo Gasparini Institute for Economic Research Working Paper No 420. See also M Lemley, 'Industry-Specific Antitrust Policy for Innovation' [2011] *Columbia Business Law Review* 637,

However, the Court of Justice does not seem to endorse dynamic efficiencies as a matter of law in its analysis under Article 102 TFEU. For example, the most recent manifestation of the said trade-off between future and present consumers is a case concerning parallel trade in pharmaceuticals.[15] In *Sotirios Lélos*, Glaxo refused to supply wholesalers in Greece engaging in parallel exports and argued, inter alia, that:

> [P]arallel trade in medicines reduces the profits that pharmaceutical companies can invest in research and development activities. By contrast, distributors which profit from parallel trade make no contribution to pharmaceutical innovation.[16]

However, the Court rejected the argument and insisted on the static (price) efficiency gains of parallel trade.[17] By contrast, AG Jacobs in his Opinion in *Syfait* had suggested that:

> [D]ominant pharmaceutical undertakings would respond to an obligation to supply parallel traders within a given Member State by removing existing products from the market in that State, if they were able to do so, and by delaying the launch of new products there. Price differentials would be replaced by a greater fragmentation of the market, with a differing range of products available from State to State.[18]

Nevertheless, both sides of the debate align concerning one feature. The substantive value underlying protection of competition against monopoly power is wealth, economic growth and its contribution to raising the standards of living. In the case of productive efficiency, this appears straightforward; it is the production of maximum outputs from minimum inputs, thereby increasing society's overall wealth.[19] Allocative efficiency allocates goods to those who value them the most; thus, one interpretation could be based on some egalitarian basis in the sense that

who is in favour of an industry-specific antitrust policy for innovation; *cf* J Kirkwood and R Lande, 'The Fundamental Goal of Antitrust: Protecting Consumers, Not Efficiency' (2008) 84 *Notre Dame Law Review* 239–40, who view the total surplus standard as a form of 'trickle-down economics'.

[15] The case first came before the Court of Justice as a reference for preliminary ruling from the Hellenic Competition Commission, but was rejected on jurisdictional grounds; Case C-53/03 *Syfait and others v Glaxosmithkline AEVE* [2005] ECR I-4609. The same reference was then made by the Athens Court of Appeal in Joined Cases C-468/06–C-478/06 *Sotirios Lélos and others v GlaxoSmithKline AEVE Farmakeftikon Proionton, formerly Glaxowellcome AEVE* [2008] ECR I-7139.

[16] *Sotirios Lélos and others v GlaxoSmithKline* (n 15) [44].

[17] '[T]he attraction of the other source of supply which arises from parallel trade in the importing Member State lies precisely in the fact that that trade is capable of offering the same products on the market of that Member State at lower prices than those applied on the same market by the pharmaceutical companies': ibid [55].

[18] *Syfait and others v Glaxosmithkline AEVE* (n 15), Opinion of AG Jacobs [95]. A similar tension arises in refusal to supply cases in the electronic communications markets. See, eg, Case T-201/04 *Microsoft Corporation v Commission* [2007] ECR II-3601 [647]–[648], [710]. *Cf* the approach of the US Supreme Court in a refusal to supply case in the electronic communications market. 'The opportunity to charge monopoly prices … induces risk taking, that produces innovation and economic growth': *Verizon Communications Inc v Law Offices of Curtis V Trinko*, LLP 540 US 398, 124 SCt 872 (2004) [407].

[19] T Prosser, *The Limits of Competition Law: Markets and Public Services* (Oxford University Press, 2005) 28.

each consumer takes responsibility for the true costs of his or her actions and there is no discrimination between individuals.[20]

However, in both cases, members of society are solely treated in their capacity as 'consumers', and in economic terms this is labelled 'surplus' rather than 'welfare', which also conveys the preliminary question as to the value of the market to society.[21] Therefore, any distribution trade-off between present consumers, future consumers and 'consumers-producers' is internal to the concept of competition as a vehicle to economic growth.[22] Under the efficiency standard, the sets of consumers whose interests may conflict are not related to the distinction between final/end-consumers and intermediate buyers as such, but, rather, to the degree that each group of interests contributes to the economic growth of the industry at stake.

B. Competition and Economic Freedom: A Trade-Off between Intermediate Buyers and End-Consumers

An alternative justification for protecting competition under Article 102 TFEU is the protection of individual choice in itself on libertarian grounds.[23] Competition in the market is considered to be an expression of individual freedom. Individuals

[20] This holds true under the Chicagoan view of 'producers' as 'consumers' whose interests count on the same basis as those who are not producers; ie, it is a formal equality among all economic agents. See Nazzini (n 3) 40. However, it is the consumer surplus standard that is treated in the literature as reflecting economic equality concerns; see, eg, K Cseres, 'The Controversies of the Consumer Welfare Standard' (2007) 3 *Competition Law Review* 126–29; R Ahdar, 'Consumers, Redistribution of Income and the Purpose of Competition Law' (2002) 23 *European Competition Law Review* 345–49; J Farrell and M Katz, 'The Economics of Welfare Standards in Antitrust' (2006) 2 *Competition Policy International* 9–10. The latter standard is conceptually distinct from an overall distribution of wealth in society: Kirkwood and Lande (n 14) 200–01.

[21] B Orbach, 'The Antitrust Consumer Welfare Paradox' (2010) Arizona Legal Studies Discussion Paper No 10-07 [28]; see, in particular, the early debate between R Dowrkin, 'Is Wealth a Value?' (1980) 9 *Journal of Legal Studies* 191 and R Posner, 'The Value of Wealth: A Comment on Dworkin and Kronman' (1980) 9 *Journal of Legal Studies* 243 with regard to the question as to why wealth is a worthy social value. More recently, the distinction is more often expressed in terms of 'consumer welfare' as opposed to 'citizen/social welfare'; see, eg, M Lodge, 'Regulatory Accountability: Towards a Single Citizen-Consumer Model?' in K Dowding, J Hughes and H Margetts (eds), *Challenges to Democracy: Ideas, Involvement and Institutions—The PSA Yearbook 2000* (Palgrave, 2001) 205; J Davies, *The European Consumer Citizen in Law and Policy* (Palgrave Macmillan, 2011) 68–109. See also, eg, M Freedland, 'Law, Public Services, and Citizenship: New Domains, New Regimes?' in M Freedland and S Sciarra (eds), *Public Services and Citizenship in European Law* (Clarendon Press, 1998) 1; D Lewinsohn-Zamir, 'Consumer Preferences, Citizen Preferences, and the Provision of Public Goods (1998–99) 108 *Yale Law Journal* 377 in the specific context of public services or public goods.

[22] However, see challenges to this proposition by O Black, *Conceptual Foundations of Antitrust* (Cambridge University Press, 2005) 40–61, in particular 58–61, as well as by the advocates of libertarian paternalism and the theory of nudge, eg, C Sunstein, 'Willingness to Pay vs Welfare' [2007] *Harvard Law and Policy Review* 328–30; R Thaler and C Sunstein, *Nudge* (Yale University Press, 2008) 1–14.

[23] Prosser (n 19) 19–20; O Odudu, *The Boundaries of EC Competition Law: The Scope of Article 81* (Oxford University Press, 2006) 14–16.

are free to make choices as to what to produce and what to consume, and prices comprise the coordinating mechanism of supply and demand via market transactions: these permit individuals to reveal their preferences, which may result in exit from the market and in rejecting the products of one supplier in favour of another.[24] Therefore, competition-as-a-process is promoted and protected against 'private market power as a degeneration of freedom, against which the freedoms of all must be guaranteed, and competition law is seen not as a negation but a limitation of that power'.[25]

This perception of competition as safeguarding the conditions of operation in the market is not uniquely European. Market openness, setting fair rules of the game and giving access rights and opportunities have occasionally been perceived to be the goals of US antitrust law[26] and have, more recently, been interpreted as ensuring that individual (and, in particular, consumer) choices determine the market outcomes.[27]

However, competition has been strongly associated, through what is known as 'Ordoliberalism', with protecting the individual freedom of market players as a value in itself from undue economic power in the EU regulation of unilateral anti-competitive conduct. A 'constitutionalised'[28] competitive order guarantees price stability,[29] which, in turn, ensures a prosperous and human society.[30] Economic efficiency is only an indirect and derived goal, while the competition process has

[24] R Sally, *Classical Liberalism and International Economic Order: Studies in Theory and Intellectual History* (Routledge, 1998) 17–21; A Shipman, *The Market Revolution and its Limits: A Price for Everything* (Routledge, 1999) 13.

[25] J Amato, *Antitrust and the Bounds of Power: The Dilemma of Liberal Democracy in the History of the Market* (Hart Publishing, 1997) 76, 113. See also F Böhm's aphoristic formula 'The one who has power has no right to be free and the one who wants to be free should have no power', as quoted in W Möschel, 'The Proper Scope of Government Viewed from an Ordoliberal Perspective: The Example of Competition Policy (2001) 157 *Journal of Institutional and Theoretical Economics* 4.

[26] E Fox, 'The Modernization of Antitrust: A New Equilibrium', (1981) 66 *Cornell Law Review* 1182; E Fox and L Sullivan, 'Antitrust—Retrospective and Prospective: Where Are We Coming from? Where Are We Going?' (1987) 62 *New York University Law Review* 959.

[27] Termed 'consumer sovereignty' by N Averitt and R Lande, 'Consumer Sovereignty: A Unified Theory of Antitrust and Consumer Protection Law' (1997) 65 *Antitrust Law Journal* 713; N Averitt and R Lande, 'Using the "Consumer Choice" Approach to Antitrust Law' (2007) 74 *Antitrust Law Journal* 176. I Lianos and A Matteus, 'Antitrust in the New US Administration: A Transatlantic View' (2009) 2 *Global Competition Policy* 32–33 suggest that the European concept of a dominant firm's 'special responsibility' should be understood as a proxy for 'consumer sovereignty', since open markets are a prerequisite for consumer empowerment.

[28] The concept of an 'Economic Constitution' was the means by which Ordoliberals integrated economic and legal/political thought; its role was to provide basic principles of economic conduct, shaped into a Rule of Law, rather than a mechanism of ad hoc discretionary political decisions. See D Gerber, 'Constitutionalizing the Economy: German Neo-Liberalism, Competition Law and the "New" Europe' (1994) 42 *American Journal of Comparative Law* 44–47.

[29] See Eucken's structural and regulating principles in S Karsten, 'Eucken's "Social Market Economy" and its Test in Post-War West Germany: The Economist as Social Philosopher Developed Ideas that Paralleled Progressive Thought in America' (1985) 44 *American Journal of Economics and Sociology* 175–77.

[30] The Ordoliberal 'economic order' is realising the Kantian ethic of ensuring freedom of citizens against other citizens and the state by guaranteeing equality of individuals and civil liberties: Möschel

an intrinsic value for guaranteeing the basic equality of individuals as economic subjects.[31] In regard to the exercise of monopoly power, the Ordoliberal standard for assessing its legality is the 'as-if-they-were-subject-to-competition' standard, as opposed to conduct designed to impede the rivals' ability to compete and perform.[32]

As a matter of law, this conception of competition as a process can nevertheless lead to interventions that protect choice as the main constituent element of individual economic freedom. There are two categories of consumers whose freedom of choice is protected under the process-based conception of competition: end-consumers and intermediate buyers.[33] The economic freedom of end-consumers is often presumed to be restricted when their choice as to the source of supply is limited, once a competitor of the dominant undertaking is squeezed out of the market.[34] The often-quoted assumption that Article 102 TFEU protects the dominant undertaking's competitors rather than competition or consumers stems from this,[35] as is illustrated in most Article 102 TFEU cases dealing with allegedly exclusionary abuses.[36]

In addition, the protected economic freedom under Article 102 TFEU could be the economic freedom of intermediate buyers, who are customers but not competitors of the dominant undertaking. For example, in *British Airways*, a case concerning loyalty-inducing rebates, the General Court held that it is sufficient to examine whether the scheme tended to remove or restrict the travel agents'

(n 25) 6–7; Sally (n 24) 111; L Gormsen, 'The Conflict between Economic Freedom and Consumer Welfare in the Modernisation of Article 82 EC' (2007) 3 *European Competition Journal* 332–36.

31 The deontological and rights-based approach of protecting 'competition-as-a-process' is often contrasted with utilitarianism on a philosophical basis: W Möschel, 'Competition Policy from an Ordo Point of View' in H Willgerodt and A Peacock (eds), *German Neo-liberals and the Social Market Economy* (Macmillan for the Trade Policy Research Centre, 1989) 146; C Wartin, 'Germany's Social Market Economy' in A Kilmarnock (ed), *The Social Market and the State* (Social Market Foundation, 1999) 92–95.

32 Gerber (n 1) 252–53; *cf* H Schweitzer, 'The History, Interpretation and Underlying Principles of Section 2 Sherman Act and Article 82 EC' in C-D Ehlermann and M Marquis (eds), *European Competition Law Annual 2007: A Reformed Approach to Article 82 TEC* (Hart Publishing, 2008) 133–34.

33 See Case T-168/01 *GlaxoSmithKline Services Unlimited v Commission* [2006] ECR II-2969 [170]–[171] on the distinction between the freedom of action of an intermediate consumer to choose his or her customers, and the freedom of action of the end-consumer to choose his or her source of supply.

34 L Gormsen, 'The Parallels between the Harvard Structural School and Article 82 EC and the Divergences between the Chicago and the Post-Chicago Schools and Article 82 EC' (2008) 4 *European Competition Journal* 232–36, 249–50; E Rousseva, *Rethinking Exclusionary Abuses in EU Competition Law: Rethinking Article 82 of the EC Treaty* (Hart Publishing, 2010) 194.

35 D Gerber, 'The Future of Article 82: Dissecting the Conflict' in Ehlermann and Marquis (n 32) 45 places this claim among the misconceptions concerning the objectives of Article 102 TFEU.

36 See, eg, *Microsoft Corporation v Commission* (n 18) [651]–[652]; Case C-202/07P *France Telecom v Commission* [2009] ECR I-2369 [112]; Case C-280/08P *Deutsche Telekom v Commission* [2010] ECR I-09555 [182]. See Case C-209/10 *Post Danmark A/S v Konkurrencerådet*, Judgment of 27 March 2012 (NYR) [22] for a more recent reaffirmation: 'Competition on the merits may, by definition, lead to the departure from the market or the marginalisation of competitors that are less efficient and so less attractive to consumers from the point of view of, among other things, price, choice, quality or innovation.'

freedom to sell their services to the airlines of their choice and, thereby, whether it hindered the access of British Airways' competitors to the market.[37] This approach seems deeply rooted in EU competition law. Even in the Commission's policy documents with regard to an economics-based approach to Article 102 TFEU, it is stated that 'harm to intermediate buyers is generally presumed to create harm to final consumers'.[38]

The standard for an assessment of the restriction to their economic freedom seems to vary between these different sets of 'consumers', namely end-consumers and intermediate buyers, in particular in intermediate goods markets.[39] However, as long as the guiding principle is economic freedom, the distinction is internal to the concept of 'competition-as-a-process'.

III. LINKING THE OBJECTIVES OF ARTICLE 102 TFEU TO EU TRADE LIBERALISATION

The research presented in this section links the two objectives of Article 102 TFEU to EU trade liberalisation, based on a historical analysis of the early years of enforcement of Article 102 TFEU. The analysis is preceded by a note on terminology, due to the interdisciplinary connotation of the term 'market integration' in the EU, which spans the areas of political science, international economics and law.

A. Delimitation of the Notion of 'Market Integration' in the EU

In this chapter, 'market integration' in the EU refers to the form of economic integration sought by Member States before the Commission's White Paper on the completion of the Internal Market in 1985.[40] In international economics, economic integration is concerned with 'the discriminatory removal of all trade impediments between at least two participating nation-States and with the

[37] Case T-219/99 *British Airways plc v Commission* [2003] ECR II-5917 [270].

[38] Commission (EC), 'DG Competition Discussion Paper on the application of Article 82 of the Treaty to exclusionary abuses' (December 2005) [55]. In Commission (EC), 'Guidance on Commission's enforcement priorities in applying Article 82 of the EC Treaty to abusive exclusionary conduct by dominant undertaking' [2009] OJ C45/7 [19], it is suggested that harm will be addressed at either level or at both levels.

[39] See, eg, P Evans, 'Assessing Consumer Detriment' (2007) 28 *European Competition Law Review* 26; P Akman, '"Consumer" v "Customer": The Devil in the Detail' (2008) Centre for Competition Policy Working Paper 08-34, Rousseva (n 34) 469–70. See also P Akman, *The Concept of Abuse in EU Competition Law: Law and Economic Approaches* (Hart Publishing, 2012) 246–57, who uses the specific example of price discrimination.

[40] Commission of the European Communities (n 2).

establishment of certain elements of coordination between them'.[41] Balassa has identified five conventional stages of economic integration.[42] Market integration in the EU, in light of the 1992 project to 'create an area without internal frontiers', constituted a 'common market', out of Balassa's five stages of economic integration, which involved the freedom to provide goods and services as well as free factor mobility across national member frontiers.[43] However, the term used in policy documents, in particular in the 1985 White Paper and later in the TEC itself, was 'Internal Market', in recognition that the prescriptions of the Treaty of Rome had not been achieved because non-tariff (or technical) barriers to trade persisted, and as an attempt to signal a new impetus to the then European Community.[44] Therefore, internal trade liberalisation comprises the core of market integration in the EU.

The distinction between 'negative' and 'positive' (market) integration,[45] as well as its intersection with the ambiguous notion of policy integration,[46] will be analysed in chapter three and, largely, in chapter four, from a legal perspective.[47] In those early years, the only relevant concept of policy integration was that of a 'collective decision making' to achieve market integration.[48] In legal terms, this is reflected both in the constitutional principles of supremacy and direct effect of

[41] A El-Agraa, 'General Introduction: The EU within the Global Context of Regional Integration' in A El-Agraa (ed), *The European Union: Economics and Policies* (Cambridge University Press, 2007) 1.

[42] B Balassa, *The Theory of Economic Integration* (Allen & Unwin, 1962) identifies five forms of economic integration: a free trade area, a customs union, a common market, an economic union and complete economic integration.

[43] See n 42. Elimination of customs duties and quantitative restrictions to trade was introduced in 1958 and a common external tariff in 1968.

[44] The term 'Common Market' was retained in Article 94 TEC, concerning the approximation of laws which 'directly affect the establishment or functioning of the Common Market', as opposed to the use of the term 'Internal Market' in Article 95 TEC, concerning the approximation of laws which 'have as their object the establishment and functioning of the Internal Market'. See ch 6, text to nn 6–12 for the legal debate as to whether the 'Common Market' and the 'Internal Market' under these two provisions was the same concept.

[45] The distinction was introduced by J Tinbergen, *International Economic Integration* (Elsevier, 1965) 76 on the basis that (national) policy instruments are simply eliminated or new (common/centralised) instruments are formed. It was subsequently used in the context of the then EEC by J Pinder, 'Problems of European Integration' in G Denton (ed), *Economic Integration in Europe* (Weidenfeld & Nicolson, 1969) 145, on the basis that the purpose of market integration is to remove discrimination or maximise the welfare optimum of the integrated area in other ways.

[46] In light of the traditional economic integration theories, policy integration is associated with the achievement of economic unions, as opposed to market integration which is associated with earlier stages of economic integration (eg, common markets); see J Pelkmans, 'Economic Theories of Integration Revisited' (1980) 18 *Journal of Common Market Studies* 334–35. Other scholars equate policy integration with 'positive' integration; see R Bouterse, *Competition and Integration: What Goals Count?: EEC Competition Law and Goals of Industrial, Monetary, and Cultural Policy* (Kluwer Law and Taxation, 1994) 7.

[47] See ch 3, section III.A and ch 4, section II.A, which address the mismatch between the European market and a European polity.

[48] L Lindberg, *The Political Dynamics of European Economic Integration* (Oxford University Press, 1963) 4–8. See also F Scharpf, *Governing in Europe: Effective and Democratic?* (Oxford University Press, 1999) 43–83 on the concepts of positive and negative integration until the entry into force of the Treaty of Maastricht. This 'old constitutionalism' is central to the understanding of the EU as a

the Treaty free movement provisions, and in the conferral of law-making powers to the EU for enacting relevant harmonisation measures.[49]

B. Market Integration: Not a Stand-Alone Objective of Article 102 TFEU

The purpose of the historical inquiry is to highlight that market integration was not a distinct objective of Article 102 TFEU, alongside efficiency and economic freedom, on the spectrum of values that underlie the enforcement of this article. Market integration is an external value that influenced the interpretation of either efficiency or economic freedom as the objectives of Article 102 TFEU. Therefore, the historical inquiry does not attempt to identify either efficiency or economic freedom as the prevailing objective of the enforcement of Article 102 TFEU. This may have been the case over some period of time, depending on various influences and factors, such as the prevailing economic schools of thought or institutional arrangements or the power politics within the Commission at the time.

For example, in the early years, there was virtually no enforcement of Article 102 TFEU. It is well documented early on, since the Treaty establishing the European Coal and Steel Community (hereinafter the 'ECSC Treaty')[50] and the Spaak Report,[51] that the reason for this was, in part, the post-war policy to strengthen the productive efficiency of European firms to compete internationally and the widespread assumption that the growth and the size of the firms are instrumental to higher productivity.[52] However, over the following decades, there was enforcement of Article 102 TFEU based on a structural interpretation

constitutionalised polity; see J Shaw, 'Citizenship: Contrasting Dynamics at the Interface of Integration and Constitutionalism' in Craig and De Búrca (n 1) 585.

[49] Until the enactment of the SEA, it was limited by unanimity vote in Council: see n 2.

[50] Article 102 TFEU contains similar wording to Article 66(7) ECSC Treaty. Cases under the competition provisions of the ECSC Treaty show that large production and sales units were seen as a requirement for technical and commercial evolution. See, eg, Case 13/60 *'Geitling', Ruhrkohlen-Verkaufsgesellschaft mbH and others v High Authority of the ECSC* [1962] ECR 83, 110 (English special edition). It is documented that the competition law provisions in the ECSC Treaty were inserted under strong American intellectual influence; see J Gillingham, *Coal, Steel and the Rebirth of Europe: 1945–1955: The Germans and French from Ruhr Conflict to Economic Community* (Cambridge University Press, 1991) 266–83.

[51] 'While on the one hand the United States, in almost every sector, produces one-half of the world's goods, and on the other the Communist countries, counting a third of the world's population, are increasing their production annually by ten or fifteen per cent, Europe, which once had a monopoly in the manufacturing industries and could count on its overseas possessions for considerable resources, now finds its external position weakening, its influence declining and its capacity for progress diminished by internal divisions': Intergovernmental Committee of the Messina Conference, Report by the Heads of Delegations to the Foreign Ministers (hereinafter 'Spaak Report') 21 April 1956 [9] (translation from the French).

[52] H Thorelli, 'Antitrust in Europe: National Policies after 1945' (1958–59) 26 *University of Chicago Law Review* 233; B Hawk, 'Antitrust in the EEC: The First Decade' [1972–73] *Fordham Law Review* 231–35.

of the notion of 'abuse of the dominant position'.[53] This interpretation arguably embraced the view that the individual economic freedom of third parties and their opportunities to compete on the merits are protected from the harm that they would not risk suffering in a competitive market.[54] At the time, E-J Mestmäcker, an Ordoliberal scholar, was advising the Commission, which was already known as 'the German DG'.[55]

Therefore, at different times, efficiency or economic freedom was predominant as the objective of European competition law and policy. However, it is argued that the attainment of either objective has historically been linked to market integration. In particular, market integration, conceptualised as promoting economic efficiency or economic freedom, has been the 'first principle' of European competition law and policy from the foundational period until the setting of the '1992 benchmark'. This is aptly revealed in the Commission's policy documents in the early years of competition law enforcement. In the Commission's first Competition Policy Report, it is stated that 'with regard to rules of competition applicable to enterprises, the Community's policy must, in the first place, prevent governmental restrictions and barriers—which have been abolished—from being replaced by similar measures of a private nature'.[56] Similarly, according to the Commission's eighth Competition Policy Report: 'The Commission's administrative practice, supported by the Court of Justice in its judgments, has made it possible gradually to introduce a body of rules governing fair conduct, which give market operators an idea of how they must behave if equality of opportunity, freedom of access to business and freedom of choice are to be guaranteed within the Common Market.'[57]

The two statements above, taken from the Commission's Competition Policy Reports, correspond to the two sides of the historical link between competition and market integration: that of economic efficiency and of economic freedom.

[53] In Case 6/72 *Europemballage Corp and Continental Can Co Inc v Commission* [1973] ECR 215, the European Court of Justice held that Article 102 TFEU could be applied to a situation in which a dominant undertaking eliminates competition by acquiring a competitor. At the time, legal writers and in particular R Joliet, *Monopolization and Abuse of Dominant Position: A Comparative Study of the American and European Approaches to the Control of Economic Power* (Nijhoff, 1970) 252 favoured a purely behavioural interpretation of the notion of 'abuse of a dominant position', on the basis that a dominant position, as such, is legal.

[54] Case 85/76 *Hoffmann-La Roche AG v Commission* [1979] ECR 461 [91]; Case 322/81 *Nederlandsche Banden-Industrie Michelin NV v Commission* [1983] ECR 3461 [57], [70]. See also E-J Mestmäcker, 'Concentration and Competition in the EEC (Part I)' (1972) 6 *Journal of World Trade Law* 639–43.

[55] Gerber (n 1) 263–65; Gormsen (n 34) 233; M Cini and L McGowan, *Competition Policy in the European Union* (Palgrave Macmillan, 2009) 49. In addition, some authors find parallels between the Ordoliberal approach towards market power and the Harvard School of thought, which, at the end of 1960s, refuted the assumption that concentration of market power is the key factor to higher productivity, based on empirical research. See Gormsen (n 34); Rousseva (n 34) 37–38.

[56] Commission (EEC), 'First Report on Competition Policy' (annexed to the 'Fifth General Report on the Activities of the Communities') April 1972 [13].

[57] Commission (EEC), 'Eighth Report on Competition Policy' (published in conjunction with the 'Twelfth General Report on the Activities of the Communities') April 1979 [9].

The first statement sees economic efficiency as an objective of EU competition law, because economic efficiency is an objective of market integration in the first place. This is based on the assumption that the economic benefits derived from the integration project would only occur because private economic agents would take advantage of changes in the market structure, rather than acting strategically to protect their home markets.[58] From an economic point of view, this is a one-way relationship, since the reverse assumption, namely that changes in competitive intensity affect trade patterns, does not seem to be confirmed.[59]

The second statement sees economic freedom as an objective of EU competition law, because economic freedom is an objective of market integration in the first place. This assumes that the legitimacy of market integration in the EU is founded on individual rights, including the freedom to compete, as opposed to all forms of public power.[60]

The following sections assess the validity of the assumptions which underpin the two sides of the historical link between market integration and competition, before arguing that this link was achieved, in law, through recourse to ex-Article 3(1)(g) TEC. Therefore, market integration is treated as the interpretative lens through which the two objectives of Article 102 TFEU are viewed, and not as a third, stand-alone objective of competition law that may, in some instances, conflict with the other objectives.[61]

Finally, it is not contested that European market integration in itself had long-term non-economic objectives since its inception, one of which was the objective to foster solidarity between the European nations so that war would be prevented.[62] However, these objectives presupposed the achievement of the immediate

[58] M Egan, *Constructing a European Market: Standards, Regulations, and Governance* (Oxford University Press, 2001) 44–46; Bouterse (n 46) 5 speaks of the assumption that market integration will result in more intense competition in national markets; Wesseling (n 1) 12 points to the 'functional' character of the European competition rules, on the basis of the same assumption.

[59] See M Levenstein, J Sivadasan and V Suslow, 'The Effect of Competition on Trade Patterns: Evidence from the Collapse of International Cartels' (2010) Research Seminar in International Economics Discussion Paper No 603, University of Michigan.

[60] E-J Mestmäcker, 'On the Legitimacy of European Law' (1994) 58 *Rabels Zeitschrift für ausländisches und internationales Privatrecht* 631; M Streit and W Mussler, 'The Economic Constitution of the European Community: From "Rome" to "Maastricht"' (1995) 1 *European Law Journal* 14–15; E-U Petersmann, National Constitutions, Foreign Trade Policy and European Community Law' (1992) 3 *European Journal of International Law* 4–15.

[61] The prevailing approach in virtually all competition law textbooks is to view market integration as a third, stand-alone objective of competition law. A notable exception seems to be Nazzini (n 3) 113–21, who takes the Internal Market into account as a factor which influences the interpretation of Article 102 TFEU. He also acknowledges that the relevant elements in that regard are only the economic objectives of the Internal Market specifically because the competition rules are a key element of economic policy.

[62] See the Schuman Declaration, 9 May 1950. See also ch 4, text to n 9.

economic task of integrating the markets of the Member States[63] and are not relevant with regard to the interface between market integration and competition.[64]

i. Market Integration and Economic Efficiency: A Uniform Level of Protection

The main and immediate objective of European market integration since its inception was to enhance the allocational efficiency of the economies of Member States.[65] According to the Spaak Report, 'the merging of the markets ... will allow, through increased division of labour, to eliminate the wasteful use of resources, and, through increased certainty of supplies, to give up the production at uneconomic cost'.[66] At the same time, 'while in many industries, no national market can allow firms to reach their optimum size, unless they enjoy a virtual monopoly ... this merging of the markets creates large enough outlets to permit the use of advanced production techniques'.[67]

In economic terms, the static effects of trade liberalisation stem from the combined effect of 'trade creation' and 'trade diversion',[68] as well as the ability of Member States to cooperate to distribute the gains, so that all partners may benefit, unlike the results of independent action.[69] The effects are static, since they represent a one-shot increase in the levels of welfare gain, principally affecting the prices of the traded products. The underlying comparative advantage of the Member States, subsequent to the removal of trade barriers, determines the allocation of production to those countries that are relatively more efficient at providing output, because of the decrease in transaction costs and increased specialisation.[70]

At the same time, trade liberalisation has dynamic effects that stem from the exploitation of economies of scale and increased competition.[71] On the one hand, if the minimum efficient scale exceeds national demand, market integration

[63] At least, this was the assumption at the initial stage of market integration in the EU. Therefore, Article 2 EEC Treaty specified that: 'The Community shall have as its task, by establishing a Common Market and progressively approximating the economic policies of Member States, to promote throughout the Community a harmonious development of economic activities, a continuous and balanced expansion, an increase in stability, an accelerated raising of the standard of living and closer relations between the States belonging to it.'

[64] See ch 4, section II.A on the non-economic values embedded in the process of market integration.

[65] See W Molle, *The Economics of European Integration: Theory, Practice, Policy* (Ashgate, 2006) 235.

[66] Spaak Report (n 51) [13] (translation from the French).

[67] ibid.

[68] 'Trade creation' denotes the movement of trade from a high-cost domestic producer to a low-cost partner producer and 'trade diversion' is the reverse situation; F McDonald, 'Market Integration in the European Union' in F McDonald and S Dearden (eds), *European Economic Integration* (3rd edn, Longman, 1999) 45.

[69] A El-Agraa, 'The Theory of Economic Integration' in El-Agraa (ed) (n 41) 128.

[70] Egan (n 58) 47; McDonald (n 68) 48, Figure 1.5 (reaping comparative advantage), showing the distributional effects between consumers and producers in each (export and import) country.

[71] T Scitovsky, 'Economies of Scale, Competition and European Integration' [1956] *American Economic Review* 71.

permits larger product markets and internal economies of scale for firms.[72] On the other hand, market integration increases the possible sources of supply within a Member State by including trade from other Member States. Therefore, the competitive pressure in the national market is intensified or firms are induced to form networks, which results in reduced transaction costs when firms conduct their business (external scale economies).[73]

The Commission estimated both the static and the dynamic potential gains of market integration in 1988 in a project named 'The Costs of Non-Europe' (or the so-called 'Cecchini Report'),[74] which largely focused on efficiency gains from removing 'non-tariff barriers' to trade.[75]

The realisation of the above-mentioned static or dynamic efficiency gains of market integration occurs specifically because the gain is uniform across the Member States involved. This is exemplified by parallel imports, which occur when goods intended for sale in one national market are exported from their original destination to another Member State that has a pre-existing source of supply for the same goods.[76] From an economic point of view, parallel imports are deemed to be efficient when the interference with the manufacturer's retail discriminatory pricing takes place among countries with similar consumer demand structure,[77] because this leads to lower prices. On the other hand, unrestricted parallel trade, and price uniformity in the EU stemming from this, may impair

[72] McDonald (n 68) 48, 51, Figure 1.8 (economies of scale) showing the importance of the technical relationship between cost and output for the magnitude of the cost reduction of any output increase that might arise from economic integration.

[73] Molle (n 65) 242; Egan (n 58) 48–49; McDonald (n 68) 47, 49. See also Spaak Report (n 51) 14: 'National protection that eliminates external competition is particularly harmful ... In a wider market, it is no longer possible to maintain outdated methods of production that lead to both high prices and low wages; companies, instead of remaining static, are subject to a constant pressure to invest, in order to increase production, improve the quality of their products and modernise their production methods: they must progress, or they fail' (translation from the French).

[74] P Cecchini, *The European Challenge 1992: The Benefits of a Single Market* (Wildwood House, 1988). The report uses predictive models to estimate the net benefits of trade liberalisation, as indicated by economic theory, by measuring departures from it. It is treated with caution for that reason. See McDonald (n 68) 53–60; B Ardy and A El-Agraa, 'The Economics of the Single Market' in El-Agraa (ed) (n 41) 140–42.

[75] Non-tariff barriers are non-tariff government policy measures that intentionally or unintentionally alter the quantity or direction of trade. Therefore, they are artificial, not natural conditions; see Ardy and El-Agraa (n 74) 133.

[76] S Horner, *Parallel Imports* (Collins Professional Books, 1987) 1; C Stothers, *Parallel Trade in Europe: Intellectual Property, Competition and Regulatory Law* (Hart Publishing, 2007) 2.

[77] K Maskus, 'Parallel Imports' in P Lloyd and C Milner (eds), *The World Economy: Global Trade Policy 2000* (Blackwell, 1998) 1276–77 points to the redistribution, under price discrimination, of consumer benefits in high-price countries to consumers in low-price countries, and to the redistribution from consumers in high-price countries that are net importers to producers in countries that are net exporters; see also Stothers (n 76) 21. C Stevenson, 'Exhausting All the Arguments: A Short Guide to the Economics of Trademark Exhaustion' in J Grayston (ed), *European Economics and Law-Competition, Single Market, Trade* (Palladian Law, 1999) 92–93 specifically points out that the existing level of competition in the market concerned is crucial to whether regulation of parallel imports permits unfair price discrimination to occur.

the manufacturer's profits and hinder the dynamic benefits of launching new products in the long run, at least in low-price Member States.[78] In both cases, the efficiency gain is uniform across each category of consumers in the EU: present consumers or future consumers. The trade-off between product or price market fragmentation is internal to the decision as to whether or not to regulate parallel imports.[79]

ii. Market Integration and Economic Freedom: A Uniform Level of Protection

Market integration in the EU is closely associated with individual economic freedoms, which guarantee open markets against public power.[80] According to the definition of a 'trade barrier' in *Dassonville*, 'all trading rules enacted by Member States which are capable of hindering, directly or indirectly, actually or potentially, intra-[EU] trade are to be considered as measures having an effect equivalent to quantitative restrictions'.[81] The Court of Justice has gradually expanded the scope of the free movement provisions based on this definition, as guarantees of a 'substantive economic due process' or of an 'unhindered pursuit of commerce in individual Member States'.[82]

The expansion of the scope of free movement of goods to cover national rules which aim to restrict the freedom to compete is arguably the best illustration of the interface between competition and market integration through the objective of economic freedom. Such national laws that, for example, regulate prices are caught by Article 34 TFEU when they result in a loss of the competitive advantage

[78] Maskus (n 77) 1275–76; T Valletti, 'Differential Pricing, Parallel Trade, and the Incentive to Invest' (2006) 70 *Journal of International Economics* 314. See also Motta (n 4) 23: 'price uniformity may even induce a monopolist not to sell at all in countries where it would sell under price discrimination'.

[79] See, in particular, the debate with regard to the question of international or regional exhaustion of intellectual property (IP) rights, which normally confer exclusive export and import rights to the owner; I Avgoustis, 'Parallel Imports and Exhaustion of Trade Mark Rights: Should Steps Be Taken towards an International Exhaustion Regime?' (2012) 34 *European Intellectual Property Review* 108; E Bonadio, 'Parallel Imports in a Global Market: Should a Generalised International Exhaustion Be the Next Step?' (2011) 33 *European Intellectual Property Review* 153; A Feros, 'Free Movement of Pharmaceuticals within the EU: Should Rights Be Exhausted Regionally? (2010) 32 *European Intellectual Property Review* 486; G Grossman and E Lai, 'Parallel Imports and Price Controls' (2008) 39 *RAND Journal of Economics* 378.

[80] See n 60.

[81] Case 8/74 *Procureur du Roi v Benoît and Gustave Dassonville* [1974] ECR 837 [5].

[82] These are the words of AG Tesauro in Case 292/92 *Hünermund v LandesapothekerkammerBaden-Württemberg* [1993] ECR I-6787, Opinion of AG Tesauro [1], who was, in fact, denying that Article 34 TFEU should be treated as a basis for 'unhindered pursuit of commerce'. The analysis by AG Tesauro focuses on measures which, 'by affecting the supply (eg, by a channelling of imports) or demand (eg, by restricting opportunities to advertise) for the products concerned, including imports, may bring about a decrease in sales': ibid [9]. The Opinion of AG Tesauro to exclude these measures from the scope of Article 34 TFEU was followed by the Court of Justice in Joined Cases C-267/91 and C-268/91 *Criminal Proceedings against Bernard Keck and Daniel Mithouard* [1993] ECR I-6097 [14]: 'in view of the increasing tendency of traders to invoke [Article 34 TFEU] as a means of challenging any rules whose effect is to limit their commercial freedom'.

enjoyed by imports, either because the minimum fixed price does not allow the lower cost price of imports to be reflected or because the maximum fixed price only allows imports to be marketed at a loss.[83]

The core of the conceptualisation of market integration in the EU as a process of ensuring economic freedoms is to afford a uniform level of protection in all Member States to a particular class of traders. This can be exemplified by parallel imports, where such parallel trade flows between distributors in different Member States, or between distributors and retailers, and not just between manufacturers who exercise price discrimination directly at the retail level.[84] In these cases, the restrictions that, for example, an intellectual property (IP) rights owner may impose over the distribution chain or its licensees in order to secure some vertical control[85] are treated as trade barriers because they impair the subjective right to EU-wide movement of a particular class of traders, the parallel traders, in absolute, not comparative terms.[86]

The rights-based approach to trade liberalisation has an additional dimension that extends beyond the substance of the market freedoms. The Court of Justice has interpreted the objective prohibitions of trade restrictions as directly enforceable individual rights since *Van Gend & Loos*.[87] The recognition of EU trade law as a source of individual (economic) rights has given further rise to neoliberal interpretations of market integration in the EU as a 'self-organising system'.[88] The freedom of trade is directed against the public power of the sovereign state, so this interpretation has rendered competition among national rules subject to market choice as the prevailing method of market integration.[89] This was also the initial meaning of the principle of mutual recognition, which was introduced by

[83] Case 82/77 *Openbaar Ministerie of the Kingdom of the Netherlands v Jacobus Philippus van Tiggele* [1978] ECR 25 [18]; Joined Cases 177 and 178/82 *Criminal Proceedings against Jan van de Haar and Kaveka de Meern BV* [1984] ECR 1797 [19]; Case 231/83 *Henri Cullet and Chambre syndicale des réparateurs automobiles et détaillants de produits pétroliers v Centre Leclerc à Toulouse and Centre Leclerc à Saint-Orens-de-Gameville* [1985] ECR 305 [23], [25]–[27]; Case 181/82 *Roussel Laboratoria BV and others v État Néerlandais* [1983] ECR 3849 [17], [21]–[23]. See also Joined Cases C-267/91 and C-268/91 *Criminal Proceedings against Bernard Keck and Daniel Mithouard* [1993] ECR I-6097, Opinion of AG van Gerven [4]–[5], who distinguishes between prohibitions of sales at a loss at the level of retail trade and at the level of manufacturer, importer or wholesaler as a marketing strategy. *Cf Jan van de Haar* [18] and Case 231/83 *Cullet v Leclerc* [28].

[84] Maskus (n 77) 1277–78.

[85] This is because it permits quality consistency or maintenance of pre-sales (eg, advertising) and post-sales (eg, repair services) services; see JS Chard and CJ Mellor, 'Intellectual Property Rights and Parallel Imports' (1989) 12 *World Economy* 73–74; Stothers (n 76) 22.

[86] See Commission (EEC), 'Sixth Report on Competition Policy' (published in conjunction with the 'Tenth General Report on the Activities of the Communities') April 1977 [45]–[52].

[87] Case 26/62 *Van Gend & Loos v Netherlands Inland Revenue Administration* [1963] ECR 1, 12.

[88] Streit and Mussler (n 60) 9–10, 14–15.

[89] M Maduro, *We the Court: the European Court of Justice and the European Economic Constitution-A Critical Reading of Article 30 of the EC Treaty* (Hart Publishing, 1998) 129–30. Wesseling (n 1) 13 refers to the normative, socio-political role of competition as a means of integrating national economies; C Joerges, 'What is Left of the European Economic Constitution?' (2004) EUI Working Paper LAW No 2004/13 17–19.

the Court of Justice in *Cassis de Dijon*[90] and was included in the new approach to harmonisation following the 1985 White Paper.[91] According to Mestmäcker, the economic freedoms have this dual function, as they protect individuals against interference with their right to participate in trade between Member States and, simultaneously, they establish the legislative powers of the EU for implementing those economic liberties. These legislative powers are inherently limited by the purpose of the underlying individual rights.[92]

C. Teleological Interpretation of 'Abuse of a Dominant Position': The Vehicle Linking Competition to Market Integration

The two objectives of market integration—efficiency and economic freedom—influenced the early enforcement of Article 102 TFEU through the use of teleological interpretation as the preferred method for interpreting the notion of 'abuse of a dominant position'. The teleological (or functional) method has a polysemous character and consists of interpretation by reference to the context, the whole system of the Treaty, its general objectives and philosophy.[93]

The teleological reasoning was employed by the Court of Justice within the domain of Article 102 TFEU, by going back to 'the spirit, general scheme, and wording of [Article 102 TFEU] as well as to the system and objectives of the Treaty'.[94] In *Continental Can*, the Court of Justice affirmed the Commission's structural interpretation of 'abuse of a dominant position' to cover exclusionary abuses, including the acquisition of a competitor by the dominant undertaking, which 'practically leads to elimination of competition in a substantial part of the common market'.[95] The Court did so by reference to the objectives of the Treaty and in particular to Article 3(f) EEC, which was the *pre*-Lisbon Article 3(1)(g) TEC. According to Article 3(1)(g) TEC, the (then) Community's activities were to include the institution of a system ensuring that competition in the Internal Market was not distorted. The Court of Justice rejected the applicant's

[90] Case 120/78 *Rewe-Zentral AG v Bundesmonopolverwaltung für Branntwein* [1979] ECR 649.

[91] Commission (EEC) (n 2) [17]–[23]. See ch 4, text to nn 21–24 for the evolution of the principle of mutual recognition and its place in a reformed approach to the free movement provisions.

[92] Mestmäcker (n 60) 632; in a similar vein, see Petersmann (n 60); E-U Petersmann, 'Proposals for a New Constitution for the European Union: Building-Blocks for a Constitutional Theory and Constitutional Law of the EU' (1995) 32 *Common Market Law Review* 1154.

[93] A Bredimas, *Methods of Interpretation and Community Law* (Elsevier, 1978) 77, with further citations. This is also the core component of Barak's 'purposive interpretation': A Barak, *Purposive Interpretation in Law* (Princeton University Press, 2005) 85–96. In the context of the legal reasoning of the Court of Justice, see J Bengoetxea, N MacCormick and L Moral Soriano, 'Integration and Integrity in the Legal Reasoning of the Court of Justice' in G De Búrca and H Weiler (eds), *The European Court of Justice* (Oxford University Press, 2001) 44–47.

[94] *Europemballage Corp and Continental Can* (n 53) [22].

[95] ibid [18], [26].

arguments that 'this provision merely contains a general programme devoid of legal effect' and recalled that '[Article 102 TFEU] is part of the common rules on the [EU's] competition policy', which, in turn, is based on ex-Article 3(1)(g) TEC.[96] The Court then read ex-Article 3(1)(g) TEC, which provides for a system of undistorted competition, as requiring a fortiori that competition must not be eliminated:

> Any restraints on competition which the Treaty allows ... are limited by the requirements of [ex-Articles 2 and 3 TEC]; going beyond these limits involves the risk that the weakening of competition would conflict with the aims of the Common Market.[97]

The important role played by the teleological method of interpretation in European law has been attributed to the autonomy and comprehensiveness of the European legal order in which there is no place for 'silent' judges, in conjunction with the open-ended wording of the Treaty provisions.[98] The function of the method is to fill in gaps in the legislation.[99] In *Continental Can*, the Court of Justice did so by introducing limited merger control, since the relevant provisions in the ECSC Treaty[100] were not included in the EEC Treaty. The Court rejected the applicant's argument that the absence of a merger control provision similar to that in the ECSC Treaty was explicitly intended by the legislator,[101] implying that the underlying policy assumption regarding market power had changed.[102]

The example above highlights the benefits of the teleological method of interpretation. During the early years of the development and enforcement of Article 102 TFEU, its flexibility allowed the Court of Justice to link competition to market integration. In many Article 102 TFEU cases, the Court of Justice makes reference to ex-Article 3(1)(g) TEC for the purpose of establishing an 'abuse of the dominant position'.[103] The underlying assumption is that the total exclusion of competition leads to market isolation, as explained in the previous sections. In that way, either efficiency or economic freedom, as objectives of market integration, was

[96] ibid [23].

[97] ibid [24].

[98] B van der Esch, 'The Principles of Interpretation Applied by the Court of Justice of the European Communities and their Relevance for the Scope of the EEC Competition Rules' (1991–92) 15 *Fordham International Law Journal* 366–67; Bredimas (n 93) 70–71.

[99] See G Conway, *The Limits of Legal Reasoning and the European Court of Justice* (Cambridge University Press, 2012) 1–85 for a comprehensive overview of the role and the critiques of the Court engaging in interpretation and, allegedly, invading the legislative domain.

[100] Article 66(1)–(6) ECSC Treaty.

[101] *Europemballage Corp and Continental Can Can* (n 53) 224 (submissions of the parties), [22].

[102] See W van Gerven, 'Twelve Years of EEC Competition Law (1962–1973) Revisited' (1974) 11 *Common Market Law Review* 46–50, who argues that the judgment is well motivated in law, but that the Court of Justice could have equally applied the opposite view and decided not to install imperfect merger control.

[103] Joined Cases 6 and 7/73 *Istituto Chemioterapico Italiano SpA and Commercial Solvents Corporation v Commission* [1974] ECR 223 [25]; Case 27/76 *United Brands Company and United Brands Continentaal BV v Commission* [1978] ECR 207 [63], [183]; *Hoffmann-La Roche* (n 54) [125], [132]; Case 322/81 *NV Nederlandsche Banden Industrie Michelin v Commission* [1983] ECR 3461 [29]. Article 3(1)(g) TEC used to be Article 3(f) EEC.

linked to European competition policy. The link between the two means that the protection afforded to the various categories of consumers under the efficiency or economic freedom standard under Article 102 TFEU is uniform across the EU, since uniformity is the key feature of market integration, as discussed earlier.

However, the very same quality feature of the teleological method of interpretation, namely its flexibility, that historically linked competition to market integration in Europe equally makes teleological interpretation receptive to introducing new policy developments into Article 102 TFEU. Such a change can be fuelled by the relocation of ex-Article 3(1)(g) TEC after the Lisbon Treaty came into force.[104] Therefore, the historical link identified in this chapter between competition and integration—ie, viewing the protection, under an efficiency- or freedom-oriented approach to competition, as uniform across an EU-wide market—does not necessarily dictate the current link between Article 102 TFEU and market integration. The notion of 'abuse of a dominant position' is amenable to change because of the flexibility of the interpretative method used. However, the historical link cannot be ignored, inasmuch as it is expressly echoed in the requirement of 'effect on *inter*-state trade'. This is explored in the following section.

IV. 'EFFECT ON TRADE': AN ANALYTICAL APPROACH TO JURISDICTIONAL ELEMENTS WITH THE ADVANTAGE OF HINDSIGHT

It is argued in this section that market integration remains a concept relevant for the interpretation of Article 102 TFEU. In particular, the historical link between competition and market integration is, and should be, taken into account to determine whether the conduct in question 'may affect trade between Member States'. The requirement of 'effect on trade' represents the minimum of a legitimate link between market integration and competition under Article 102 TFEU on jurisdictional grounds.

A. The Jurisdictional Function of the Requirement of 'Effect on Trade'

The link between competition and market integration originates from the early years of the development and enforcement of Article 102 TFEU until the formal completion of the Internal Market. Twenty years after the formal completion of the Internal Market, it is still legitimate to take this link into account when establishing the 'effect on trade' condition under Article 102 TFEU. The reason

[104] The question of potential changes in the interpretation of Article 102 TFEU in light of the enactment of the Lisbon Treaty is explored throughout the remainder of this book and, in particular, it is discussed in ch 3, section V.B and ch 6, section II.

for this is the jurisdictional function of this requirement within the scheme of Article 102 TFEU.

The core component of the historical link between competition and market integration is the uniformity of the protection afforded to various categories of consumers across a market which is EU-wide. Accordingly, if the threshold of 'effect on trade' is crossed, the allegedly abusive conduct is assessed against a uniform level of competition law protection across the EU. This is because of the jurisdictional function of the requirement of 'effect on trade', which delimitates the sphere of application of EU and national competition laws.[105]

A statement of the jurisdictional function of the requirement of 'effect on trade' under Article 102 TFEU and its interconnection with market integration is traced in *Hugin*:

> The interpretation and application of the condition relating to effects on trade between Member States contained in [Articles 101 and 102 TFEU] must be based on the purpose of that condition which is to define, in the context of the law governing competition, the boundary between the areas respectively covered by [EU] law and the law of the Member States. Thus [EU] law covers any agreement or any practice which is capable of constituting a threat to freedom of trade between Member States in a manner which might harm the attainment of the objectives of a single market between the Member States, in particular by partitioning the national markets or by affecting the structure of competition within the common market.[106]

This basic test for establishing an 'effect on trade' was explained by the Court of Justice in two alternative tests, namely a test of 'altering the patterns of *inter*-state trade' or one of 'altering the competitive structure of the market'. The first test ('altering the patterns of *inter*-state trade') is examined in relation to its link with the test under Article 34 TFEU for Measures Equivalent to Quantitative Restrictions (MEQR) in section IV.B. The second test ('altering the competitive structure of the market') is examined in relation to its link with the substantive test of 'abuse of the dominant position' in section IV.C.[107] However, both tests

[105] Commission (EC), 'Guidelines on the Effect on Trade Concept Contained in Articles 81 and 82 of the Treaty' (Notice) [2004] OJ C101/81 [12]. The test for 'effect on trade' and its role are common to Articles 101 and 102 TFEU. It should be noted, though, that according to Article 3(2) Regulation 1/2003, Member States are not precluded from adopting stricter national laws only for unilateral anti-competitive conduct.

[106] Case 22/78 *Hugin Kassaregister AB and Hugin Cash Registers Ltd v Commission* [1979] ECR 1869 [17]. In the same vein, see Case 73/74 *Groupement des fabricants de papiers peints de Belgique and others v Commission* [1975] ECR 1491, Opinion of AG Trabucchi [6]: 'the criterion ... must be interpreted in such a way as to bring within the prohibitions of [Article 101 TFEU] agreements in restraint of competition which affect the attainment of the objectives for which the common market was established. ... Even from this wider standpoint, this requirement would still perform the function of tracing the dividing line between the area exclusively within national jurisdiction and that subject to [EU] law on competition'.

[107] This division reflects the similarity of the wording of the tests being compared, as is explained in sections IV.B and IV.C.

link competition and market integration on jurisdictional grounds,[108] and, for the purposes of the research presented in this book, emphasis is placed on this element.[109]

B. The 'Effect on Trade' Test: Identical to or Distinct from the Test under Article 34 TFEU for MEQR?

'Effect on trade' between Member States requires that the conduct in question 'is capable of constituting a threat, direct or indirect, actual or potential, to freedom of trade between Member States in a manner which might harm the attainment of the objectives of a Single Market between States'.[110] It is striking that the wording in *Dassonville* used by the Court of Justice to define 'trade barriers' under Article 34 TFEU is virtually identical to the above definition of 'effect on trade'.[111] However, the Court of Justice rejected an interpretation of the notion of 'measures having an equivalent effect to quantitative restrictions' under Article 34 TFEU on the basis of the case law on 'effect on trade' when it was asked to do so.[112] In particular, it distinguished between the aims of the two sets of provisions, even though its emphasis was on rejecting a de minimis requirement under the free movement provisions, as opposed to the condition that the effect on trade needs to be appreciable under the competition law provisions.[113] In any case, under the 'effect on trade' requirement, there is no need to calculate the actual volume of trade or what the level of trade would have been in the absence of the conduct.[114] It is sufficient that the conduct is capable of having such an effect.[115]

The comparison, as regards the quantitative magnitude of the conduct in question, between the 'effect on trade' under Article 102 TFEU and the substantive test for MEQR under Article 34 TFEU is guided by the similarity in the wording of the tests as they are formulated by the Court of Justice. However, the comparison

[108] J Faull, 'Effect on Trade between Member State and Community: Member State Jurisdiction' [1989] *Fordham Corporate Law Institute* 488–89.

[109] Rather than on the notions of 'trade between Member States' and 'appreciable effect'.

[110] Joined Cases 56 and 58/64 *Établissements Consten SàRL and Grundig-Verkaufs-GmbH v Commission* [1966] ECR 299, 341 (English special edition).

[111] See n 81 on the wording of the *Dassonville* definition of MEQR. See also Case C-145/88 *Torfaen Borough Council v B & Q plc* [1989] ECR 3851, Opinion of AG Van Gerven [21]–[22].

[112] Joined Cases 177 and 178/82 *Jan van de Haar* (n 83) [11]–[14].

[113] The development of the case law under the free movement provisions shows, however, that the rejection of a de minimis threshold under Article 34 TFEU is contested, in particular after the judgments in Case C-142/05 *Åklagaren v Percy Mickelsson and Joakim Roos* [2009] ECR I- 4273 and Case C-110/05 *Commission v Italian Republic* [2009] ECR I- 519. See ch 3, text to nn 91–92.

[114] Commission (EC), 'Guidelines on the Effect on Trade Concept Contained in Articles 81 and 82 of the Treaty' (Notice) [2004] OJ C101/81 [27].

[115] Joined Cases T-24/93, T-25/93, T-26/93 and T-28/93 *Compagnie maritime belge transports SA and Compagnie maritime belge SA et al v Commission* [1996] ECR II-1201 [201]–[203]; Case T-228/97 *Irish Sugar plc v Commission* [1999] ECR II-2969 [170].

seems misleading, because the objective of the competition law provisions is dictated by the substantive prohibitions rather than the jurisdictional requirement of 'effect on trade'. A more principled comparison as regards the magnitude of the prohibited effect would be between MEQR under Article 34 TFEU and the condition, under the competition law provisions, that the restriction on competition be appreciable.[116]

However, the comparison between the 'effect on trade' and the test for MEQR under Article 34 TFEU is valuable and justified, due to their common wording in the Court's formulation. The common wording is, further, explained on the basis that the very same jurisdictional function of the 'effect on trade' under the competition law provisions is assumed under the substantive tests in the free movement provisions, even though they do not expressly mention it. It is settled case law that the free movement provisions do not apply to situations in which all the relevant facts of the case are confined within a single Member State ('purely internal situations').[117] However, in the case of the free movement of goods, the 'purely internal situations' test is conflated with the substantive test of MEQR, because the Court of Justice seems to require not only that a cross-border element *exists*, but also that the measure in question *impedes* this cross-border movement.[118]

It could be argued that 'effect on trade' is more broad than 'purely internal situations' as reflected in the MEQR test, even though no conclusive remarks can be drawn from the existing case law.[119] One way to argue that 'effect on trade' is more

[116] See, eg, Commission (EC), 'Notice on agreements of minor importance which do not appreciably restrict competition under Article 81(1) of the Treaty establishing the European Community (de minimis)' [2001] OJ C368/07.

[117] For a somewhat more recent reaffirmation, see Case C-245/09 *Omalet NV v Rijksdienst voor Sociale Zekerheid* [2010] ECR I-13771 [12].

[118] This approach originates from Joined Cases 314/81, 315/81, 316/81 and 83/82 *Procureur de la République and Comité national de défense contre l'alcoolisme v Alex Waterkeyn and others* [1982] ECR 4337 [11]–[12]. See A Tryfonidou, 'The Outer Limits of Article 28 EC: Purely Internal Situations and the Development of the Court's Approach through the Years' in C Barnard and O Odudu (eds), *The Outer Limits of European Union Law* (Hart Publishing, 2009) 199–201. This conflation of the 'cross-border element' with the MEQR test is also evidenced by comparing and contrasting the 'purely internal situations' test in the goods cases with the 'purely internal situations' test in the context of the movement of natural persons. In the latter cases, the Court of Justice has dissociated the 'cross-border element' test from the scope of application of the substantive test under the relevant free movement provision and has attached a wider significance to it by associating it with the scope of the Treaty, including the EU citizenship provisions and the fundamental rights. It could be said that this is reflected in the case law since Case C-60/00 *Mary Carpenter v Secretary of State for the Home Department* [2002] ECR I-6279. See N Nic Shuibhne, 'The Outer Limits of EU Citizenship: Displacing Economic Free Movement Rights?' in C Barnard and O Odudu (eds), *The Outer Limits of European Union Law* (Hart Publishing, 2009) 170–74 on the relationship between the EU citizenship provisions and the specific free movement provisions, as regards their outer limit of a 'cross-border movement' requirement. Similarly, S O'Leary, 'The Past, Present and Future of the Purely Internal Rule in EU Law' in M Dougan, N Nic Shuibhne and E Spaventa (eds), *Empowerment and Disempowerment of the European Citizen* (Hart Publishing, 2012) 46–64. In that regard, see also ch 5, text to n 137, on the development of the case law.

[119] A conclusive way to test this proposition would be to find cases in which both the free movement and the competition law provisions were invoked, namely state action doctrine cases, and

broad is by identifying competition law cases in which the conduct in question boosts rather than impedes trade.

In particular, 'effect on trade' is established if it is shown that it is 'possible to foresee with a sufficient degree of probability on the basis of a set of objective factors of law or of fact that the [conduct] in question may have an influence, direct or indirect, actual or potential, on the pattern of trade between Member States'[120] and the term 'pattern of trade' is neutral. This test for 'effect on trade' is more commonly used under Article 101 TFEU, but it has also been used in Article 102 TFEU cases, in particular in cases which concern contractual abuses.[121]

In *Consten and Grundig*, the Court of Justice ruled that an increase in the volume of trade between Member States is not sufficient to exclude the possibility that trade may be affected.[122] However, it should be noted that the conduct in question in *Consten and Grundig* was one that impeded parallel trade and had the effect of isolating a national market. Therefore, it was hostile to market integration. By contrast, in the Commission's decision in *Napier Brown/British Sugar*, there was an increase in the level of trade between Member States as a result of the dominant firm's refusal to sell domestically produced industrial sugar to Napier Brown, an undertaking active in the retail sugar market. In reaction, Napier Brown purchased large quantities of imported industrial sugar from France, Denmark and the Netherlands, instead of purchasing cheaper domestic industrial sugar.[123] The Commission, citing *Consten and Grundig*, found that such an increase in imports was not an obstacle in establishing that trade was affected for the purpose of applying Article 102 TFEU. Despite the seemingly pro-market integration effect of the refusal to sell domestically produced industrial sugar, this was in fact combined with the likely exclusion of Napier Brown from the retail sugar market in Great Britain. The exclusion would lead to the elimination of the link between the price of industrial sugar, which was limited by the price of

in which the free movement question is inadmissible ('purely internal situation'), while Article 4(3) TEU-L, read together with Articles 101 or 102 TFEU, is breached and therefore an 'effect on trade' is established. Case C-393/08 *Emanuela Sbarigia v Azienda USL RM/A and others* [2010] ECR I-6337 is the only case found to date. However, in this case the free movement question is inadmissible ('purely internal situation'), while Article 4(3) TEU-L, read together with Article 101 or 102 TFEU, is not breached because the condition of 'effect on trade' is not established; see ch 5, text to nn 135–36 (more generally, in ch 5, section III.D, the relationship between the state action doctrine and the free movement provisions is addressed). In addition, there has not been found any state action doctrine case in which 'effect on trade' is not established, while the free movement question is admissible.

[120] Case 56/65 *Société Technique Minière (LTM) v Maschinenbau Ulm GmbH (MBU)* [1966] ECR 235, 249 (English special edition).

[121] Case T-65/89 *BPB Industries Plc and British Gypsum Ltd v Commission* [1993] ECR II-389 [135]; Joined Cases C-215/96 *Carlo Bagnasco and others v Banca Popolare di Novara soc coop arl (BNP)* and C-216/96 *Cassa di Risparmio di Genova e Imperia SpA (Carige)* [1999] ECR I-135 [47], [60].

[122] See n 110. Similarly (under Article 101TFEU), see Case T-141/89 *Tréfileurope Sales SARL v Commission* [1995] ECR II-00791 [57]; and, somewhat more recently, C-238/05 *Asnef-Equifax, Servicios de Información sobre Solvencia y Crédito, SL v Ausbanc* [2006] ECR I-11125 [38].

[123] *Napier Brown-British Sugar* (Case No IV/30.178) Commission Decision 88/518/EEC [1988] OJ L284/41 [80].

imports,[124] and retail sugar, the price of which was not equally limited by the price of imported sugar.[125] Therefore, the increase in imports was combined with the likely elimination of a competitor, 'which would have repercussions on the competitive structure within the common market'.[126] Thus, whether the requirement of 'effect on trade' is established in purely internal situations, which are outside the scope of free movement provisions, when the cross-border movement either does not exist or is not impeded is inconclusive.[127]

A second argument that 'effect on trade' is broader than the 'purely internal situations' test under Article 34 TFEU is obtained by observing that the latter test assumes functions that are undertaken at three different stages in the application of the competition law provisions (in the context of preliminary references). The first function is to permit the Court of Justice to determine whether a question referred to the Court as a preliminary reference is admissible.[128] The second is the jurisdictional function of delimiting the spheres of application of EU and national law, while the third function is the actual application of the free movement provision (as a matter of substance), as discussed above. A very clear illustration of these three different stages in the application of EU competition law is *Ausbanc*, in which the three stages, namely admissibility criteria for a preliminary reference, 'effect on trade' and restriction of competition under Article 101(1) TFEU, build from the broader to the narrower.[129] The 'effect on trade' requirement, which performs only the second of the above-mentioned functions, can be broad enough, because there is a distinct substantive test to narrow down further the scope of the competition law provisions. This is analysed in section IV.C on the basis of cases in which the conduct covers only a single Member State, yet the 'effect on trade

[124] ibid [78]; Napier Brown was free to choose its source of industrial sugar for repackaging, either domestic or imported, whichever was cheaper at any moment in time, mainly depending upon currency fluctuations.

[125] Mainly because of higher transport costs compared with imported industrial sugar: ibid [44].

[126] ibid [79].

[127] S Weatherill, 'Case C-415/93 *Union Royale Belge des Sociétés de Football Association and others v Bosman and others.* Article 177 Reference by the Cour d'Appel, Liège, on the Interpretation of Articles 48, 85 and 86 EC. Judgement of the European Court of Justice of 15 December 1995 (Case Comment)' (1996) 33 *Common Market Law Review* 1022–23 submits that the purely internal character of the market distortion should not be an obstacle in triggering the application of the EU competition law provisions. A Tryfonidou, *Reverse Discrimination in EC Law* (Kluwer Law International, 2009) 67–71 seems to approach the issue from the opposite direction. She argues that because an 'effect on trade' can be established even when the conduct in question is applied to products confined within the territory of a single Member State, the test under free movement provisions should also not be restricted to the specific goods and services that are involved in the facts of the case and that have moved or (are going to move) between Member States.

[128] See Tryfonidou (n 127) 215 on the traditional implicit assumption that in purely internal situations, EU (substantive) law does not apply, but also that the Court of Justice does not have jurisdiction to answer a preliminary reference. Similarly, see O'Leary (n 118) 37.

[129] See Case C-238/05 *Asnef-Equifax, Servicios de Información sobre Solvencia y Crédito, SL v Ausbanc* [2006] ECR I-11125 [17], [20]–[21] on the admissibility criteria for a preliminary reference, [33]–[39] on the 'effect on trade requirement' and [61] on the 'restriction of competition' under Article 101(1) TFEU, which was not established in that case.

requirement' is established, without necessarily leading to a finding of an 'abuse of a dominant position'. Arguably, in those cases it can be assumed that the Internal Market is already established and competition law is a tool for the proper functioning of this Internal Market. In that case, the concept of 'serious impediments to the proper functioning of the Internal Market' is distinct from the concept of an 'effect on *intra-*[EU] trade' and it 'may constitute one of the criteria for evaluating whether there is sufficient [European] interest to necessitate the investigation of a complaint by the Commission'.[130]

For the very same reason, it is easier for the Court of Justice to assert a real link between the facts of the specific case and EU law in order to answer a preliminary reference under Article 102 TFEU.[131] This could lead to a wide interpretation of 'effect on trade', even where the Court does not have all the necessary factual information as regards 'effect on trade'. For example, in *TeliaSonera*, the Court suggested that the reference was admissible, even though the procedural rules of Sweden did not permit the national court to assess in advance questions of fact such as whether trade between Member States has been affected.[132] However, regardless of this, an abuse of a dominant position may or may not be established.

The Court of Justice is, by contrast, more careful in assuming jurisdiction to address the 'purely internal situations' at the admissibility stage of a preliminary reference under the free movement provisions, the reason being that the 'purely internal situations' test is conflated with the substantive test under the free movement of goods. It is true that the Court of Justice has held that, even in a purely internal situation, it is useful to answer the question referred if, in essence, the national law prohibits reverse discrimination and, hence, the rights depend on the interpretation of EU law.[133] However, this test has been applied in a way that the Court of Justice requests the referring court to show that the national law actually prohibits reverse discrimination.[134] Therefore, the Court of Justice seems

[130] Case C-425/07 P *AEPI AE v Commission* [2009] ECR I-3205 [49]–[50], [52].

[131] In Case C-7/97 *Oscar Bronner GmbH & Co KG v Mediaprint Zeitungs- und Zeitschriftenverlag GmbH & Co KG, Mediaprint Zeitungsvertriebsgesellschaft mbH & Co KG* [1998] ECR I-7791 [10], [12]–[22], the Court held that the question referred was admissible on the basis that the national court was concerned 'to ensure compliance with the rule of the primacy of [EU] law and, consequently, not to tolerate a situation in national law contrary to [EU] law'. It stated that 'whether trade between Member States was genuinely affected concerns the applicability of [Article 102 TFEU] to the factual situation forming the subject-matter of the main proceedings … and is irrelevant for the purposes of verifying whether the questions referred to the Court are admissible', even though the national court had found that the condition was met in the main proceedings.

[132] Case C-52/09 *Konkurrensverket v TeliaSonera Sverige AB* [2011] ECR I-527 [10], [17].

[133] See Case C-245/09 *Omalet NV v Rijksdienst voor Sociale Zekerheid* [2010] ECR I-13771 [15] for a relatively recent reaffirmation: 'even in such a purely internal situation, the Court's answer may nevertheless be useful to the referring court, in particular if its national law required it to grant the same rights to a national of a given Member State as those which a national of another Member State in the same situation would derive from European Union law'.

[134] ibid [16]–[17]. However, this check has not been applied consistently. See, eg, Joined Cases C-94/04 and C-202/04 *Federico Cipolla v Rosaria Fazari, née Portolese and Stefano Macrino and Claudia Capoparte v Roberto Meloni* [2006] ECR I-11421 [30]–[31] for a counter-example. See C Ritter, 'Purely

to require an explicit 'renvoi' technique employed by the national law under the free movement provisions,[135] which should actually prohibit reverse discrimination for the Court to answer a preliminary question on a 'purely internal situation'.

C. The 'Effect on Trade' Test as Distinct from the Substantive Test of 'Abuse of the Dominant Position'

In most Article 102 TFEU cases, the Court of Justice uses the test of 'altering the competitive structure of the market' in order to establish the 'effect on trade' requirement. According to the Court:

> [W]hen an undertaking in a dominant position within the common market abuses its position in such a way that a competitor in the common market is likely to be eliminated, it does not matter whether the conduct relates to the latter's exports or its trade within the common market, once it has been established that this elimination will have repercussions on the competitive structure within the common market.[136]

The underlying support for market integration in these cases is evidenced when the geographic market in question covers more than one Member State and thus the affected competitor ceases to be a source of supply within those Member States.[137] When the geographic market concerned covers a single Member State, the condition of 'effect on trade' is also normally established,[138] either because the abusive conduct makes it more difficult for competitors from other Member States to penetrate the market, thereby leading to isolation of national markets, or because the affected undertaking imports from, or exports to, other Member States. For example, in *Michelin I*, the Court of Justice held that a system of loyalty rebates operating solely in the Netherlands reduced the chances for competitors of significant size established in other Member States to penetrate the Dutch

Internal Situations, Reverse Discrimination, *Guimont*, *Dzodzi* and Article 234' (2006) 31 *European Law Review* 696–703 for a critique against the 'relaxed version' of the test.

[135] The terminology is borrowed from Johnston's typology/taxonomy of 'spillover'-type situations from EU law into national law: A Johnston, '"Spillovers" from EU Law into National Law: (Un)intended Consequences for Private Law Relationships' in D Leczykiewicz and S Weatherill (eds), *The Involvement of EU Law in Private Law Relationships* (Hart Publishing, 2013) 376–82.

[136] *Istituto Chemioterapico Italiano SpA* (n 103) [33]; on that basis, the Court also rejected the undertaking's arguments that 90 per cent of the affected competitor's production is traded outside the common market: ibid [30]–[35]. The same approach was followed, inter alia, in *Hoffmann-La Roche* (n 54) [124]–[126]; *United Brands Company* (n 103) [201]; and Case T-69/89 *Radio Telefis Eireann v Commission* [1991] ECR II-485 [76]–[78].

[137] See all cases cited above in n 136. See also Commission (EC), 'Guidelines on the Effect on Trade Concept Contained in Articles 81 and 82 of the Treaty' (Notice) [2004] OJ C101/81 [75].

[138] Commission (EC) (n 137) [93]–[95]. See also, as counter-examples in a case in which 'effect on trade' was not established, Case T-229/05 *AEPI AE v Commission* [2007] ECR II-00084 [49]–[50], [51] (in Greek and in French).

market.[139] In *Irish Sugar*, the General Court upheld that a scheme of 'sugar export rebates' which discriminated between the dominant undertaking's industrial sugar customers according to whether or not they exported their own processed products affected trade between Member States. The geographic market concerned was Ireland, and the General Court rejected the applicant's arguments that the Commission did not assess the scheme's beneficial effects on exports outside Ireland and also that the Commission rested on the false premise that the Irish market was already isolated.[140]

However, not all allegedly abusive conduct affects the competitive structure of the market. In *Hugin*, a Swedish undertaking (Hugin)[141] refused to supply cash register spare parts to an independent servicing and repair undertaking in London (Liptons), which, according to the Commission, was an example of Hugin's EU-wide policy not to allow distribution of spare parts outside its own network and thus prevented Liptons from importing Hugin spare parts bought elsewhere in the EU.[142] The Court of Justice annulled the Commission's decision on the ground that there was no effect on trade. In particular, after establishing that 'the refusal to supply independent undertakings applied whatever the geographic location of the undertaking',[143] the Court focused on the activities of the affected undertaking, Liptons, whose activities had never extended beyond the UK, nor would in the future, because of the nature of these commercial activities. Therefore, it held that:

> [I]f Liptons had been able to obtain spare parts from a Hugin subsidiary in another Member State, it would have been because Hugin was willing to sell those parts outside its own distribution network. In such a case, however, it would be customary for Liptons to apply to the Hugin subsidiary in its own country rather than to a subsidiary in another Member State.[144]

Therefore, the 'effect on trade' requirement is linked to the Internal Market, but it is arguably broader than the substantive test under the free movement provisions (see section IV.B). However, this broad scope of the 'effect on trade' does not necessarily mean that the objectives of market integration are transcended into the notion and the substantive test of 'abuse of a dominant position'.[145] The reason is

[139] *NV Nederlandsche Banden Industrie Michelin* (n 103) [100]–[105].

[140] *Irish Sugar plc v Commission* (n 115) [125] et seq and [145]–[148]: 'By securing the loyalty of its exporting customers for their supplies of industrial sugar, the applicant prevented those of them who were the most open to inter-State trade from seeking supplies from competitors established in other Member States'. ibid [147].

[141] Prior to Sweden joining the EU.

[142] *Hugin Kassaregister AB* (n 106) 1888 (submissions and arguments of the parties); *Hugin/Liptons* Case No IV/29.132 Commission Decision 78/68/EEC [1978] OJ L22/23, 32.

[143] *Hugin Kassaregister AB and Hugin Cash Registers Ltd v Commission* (n 106) [21]: 'it has not been alleged that Hugin applies differentiated prices at various locations' (ibid [23]).

[144] ibid [24].

[145] This seems to be the assumption made by K Mortelmans, 'Towards Convergence in the Application of the Rules on Free Movement and on Competition?' (2001) 38 *Common Market Law Review* 623, inasmuch as he makes out of the common wording of the 'effect on trade' test and the

that some but not necessarily all of the conduct that has an 'effect on trade' will be found to be abusive. 'Abuse of the dominant position' exists as an additional element in the scheme of Article 102 TFEU. It cannot be assumed that it is not an independent condition for the application of Article 102 TFEU, nor that its role is limited to internal situations, in which 'effect on trade' is established, as analysed above.[146]

D. Geographic Market Definition as an Example of the Likely Different Roles of Market Integration at the Jurisdictional and Substantive Levels

The link between market integration and 'effect on trade' upon jurisdictional grounds is fairly uncontested. The broad interpretation of 'effect on trade' does not necessarily mean that market integration also affects the substantive analysis under Article 102 TFEU; it may or, equally, it may not. In this section, geographic market definition is used as an example to illustrate how market integration may influence the substantive analysis under Article 102 TFEU or, conversely, may not do so. The purpose is to highlight that the geographic market involved and the geographic coverage of the effect of the allegedly abusive conduct coincide or diverge based on whether market integration is a valid consideration for establishing an 'abuse of the dominant position'. Similarly, the geographic market definition and the geographic coverage of the 'effect on trade' do not necessarily coincide, because the latter is influenced by market integration considerations.

In free movement cases, the geographic market definition is not part of the process of applying the aforementioned rules. Inasmuch as purely internal situations are outwith the scope of the free movement provisions, any fragmentation that is condemned takes place along national lines, because the targeted measure has only national territorial scope at most (eg, it is the Member State's legislation or administrative practice). Even if the MEQR test under Article 34 TFEU moves towards an 'appreciable restriction to market access' test for non-discriminatory measures,[147] market access would still need to be delineated by reference to one Member State, because the restrictive measure is of a regulatory nature.

Geographic market definition under Article 102 TFEU has a specific purpose, namely to identify the competitive constraints that the undertaking faces, in order to assess the degree of its market power.[148] Therefore, the geographic market

definition of MEQR that the 'primary and overriding objective of the provisions on free movement and competition [is] the establishment and operation of the Common Market'.

[146] See text to nn 129–30. Besides, in these cases, market integration considerations should not normally come into play because the Internal Market has already been established and competition law is a tool for its proper functioning (as mentioned earlier).

[147] See ch 3, section III.B.

[148] Commission (EC), Notice on the Definition of Relevant Markets for the Purposes of Community Competition Law [1997] OJ C372/5 [2].

context in which the undertaking operates and coverage of the conduct's object or effect should, in principle, coincide. This has been pointed out by the General Court, by reference to the example of abusive discrimination under Article 102(c) TFEU.[149] The General Court, by reference to *United Brands* and *Tetra Pak II*, clarified that charging different prices:

> [M]ay, in the absence of objective explanation, constitute an indicium of discrimination where those prices are applied on a particular geographic market, characterised by sufficiently homogeneous conditions of competition, [but] this is not the case where they are applied on separate geographic markets, characterised by insufficiently homogeneous conditions of competition, regard being had in particular to the relevant regulatory framework.[150]

Therefore, if a product market is not integrated, so is not already EU-wide, because the regulatory framework is fragmented, but the incumbent undertaking is active at an EU-wide level, the geographic market cannot consist of more than one Member State, since the conditions of competition are not homogeneous. In such a case, let us assume that market integration influences Article 102 TFEU by determining the object or effect of the unilateral conduct in question. In that case, a paradox is revealed, namely that the geographic market definition and the market coverage of the conduct's effect do not coincide, and this diversification defeats the purpose of defining the market in the first place in order to apply Article 102 TFEU.

For example, in *Syfait*, the Greek Competition Commission found that the geographic market involved in Glaxo's refusal to supply specific medical products to Greek distributors involved in parallel trade was Greece, because of the special regulatory regime regarding the distribution and the prices of the medical products.[151] However, according to the dissenting opinion of two members of the Greek Competition Commission, in parallel trade cases the geographic market comprises the entire EU, because the effects of either sanctioning or allowing the unilateral conduct are felt throughout the EU, where Glaxo is active.[152] Equally, in *Deutsche Telekom*, the geographic market was solely Germany, because of the telecoms network geographic coverage and the existence of regulatory arrangements along national lines.[153] However, the Commission established an abusive margin

[149] *GlaxoSmithKline Services Unlimited* (n 33) [177]–[179].

[150] ibid [177], citing *United Brands Company* (n 103) [44]–[56], [207], [208], [225], [228] and [233]; Case T-83/91 *Tetra Pak v Commission* [1994] ECR II-755 [92]–[96], [161], [164], [165], [167], [170].

[151] Hellenic Competition Commission, Decision No 229/III/2003 of 28 February 2002 [16] (text in Greek).

[152] ibid. Interestingly, there is a case at the EU level in which the Commission has essentially presented the same opinion, namely that, because parallel trading is highly likely between the Member States, the relevant geographic market is the EU as a whole. See Case T-30/89 *Hilti AG v Commission* [1991] ECR II-01439 [79]–[81]. However, in this case there was no fragmented regulatory framework, parallel trade being due to low transport costs for the traded goods.

[153] *Deutsche Telekom AG* (Case COMP/C-1/37.451, 37.578, 37.579) Commission Decision 2003/707/EC [2003] OJ L263/9 [92]–[95]; Case T-271/03 *Deutsche Telekom v Commission* [2008] ECR II-477 [35].

squeeze in light of the fact that the prices charged by the incumbents would not allow equally efficient competitors established in another Member State to enter the German market.[154]

The same paradox is observed when the 'effect on trade' requirement is established but the geographic market under Article 102 TFEU comprises a single Member State. The paradox is that the geographic market definition and the geographic coverage of the 'effect on trade' diverge. It is noteworthy that in *Michelin I* and *Irish Sugar*, the dominant undertakings challenged the Commission decisions, complaining about, inter alia, the geographic market definition.[155]

Highlighting this paradox does not necessarily serve the purpose of arguing that, for example, in parallel trade cases the geographic market should be broader. This depends on whether market integration is a valid consideration for substantiating an 'abuse of a dominant position', which is the main question to be explored in the remainder of this book.[156] Conversely, with regard to the 'effect on trade' requirement, the same paradoxical situation is justified and confirms the claim that market integration plays a legitimate role in establishing this jurisdictional requirement, as discussed earlier.

V. CONCLUSIONS

This chapter has explored the objectives of Article 102 TFEU and their relationship to market integration. Two main objectives have been identified, namely economic efficiency and economic freedom. The analysis shows that, in both cases, there are trade-offs between various categories of consumers as regards the protection that is afforded to them, for example, between present and future consumers under an efficiency standard or between intermediate and end-consumers under a freedom-oriented standard.

Subsequently, the historical link of these two objectives with market integration is identified, based on policy documents and early case law, until the formal completion of the Internal Market in 1992. The analysis shows that far from being a stand-alone, third objective of Article 102 TFEU, market integration served, traditionally, as the lens through which the two objectives of Article 102 TFEU were interpreted, via ex-Article 3(1)(g) TEC. Efficiency and economic freedom were the objectives of market integration in the first place, affording a uniform level of protection to the various categories of consumers identified above.

[154] *Deutsche Telekom AG* (Case COMP/C-1/37.451, 37.578, 37.579) (n 153) [183], [201]–[203].

[155] *NV Nederlandsche Banden Industrie Michelin* (n 103) [22]–[23]; *Irish Sugar plc v Commission* (n 115) [69]–[79].

[156] A conclusion drawn from research presented in this book is that market integration should be taken into account under Article 102 TFEU if regulatory intervention is in conformity with the free movement provision and, further, that such assessment is better accommodated under the geographic market definition; see ch 6, section II.B.

The historical link between competition and market integration is not conclusive, with regard to the interpretation of 'abuse of the dominant position' in the future, because of the flexibility of the teleological method of interpretation employed by the Court of Justice. In section IV, however, it is argued that the historical link is legitimately echoed in the requirement of 'effect on trade' under Article 102 TFEU, because of that Article's jurisdictional function to delineate the boundaries between EU and national competition law. The analysis of the Commission's and European courts' case law regarding the 'effect on trade' test reveals that a broad approach is adopted, since 'effect on trade' is established even when the goods in question do not actually cross national frontiers or when a cross-border movement exists but is not impeded by the conduct in question. However, the case law does not endorse the view that all allegedly abusive conduct has an 'effect on trade', nor that the substantive test under the notion of 'abuse of the dominant position' is rendered redundant, once 'effect on trade' is established.

This confirms that, for market integration to be taken into account, 'effect on trade' is the minimum legitimate requirement under Article 102 TFEU, which leaves open the question as to what extent market integration should affect the substantive analysis of finding an 'abuse of the dominant position'. The example of the geographic market definition is advanced to show the likely different influences of market integration upon the substantive analysis under Article 102 TFEU.

2

Market Separation under Article 102 TFEU: The Role of Dominance

I. INTRODUCTION

The assessment of the effects on competition of the conduct by a dominant undertaking is placed under the European market regulatory framework, rather than a national one, once it is established that such conduct 'affects trade between Member States' (Chapter one above). This chapter explores the question as to which is the correct regulatory instrument—the free movement provisions or Article 102 TFEU—under which to address alleged market separation by dominant undertakings. Cases in which conduct by dominant undertakings is condemned under Article 102 TFEU, because there is a protectionist intent or effect (market separation), are identified in section II.[1] Therefore, 'abuse of the dominant position', which has the intent or effect of hindering cross-border trade, can be conducted by dominant undertakings. On the face of it, such conduct seems materially similar to a 'restriction on free movement'. However, conduct by private actors has also been condemned under the free movement provisions. These cases, which are often referred to as cases of horizontal (direct) application of the freedoms,[2] are examined in this chapter as a category of regulation of private conduct that involves, potentially, market separation by dominant undertakings as one of its specific manifestations. The purpose of this examination is to support the view that Article 102 TFEU, with its distinct conditions of application and, in particular, the requirement of significant market power, constitutes a meaningful limitation to any expansive view of the horizontal application of the freedoms.[3] Therefore, market separation by dominant undertakings is not a

[1] Therefore, cases in which the undertaking's conduct, such as discrimination on the grounds of nationality, is assessed under Article 102 TFEU in conjunction with Article 106 TFEU are outside the scope of this chapter. See, for example, Case C-18/93 *Corsica Ferries Italia Srl v Corpo dei Piloti del Porto di Genova* [1994] ECR I-1783; Case C-163/99 *Portuguese Republic v Commission* [2001] ECR I-2613; and *Deutsche Post AG- Interception of Cross-Border Mail* (Case COMP/C-1/36.915) Commission Decision 2001/892/EC [2001] OJ L331/40.

[2] See J Baquero Cruz, *Between Competition and Free Movement: The Economic Constitutional Law of the European Community* (Hart Publishing, 2002) 106–08 for a critique of the use of the term.

[3] Contra C Krenn, 'A Missing Piece in the Horizontal Effect "Jigsaw": Horizontal Direct Effect and the Free Movement of Goods' (2012) 49 *Common Market Law Review* 203–06, with very poor argumentation.

specific manifestation of a generic application of the freedoms to private actors. Three arguments are advanced to support this, following a brief description of the asymmetry between the addressees of the competition law provisions and the addressees of the free movement provisions (see section III). This description assumes that the functional definition of the notion of 'undertaking' under Article 102 TFEU is employed in accordance with the case law.[4]

First, the existing cases that apply, simultaneously, both the freedoms and the competition law provisions to the same conduct are to be read in the context of a mutually exclusive, functional understanding of 'state-actors' and 'undertakings', namely on the basis of 'regulatory power' and 'economic activity'. The fact that there are cases of false classification of the actor can arguably be explained by the significance of public enforcement of the competition law provisions as opposed to the prevailing private enforcement of the freedoms (see section IV).

Second, the recent cases in which the Court of Justice does not seem to require a link between the power of the actor to obstruct the freedom and a regulatory function do not negate the significance of 'dominant undertakings' for the purposes of applying Article 102 TFEU. These cases erode one side of the 'mirror image' of 'regulation' and 'economic activity' as the benchmarks of the personal scope of the two sets of provisions. The personal scope of the free movement provisions has expanded beyond regulatory functions, but it has never crossed the line of an 'undertaking' as set by the concept of 'economic activity'. This argument is complemented by a normative and a legal analysis that shows dominance as a condition *sine qua non* under which the anti-competitive effect of market separation occurs under Article 102 TFEU. By contrast, no quantitative threshold as regards the ability of 'state measures' to obstruct the freedoms has been established (see section V).

Third, a textual argument, drawn from the Treaty itself, and in particular Article 106(2) TFEU, confirms the view that alleged market separation by dominant undertakings was intended to be subject to Article 102 TFEU alone (see section VI).

II. CASES OF MARKET SEPARATION BY DOMINANT UNDERTAKINGS UNDER ARTICLE 102 TFEU

The Commission and the European courts have condemned market separation along national lines within the EU as an abuse of a dominant position under Article 102 TFEU. A distinction is drawn, for reasons of systematic presentation,

[4] In Case C-41/90 *Klaus Höfner and Fritz Elser v Macrotron GmbH* [1991] ECR I-1979 [21], the Court of Justice construed the definition of the concept of an undertaking as 'encompassing every entity engaged in an economic activity, regardless of the legal status of the entity and the way in which it is financed'. See O Odudu, *The Boundaries of EC Competition Law: The Scope of Article* 81 (Oxford University Press, 2006) 23–56 for an analysis of the functional approach to the definition of an undertaking.

between cases that deal with geographic price discrimination and those with exclusionary practices which hinder competition across national borders, in light of the four categories listed in Article 102 TFEU as examples of abusive conduct. Although the distinction implies that geographic price discrimination has been treated as an independent ground of abuse under Article 102(c) TFEU, it will be revealed that the Commission and the European courts have, only formally, condemned this as unlawful in itself. Rather, discrimination under Article 102(c) TFEU is the inherent result of another independent, either exclusionary or exploitative, abuse.[5] Therefore, the focus of the case law description in this section is not placed on the distinct—legal and economic—guiding principles of abusive discrimination.[6] The section presents the cases of any abuse of a dominant position, regardless of its form, that has been found to have an effect, or intent, of creating artificial barriers to trade between Member States.

A. Geographic Price Discrimination

The first case to address geographic price discrimination is *United Brands*.[7] The Commission, confirmed by the Court of Justice, condemned as abusive the policy of United Brands Company (UBC) to charge different prices for the sale of its branded bananas to distributors, according to the Member State in which the distributor was established and, thus, where it was intended to sell the bananas. At the same time, UBC's general sales conditions incorporated a clause which prohibited the resale, within a single state or between Member States, of bananas while still green, which had a similar effect of export prohibition. The Court of Justice held that:

> The discriminatory prices, which varied according to the circumstances of the Member States, were just so many obstacles to the free movement of goods and their effect was intensified by the clause forbidding the resale of bananas while still green and by reducing the deliveries of the quantities ordered.
>
> A rigid partitioning of national markets was thus created at price levels, which were artificially different, placing certain distributor/ripeners at a competitive disadvantage, since compared with what it should have been competition had thereby been distorted.[8]

[5] Conversely, price discrimination cannot in itself constitute an exclusionary abuse; see Case C-209/10 *Post Danmark A/S v Konkurrencerådet*, Judgment of 27 March 2012 (NYR) [30].

[6] See R O'Donoghue and J Padilla, *The Law and Economics of Article 82 EC* (Hart Publishing, 2006) 202–06, 552–55; D Geradin and N Petit, 'Price Discrimination under EC Competition Law' in Swedish Competition Authority (eds), *The Pros and Cons of Price Discrimination* (Elanders Gotab, 2005) 21; D Gerard, 'Price Discrimination under Article 82(2)(c) EC: Clearing Up the Ambiguities' (2005) Global Competition Law Centre, Research Paper on the Modernisation of Article 82 EC, on the use of Article 102(c) TFEU as a legal basis for various categories of price discrimination.

[7] Case 27/76 *United Brands Company and United Brands Continentaal BV v Commission* [1978] ECR 207.

[8] ibid [232]–[233].

The Court of Justice seems to suggest that UBC segregated the Internal Market along national lines from the outset through contractual clauses prohibiting exports, thereby being able to charge artificially different prices in each Member State.[9] It seems that charging different prices in each Member State was then found to be abusive in itself, because its market partitioning effect allegedly placed the distributors at a competitive disadvantage, even though distributors/ripeners from different Member States were not in competition with one another once the geographic market had been segregated.

Similarly, in *Tetra Pak II*, the Commission, confirmed by the General Court, found discriminatory pricing contrary to Article 102 TFEU on the basis of the different selling prices of the Tetra Pak cartons and machines between Italy and the other Member States.[10] However, the Commission and the General Court did not focus on establishing the competitive disadvantage flowing from Tetra Pak's policy of applying different prices within the same geographic market. Rather, they found various contractual resale restrictions to be abusive because they comprised a 'market compartmentalisation policy … thereby creating the right conditions for the success of policies such as a profit maximization policy, based on discrimination, or a policy of eliminatory prices intended to preserve or strengthen a dominant position'.[11] It seems that geographic price discrimination was the result of (or a proof of) the market partitioning effect of Tetra Pak's contractual abuses.

British Leyland is another case of geographic price discrimination under Article 102 TFEU.[12] British Leyland, which had a statutory monopoly for the issue of certificates of conformity for British Leyland vehicles in the UK, marketed its vehicles in the UK through a selective distribution network. Parallel trade in the reimportation of British Leyland cars, mainly from Belgium, was developed as a result of the differences between the prices charged by British Leyland in the UK for right-hand-drive vehicles and in the continental European Member States for left-hand-drive vehicles, because conversion of left-hand-drive to right-hand-drive vehicles was easy. The Commission found that the non-renewal of conformity certificates for reimported left-hand-drive vehicles, in addition to the charging of higher fees for the grant of conformity certificates for such vehicles, was abusive as a result of British Leyland's intent to create barriers to reimportation to the UK of left-hand-drive cars and to protect its domestic distributors, a

[9] The Court of Justice held that the contractual clause, in itself, is 'an abuse of the dominant position since it limits markets to the prejudice of consumers and affects trade between Member States, in particular by partitioning national markets. Thus UBC's organization of the market confined the ripeners to the role of suppliers of the local market and prevented them from developing their capacity to trade vis-à-vis UBC', ibid [159]–[160].

[10] *Tetra Pak II* (Case IV/31043) Commission Decision 92/163/EEC [1992] OJ L72/1 [154]–[155], [160]; Case T-83/91 *Tetra Pak v Commission* [1994] ECR II-755 [160]–[173].

[11] *Tetra Pak II* (Case IV/31043) (n 10) [154]; *Tetra Pak v Commission* (n 10) [170]–[171].

[12] Case 226/84 *British Leyland Public Limited Company v Commission* [1986] ECR 3263.

decision that was confirmed by the Court of Justice.[13] The Commission found that the fee charged was both excessive and discriminatory.[14] However, the Court of Justice focused not on discrimination itself, but rather on the 'disproportionate [price level of the fee] to the economic value of the service provided'.[15] In addition, it is noteworthy that it was British Leyland's own conduct which 'allowed a trade in the re-importation of [left-hand-drive] cars to develop. That trade came about as a result of its pricing policy'.[16]

This is in contrast with the somewhat more recent *Sotirios Lélos* case, which involved parallel trade in pharmaceuticals.[17] In this case, despite Glaxo's undisputed intent to limit parallel trade in the market for specific prescription medicines,[18] the Court of Justice said that, in assessing Glaxo's refusal to supply wholesalers in Greece involved in parallel exports, 'it cannot be ignored that State intervention [price regulation in the pharmaceuticals sector] is one of the factors liable to create opportunities for parallel trade'.[19] It seems that the Court of Justice did not consider Glaxo's conduct, which was aimed at neutralising the benefits in terms of prices that parallel exports could bring to other Member States, to be abusive per se, as was the case in *British Leyland*.[20] This was precisely because the price differences allowing for the development of parallel trade did not stem from Glaxo's own pricing policy. However, the Court of Justice seems to infer that Glaxo's practice, which was aimed at limiting parallel exports, was liable to eliminate competition in Member States other than Greece and therefore was abusive prima facie.[21] In exceptional circumstances, it could be justified and, hence, the Court focused its analysis on the question whether the conduct was a reasonable and proportionate way of protecting Glaxo's legitimate commercial interests.[22]

A final case involving, indirectly, geographic price discrimination along national lines is the *Swedish Interconnectors* Commission Decision, on the basis of which the Commission accepted as binding commitments under Article 9 of Regulation 1/2003. According to the Commission, SvK, the state-owned Transmission System Operator of Sweden, allegedly abused its dominant position on the Swedish electricity transmission market by curtailing capacity on the Swedish interconnectors when it anticipated internal congestion within the Swedish transmission system,

[13] ibid [18], [21], [24] and [29].

[14] *British Leyland* (Case IV/30.615) Commission Decision 84/379 [1984] OJ L207/11 [26].

[15] *British Leyland* (n 12) [31].

[16] ibid [13].

[17] Joined Cases C-468/06–478/06 *Sotirios Lélos kai Sia EE and others v GlaxoSmithKline AEVE Farmakeftikon Proïonton, formerly Glaxowellcome AEVE* [2008] ECR I-7139.

[18] ibid [36].

[19] ibid [67].

[20] ibid [37], [66], in which *British Leyland* is being cited.

[21] *Sot Lélos kai Sia EE and others* (n 17) [35].

[22] ibid [69].

thereby discriminating between different network users located inside and outside Sweden. According to the Commission:

> SvK's practice of restricting exports by reducing interconnection capacity between Sweden and neighbouring Member States as well as Contracting Parties to the EEA Agreement due to internal congestion leads, de facto, to discrimination between the customers in Sweden and customers in the Member States and Contracting Parties to the EEA Agreement importing electricity from Sweden. Discrimination between customers based on residence constitutes, in view of the Court [of Justice] case law, an abuse of dominant position in violation of Article 102 TFEU ...[23]

> Moreover, Article 35 TFEU expressly prohibits quantitative restrictions on exports and all measures having equivalent effect. It is thus clear that a Member State would not be entitled to restrict exports of electricity so as to reserve such electricity for domestic consumption. Similarly, a dominant undertaking cannot seek to achieve the same objective through its conduct on the market without falling foul of Union competition rules.[24]

B. Exclusionary Abuses Hindering Competition across National Borders

The Commission and the European courts condemn certain conduct because of its exclusionary effects under Article 102 TFEU. In a stream of cases, the exclusionary effect of the dominant undertaking's conduct is, in part, equated with hindering competition across national borders or raising barriers to market entry for out-of-state competitors.

For example, in *British Gypsum*, the dominant undertaking decided to withdraw the four per cent rebate that it had granted to Northern Ireland merchants who intended to import plasterboard from Spain and, at the same time, it decided to grant a rebate of five per cent to the merchants who agreed to obtain their supplies exclusively from British Gypsum (BG).[25] The General Court held that:

> Such a practice, by virtue of its discriminatory nature, was clearly intended to penalize those merchants who intended to import plasterboard and to dissuade them from doing so, thus further supporting BG's position in the plasterboard market.[26]

It seems that the exclusionary effect of the loyalty rebates stems from the fact that the rebates were conditional on the recipients not handling imported products and that the rebates necessarily made it more difficult for plasterboard importers to penetrate the Northern Ireland market. At the same time, the dominant undertaking implemented a policy of giving priority to orders for plaster placed by

[23] *Swedish Interconnectors* (Case 39351) Commission Decision of 14 April 2010 (NYR) [42].
[24] ibid [43].
[25] Case T-65/89 *BPB Industries plc and British Gypsum Ltd v Commission* [1993] ECR II-389.
[26] ibid [119].

customers in the UK who did not handle imported plasterboard from Spain. The General Court held that:

> [T]he criterion adopted in this case by BG was based on a distinction between, on the one hand, customers who marketed plasterboard imported and produced by certain of its competitors and, on the other, 'loyal' customers who obtained their supplies from BG. Such a criterion, which results in the provision of equivalent services on unequal terms, is in itself anti-competitive by reason of the discriminatory purpose which it pursues and the exclusionary effect which may result from it.[27]

In *Irish Sugar*, the dominant undertaking operated a system of 'sugar export rebates' which discriminated between its industrial sugar customers according to whether or not they exported their own processed products. Also, it operated a system of 'border rebates', which were granted to certain retailers established in the border area between Ireland and Northern Ireland and which aimed to 'confront' competition from sugar imported from Northern Ireland.[28] As regards the system of 'export rebates', the General Court pointed out that:

> [T]he Commission did not simply rely on the discriminatory character of the [export rebates] in order to find them contrary to [Article 86]: it has also demonstrated that granting them placed the applicant's competitors on the industrial sugar market who were based outside Ireland at a competitive disadvantage[29] ... granting such [rebates] prevents other potential suppliers from competing, on a fair basis, with the services offered by the applicant to its exporting customers. In any event, the Commission has shown that the [export rebates] constituted a hindrance to importations of industrial sugar into Ireland, inasmuch as they reinforced the isolation of the Irish market.[30]

In relation to the 'border rebates' scheme, the General Court found the scheme discriminatory and thus abusive, on the basis of the dominant undertaking's own submission that:

> [I]ts economic capacity to offer rebates in the region [where retailers faced competition from cheap imports from another Member State] depended on the stability of its prices in other regions, which amounts to recognition that it financed those rebates by means of its sales in the rest of Irish territory.[31]

In addition, the General Court held that:

> [T]he influence of the pricing policy of operators active principally on a neighbouring market, in this case the British and Northern Ireland market, on that of operators active on another national market is of the very essence of a common market. Anything which restricts that influence must therefore be regarded as an obstacle to the achievement of

[27] ibid [94].
[28] Case T-228/97 *Irish Sugar plc v Commission* [1999] ECR II-2969.
[29] ibid [145].
[30] ibid [148].
[31] ibid [188].

> that common market and prejudicial to the outcome of effective and undistorted competition, especially with regard to the interests of consumers.[32]

More recently, in *Deutsche Telekom*, the Commission, in a decision confirmed by the General Court and the Court of Justice, equated the competitive harm flowing from a margin squeeze practice with raising barriers to market entry for competitors, in particular those aiming at a 'geographically extended competition'.[33] The Commission held that:

> The abuse involves the whole territory of the Federal Republic of Germany and jeopardises the proper functioning of the common market by raising barriers to effective entry to the relevant telecommunications markets in Germany, thus impeding the establishment of transnational markets.
>
> Through this abuse, DT is jeopardising the objective of achieving EU-wide establishment of an Internal Market for telecommunications networks and services with undistorted competition.[34]

C. Comment: The Significance of Geographic Market Definition

The preceding description of the case law under Article 102 TFEU shows that there are, indeed, cases in which market separation by dominant undertakings has been condemned as abusive, because it has the intent, or effect, of creating artificial trade barriers between Member States and leads to the isolation of national markets; therefore it falls under the material scope of Article 102 TFEU. In some of these cases, such as *United Brands* and *Tetra Pak II*, the application of Article 102 TFEU is qualified by the assumption that the geographic market in which the dominant position is established involves more than one Member State.[35] However, in most cases, the geographic market involved comprises a single Member State, even though the effect of the abusive practice is felt throughout the territory of more than one Member State. In such cases, the starting point is that the Member States are geographically distinct markets, based on objective factors such as the regulatory framework[36] or transport costs.[37] The exclusionary effect of the abusive conduct is equated to raising the barriers to enter a national market for out-of-state competitors.

[32] ibid [185].

[33] *Deutsche Telekom AG*, Commission Decision 2003/707/EC [2003] OJ L263/9 [183]; Case T-271/03 *Deutsche Telekom v Commission* [2008] ECR II-477 [235]; Case C-280/08 P *Deutsche Telekom v Commission* [2010] ECR I-09555 [255].

[34] *Deutsche Telekom AG*, Commission Decision 2003/707/EC (n 33) [202]–[203].

[35] See also ch 1, text to nn 149–50.

[36] Hellenic Competition Commission, Decision No 229/III/2003 of 28 February 2002 [16] (text in Greek); *Deutsche Telekom AG* (Case COMP/C-1/37.451, 37.578, 37.579) Commission Decision 2003/707/EC [2003] OJ L263/9 [92]–[95].

[37] *Irish Sugar plc v Commission* (n 28) [80]–[84], in which the General Court rejected the applicant's argument that the Commission failed to take into account potential (out-of-state) competition when assessing the undertaking's market power in Ireland.

III. AN ANALYTICAL APPROACH TO MARKET SEPARATION BY PRIVATE ACTORS UNDER THE FREE MOVEMENT PROVISIONS AND ITS RELATIONSHIP TO MARKET SEPARATION BY DOMINANT UNDERTAKINGS

Section II identified the cases in which conduct that creates artificial barriers to trade between Member States by dominant undertakings was held to be abusive under Article 102 TFEU. Therefore, 'abuse of the dominant position', which has the intent or effect of hindering cross-border trade, can be conducted by dominant undertakings. On the face of it, such conduct seems materially similar to a 'restriction on free movement'. However, there is also conduct by private actors which has been condemned under the free movement provisions.

The discussion, as such, of the horizontal direct applicability of the free movement provisions is beyond the scope of this book. The question addressed here is whether conduct by dominant undertakings, which separates the Internal Market, should, at a normative level, qualify as an abuse. However, the discussion of the addressees of the freedoms touches upon this question insofar as horizontal direct applicability of the free movement provisions is identified by reference to conduct which is not within the compass of the competition law provisions, namely conduct by private actors which are not caught by Article 102 TFEU. For that reason, the discussion of the case law on the horizontal direct applicability of the freedoms is a necessary exercise in order to assess whether the competition law provisions should be retained as a meaningful limitation to horizontal applicability of the freedoms. Accordingly, it can be determined whether undertakings with significant market power should, or should not, be subject to the free movement provisions, as the obvious candidate to comprise an additional category of private actors, which are subject to the freedoms.[38]

The following sections, in effect, provide arguments to support a view that obstacles to trade between the Member States created by dominant undertakings ought, in principle, to be assessed under Article 102 TFEU alone rather than by applying both sets of provisions to the same conduct, or the free movement provisions in place of Article 102 TFEU. The fact that the intermediate category of cases in which the freedoms apply horizontally is itself subject to criticism at a normative level[39] does not preclude the descriptive use of the relevant case law, to the extent that it is still good law.

[38] See the question as set by G Davies, 'Freedom of Movement, Horizontal Effect, and Freedom of Contract' (2012) 3 *European Review of Private Law* 821–22, who seems to suggest the view that the freedoms should, potentially, apply to dominant undertakings. O Odudu, 'The Public/Private Distinction in EU Internal Market Law' (2010) 46 (4) *Revue Trimestrielle de Droit Européen* 836 uses the same assumptions to make an argument in regard to the horizontal direct applicability of the free movement provisions itself, namely that the obligations established by the case law which applies the free movement provisions to private parties (outwith the competition law provisions) ought to be distinct and narrower than the obligations imposed under the same provisions to state actors.

[39] See, eg, H Schepel, 'Constitutionalising the Market, Marketising the Constitution, and to Tell the Difference: On the Horizontal Application of the Free Movement Provisions in EU Law' (2012) 18

A. The Asymmetry between the Addressees of the Competition Law Provisions and the Free Movement Provisions

While the competition law provisions are expressly addressed to undertakings, the same does not apply to the free movement provisions. The Court of Justice implied a distinction between Treaty provisions which impose obligations upon individuals and Treaty provisions which impose obligations upon Member States, in its seminal judgment in *Van Gend & Loos*.[40] What the Court aimed to do was to establish directly enforceable rights of individuals stemming from Treaty provisions that impose obligations upon Member States. However, the Court was able to do so because of the presence in the Treaty of provisions that impose obligations upon individuals.[41]

The wording of the Treaty free movement provisions does not dictate that the addressees of the obligations are only Member States and not individuals. For that reason, academic debate has centred on the question as to whether private actions having the aim or effect of creating artificial barriers to *inter*-state trade fall exclusively under the competition law provisions or whether private actions that do not fall under the competition provisions are nevertheless assessed under the free movement provisions. In other words, if the specific requirements of Articles 101 and 102 TFEU are not established, should private actors escape both sets of provisions or is this an unwarranted gap or asymmetry in the scheme of the Treaty?[42]

The question remains unresolved, despite the evolution of the definition of the notion of 'undertaking' under the competition law provisions, on the basis of which the Court of Justice embraced a functional approach to the notion and defined it by reference to an 'economic activity'.[43] Arguably, this is because the alleged asymmetry is related to the abstract determination of the personal scope of

European Law Journal 177, who argues that this sometimes leads to a constitutionalised market and sometimes to a marketised constitution, without there being any principled way of distinguishing between the two.

40 Case 26/62 *Van Gend & Loos v Netherlands Inland Revenue Administration* [1963] ECR 1, 12. The same distinction is made more clearly in the Opinion of AG Roemer at [20].

41 See R Lane, 'The Internal Market and the Individual' in N Nic Shuibhne (ed), *Regulating the Internal Market* (Edward Elgar, 2006) 246.

42 See, in particular, the vigorous discussion between Judge P Pescatore, 'Public and Private Aspects of European Community Competition Law' (1987) 10 *Fordham International Law Journal* 373 and an advisor (at the time) of the Commission, G Marenco, 'Competition between National Economies and Competition between Businesses: A Response to Judge Pescatore' (1987) 10 *Fordham International Law Journal* 420, the former arguing in favour of a cross-application of both sets of provisions based on an 'eventual unity of purpose', while the latter argued against such gap-closing interpretation, on the basis that the asymmetry is deliberate and justified. See also R Joliet, 'National Anti-Competitive Legislation and Community Law' (1989) 12 *Fordham International Law Journal* 163; and R Joliet (in collaboration with D Keeling), 'Trade Mark Law and the Free Movement of Goods: The Overruling of the Judgment in Hag I' (1991) 22 *International Review of Industrial Property and Copyright Law* 313, who are in favour of keeping the distinction based on the addressee of the provision.

43 See Odudu (n 4) 45–56, who uses the functional approach as a means for maintaining the private/public divide of the Treaty provisions. Baquero Cruz (n 2) 121–25 is in favour of determining

the competition law provisions and the free movement provisions. Undertakings that hold a dominant position is a narrower concept than the notion of private parties. This is not the case under the free movement provisions. There is no further qualification to the notion of 'state measure', even if a functional definition of the 'state' is employed.

In addition, the concept of 'economic activity' is associated with the definition of 'undertaking' under the competition law provisions. By contrast, under the free movement provisions, the term 'economic activity' is associated with the much broader market element as referred to in ex-Article 2 TEC,[44] which is necessarily established if it is established that there is an 'undertaking'.[45] Moreover, 'economic activity' under the free movement provisions is associated with the interplay between economic and non-economic values under the prohibition–justification scheme of the Treaty provisions, inasmuch as purely economic grounds can never serve as a justification.[46] An example of this double use of 'economic activity' in the same judgment is *Walrave*.[47] The reference to the practice of sports as an 'economic activity' is made in paragraph [4] in relation to ex-Article 2 TEC, whereas in paragraph [8], it is made in relation to the material scope of the prohibition of discriminatory barriers to the free movement of workers. This double use of the term 'economic activity' under the freedoms has led to misunderstandings in regard to its relationship with the notion of 'undertaking'.[48] Article 3 TEU-L, which in substance replaced Article 2 TEC, omits the reference to 'economic activities' in ex-Article 2 TEC, after the entry into force of the Lisbon Treaty.[49] This leaves 'economic activity' as relevant only to the material scope of the free movement provisions and hence suggests an asymmetry, in that the core of the defini-

the personal scope of free movement provisions based on the nature of the action, but he is against the maintenance of a private/public divide.

[44] 'The Community shall have as its task … to promote throughout the Community a harmonious, balanced and sustainable development of economic activities.'

[45] A similar, confusing, double use of the notion of 'economic activity' is provided by the Court of Justice under the Sixth (VAT) Directive 77/388/EEC in Case C-369/04 *Hutchison 3G UK Ltd and others v Commissioners of Customs and Excise* [2007] ECR I-5247 [34]–[42]. The Court of Justice seems to confirm that there is a broader concept of 'economic activity' (at [42]), under which both regulatory activities and economic activities fall based on their purpose (at [38]). This second notion of 'economic activity' is, based on its purpose, defined by reference to the case law on the notion of 'undertaking' under the competition law provisions.

[46] See ch 3, section III.A.

[47] Case 36/74 *BNO Walrave and LJN Koch v Association Union Cycliste Internationale and others* [1974] ECR 1405.

[48] The most prominent example of a misunderstanding of the relationship between the two concepts of 'economic activity' under the free movement provisions and the notion of 'undertaking' is Case T-193/02 *Laurent Piau v Commission* [2005] ECR II-209 [69]–[70], [73]. See also P Ibáñez Colomo, 'The Application of EC Treaty Rules to Sport: The Approach of the European Court of First Instance in the Meca-Medina and Piau Cases' (2006) 3(2) *Entertainment and Sports Law Journal* 4, 7 on the confusing, double, use of the notion of 'economic activity' in *Piau*.

[49] This confirms the theory endorsed in this book of inclusiveness of any non-economic value under the free movement provisions and the emphasis on the 'internal' element of the internal market, since the threshold for the market element is very low; see ch 3, n 47 and ch 4, section II.A.

tion of the *personal* scope of the competition law provisions is only associated with the *material* scope of the free movement provisions.[50] Therefore, anything that is outside the scope of the competition law provisions because it is not an 'economic activity' as defined under the notion of 'undertaking' can potentially be caught by the provisions on free movement of goods, workers or freedom to provide services.

The question remains as to whether conduct by dominant undertakings can also be put to the same test, as a more specific type of conduct by private parties subject to the freedoms. The following three sections provide three arguments against such an expansive view of the horizontal applicability of the freedoms and, in effect, support the view that the intended and principled difference in the personal scope of the freedoms and the competition law provisions spills over into their material scope of finding a restriction. Therefore, market separation by dominant undertakings cannot be assimilated with restrictions of the free movement provisions.

IV. FUNCTIONALISM AND THE SIGNIFICANCE OF PUBLIC ENFORCEMENT OF THE COMPETITION LAW PROVISIONS

The majority of cases of horizontal applicability of the freedoms are seemingly about an expansion of the personal scope of the freedoms to private parties, but, in fact, they are about a functional understanding of a 'state-actor'.[51] Interestingly enough, it is in these cases in which the Court of Justice has been invited to apply simultaneously both the free movement provisions and the competition law provisions to the same conduct.

For example, in *Walrave* and *Bosman*, the Court of Justice applied Article 45 TFEU to private sports associations' rules, which are 'aimed at regulating in

[50] See also V Hatzopoulos, 'The Economic Constitution of the EU Treaty and the Limits between Economic and Non-economic Activities' [2012] *European Business Law Review* 973, who delves into a mapping exercise of the various technical criteria used by the Court of Justice to define 'economic' in the context of different legal provisions, including the competition law provisions and the freedoms. His assumption seems to be that there is a single notion of 'economic activity' in the Treaty and that this notion is political in nature. However, his analysis precisely illustrates that the term 'economic' carries different labels and roles in different legal contexts. Thus, the interesting question would be to identify the relationship between those different roles in order to assess whether there is a single or multiple definitions of 'economic'.

[51] Typically, critical for the applicability of the free movement provisions is the nature of the actor involved rather than the nature of the activity; namely, whether there is an organic element of state involvement or of formal delegation of state powers. See, eg, Case 249/81 *Commission v Ireland* [1982] ECR 4005; Case 222/82 *Apple and Pear Development Council v KJ Lewis Ltd and others* [1983] ECR 4083; Case C-292/92 *Ruth Hünermund and others v Landesapothekerkammer Baden-Württemberg* [1993] ECR I-6787; and Case 325/00 *Commission v Federal Republic of Germany* [2002] ECR I-09977. In these cases, the Member State has a decisive influence over the setting up or the funding of the body involved. Accordingly, the body's function, which is not necessarily of a regulatory nature, does not seem to matter to the Court of Justice for the applicability of Article 34 TFEU.

a collective manner gainful employment and the provision of services'.[52] In addition, it held in *Bosman* that 'there is nothing to preclude individuals from relying on justifications on grounds of public policy, public security or public health'.[53] In these judgments, the Court seems to extend the personal scope of Article 45 TFEU to private parties, which have 'regulatory power' regardless of any formal delegation by the state, because regulatory power is inherently a 'state-like' activity.[54]

The Court of Justice did not answer the competition law questions raised in these cases.[55] In *Bosman*, AG Lenz considered that the rules of private sports associations permitting a football club, after receiving a transfer fee, to release a player even after the expiry of his contract could be subject to both the provision on the free of movement for workers and Articles 101 and 102 TFEU. According to Lenz, the two sets of provisions may be applicable to a single factual situation, in the absence of a Treaty provision 'regulating the inter-relationship of the two'.[56] Lenz first asserted that professional football clubs are likely to be considered as undertakings and then found that the transfer rules constituted a 'restriction on competition'. However, Lenz seems to assume that professional football clubs are 'undertakings' insofar as the exercise of sport constitutes an 'economic activity' within the meaning of ex-Article 2 TEC, which is a logical fallacy inasmuch as 'economic activity' under ex-Article 2 TEC is more broad than 'undertakings'.[57] The Court of Justice held that it was not necessary to rule on the application of the competition law provisions since the transfer rules were unlawful under Article 45 TFEU.

Similarly, in *Wouters*, the Court of Justice found that Articles 49 and 56 TFEU are potentially applicable to the rules of the Dutch Bar Association, which prohibit any multi-disciplinary partnerships between members of the Bar and

[52] *BNO Walrave and LJN Koch* (n 47) [17]; Case C-415/93 *Union royale belge des sociétés de football association ASBL v Jean-Marc Bosman, Royal club liégeois SA v Jean-Marc Bosman and others and Union des associations européennes de football (UEFA) v Jean-Marc Bosman* ('*Bosman*') [1995] ECR I-4921 [82]. Similarly, see Joined Cases C-51/96 and C-191/97 *Christelle Deliège v Ligue francophone de judo et disciplines associées ASBL, Ligue belge de judo ASBL, Union européenne de judo and François Pacquée* ('*Deliège*') [2000] ECR I-2549 [47]; Case C-176/96 *Jyri Lehtonen and Castors Canada Dry Namur-Braine ASBL v Fédération royale belge des sociétés de basket-ball ASBL (FRBSB)* ('*Lehtonen*') [2000] ECR I-2681 [35]; and Case C-325/08 *Olympique Lyonnais SASP v Olivier Bernard and Newcastle UFC* [2010] ECR I-2177 [30]–[32].

[53] *Bosman* (n 52) [85]–[86].

[54] This seems to be confirmed by Case C-379/09 *Maurits Casteels v British Airways plc* [2011] ECR I-01379 [19]–[20], [22]–[23], in which the Court of Justice applied Article 45 TFEU to a collective labour agreement governing the supplementary pension rights of the employees and held that Article 45 TFEU applies to any measure hindering or rendering less attractive the exercise of the fundamental freedoms. However, Schepel (n 39) 185–86 seems to challenge the assumption that 'collective regulation' is significant because it is a 'state-like' activity.

[55] *Bosman* (n 52) [138]; *Deliège* (n 52) [36]–[40]; and *Lehtonen* (n 52) [28]–[30].

[56] *Bosman* (n 52), Opinion of AG Lenz [253]. In principle, the opinion of AG Lenz is repeated in *Deliège* (n 52), Opinion of AG Cosmas [103]–[114] as regards freedom to provide services.

[57] *Bosman* (n 52), Opinion of AG Lenz [255], cross-citing [125].

accountants.[58] The regulatory powers of the Dutch Bar Association were delegated by the national constitution and secondary legislation.[59] However, the functional understanding of the public realm in this judgment is evidenced in the application of essentially the same reasoning under the competition law provisions, in particular Article 101(1) TFEU.[60] The Court of Justice found that the restriction of competition was necessary for achieving a regulatory function—the proper practice of the legal profession—by citing a free movement of services case.[61] Therefore, *Wouters* is arguably a case of false classification of the actor and shows that subjecting the same factual situation to both sets of provisions is superfluous, inasmuch as the Court applied the reasoning underlying the application of the correct norm (Article 49 TFEU) under both Articles 49 and 101(1) TFEU.[62]

The *Wouters* approach under Article 101(1) TFEU was repeated in *Meca-Medina*, in which arguments based on both sets of provisions were advanced. However, unlike *Wouters*, *Meca-Medina* did not come before the Court of Justice as a preliminary reference, but originated in a Commission decision which rejected a complaint under Regulation 1/2003; as such, the Court of Justice could not but hold that Article 56 TFEU was inapplicable,[63] while it repeated the *Wouters* approach under Article 101(1) TFEU. In that sense, *Meca-Medina* is not unusual or any different from *Wouters* and this is confirmed by the fact that it is cited in *Viking* in support of the proposition that if something is excluded from the scope of the competition rules, it does not necessarily fall outside the scope of the freedoms.[64] Arguably, *Wouters* is an unfortunate judgment as regards

[58] Case C-309/99 *JCJ Wouters, JW Savelbergh and Price Waterhouse Belastingadviseurs BV v Algemene Raad van de Nederlandse Orde van Advocaten* [2002] ECR I-1577 [119]–[123].

[59] ibid [3]–[12].

[60] See R Whish, *Competition Law* (6th edn, Oxford University Press, 2009) 127–28: 'it is possible that the Court was deliberately trying to reach a similar outcome under [Article 101 TFEU] to that which would have been achieved under [Article 56 TFEU] had the case been argued under the provisions on the free movement of services'; Odudu (n 4) 166: 'classification as public or private activity is then of less importance, since the correct norm is applied regardless of how the activity is initially classified'.

[61] *JCJ Wouters, JW Savelbergh and Price Waterhouse Belastingadviseurs BV* (n 58) [97], [110], citing Case C-3/95 *Reisebüro Broede v Gerd Sandker* [1996] ECR I-6511. This makes *Wouters* 'a clear-cut example of convergence'; see J van de Gronden, 'Rule of Reason and Convergence in Internal Market Law and Competition Law' in A Schrauwen (ed), *Rule of Reason: Rethinking Another Classic of European Legal Doctrine* (Europa Law, 2005) 84; similarly, R O'Loughlin, 'EC Competition Rules and Free Movement Rules: An Examination of the Parallels and their Furtherance by the ECJ Wouters Decision' (2003) 24 *European Competition Law Review* 68–69.

[62] See the references in n 60.

[63] Case C-519/04 P *David Meca-Medina and Igor Majcen v Commission* [2006] ECR I-6991 [58].

[64] Case C-438/05 *International Transport Workers' Federation and Finnish Seamen's Union v Viking Line ABP and OÜ Viking Line Eesti* [2007] ECR I-10779 [53] (*Viking Line ABP*). See ch 5, text to n 143 on the rejection of the '*Albany* exclusion' under the free movement provisions. The oddity concerning the Court of Justice judgment in *Meca-Medina* is that it equally implies the reverse relationship, namely that if something is excluded from the scope of the freedoms because it does not constitute an 'economic activity', this does not necessarily mean that it falls outside the (personal) scope of the competition law provisions; *David Meca-Medina and Igor Majcen v Commission* (n 63) [31], [33]. This is unreasonable, since the notion of 'undertaking' under the competition law provisions is included in the broader notion of 'economic activity' as was referred in ex-Article 2 TEC.

the choice of the legal provision under which the given test was applied, since both Articles 49 and 101 TFEU were advanced by private litigants. Like in *Meca-Medina*, the *Wouters* approach under Article 101(1) TFEU was repeated by the Court of Justice in *OTOC*, a recent preliminary ruling that originated in public enforcement of competition law at the national level. The Court of Justice rejected as inadmissible questions referred by the national court as to the applicability of the freedom to provide services, conjunctively or alternatively to the competition law provisions, since they were not relevant to the resolution of the dispute at the national level.[65]

More recently, the Court of Justice confirmed the mirror-image definition of the personal scope of the free movement and the competition law provisions in *Fra.bo*, on the basis of a functional understanding of regulatory and economic activities.[66] In *Fra.bo*, the Court of Justice asserted the applicability of Article 34 TFEU to the standardisation and certification activities of a private law body (DVGW) given a legislative presumption of compliance for certified products with national legislation regulating the drinking water supply sector.[67] At the same time, the Court of Justice ruled that there was no need to answer the competition law questions raised by the referring national court and, accordingly, no need to address the relevant arguments advanced by the private litigants, inasmuch as Article 34 TFEU applied to the standardisation and certification activities of the DVGW. The questions, in essence, considered whether the very same standardisation and certification activities of the DVGW qualified as economic activities and,

[65] See Case C-1/2012 *Ordem dos Técnicos Oficiais de Contas (OTOC) v Autoridade da Concorrência*, Judgment of 28 February 2013 (NYR) [23]–[24], [29]–[31]. Nevertheless, the Court of Justice established a restriction of competition under Article 101(1) TFEU by making an explicit analogy to its reasoning in Case C-49/07 *Motosykletistiki Omospondia Ellados NPID (MOTOE) v Elliniko Dimosio* [2008] ECR I-4863, which is a state action case under Article 106(1) TFEU, applied in conjunction with Article 102 TFEU; ibid [88]–[91]. Similarly, in Case C-136/12 *Consiglio Nazionale dei Geologi (CNG) v Autorità garante della concorrenza e del mercato*, Judgment of 18 July 2013 (NYR), which originated in public enforcement of competition law at the national level, the *Wouters* approach was applied under Article 101(1) TFEU, but the referring court was not so explicit as to invoke the free movement provisions; rather, it formulated the questions in terms of 'Article 101 TFEU or any other provision of EU law'. The inadmissibility of the free movement questions referred to the Court of Justice, which is fleshed out so strikingly in cases of public enforcement of competition law at either the EU level (like *Meca-Medina*) or the national level (like *OTOC*), highlights the need to reformulate the state action defence in a manner that makes the assessment of state action legality under the freedoms an integral part of the application of the competition law provisions; see the analysis in ch 6.

[66] Case C-171/11 *Fra.bo SpA v Deutsche Vereinigung des Gas- und Wasserfaches eV (DVGW)—Technisch-Wissenschaftlicher Verein*, Judgment of 12 July 2012 (NYR).

[67] ibid [27]–[31]. There is also a strong parallel between this and the Court of Justice judgments under the competition law provisions, which preclude the qualification of technical standardisation activities (*SELEX*) or surveillance activities (*Calì & Figli*) as economic activities; Case C-113/07P *SELEX Sistemi Integrati SpA v Commission and Eurocontrol* [2009] ECR I-02207 [86]–[93]; Case C-343/95 *Diego Calì & Figli Srl v Servizi ecologici porto di Genova SpA (SEPG)* [1997] ECR I-01547 [15], [22]–[24]. See R van Gestel and H-W Micklitz, 'European Integration through Standardization: How Judicial Review is Breaking Down the Club House of Private Standardization Bodies' (2013) 50 *Common Market Law Review* 145 for a comprehensive analysis of the question as to whether private standards are, and should be, treated as public law by mere reference to them in legislation.

therefore, whether DVGW qualified as an 'undertaking' under the competition law provisions.[68] *Fra.bo* is similar to *Wouters*. Both cases illustrate that in a private enforcement setting with no restrictive framework of advancing arguments with regard to one set of provisions, as is the case in the public enforcement of the competition law provisions, there is no added value in addressing the same function under both the competition law and the free movement provisions.[69]

Therefore, as long as a functional definition of the personal scope of the free movement provisions is adopted, the mutually exclusive classification of the actor as an undertaking or an actor with regulatory powers as regards goods, services or workers determines the line between the free movement provisions and the competition law provisions. Both these categories of actors fall under the broader category of 'economic activities', the term used in ex-Article 2 TEC, which is now omitted. The classification of the actor matters, as it determines the rule under which the response to a question is given. However, the fact that the competition law provisions were exclusively enforced, prior to the enactment of Regulation 1/2003, by the Commission also means that the Commission could be forced to answer a question that is asked under the wrong rule. This is the reason why the cases which support a mutually exclusive understanding of the personal scope of the two sets of provisions also support the claim of substantive convergence between the free movement provisions and the competition law provisions when they are applied simultaneously to one and the same conduct. Therefore, these cases do not provide an argument for a cumulative and complementary application of the two sets of provisions to conduct by dominant undertakings.

V. BEYOND FUNCTIONALISM: THE SIGNIFICANCE OF A QUANTITATIVE THRESHOLD FOR POWER

The current state of case law suggests that the mirror-image definition of 'state-measures' and 'undertakings' on the basis of the mutually exclusive notions of 'regulation' and 'economic activity' is, in part, distorted. This section describes how the functional approach to the personal scope of the freedom of establishment in *Viking*[70] and of the freedom to provide services in *Laval*[71] has, indeed, been

[68] *Fra.bo SpA* (n 66) [16], [33].

[69] Yet, *Fra.bo* and *Wouters* are contrasted inasmuch as in *Fra.bo*, the Court of Justice opted for mutually exclusive applicability thresholds, namely that of 'regulatory' and 'economic' activity, while in *Wouters*, it opted for a concomitant applicability of both sets of provisions to one and the same activity (of regulatory nature) in a manner that reflects substantive convergence of the actual application of the two provisions. This leaves one to think about the role of the national courts in formulating the preliminary references as regards both sets of provisions, which are freely advanced by private litigants, and how the formulation of the questions by the national courts influences and feeds back to the answers given by the Court of Justice.

[70] *Viking Line ABP* (n 64).

[71] Case C-341/05 *Laval un Partneri Ltd v Svenska Byggnadsarbetareförbundet and others* [2007] ECR I-11767.

eroded. There is no need for a positive assertion of a link with a function equivalent to regulation for conduct to fall under the scope of the free movement provisions. In that regard, Schepel argues that the case law applying the free movement of workers (*Angonese*),[72] the freedom of establishment (*Viking*) and the freedom to provide services (*Laval*) to private actions seems to suggest that the significant element is rather 'the ability to obstruct free movement, an ability that could also find its source in market power or in the mobilisation of people to picket or lay their bodies on a motorway'.[73]

It is, however, disputed that because the Court of Justice did not require a positive link with some regulatory function in these judgments, the pragmatic ability of the actor, including the market power of an undertaking, to obstruct the free movement is the trigger mechanism for the application of freedoms. No matter how distinct from some form of regulation the application of the freedoms has been, this application has never crossed the outer limit as set by 'conduct by dominant undertakings', even though the Court of Justice was asked to do so. In particular, the Court of Justice did not follow the opinion of AG Maduro in *Roaming Regulation*, which addressed the EU's competence under Article 114 TFEU to adopt legislation aimed at tackling restrictions to free movement arising from the behaviour of *undertakings*.[74] This argument is further complemented by a contrast fleshed out in the following section. Whereas dominance is a necessary condition for abusive market separation under Article 102 TFEU, no quantitative threshold is required under the freedoms, as regards the ability of 'state measures' to obstruct the free movement (see section V.A).

Both *Viking* and *Laval* concern unilateral behaviour by trade unions. In *Viking*, a Finnish trade union, supported by an international association of trade unions, threatened strike action and boycotts in light of the Finnish ferry operator's plans to reflag a Finnish ship to Estonia, in order to force the operator to enter into a collective agreement maintaining its current wage levels. Similarly, in *Laval*, a Swedish trade union took collective action in the form of a blockade against a Latvian construction company in order to force it to negotiate the rates of pay for its workers posted in Sweden and sign a collective agreement in the building sector.

[72] Case C-281/98 *Roman Angonese v Cassa di Risparmio di Bolzano SpA* [2000] ECR I-4139. This is first judgment to erode the functional understanding of the personal scope of the free movement of workers. The Court held that the possession of a certificate of bilingualism as a condition for taking part in a competition for a post with an Italian private bank was indirectly discriminatory on grounds of nationality and, hence, in breach of Article 45 TFEU. Thus Article 45 TFEU was applied to a unilateral conduct by a private party, as opposed to collective regulations and private contracts. However, Article 45 TFEU is a special case, because it contains a textual prohibition on discrimination in Article 45(2) TFEU.

[73] Schepel (n 39) 187. See also W Sauter and H Schepel, *State and Market in European Union Law: The Public and Private Spheres of the Internal Market before the EU Courts* (Cambridge University Press, 2009) 102–03 for an earlier articulation of the same proposition.

[74] Case C-58/08 *Vodafone Ltd and others v Secretary of State for Business, Enterprise and Regulatory Reform* [2010] ECR I-4999, Opinion of AG Maduro.

In both cases, the approach adopted by the Court of Justice is pragmatic as regards the applicability of Articles 49 and 56 TFEU. The applicability of these Treaty provisions seems to be based on the factual ability of the trade unions to impose restrictions on the freedom of establishment or freedom to provide services, even if there is no apparent link with regulatory competence and power.[75] In *Viking*, the wording of the judgment may indicate a concern by the Court to link the collective action of the trade union with the conclusion of the intended collective agreement.[76] However, the Court of Justice expressly rejected an interpretation of the case law on horizontal application that restricts such application 'to associations or to organisations exercising a regulatory task or having quasi-legislative powers'.[77]

In *Laval*, the question as to the regulatory nature of the conduct of the trade union was more complex because of the additional question as to whether Sweden had correctly transposed Directive 96/71/EC concerning the posting of workers in the framework of the provision of services, since it had not:

> [M]ade use of the arrangements provided for in the Directive to extend or endorse, by a measure vested with public authority, the application of collective agreements concluded in its territory to foreign service providers which post workers there temporarily.[78]

[75] It is noteworthy that in both cases, it was the employees' rather than the employers' organisations that took action, which defeats the 'imbalance of power' argument that is often used to equate labour relationships with the relationship between private parties and the state, and thus to link such behaviour to the public interest. See C Semmelmann, 'The European Union's Economic Constitution under the Lisbon Treaty: Soul-Searching among Lawyers Shifts the Focus to Procedure' (2010) 35 *European Law Review* 529.

[76] *Viking Line ABP* (n 64) [35]–[37], [60], particularly [36]: 'collective action … which may be the trade unions' last resort to ensure the success of their claim to regulate the work of Viking's employees collectively, must be considered to be inextricably linked to the collective agreement the conclusion of which FSU is seeking'. D Wyatt, 'Horizontal Effect of Fundamental Freedoms and the Right to Equality after Viking and Mangold, and the Implications for Community Competence' [2008] *Croatian Yearbook of European Law and Policy* 8: 'this is presumably legally significant or the Court would not emphasise it'. Similarly, A Dashwood, 'Viking and Laval: Issues of Horizontal Direct Effect' [2007–08] *Cambridge Yearbook of European Legal Studies* 235–36. Contra Schepel (n 39) 187; J Krzeminska-Vamvaka, 'Horizontal Effect of Fundamental Rights and Freedoms: Much Ado About Nothing? German, Polish and EU Theories Compared after *Viking Line*' (2009) Jean Monnet Working Paper 11/09 28–29; M Karayigit, 'The Horizontal Effect of the Free Movement Provisions' (2011) 18 *Maastricht Journal* 324, who dispute the relevance of a link between the restriction and collective regulation in the judgment at a descriptive level.

[77] *Viking Line ABP* (n 64) [64]–[65]. L Azoulai, 'The Court of Justice and the Social Market Economy: The Emergence of an Ideal and the Conditions for its Realisation' (2008) 45 *Common Market Law Review* 1335 seems to assume that the trade union's conduct in *Viking* and the Bar Association's conduct in *Wouters* are comparable and, based on this, concludes that the Court of Justice made the choice to treat *Viking* differently. However, his assumption is unfortunate because, in *Wouters*, there are references to the national law which granted legal autonomy and thus regulatory power to the Bar Association. See n 59. This is not the case in *Viking* at a descriptive level.

[78] *Laval un Partneri Ltd* (n 71), Opinion of AG Mengozzi [133]. See also ibid [135], [136], in which AG Mengozzi rejected Laval's argument 'to widen the concept of a State in such a way that, in the present case, trade unions are regarded as a subdivision of the Swedish State, against which Laval could then directly invoke Directive 96/71'. He observed that 'those unions are certainly not public authorities and they are not entrusted, by an act of a public authority, with performing, under the

The Court of Justice provided a negative answer and held that:

> [T]he national authorities in Sweden have entrusted management and labour with the task of setting, by way of collective negotiations, the wage rates which national undertakings are to pay their workers.[79]

After repeating the case law on the application of the freedoms to collective regulation, the Court concluded straight away that:

> [I]t must be pointed out that the right of trade unions of a Member State to take collective action by which undertakings established in other Member States may be forced to sign the collective agreement for the building sector ... is liable to make it less attractive, or more difficult, for such undertakings to carry out construction work in Sweden, and therefore constitutes a restriction on the freedom to provide services within the meaning of [Article 56 TFEU].[80]

Therefore, the Court seems to deduce that the freedom of movement is applicable *rationae personae* from the material finding of a restriction on the freedom.

However, it cannot be assumed that, based on those two cases, the qualitative type of the power of the actors has lost its significance as the trigger mechanism for the application of the free movement provisions, nor that it has been replaced by the quantitative significance of the conduct as regards a restriction of the free movement. First, the Court seems to restore the balance in the more recent *Fra.bo* case by stressing the legislative presumption of compliance with the sector regulation, which is carried by products certified by the body involved, DVGW.[81] It is true that the Court seems to merge in one set of reasoning considerations as to whether Article 34 TFEU, which is applicable, is also breached and, in particular, whether 'the lack of certification by the DVGW places a *considerable* restriction on the marketing of the products concerned on the German market'.[82] However, the fact remains that in *Fra.bo*, there was a regulatory function exercised by the DVGW and this, according to the Court, is legally significant for ascertaining the applicability of Article 34 TFEU.

Second, the trade unions' conduct in *Viking* and *Laval*, no matter how distinct from some form of collective regulation, did not constitute conduct by 'undertakings' under the competition law provisions. Regardless of how loosely defined 'state' is, the notion of 'undertaking' remains a well-defined concept with its underlying policy concerns regarding private autonomy in the market sphere, so far outwith the scope of application of the freedoms. Indeed, in cases in which

latter's control, a service of public interest, nor are they vested, for such a purpose, with powers that go beyond the rules applicable to relations between private individuals'.

[79] *Laval un Partneri Ltd* (n 71) [68]–[69].
[80] ibid [98]–[99].
[81] *Fra.bo SpA* (n 66) [27].
[82] ibid [29], emphasis added.

the Court of Justice has expressly rejected a horizontal direct applicability of Article 34 TFEU, the private party involved was, unequivocally, an undertaking.[83]

Roaming Regulation is the most striking example of the Court of Justice not going down the path of a generalised application of the free movement provisions based exclusively on their distinct material scope and regardless of the very existence of Article 102 TFEU. In *Roaming Regulation,* the Court was called to assess the competence of the EU under Article 114 TFEU to set a Europe-wide maximum price limit for the provision of inter-state voice calls at both the wholesale and retail levels (*Eurotariff*).[84] Article 114 TFEU grants the European legislature the competence to approximate differences in Member States' laws should the perceived disparity affect the functioning of the Internal Market, such that EU intervention 'actually contributes to eliminating obstacles to free movement and to the freedom to provide services, and to removing distortions of competition'.[85]

AG Maduro asked the Court of Justice to apply the logical consequences of its case law on the horizontal application of the free movement rules to its analysis under Article 114 TFEU. He argued in favour of such regulatory intervention on the basis that certain private actions directly disfavour a cross-border economic activity (here, roaming) compared with *intra*-state economic activity (here, domestic use of mobile phone services).[86] This view disregards the existence of Article 102 TFEU with its distinct conditions of application, including dominance, since the mobile operators are unequivocally 'undertakings'. It is noteworthy that, before the enactment of the Roaming Regulation, the Commission had initiated Article 102 TFEU infringement proceedings against O2 and Vodafone UK as well as against T-Mobile and Vodafone Germany.[87] However, the competition law proceedings were stayed for a long period and finally withdrawn because, after

[83] See more on these cases in ch 6, text to nn 14–17, which address the question of attribution of the market-distorting effect to the undertaking's conduct and/or the state conduct, because the decisive element in these cases seems to be the existence of a national law merely permitting the undertaking to adopt the conduct in question.

[84] *Vodafone Ltd and others* (n 74).

[85] See Case C-376/98 *Federal Republic of Germany v Parliament and Council* [2000] ECR I-8419 [95], in which the Court of Justice held, in effect, that Article 114 TFEU is not a source of general regulatory competence but a competence to harmonise for defined ends associated with market building, in compliance with the principle of attributed powers provided for in ex-Article 5(1) TEC.

[86] *Vodafone Ltd and others* (n 74), Opinion of AG Maduro [19]–[23]. To ascertain the existence of EU competence to regulate the Internal Market under Article 114 TFEU may require an examination of the difficult question as to whether such competence extends to measures that do not qualify as restrictions of the free movement provisions. However, in that case, AG Maduro seems to assume that the mobile operators' actions would be caught by the freedom to provide services and, for that reason, the EU has competence under Article 114 TFEU.

[87] Commission (EC), 'Staff Working Paper—Impact Assessment of policy options in relation to a Commission proposal for a Regulation on roaming on public mobile telephone networks within the Community' (Impact Assessment) COM(2006) 386 final, 12 July 2006 [1.2.1].

2004, the introduction of new tariff direction technology has made it difficult to sustain findings of dominance on the wholesale international roaming market.[88]

The Court of Justice did not go down the same path as the Advocate General. Instead, it upheld the EU's competence under Article 114 TFEU to address:

> [L]ikely national measures aiming to address the problem of the high level of retail charges for [EU]-wide roaming services through rules fixing the rate of retail charges ... taken by the Member States based on their residual competence as regards consumer protection rules.[89]

This confirms that the current state of the case law under the freedoms does not negate Article 102 TFEU, with its distinct conditions of application and, in particular, significant market power, which is the outer limit to any expansive view of horizontal application of the freedoms.

A. Dominance as a Condition *Sine Qua Non* for Anti-competitive Market Separation under Article 102 TFEU: Normative and Legal Considerations

The cases described above indicate that, no matter how remote from a regulatory function, the 'private actors', which are subjected so far to the freedoms, are not considered to be undertakings. Therefore, the distinction between the addressee of Article 102 TFEU and 'state measures' under the free movement provisions seems to be retained and to be intentional. This analysis is complemented by the normative considerations which underpin the legal condition of significant market power akin to dominance under Article 102 TFEU in market separation cases. By contrast, there is no similar quantitative threshold as regards the ability of 'state measures' to obstruct the freedoms when the free movement provisions are applied beyond regulatory functions by the Court of Justice.[90]

Interestingly enough, in *Viking*, it is AG Maduro who draws a distinction, at a normative level, between states and private actors as regards the power they

[88] See M Martino, 'Effectiveness of Traffic Direction Techniques in Mobile International Roaming and Implications for Market Definition' (2007) 66 *Communications and Strategies* 137 for a technical discussion of the effectiveness of this technology and its regulatory implications, in particular upon market definition and hence dominance.

[89] *Vodafone Ltd and others* (n 74) [45]–[46]. The Court's ruling seems to imply that undertakings are permitted under the Treaty provisions to take advantage of 'gaps' in non-economic regulations, such as consumer protection, at the national level, while it rests upon the legislator at the national or the EU level to address these issues. This fits into the argument presented in ch 4, namely that non-economic considerations should be excluded from the scope of the competition law provisions, because there is always the potential for state involvement to occur.

[90] *Viking Line ABP* (n 64), Opinion of AG Maduro [49] seems to suggest such a quantitative threshold as a corollary to his suggestion that the only significant element for the application of Article 56 TFEU is the factual ability to obstruct the freedom to provide services.

possess.[91] According to him, 'the normative and socio-economic power inherent in State authorities entails that these authorities have, by definition, significant potential to thwart the proper functioning of the Common Market'.[92] He then gives the counter-example that:

> [A]n individual shopkeeper who refuses to purchase goods from other Member States would not be liable to obstruct the functioning of the Common Market. The reason is that suppliers from other Member States would still have the opportunity to market their goods through alternative channels.[93]

Indeed, it is a fundamental assumption of neoclassical economics that undertakings are guided by profit maximisation incentives[94] and that market-distorting practices can be profitable if the undertaking has significant market power.[95] This is fully reflected in the definition of dominance adopted by the European courts, as 'a position of economic strength enjoyed by an undertaking, which enables it to prevent effective competition being maintained on a relevant market, by affording it the power to behave to an appreciable extent independently of its competitors, its customers and ultimately of consumers'.[96]

The Court of Justice has unequivocally confirmed the significance of a quantitative threshold of market power under Article 102 TFEU in the specific case of abusive market separation, as opposed to state action under the freedoms. It did so in *Bayer*, a parallel trade case which concerned successive reductions in the volumes of medicinal products supplied by Bayer to its exporting wholesalers.[97]

[91] Private actors, in general rather than between states and undertakings: ie, he draws the distinction within the free movement provisions, after he has rejected the relevance of the competition law provisions. However, this is implicitly self-defeating because it contradicts his initial assumption, as set out in [33]–[34] of his Opinion, namely that the Treaty provisions on free movement and on competition constitute a systematic whole.

[92] *Viking Line ABP* (n 64), Opinion of AG Maduro [41].

[93] ibid [42]. See Wyatt (n 76) 22–24, who rejects the application of Article 34 TFEU to the purchasing choices of private market operators as opposed to their sale choices, even when they hold a significant market position.

[94] See C Mantzavinos, *Individuals, Institutions, and Markets* (Cambridge University Press, 2001) 10–15 for the general hypothesis of individuals striving to increase their own utility, which is based on the assumption that we are very ignorant about the motivational system of humans. Similarly, see G Mitchell, 'Taking Behavioralism Too Seriously? The Unwarranted Pessimism of the New Behavioral Analysis of Law' (2002) 43 *William and Mary Law Review* 1912–13, who attributes a 'pessimism bias' to behavioural law and economics literature, because 'a rational review of the evidence on ... human decision making should lead one to agnosticism'. See J Persky, 'Retrospectives: The Ethology of Homo Economicus' (1995) 9(2) *Journal of Economic Perspectives* 221; S Bowles and H Gintis 'The Revenge of Homo Economicus: Contested Exchange and the Revival of Political Economy' (1993) 7(1) *Journal of Economic Perspectives* 83 for the *homo economicus* hypothesis.

[95] Similarly, even if one adopts a behavioural economics perspective, only dominant undertakings may be in a position to directly influence the market activities of other economic agents and therefore constitute informal institutions, shaping consumers' ultimate choices. See I Lianos and A Matteus, 'Antitrust in the New US Administration: A Transatlantic View' (2009) 2 *Global Competition Policy* 32.

[96] *United Brands Company* (n 7) [65]; Case 85/76 *Hoffmann-La Roche AG v Commission* [1979] ECR 461 [38].

[97] Joined Cases C-2/01P and C-3/01P *Bundesverband der Arzneimittel-Importeure eV and Commission v Bayer AG* [2004] ECR I-23.

Bayer is an Article 101 TFEU case and the ruling is confined to the notion of 'agreement' under Article 101 TFEU. However, the Court of Justice held, obiter, that:

> Under the general system of the Treaty, measures adopted by a Member State which prevent parallel exports are indeed prohibited by [Article 34 TFEU], but unilateral measures taken by private undertakings are subject to restrictions, by virtue of the principles of that Treaty, only if the undertaking in question occupies a dominant position on the market, within the meaning of [Article 102 TFEU], which is not the case here.[98]

In addition, the general case law of the European courts requires a link between the dominant position and the alleged abuse as a condition for the application of Article 102 TFEU. In *Continental Can* and in *Hoffmann-La Roche*, the Court of Justice rejected the applicants' argument that there must be causality between the dominant position and the abuse, in the sense that the economic power should be the means by which the abuse is brought about.[99] However, this does not mean that there is no need, in principle, to establish any connection whatsoever between dominance and abuse.[100] Indeed, the Court of Justice has expressly confirmed the need for a link between dominance and abuse in the more recent *TeliaSonera* case.[101] In addition, it has been suggested that the Court's reasoning in *Continental Can* and *Hoffmann-La Roche* did not rule out the need for such a link in general; it only concerned the link between dominance and the conduct element of the abuse, namely the acquisition (in *Continental Can*) and the exclusive agreement (in *Hoffmann-La Roche*), as opposed to the link between dominance and the anti-competitive effect of the abuse.[102]

An additional challenge to the requirement of significant market power as a distinct condition for the application of Article 102 TFEU arose during the consultation process for reviewing the policy, which underpins Article 102 TFEU enforcement. The focus was especially on cases in which there is a link between dominance and the effect element of the alleged abuse. It was argued that the continuous widening of the notion of dominance by the European courts, in conjunction with the notion of 'special responsibility of the dominant undertaking

[98] ibid [70].

[99] Case 6/72 *Europemballage Corp and Continental Can Co Inc v Commission* [1973] ECR 215 [27]; *Hoffmann-La Roche* (n 96) [91].

[100] O'Donoghue and Padilla (n 6) 215–17.

[101] Case C-52/09 *Konkurrensverket v TeliaSonera Sverige* [2011] ECR I-00527 [86]: 'the application of Article 102 TFEU presupposes a link between the dominant position and the alleged abusive conduct'.

[102] E Rousseva, *Rethinking Exclusionary Abuses in EU Competition Law: Rethinking Article 82 of the EC Treaty* (Hart Publishing, 2010) 73–79. Rousseva builds on an early article by P Vogelenzang 'Abuse of Dominant Position in Article 86: The Problem of Causality and Some Applications' (1976) 13 *Common Market Law Review* 66–72, who distinguishes between three categories of 'dominance-abuse' types of connection: a connection between dominance and the act of abuse (eg, in excessive pricing); a connection between dominance and the anti-competitive effect of abuse (eg, in refusal to supply, discriminatory pricing); and a connection between dominance and a worsening effect on competition (eg, exclusive dealing, rebates, contractual tying).

not to allow its conduct impair undistorted competition',[103] had led to certain forms of practices being prohibited virtually per se once an undertaking is found to be dominant. This concern was voiced, in particular, by the Economic Advisory Group on Competition Policy (EAGCP) in its report on 'An Economic Approach to Article 82EC'. The EAGCP suggested that the substantive assessment of the undertaking's market power should be integrated with the assessment for establishing competitive harm.[104] This proposal provoked academic debate as regards the link between dominance and the effects of the alleged abuse.[105]

Ultimately, the Commission's Guidance Paper retained the assessment of the undertaking's market power as a separate first step in the application of Article 102 TFEU.[106] After the publication of the Guidance Paper, the Court of Justice confirmed in *TeliaSonera* that when the threshold for establishing dominance is crossed, the degree of market power is, as a general rule, significant not as regards the existence of the alleged abuse as such, but only as regards the extent of the effects of the conduct.[107] The question of dominance is, then, significant because it impacts on the level of intervention and the risk of chilling competition, since the establishment of a violation depends on the strength of evidence of consumer harm and the robustness of the relevant economic theory.[108] In addition, merging the two steps of the analysis would also involve the risk of over-reliance on the 'monopoly-explanation', which was first expressed by Coase.[109]

[103] The Court of Justice first referred to the 'special responsibility' of the dominant firm in Case 322/81 *NV Nederlandsche Banden Industrie Michelin v Commission* [1983] ECR 3461 [57] at the stage of assessing whether Michelin was in a dominant position. It is in subsequent case law that the notion of 'special responsibility' has been applied to indicate normative examples of abuses; see R Allendesalazar, 'Can We Finally Say Farewell to the "Special Responsibility" of Dominant Companies?' in C-D Ehlermann and M Marquis (eds), *European Competition Law Annual 2007: A Reformed Approach to Article 82 EC* (Hart Publishing, 2008) 319–20.

[104] EAGCP, 'An Economic Approach to Article 82EC' (Report) July 2005 http://ec.europa.eu/dgs/competition/economist/eagcp_july_21_05.pdf [14]–[15].

[105] See, eg, G Niels and H Jenkins, 'Reform of Article 82: Where the Link between Dominance and Effects Breaks Down' (2005) 26 *European Competition Law Review* 605, A Majumdar, 'Whither Dominance?' (2006) 27 *European Competition Law Review* 161; T Eilmansberger, 'Dominance—The Lost Child: How Effects-Based Rules Could and Should Change the Dominance Analysis' (2006) 2 *European Competition Journal* 15.

[106] Commission (EC), 'Guidance on Commission's enforcement priorities in applying Article 82 of the EC Treaty to abusive exclusionary conduct by dominant undertaking' (Communication) [2009] OJ C45/7 [9].

[107] *Konkurrensverket v TeliaSonera Sverige* (n 101) [78]–[82].

[108] Majumdar (n 105) 163–64. For example, I Kokkoris, 'Are We Underenforcing Article 102 TFEU?' in F Etro and I Kokkoris (eds), *Competition Law and the Enforcement of Article 102 TFEU* (Oxford University Press, 2010) 139 argues that there is, indeed, a case for under-enforcement of Article 102 TFEU in cases of consumer harm induced by the conduct of non-dominant firms. However, it is very difficult to identify gap cases because the Commission does not publish detailed decisions in which the undertaking is not found to be dominant and, hence, an abuse is not substantiated.

[109] 'If an economist finds something—a business practice of one sort or another—that he does not understand, he looks for a monopoly explanation. And, as in this field we are very ignorant, the number of un-understandable practices tends to be very large, and the reliance on monopoly explanation, frequent', as cited in J Vickers, 'Abuse of Market Power' (Speech to the 31st Conference of the European Association for Research in Industrial Economics, Berlin, 3 September 2004) 4.

Therefore, the question of keeping or discarding dominance as a separate step in the analysis arises in cases in which dominance is a condition for the anti-competitive effect to occur, rather than the act of abuse itself. The cases presented in section II show that market separation by dominant undertakings is one such category of abuses in which dominance is linked to the anti-competitive effect rather than to the conduct as such.

For example, if an undertaking is dominant and refuses to supply parallel traders, the latter may find it impossible to find alternative supplies. Any undertaking may refuse to provide them with supplies, but it is only if the supplier is dominant that it may be the case that the refusal has an anti-competitive effect. In addition, there are cases in which market separation is conducted as a contractual abuse, as in *British Gypsum* and *Irish Sugar*, in which it takes the form of rebates, or is conducted as geographic price discrimination tied to some other contractual abuse, such as the clauses which prohibit exports in *United Brands* and *Tetra Pak II*. In these cases, dominance is not a condition for the worsening of the negative effect on competition, as is argued by Rousseva, but rather a condition for the negative effect to occur in the first place.[110] The reason is the disproportionate lack of parity of the parties to the agreements, which matters only once the conduct is classified under Article 102 TFEU rather than Article 101 TFEU.[111] Under Article 101 TFEU, the form of the conduct, namely an 'agreement', manifests itself over the degree of the market power of the undertakings involved; the fact that one of the contracting parties is dominant simply makes that party subject to the obligation to pay damages to the other contracting party.[112] By contrast, in the case of contractual abuses, market power akin to dominance is a condition for the anti-competitive effect to occur rather than for the worsening of the anti-competitive effect.[113] The reason is that the latter situation would presuppose that there is a quantitative threshold identifiable a priori below dominance, due to which the negative effect on competition occurs.[114] Unfortunately, this is not yet the case.

[110] Rousseva (n 102) 463–64.

[111] See ch 3, section II.B on the criterion for distinguishing between the two situations.

[112] See the example of an undertaking which controls a network of similar contracts that have a negative cumulative effect on competition, but holds a 19 per cent share of the relevant market, as is the case with *Courage*; Case C-453/99 *Courage Ltd v Bernard Crehan and Bernard Crehan v Courage Ltd and others* [2001] ECR I-6297 [34]–[35]: 'In such a case, the party contracting with the person controlling the network cannot bear significant responsibility for the breach of [Article 101 TFEU], particularly where in practice the terms of the contract were imposed on him by the party controlling the network … making a distinction as to the extent of the parties' liability does not conflict with the case law of the Court to the effect that it does not matter, for the purposes of the application of [Article 101 TFEU], whether the parties to an agreement are on an equal footing as regards their economic position and function.'

[113] Contra Rousseva (n 102) 463–464, who argues that dominance worsens the negative effect, which would have been brought about anyway and therefore the dominant undertaking bears a special responsibility.

[114] See also L Ortiz Blanco, *Market Power in EU Antitrust Law* (Hart Publishing, 2012), who asks the question whether a specific quantitative limit in terms of market power must be established to apply the competition law provisions and, if so, at what level. Ortiz Blanco argues that we do not know what a reference criterion below dominance could be and hence it is better to fix the level of intervention to

The subsequent question is related to the degree of market power that is required for the undertaking to be subjected to Article 102 TFEU for alleged separation of markets along national lines. The concept of barriers to entry is particularly instructive, since market separation by private parties under the free movement provisions in the cases analysed above points to making cross-border access to a market more difficult. Entry barriers are precisely features of the market that make it difficult for a newcomer to access a market or more difficult than it was for the incumbent, depending on whether economists adopt an absolute or relative understanding of the concept.[115]

Generally, under the dominance assessment, the notion of barriers to entry serves the very specific purpose of identifying the ability of potential competition to limit the market power of the incumbent.[116] Both legal barriers and strategic barriers, including the undertaking's own conduct, are amongst the entry barriers identified in the Commission's Guidance Paper.[117] Legal barriers, such as tariffs or licensing procedures, could be subject to the free movement rules. As regards the undertaking's own conduct, in the specific case of market separation, it is important not to over-rely on behavioural indications of selectivity because of the circularity of such an approach.[118] However, both legal and strategic entry barriers are very important in market separation cases because assessment of the undertaking's market power feeds back to geographic market definition,[119] which was, in effect, identified in section II.C as the significant factor for the qualification of a conduct as abusive market separation in some of the cases described.

VI. THE SPECIFIC EXAMPLE OF ARTICLE 106(2) TFEU

Finally, a textual argument is drawn from the Treaty itself to support the view that Article 102 TFEU, with its specific conditions for application, is a meaningful limitation to the application of the freedoms to private actors. Conduct by dominant undertakings which allegedly has the intent or effect of creating artificial barriers to trade should be subjected to Article 102 TFEU alone rather than cumulatively

that of a dominant position across the competition law provisions: 'The cosy utopia [of using entirely reliable econometric techniques] does not appear to be just around the corner' (vii).

115 See P McAfee, H Mialon and M Williams, 'What is a Trade Barrier?' [2004] *American Economic Review* 461 for a review of the economic theories on entry barriers.

116 See, in particular, D Carlton, 'Why Barriers to Entry are Barriers to Understanding' [2004] *American Economic Review* 466 on the use of the (unclear) economic concept of entry barriers in antitrust or regulatory proceedings.

117 Commission (EC), 'Guidance on Commission's enforcement priorities in applying Article 82 of the EC Treaty to abusive exclusionary conduct by dominant undertaking' (Communication) [2009] OJ C45/7 [17].

118 However, see Ortiz Blanco (n 114) 64–65, who argues that the circularity can be overcome if behavioural and structural considerations are cumulatively taken into account.

119 See ch 1, text to n 148.

to both Article 102 TFEU and the freedoms.[120] Where the founders of the Treaty wanted to subject dominant undertakings to the obligations under the free movement provisions, they did so explicitly.

One such example is Article 106(2) TFEU, which makes the conduct of undertakings entrusted with (a specific type of) monopoly rights subject to the Treaty rules, *in particular* the competition law provisions. Article 106(2) TFEU is phrased as providing for an exception from the application of the Treaty provisions to which it refers. However, an exception presupposes that the conduct of the undertakings is, in principle, subject to those Treaty provisions. In addition, the example of Article 106(2) TFEU is advanced to support not a rejection of the horizontal application of the freedoms to any private action, but something more limited. The argument drawn is limited to rejecting application of the freedoms to dominant undertakings. The reason is that the undertakings concerned under Article 106(2) TFEU are entrusted with monopoly rights, which confer a dominant position if the reserved activity constitutes, on its own, a relevant market or a substantial part of it.

The wording of Article 106(2) TFEU (namely 'in particular') indicates that there are other than competition law Treaty provisions to which undertakings entrusted with (a specific type of) monopoly rights are subject. These other Treaty provisions also include the free movement provisions, as confirmed by the Court of Justice in the *Electricity Monopolies* cases. The Court held that these particular undertakings 'are subject to all the rules laid down in the Treaty' and that the scope of Article 106(2) TFEU is to be assessed in combination with Article 106(1) TFEU. The latter paragraph is 'intended to ensure that the Member States do not take advantage of their relations with those undertakings in order to evade the prohibitions laid down by other Treaty rules addressed directly to them, such as those in [Articles 34, 35 and 37 TFEU], by obliging or encouraging those undertakings to engage in conduct which, if engaged in by the Member States, would be contrary to those rules'.[121]

VII. CONCLUSIONS

This chapter has examined the question of what is, and ought to be, the correct regulatory instrument for assessing alleged market separation across national lines by dominant undertakings—Article 102 TFEU or the free movement provisions? In so doing, the functional understanding of the notion of 'undertaking' has been assumed. Hence, the focus has shifted from the question of the func-

[120] This is the mirror-image of the argument which is advanced in section V.A, namely that dominance is required for the purposes of subjecting market separation by an undertaking to the Treaty competition provisions.

[121] Case C-157/94 *Commission v Kingdom of the Netherlands* [1997] ECR I-5699 [29]–[30].

tional definition of 'undertaking' as such to the question whether the notion of 'dominant undertaking' still constitutes a meaningful limitation to an expansive view of the horizontal applicability of the freedoms. In addition, the role of significant market power ('dominant position') as a distinct condition for the application of Article 102 TFEU is addressed.

After identifying market separation cases under Article 102 TFEU as well as the asymmetry in the addressee of the competition law provisions and the freedoms, three arguments are advanced to support the view that the difference between the two sets of provisions is intended. Therefore, it is submitted that market separation by dominant undertakings is not a specific manifestation of horizontal application of the freedoms.

First, the cases of horizontal application of the freedoms, in which competition law provisions have been applied cumulatively, were examined. It is argued that those cases are to be read in the context of a mutually exclusive, functional understanding of the personal scope of the two sets of provisions; hence, these cases also support a view of substantive convergence of the cumulatively applicable provisions. The use of the inappropriate provision is justified in some instances by the public enforcement of Article 102 TFEU, which allows the Commission more discretion to control the substantive standard for responsibility under the competition law provisions.

Second, it is argued that the cases in which the application of the freedoms to private parties was triggered by their mere ability to obstruct the free movement do not discount the application of Article 102 TFEU to market separation by dominant undertakings. This is because, in these cases, the private actors involved, no matter how remote from some regulatory function, did not constitute 'undertakings'. This is confirmed by a normative and legal analysis of the quantitative threshold of market power, namely a dominant position, which is required as a separate step of analysis under Article 102 TFEU, for alleged market separation by an undertaking to be subjected to this Article. By contrast, no quantitative power threshold is established as regards the ability of 'state measures' to obstruct the freedoms.

Finally, a textual argument is drawn from Article 106(2) TFEU, because Article 106(2) TFEU, as interpreted by the Court of Justice, subjects a specific category of dominant undertakings to the freedoms, in addition to the competition law provisions.

Therefore, all three arguments support the view that market separation by dominant undertakings should only be subjected to Article 102 TFEU rather than to both Article 102 TFEU and the free movement provisions.

3

Market Separation under Article 102 TFEU: The Role of Economic Justifications

I. INTRODUCTION

Chapter two identified Article 102 TFEU as the only regulatory instrument that should be used to address alleged market separation by dominant undertakings. This chapter and those which follow examine how the assessment of such conduct under Article 102 TFEU is to be carried out and what weight is to be applied to market integration for substantiating an abuse of the dominant position.

The structure of Article 102 TFEU and how assessment of the anti-competitive effects of the market separation is to be accommodated under it are examined in section II of this chapter. Contrary to the two-step structure (prohibition–exception) of Article 101 TFEU, the definition of 'abuse of the dominant position' appears to be a one-step analysis, this having a consequence for the allocation of the burden of proof of 'efficiencies' or 'objective justifications'. The qualitative and legal difference between unilateral conduct and agreements is also addressed. The purpose of this is to distinguish between the methodology used under Articles 101 and 102 TFEU in the specific case of contractual abuses, since many market separation cases under Article 102 TFEU take the form of contractual abuses.

Section III highlights the elements which determine the scope of the provisions on free movement and are significant for assessing market separation under Article 102 TFEU, notably the interplay between economic and non-economic values. The focus of this chapter is on the economic values promoted by finding a restriction of the free movement of goods ('trade barriers') and, consequently, on the two relevant tests: discrimination and market access. Understanding the 'internal' element of the Internal Market, as reflected in the notion of 'trade barriers', will help us to understand the actual integrationist thrust of market separation cases under Article 102 TFEU.

Section IV examines the two tests for establishing market separation as an abuse of the dominant position: first, the intent-based test and, subsequently, the effects-based test, which focuses on 'efficiency' or 'objective justifications' in market separation cases under Article 102 TFEU. A comparison and an analogy are then drawn between the intent-based test and discriminatory trade barriers, as well as between the effects-based test and trade barriers failing the market access test. The analogy is drawn between each of the two tests for substantiating an 'abuse' and the two tests for broadly finding a 'trade barrier', regardless of whether the trade barrier can be justified by reference to non-economic values. The comparison is structured so as to reveal the specific areas in which the underlying values of market integration and Article 102 TFEU coincide.

It is argued in section V that the raison d'être of Article 102 TFEU and market integration, as reflected in the notion of 'trade barriers', is efficiency. Market separation cases that involve economic justifications are not cases in which a conflict of substantive values between competition and market integration can arise. Rather, they are cases in which the inherent limits of economic integration should also be respected under Article 102 TFEU enforcement, otherwise the outcome does not make sense from an economic perspective. However, two main differences in the way in which efficiency is realised under the two sets of provisions are identified. The differences are market, as opposed to regulatory, equivalence of the products concerned and, consequently, the different use of economics. Finally, this conclusion is put into the constitutional context of the Treaty *post*-Lisbon.

II. THE ANALYTICAL FRAMEWORK FOR ASSESSING MARKET SEPARATION AS AN ABUSE OF THE DOMINANT POSITION

The purpose of this section is to sketch out the framework for establishing, under Article 102 TFEU, market separation as an abuse of the dominant position. First, the structural vehicles through which assessment of conduct and effects are being carried out under Article 102 TFEU are identified; and, second, the methodology employed under Article 102 TFEU is distinguished from that employed under Article 101 TFEU. Both steps are important in the context of the present research because they determine whether market separation either can conceptually or should from a policy perspective be assessed under both Articles, particularly when it takes the form of contractual abuses. This should further provide a response to the question whether precedents under Article 101 TFEU should be used to establish a finding under Article 102 TFEU.

The terms 'objective justifications' or 'efficiency justifications' are employed interchangeably in the present section because they both refer to the structure of the analysis under Article 102 TFEU, rather than to the substantive values underpinning such justifications. In terms of substantive values, only economic justifications—which, in the traditional competition law discourse are termed 'efficiency defence', 'meeting competition defence' and 'factors beyond the control of the dominant undertaking'—are addressed in the present chapter. Therefore, economic justifications do not involve the so-called objective justifications based on public policy considerations, which are addressed in chapter four under the heading of non-economic justifications. However, the terms 'objective justifications' and 'efficiency justifications' are adopted interchangeably in the present section because the same structural analysis of Article 102 TFEU applies to both economic and non-economic justifications.[1]

A. The Structure of Article 102 TFEU: 'Objective' or 'Efficiency' Justifications and the Burden of Proof

The text of Article 102 TFEU prohibits any 'abuse of a dominant position', with no explicit provision for the exemption of a conduct otherwise falling within the scope of this Article. This is in contrast with the two-step analysis under Article 101(1) and (3) TFEU, as interpreted in a literal sense. As AG Jacobs has stated, 'the very fact that conduct is characterised as an "abuse" suggests that a negative conclusion has already been reached, by contrast with the more neutral terminology of "prevention, restriction, or distortion of competition" under [Article 101 TFEU]'.[2] This approach is confirmed by the definition of the notion of 'abuse' first given by the Court of Justice in *Hoffmann-La Roche*, according to which:

> The concept of abuse is an objective concept relating to the behaviour of an undertaking in a dominant position which is such as to influence the structure of a market where, as a result of the very presence of the undertaking in question, the degree of competition is weakened and which, through recourse to methods different from those which condition normal competition in products or services on the basis of the transactions of commercial operators, has the effect of hindering the maintenance of the degree of competition still existing in the market or the growth of that competition.[3]

The reference to 'normal competition on the basis of the transactions of commercial operators' (or 'the traders' performance')[4] indicates that this type of competition is perfectly legal and there is no presumption of responsibility for breach of

[1] Research into the structure of the analysis under Article 102 TFEU is incorporated in this chapter on economic justifications, even though the structure is common to both economic and non-economic justifications. The reason for this is that non-economic justification and conduct by the dominant undertaking are mutually exclusive, as is argued in ch 4.

[2] Case C-53/2003 *Synetairismos Farmakopoion Aitolias & Akarnanias (Syfait) and others v GlaxoSmithKline plc and GlaxoSmithKline AEVE* [2005] ECR I-4609, Opinion of AG Jacobs [72]. Similarly, see Case 66/86 *Ahmed Saeed Flugreisen and Silver Line Reisebüro GmbH v Zentrale zur Bekämpfung unlauteren Wettbewerbs eV* [1989] ECR 803 [32]; and Case T-51/89 *Tetra Pak Rausing SA v Commission (Tetra Pak I)* [1990] ECR II-309, Opinion of AG Kirschner [21].

[3] Case 85/76 *Hoffmann-La Roche & Co AG v Commission* [1979] ECR 461 [91].

[4] Case 322/81 *NV Nederlandsche Banden Industrie Michelin v Commission* [1983] ECR 3461 [70]: 'practices which, through recourse to methods different from those governing normal competition in products or services based on traders' performance, have the effect of hindering the maintenance or development of the level of competition still existing on the market'.

Article 102 TFEU.[5] On the contrary, unilateral conduct is 'inherently meritorious; it reflects the merits of an undertaking acting on its own'.[6]

This further explains the distribution of the burden of proof of an infringement of Article 101 TFEU and Article 102 TFEU according to Article 2 of Regulation 1/2003, as is demonstrated below. Whereas, in the context of Article 101 TFEU, the legal burden of persuasion shifts from the party alleging an infringement of Article 101 TFEU to the undertakings claiming the benefit of Article 101(3) TFEU, there is no such reversal in the context of Article 102 TFEU with regard to 'objective' or 'efficiency' justifications. The very text of Article 102 TFEU, and subsequently the allocation of the burden of proof according to Article 2 of Regulation 1/2003, had led the General Court to reject an 'objective' or 'efficiency' justification as a defence *proper*, in other words as a legally recognised 'excuse' that allows this conduct despite its negative effects.[7] In *Atlantic Container Line*, the General Court held that 'because [Article 102 TFEU] does not provide for any exemption, abusive practices are prohibited regardless of the advantages which may accrue to the perpetrators of such practices or to third parties'.[8]

Despite this, both the Guidance Paper on exclusionary abuses and the Court of Justice recognise an 'efficiency' justification, modelled upon the substantive conditions found in Article 101(3) TFEU, but functioning rather as a 'denial defence'.[9] This means that efficiency claims are directed against a prima facie case of abuse, which involves a shifting only of the evidential burden (or burden of production)

[5] Economists also support this view; see C Albhorn and J Padilla, 'From Fairness to Welfare: Implications for the Assessment of Unilateral Conduct under EC Competition Law' in C-D Ehlermann and M Marquis (eds), *European Competition Law Annual 2007: A Reformed Approach to Article 82 TEC* (Hart Publishing, 2008) 90–91, with further citations.

[6] D Waelbroeck, 'The Assessment of Efficiencies under Article 102 and the Commission's Guidance Paper' in F Etro and I Kokkoris (eds), *Competition Law and the Enforcement of Article 102 TFEU* (Oxford University Press, 2010) 122. See also R O'Donoghue and L Macnab, 'Dominant Firms' Duties to Deal with Pharmaceutical Parallel Traders Following Glaxo Greece' (2009) 1 *Competition Policy International* 162–63; and E Rousseva, *Rethinking Exclusionary Abuses in EU Competition Law: Rethinking Article 82 of the EC Treaty* (Hart Publishing, 2010) 467–68.

[7] On the so-called 'affirmative' defences, see A Gavil, 'Secondary Line Price Discrimination and the Fate of Morton Salt: To Save it, Let it Go' (1999) 4 *Emory Law Journal* 1119–22; and R Nazzini, 'The Wood Began to Move: An Essay on Consumer Welfare, Evidence and Burden of Proof in Article 82 EC Cases' (2006) 31 *European Law Review* 530.

[8] Joined Cases T-191/98 and T-212/98–214/98 *Atlantic Container Line AB and others v Commission* [2003] ECR II 3275 [1112]. See also Case T-340/03 *France Télécom SA v Commission* [2007] ECR II-107 [217]: 'An undertaking which charges predatory prices may enjoy economies of scale and learning effects on account of increased production precisely because of such pricing. The economies of scale and learning effects cannot therefore exempt that undertaking from liability under [Article 102 TFEU].' It is not, however, clear whether, in this case, the General Court rejected the efficiency justification as a defence on the facts or as a matter of principle.

[9] Commission (EC), 'Guidance on Commission's enforcement priorities in applying Article 82 of the EC Treaty to abusive exclusionary conduct by dominant undertaking' [2009] OJ C45/7 [30]–[31]; Case C-95/04 P *British Airways plc v Commission* [2007] ECR I-2331 [86]; Case C-52/09 *Konkurrensverket v TeliaSonera Sverige AB* [2011] ECR I-00527 [76]; Case C-209/10 *Post Danmark A/S v Konkurrencerådet*, Judgment of 27 March 2012 (NYR) [41]–[42].

and not of the legal burden.[10] In *Microsoft*, the General Court held, as a matter of principle, that:

> [A]lthough the burden of proof of the existence of the circumstances that constitute an infringement of [Article 102 TFEU] is borne by the Commission, it is for the dominant undertaking concerned, and not for the Commission, before the end of the administrative procedure, to raise any plea of objective justification and to support it with arguments and evidence. It then falls to the Commission, where it proposes to make a finding of an abuse of a dominant position, to show that the arguments and evidence relied on by the undertaking cannot prevail and, accordingly, that the justification put forward cannot be accepted.[11]

It is incumbent upon the dominant undertaking to provide all the evidence necessary to demonstrate that: 'the efficiencies have been, or are likely to be, realised as a result of its conduct'; 'the conduct is indispensable to the realisation of those efficiencies'; 'the likely efficiencies brought about by the conduct outweigh any likely negative effects on competition and consumer welfare'; and 'the conduct does not eliminate effective competition, by removing all or most existing sources of actual or potential competition'. It then falls upon the Commission, which weighs up any apparent anti-competitive effects against any advanced and substantiated efficiencies, to make the ultimate assessment as to whether the conduct is likely to result in consumer harm.[12]

Even though the suggested distribution of the burden of proof fits well with the text of Article 102 TFEU as well as of Article 2 of Regulation 1/2003, the substantive conditions that need to be demonstrated have been heavily criticised by commentators as 'manifestly ill-suited for the assessment of unilateral conduct by dominant undertakings'.[13] This is because, once dominance and the anti-competitive effect are established, the condition that the conduct 'does not eliminate competition' is, in practice, highly unlikely to be satisfied.[14] Therefore, the availability of a denial defence based on efficiencies is rather inconsistent with the basic test of (exclusionary) abuses in *Hoffmann-La Roche*. In addition, balancing

[10] The distinction between legal and evidential burden of proof is typical of denial defences in common law systems; see Nazzini (n 7) 523–26.

[11] Case T-201/04 *Microsoft Corporation v Commission* [2007] ECR II-3601 [688].

[12] Commission (EC), 'Guidance on Commission's enforcement priorities in applying Article 82 of the EC Treaty to abusive exclusionary conduct by dominant undertaking' [2009] OJ C45/7 [30]–[31].

[13] Waelbroeck (n 6) 121–26; J-F Bellis and T Kasten, 'Will Efficiencies Play an Increasingly Important Role in the Assessment of Conduct under Article 102 TFEU?' in F Etro and I Kokkoris (eds), *Competition Law and the Enforcement of Article 102 TFEU* (Oxford University Press, 2010) 131–33, 136–37; R O'Donoghue and J Padilla, *The Law and Economics of Article 82 EC* (Hart Publishing, 2006) 232–34; Rousseva (n 6) 292–93; A Albors-Llorens, 'The Role of Objective Justification and Efficiencies in the Application of Article 82 EC' (2007) 44 *Common Market Law Review* 1758–59. See also R Nazzini, *The Foundations of European Union Competition Law: The Objective and Principle of Article 102* (Oxford University Press, 2011) 304–09, who focuses his criticism of the Guidance Paper on its divergence from the case law.

[14] Contra Rousseva (n 6) 293, who suggests that the same conduct is treated more leniently under Article 102 TFEU than under Article 101 TFEU.

the pro- and anti-competitive effects of unilateral conduct is not, in practice, easy for dominant undertakings in their everyday business decisions.[15]

A solution to the assessment of 'objective' or 'efficiency' justifications under Article 102 TFEU would be: (a) to incorporate as a condition the absence of any such justification; and (b) to assess the alleged justifications independently of the conduct's likely negative effect of hindering the maintenance or growth of competition. This takes into account the qualitative difference between unilateral conduct and agreements, and considers the limitations imposed by the wording of the two Articles.[16] The *lack* of any 'objective' or 'efficiency' justification would be a necessary condition for establishing an abuse of the dominant position. However, if such a justification is proved, this would preclude the application of Article 102 TFEU and allow the unilateral conduct, *although* that conduct has the likely effect of hindering the maintenance or growth of competition. Methodologically, this solution finds support in the early case law of the Court of Justice that alludes to the notion of 'objective' justification with no systematic treatment of the relevant arguments, especially in relation to the exercise of IP rights.[17]

There is a lack of case law acceptance of 'objective' or 'efficiency' justification arguments.[18] This may indicate precisely that such arguments cannot operate

[15] D Melamed, 'Exclusionary Conduct under the Antitrust Laws: Balancing Sacrifice, and Refusals to Deal' (2005) 20 *Berkeley Technology Law Journal* 1252–55; E Elhauge, 'Defining Better Monopolization Standards' (2003) 56 *Stanford Law Review* 317.

[16] Rousseva (n 6) 480–81, 498–500 and P-J Loewenthal 'The Defence of "Objective Justification" in the Application of Article 82 EC' (2005) 28 *World Competition Law and Economics Review* 462 provide academic support for this solution. Rousseva's suggestion is based on the distinction between unilateral conduct and agreements, but places greater emphasis on the problem of inconsistencies in areas of overlapping application of Articles 101 and 102 TFEU. See also E Rousseva, 'Modernizing by Eradicating: How the Commission's New Approach to Article 81 EC Dispenses with the Need to Apply Article 82 EC to Vertical Restraints' (2005) 42 *Common Market Law Review* 587. Loewenthal suggests that the distinction between Articles 101 TFEU and 102 TFEU is not so great, since the eventual outcome under Article 102 TFEU will not differ significantly whether 'objective' justification is an exception to abusive conduct or a factor which is taken into account when determining whether an abuse has been committed. *Cf* Nazzini (n 13) 307, who considers the balancing test appropriate as 'a qualitative assessment of the comparative magnitude of the competitive harm and benefits'. Contra T van der Vijver, 'Article 102 TFEU: How to Claim the Application of Objective Justifications in the Case of Prima Facie Dominance Abuses' (2013) 4(2) *Journal of European Competition Law and Practice* 124–25, 128–29, who, instead, suggests varying degrees of standard of proof, depending on the type of 'objective' or 'efficiency' justification that the dominant undertaking wishes to invoke.

[17] Case 40/70 *Sirena Srl v Eda Srl and others* [1971] ECR 69 [17]; Case 78/70 *Deutsche Grammophon Gesellschaft mbH v Metro-SB-Großmärkte GmbH & Co KG* [1971] ECR 487 [19]; Case 395/87 *Ministère public v Jean-Louis Tournier* [1989] ECR 2521 [45]–[46]; Case 311/84 *Centre belge d'études de marché—Télémarketing (CBEM) v SA Compagnie luxembourgeoise de télédiffusion (CLT) and Information publicité Benelux (IPB)* [1985] ECR 3261 [27]. The proposed structure for incorporating efficiency or objective justifications in Article 102 TFEU analysis is also reflected in the legal construction of margin squeeze abuses, most recently confirmed in *Konkurrensverket v TeliaSonera Sverige AB* (n 9) [31].

[18] Similarly, H Friederiszick and L Gratz, 'Dominant and Efficient: On the Relevance of Efficiencies in Abuse of Dominance Cases', ESMT White Paper No WP–12–01 [28] report that the percentage of cases in which an 'objective' or 'efficiency' justification is put forward by the defendants is very low at the level of Commission Decisions, rather than Court judgments, being 42 per cent of the Article 102 TFEU cases investigated by the Commission from 2009 until 2013.

as a denial defence once the Commission has already taken up the case, because the Commission would only pursue cases of outright abuse.[19] It may be the case that, in the context of private litigation being boosted in the future, arguments based on the lack of any justification will be tested, given that there will be no initial screening of the cases being pursued. This is confirmed by the preliminary reference in *Post Danmark*, in which the Court of Justice did not examine the efficiency justifications claimed by the dominant undertaking (scale economies), but only because there was no anti-competitive effect and, hence, no abuse prima facie.[20] The receptiveness of the Court of Justice as regards efficiency justifications is contrasted with its stance regarding public policy justifications, which remains unaltered in recent private enforcement cases that culminated in preliminary references.[21]

B. The Distinction between Unilateral Conduct and Agreements: The Specific Case of Contractual Abuses

A question arises as to whether market separation can conceptually, or should from a policy perspective, be assessed under both Articles 101 and 102 TFEU or exclusively under one of them, given the different analytical framework governing the application of those Articles. Particularly in the area of contractual abuses, the established law suggests that Articles 101 and 102 TFEU can apply concomitantly to the same matter and, furthermore, that an agreement which is exempted under Article 101(3) TFEU (or block exempted), does not, for that reason, escape review under Article 102 TFEU.[22] The question is extremely important in market separation cases under Article 102 TFEU, since: (a) they often take the form of contractual abuses, such as rebates in the cases of *Irish Sugar*[23] or *British Gypsum*,[24] or of geographic price discrimination which is tied to some other contractual abuse, as

[19] Friederiszick and Gratz (n 18) 28–29 also suggest that 'efficiency' justifications might have played a significant role, but are not reported transparently, on the basis of a survey they conducted amongst competition law practitioners about the latter's perception of how often efficiency considerations are brought forward in Article 102 TFEU (and Article 101 TFEU) cases.

[20] *Post Danmark A/S* (n 9) [40], [43].

[21] See ch 4, text to nn 68–69.

[22] Case 85/76 *Hoffmann-La Roche & Co AG v Commission* [1979] ECR 461 [116]: 'the fact that agreements … might fall within [Article 101] and in particular within paragraph 3 thereof does not preclude the application of [Article 102] … so that in such cases the Commission is entitled, taking into account the nature of the reciprocal undertakings entered into and the competitive position of the various contracting parties on the market or markets on which they operate, to proceed on the basis of [Article 101] or [Article 102]'; Case T-51/89 *Tetra Pak Rausing SA v Commission (Tetra Pak I)* [1990] ECR II-0309 [20]–[21], [25]–[31]; Joined Cases C-395/96 P and C-396/96 P *Compagnie maritime belge transports SA, Compagnie maritime belge SA and Dafra-Lines A/S v Commission* [2000] ECR I-1365 [130]; *Atlantic Container Line AB and others* (n 8) [939].

[23] Case T-228/97 *Irish Sugar plc v Commission* [1999] ECR II-2969.

[24] Case T-65/89 *BPB Industries plc and British Gypsum Ltd v Commission* [1993] ECR II-389.

in the case of *United Brands*[25] and *Tetra Pak II*;[26] and (b) even in cases of genuinely unilateral conduct, as in *Sotirios Lélos*, the Court substantiates the abuse prima facie by explicit reference to the case law on anti-competitive by object agreements under Article 101 TFEU aimed at restricting parallel trade.[27]

Rousseva has recently argued that Article 102 TFEU should apply only to unilateral conduct and that the criterion for distinguishing the mutually exclusive concepts of 'unilateral conduct' and 'agreement' for the purposes of EU competition law is whether the implementation of the purchasing transaction is conditional on prior commitment on the part of customers.[28] Thus, exclusive dealing, loyalty rebates and contractual tying cases under Article 102 TFEU should be discarded and addressed under Article 101 TFEU. This criterion is in line with the definition of agreements under Article 101 TFEU. It is also in line with the distinction drawn by the General Court—and affirmed by the Court of Justice—between genuinely unilateral measures whose aims can be achieved without the express or implied participation of another undertaking, and 'merely apparent unilateral measures' which receive at least tacit acquiescence by another undertaking.[29]

There is much merit in Rousseva's analysis, in the sense that genuinely unilateral conduct, such as refusal to supply, discriminatory or excessive pricing, is liberated from the restrictions imposed by the analytical framework of Article 101 TFEU. The distinction also makes good sense from a policy perspective. Whereas agreements involve risk-sharing and are reached in relative transparency and with information exchange between the parties, unilateral conduct does not involve prior detailed assessment of its effect, precisely because a single undertaking has

[25] Case 27/76 *United Brands Company and United Brands Continentaal BV v Commission* [1978] ECR 207.

[26] Case T-83/91 *Tetra Pak v Commission* [1994] ECR II-755.

[27] Joined Cases C-468–478/06 *Sotirios Lélos kai Sia EE and others v GlaxoSmithKline AEVE Farmakeftikon Proïonton, formerly Glaxowellcome AEVE* [2008] ECR I-7139 [65]–[68].

[28] Rousseva (n 6) 460–63.

[29] Case T-41/96 *Bayer AG v Commission* [2000] ECR II-3383 [66]–[72]. A broad interpretation of the notion of 'agreement' was adopted by the Court of Justice in Case 107/82 *Allgemeine Elektrizitäts-Gesellschaft AEG-Telefunken AG v Commission* [1983] ECR 3151; Joined Cases 228 and 229/82 *Ford of Europe Incorporated and Ford-Werke Aktiengesellschaft v Commission* [1984] ECR 1129; and Case C-277/87 *Sandoz prodotti farmaceutici SpA v Commission* [1990] ECR I-45, in which an export ban was read into an agreement, even though it did not operate in the distributor's interest. However, the Court of Justice affirmed the General Court judgment in Joined Cases C-2/01 P and C-3/01 P *Bundesverband der Arzneimittel-Importeure eV and Commission v Bayer AG* [2004] ECR I-23 [101]–[102] and held that 'an agreement cannot be based on what is only the expression of a unilateral policy of one of the contracting parties, which can be put into effect without the assistance of others. To hold that an agreement prohibited by [Article 101(1) TFEU] may be established simply on the basis of the expression of a unilateral policy aimed at preventing parallel imports would have the effect of confusing the scope of that provision with that of [Article 102 TFEU]. For an agreement within the meaning of [Article 101(1) TFEU] to be capable of being regarded as having been concluded by tacit acceptance, it is necessary that the manifestation of the wish of one of the contracting parties to achieve an anti-competitive goal constitute an invitation to the other party, whether express or implied, to fulfil that goal jointly, and that applies all the more where, as in this case, such an agreement is not at first sight in the interests of the other party, namely the wholesalers'.

no detailed knowledge of the commercial strategy of its competitors.[30] Therefore, in the context of market separation, unilateral refusals to supply distributors involved in parallel trade, as in *Sotirios Lélos*, or geographic price discrimination under Article 102(c) TFEU, should not be found to be abusive on the basis of the case law on Article 101 TFEU. This applies in particular with regard to reproduction of precedents from restrictions of competition by object under Article 101 TFEU.

However, in the context of market separation cases under Article 102 TFEU, the proposal mentioned above does not seem to be operable where market separation by dominant undertakings takes the form of contractual abuses. This is because, in practice, the contractual abuse is rarely the only form of conduct which is condemned. In *United Brands*[31] and *Tetra Pak*,[32] plurality of actions by the dominant undertaking, including both contractual and genuinely unilateral abuses, occurred.[33] For example, in *United Brands*, the dominant undertaking was facing allegations not only of contractually prohibiting the resale of its products under certain conditions but also of refusal to supply, of geographic price discrimination and of charging excessive prices.[34] Similarly, in *Tetra Pak II*, the dominant undertaking was fined for contractual tying and also for geographic price discrimination and predatory pricing.[35] In such cases, even assuming that Article 101 TFEU covers contractual abuses, the question remains as to why the market distortions stemming from the contract were in fact addressed under Article 102 TFEU rather than Article 101 TFEU.

The response appears, in my view, to be more than simply practicalities. It is rather a matter of principle that the distinguishing feature of Article 102 TFEU is dominance, whereas that of Article 101 TFEU is the existence of an 'agreement' or 'concerted practice'.[36] It is not possible to demarcate the scope of the two

[30] Rousseva (n 6) 466–67.

[31] *United Brands Company* (n 25).

[32] *Tetra Pak* (n 26).

[33] More generally, this limitation to convergence (or distinction) between Articles 101 and 102 TFEU is also recognised by T Eilmansberger, 'Restrictive Agreements and Unilateral Restraints: Merging Regimes on Market Power and Exclusion' in J Drexl, L Idot and J Moneger (eds), *Economic Theory and Competition Law* (Edward Elgar, 2009) 156–57, by reference to the various examples of abusive conducts listed in Article 102 TFEU.

[34] *United Brands Company* (n 25).

[35] *Tetra Pak* (n 26).

[36] See particularly *Compagnie maritime belge transports SA* (n 22) [33]–[34]: 'Simultaneous application of [Articles 101 and 102 TFEU] cannot therefore be ruled out a priori. However, the objectives pursued by each of those two provisions must be distinguished. [Article 101 TFEU] applies to agreements, decisions and concerted practices, which may appreciably affect trade between Member States, regardless of the position on the market of the undertakings concerned. [Article 102 TFEU], on the other hand, deals with the conduct of one or more economic operators consisting in the abuse of a position of economic strength which enables the operator concerned to hinder the maintenance of effective competition on the relevant market by allowing it to behave to an appreciable extent independently of its competitors, its customers and, ultimately, consumers.'

provisions in a mutually exclusive way based on one single criterion.[37] Obviously, in the modernised approach to Article 101 TFEU, market power is central to the finding of a 'restriction on competition', particularly in relation to vertical restraints.[38] However, market power in Article 101 TFEU analysis does not perform the same screening function as dominance, but becomes important only at a later stage. This may occur at the stage of checking whether the agreement falling within the scope of Article 101 TFEU can be block exempted. The new Block Exemption Regulation for the categories of vertical agreements provides for a safe harbour when each market share of the supplier and that of the buyer is 30 per cent or less.[39] Alternatively, market power becomes important at the stage of ascertaining the obligation of the one party to pay damages to the other contracting party,[40] or of not imposing a fine on the party that acted under duress.[41] It becomes important by allowing a distinction to be drawn as to the extent of the liability of the parties to the agreement. In other words, the role of market power in the two Articles does not differ simply as a matter of degree.[42] Under Article 102 TFEU, market power amounting to dominance is the triggering factor for assessing a conduct's compatibility. The functional equivalent under Article 101 TFEU has nothing to do with the market position of the undertakings; rather, it concerns the form of the conduct that is to be scrutinised, namely an agreement (or concerted practice). It may be the case that lack of interest in the agreement does not preclude the application of Article 102 TFEU. However, it does preclude the reading into an agreement of an apparently unilateral conduct; thus, the application of Article 101 TFEU is precluded.[43] Therefore, if one were to find a mutually exclusive way of distinguishing the scope of the two Articles in the 'grey area' of contractual abuses, this should be neither on the grounds of market power nor of the form of conduct.

In practice, I would rather opt for a case-by-case analysis, which enables a determination to be made as to which criterion, ie, market power or the form of the conduct, manifests itself more profoundly in the situation under examination. This would determine which Article applies in practice, without it being

[37] Rousseva assumes that this is possible by rejecting dominance as the distinguishing feature of Article 102 TFEU applicability. She maintains that the reference to dominance is devoid of meaning, since the application of Article 102 TFEU does not require unilateral interest or the exercise of economic pressure and, also, because of the increasing relevance of market power in the assessment under Article 101 TFEU. See Rousseva (n 16) 620–24.

[38] See Commission (EU), 'Guidelines on Vertical Restraints' [2010] OJ C130/1 [96]–[99].

[39] Commission Regulation (EU) 330/2010 on the application of Article 101(3) of the Treaty on the Functioning of the European Union to categories of vertical agreements and concerted practices [2010] OJ L102/1 [Article 3].

[40] See Case C-453/99 *Courage Ltd v Bernard Crehan and Bernard Crehan v Courage Ltd and others* [2001] ECR I-6297 [34]–[35]. See also ch 2, text to nn 112–14.

[41] *Volkswagen* (Case IV/35.733) Commission Decision 98/273/EC [1998] OJ L124/60 [208].

[42] Even if one considers that the double market share threshold provided for in the Block Exemption Regulation operates at the screening level (like dominance) but as a presumption of compatibility, there is a meaningful difference of degree in the required market power.

[43] See n 29.

conceptually impossible for one to assess the conduct under the residual Article. In the market separation cases that take the form of contractual abuse, it is the disproportionate lack of parity between the parties that allows the dominant undertaking to act. This is manifested by the fact that such an act takes various forms, including agreements, refusal to supply, predatory or excessive pricing, as mentioned above. This is why market power, rather than the form of the conduct, is the centre of gravity. On the contrary, in *Van den Bergh Foods*, which may be used as an example of the redundancy of Article 102 TFEU in the area of vertical agreements,[44] it was the form of the undertaking's conduct that prevailed over its market position, as demonstrated by the fact that this was the only form of conduct that occurred and that the individual agreement was part of the network of distribution agreements fulfilling the same conditions.[45] In that respect, the existence of a network of similar vertical restraints is an indication that the form of the conduct (agreement) prevails. The new Block Exemption Regulation for categories of vertical agreements, which provides for a different screening threshold based on market power once a network of agreements has been found to operate in the market, confirms this.[46] Therefore, the difference between the two scenarios is the starting point (dominance in the first case and agreement in the second).

Based on this analysis, market separation conducted by dominant undertakings, regardless of the form of the conduct, should be exclusively assessed under Article 102 TFEU. This further requires the application of the distinctive methodology of that Article, as opposed to the methodology of Article 101 TFEU. The only qualification to this proposition would be in the grey area of contractual abuses if the form of the conduct constitutes the centre of gravity and, consequently, manifests itself over the market position of the undertaking involved, as explained above.

III. CONCEPTUAL ELEMENTS OF MEASURES CONSTITUTING A RESTRICTION ON FREE MOVEMENT

The conceptual elements of the free movement provisions, which are used to 'unpack' the oft-quoted proposition that Article 102 TFEU serves market integration

[44] Rousseva (n 16) 634–36; Case T-65/98 *Van den Bergh Foods Ltd v Commission* [2003] ECR II-4653.

[45] Therefore, as rightly pointed out by Rousseva, there was no need to apply Article 102 TFEU. However, the redundancy of Article 102 TFEU, according to the thesis advanced here, is case-specific. An example providing a counter-argument to Rousseva's generalisation is discriminatory rebates cases such as *BPB Industries plc and British Gypsum Ltd v Commission* (n 24) [40], in which the decisive factor seems to be the offer by the dominant undertaking of promotional payments to individually selected merchants, rather than offers under a general scheme.

[46] Commission Regulation (EU) 330/2010 on the application of Article 101(3) of the Treaty on the Functioning of the European Union to categories of vertical agreements and concerted practices [2010] OJ L102/1, Article 6 provides for a withdrawal of the block exemption where parallel networks of similar vertical restraints cover more than 50 per cent of a relevant market.

purposes in the EU, are examined in this section. The free movement provisions are characterised by interplay between economic and non-economic values promoted and protected by restrictions and justified restrictions. This is important for the present research because its purpose is to examine whether the same distinction is relevant for the application of Article 102 TFEU under the above-proposed structure for substantiating market separation as an abuse of the dominant position. More importantly, it is relevant because analysis of the notion of restrictions under the free movement provisions allows for an understanding of the scope of the 'internal' element of the Internal Market. This is used in section IV as the benchmark for assessing the actual integrationist thrust of the case law under Article 102 TFEU. Therefore, the analysis presented in this section does not aim at reformulating our understanding of what is, or should be, an Internal Market. Rather, whatever understanding one reaches about the proper shape of the Internal Market, interrogation of the proper application of competition law comes *after* that. Accordingly, it is critical to capture the status of the law as to what is the Internal Market, in order to assess and provide normative suggestions concerning the subsequent step of the application of Article 102 TFEU to market separation cases.

A. Distinguishing between Economic and Non-economic Values under the Free Movement Provisions

The mechanism of the Treaty provisions on the free movement involves, as a first step analysis, consideration of economic values. This step is the finding of a 'trade barrier' (or a 'restriction to the free movement'). The Treaty mechanism also involves a second step analysis, which relates to more than economic values. This is the question of whether or not the trade barrier is justified.

The link is established between the promotion of economic values and the finding of a restriction, using the example of trade barriers. The following sub-section defines these economic values promoted under the free movement provisions by identifying the two tests—discrimination or market access—for finding a trade barrier. Overall, the first step is aimed at obtaining an understanding of the nature of the 'internal' element of the Internal Market, ie, what is really internal about the Internal Market.[47]

[47] The focus is on the 'internal' element, rather than the 'market' element of the Internal Market, also because the threshold for finding a 'market' element is generally low or highly random. See, eg, Case C-159/90 *The Society for the Protection of Unborn Children Ireland Ltd v Stephen Grogan and others* [1991] ECR I-4685 [26]; and Case C-137/09 *Marc Michel Josemans v Burgemeester van Maastricht* [2011] 2 CMLR 19 [42], [47]. See also ch 2, text to nn 44–49. This first step is about obtaining an understanding of the 'internal' element of the Internal Market, rather than advancing a normative suggestion about the proper shape of the Internal Market, as explained in the Introduction to the section.

Whether the non-economic values operate as a justification (via an explicit Treaty provision) for a restriction of the freedom in question or as a negative qualification of the definition of the restriction in the first place is not of primary importance in establishing the link between economic values and restrictions. Similarly, at this stage of the research, the extensive academic debate on the scope of the non-economic values under the provisions of the free movement is not relevant. Both debates are addressed here only to the extent that they represent a challenge to the link between economic values and trade barriers (or restrictions more generally).

At first sight, the distinction between economic and non-economic values under the free movement provisions corresponds to the distinction between restrictions and justifications. The evidence for this comes from the specific justifications expressly mentioned in Articles 36, 45(3), 52, 62 and 65(1)(b) TFEU, which refer to non-economic policy objectives, such as public policy, public security and public health. At the same time, the Court has consistently held that Article 36 TFEU may not be relied upon by a Member State to protect its economic interests.[48] In addition, the scope of the general justifications for 'indistinctly applicable' measures established in the Court's case law as 'mandatory/imperative requirements' is open-ended,[49] but subject to the condition that purely economic grounds can never serve as such a justification.[50]

A first, structural challenge to the link between economic values and restrictions could be the fact that the non-economic values incorporated in the mandatory requirements concept may operate as a negative qualification to the finding of a restriction. However, this challenge is not valid because of the gradual blending of the general and the Treaty-based justifications in the Court's case law. Such

[48] See also Case 7/61 *Commission v Italian Republic* [1961] ECR (English Special Edition) 317, 329 '[Article 36 TFEU] is directed to eventualities of a non-economic kind which are not liable to prejudice the principles laid down by [inter alia Article 34 TFEU]'. Similarly, see Case 238/82 *Duphar BV and others v The Netherlands* [1984] ECR 523 [23] (in relation to a 'measure whose primary objective is budgetary in as much as it is intended to reduce the operating costs of a sickness insurance scheme'); and Case 288/83 *Commission v Ireland* [1985] ECR 1761 [28].

[49] Case 120/78 *Rewe-Zentral AG v Bundesmonopolverwaltung für Branntwein* [1979] ECR 649 [8]; Case 113/80 *Commission v Ireland* [1981] ECR 1625 [10]–[11]; Case 177/83 *Th Kohl KG v Ringelhan & Rennett SA and Ringelhan Einrichtungs GmbH* [1984] ECR 3651 [14], [19]; Case 25/88 *Criminal proceedings against Esther Renée Bouchara, née Wurmser, and Norlaine SA* [1989] ECR 1105 [10]; Joined Cases C-1/90 and C-176/90 *Aragonesa de Publicidad Exterior SA and Publivía SAE v Departamento de Sanidad y Seguridad Social de la Generalitat de Cataluña* [1991] ECR I-4151 [13]; Case C-484/93 *Peter Svensson and Lena Gustavsson v Ministre du Logement et de l'Urbanisme* [1995] ECR I-3955 [15]–[16]; Case C-55/94 *Reinhard Gebhard v Consiglio dell'Ordine degli Avvocati e Procuratori di Milano* [1995] ECR I-4165 [37].

[50] See Case C-265/95 *Commission v French Republic* [1997] ECR I-6959 [60], [62], citing the case law under Article 36 TFEU (see n 49) ('responsibility for compensation for the loss or damage sustained by the economic operators concerned'); Case C-398/95 *Syndesmos ton en Elladi Touristikon kai Taxidiotikon Grafeion v Ypourgos Ergasias* [1997] ECR I-3091 [23] ('maintaining industrial peace as a means of bringing a collective labour dispute to an end and thereby preventing any adverse effects on an economic sector, and consequently on the economy of the State'); Case C-388/01 *Commission v Italian Republic* [2003] ECR I-721 [18], [21]–[22] ('cost of managing cultural assets').

blending has been achieved either by shifting the examination of the mandatory requirements from the qualification stage to the justification stage or by examining the Treaty-based justifications at the qualification stage.[51] It has also been achieved by using the mandatory requirements for justifying (indirectly) discriminatory measures.[52] The very recent cases on rules on the use of goods confirm that there is no longer any practical significance attributed to the distinction between Treaty-based justifications and mandatory requirements, since both are being examined interchangeably, once a measure fails the market access test, at either the qualification or the justification stage.[53] Therefore, for the purposes of this book, the distinction between economic and non-economic values under the free movement provisions will be adopted as corresponding to the distinction between trade barriers (or restrictions to free movement) and justified trade barriers.

[51] The case law on the distinction between justifications under Article 36 TFEU and mandatory requirements has never been really consistent, even though the distinction bears consequences in terms of how broadly general rules and exceptions are to be interpreted as well as regarding the allocation of the burden of proof; see P Pecho, 'Good-Bye Keck? A Comment on the Remarkable Judgment in Commission v Italy, C-110/05' (2009) 36 *Legal Issues of Economic Integration* 267; and P Oliver, 'Of Trailers and Jet Skis: Is the Case Law on Article 34 TFEU Hurtling in a New Direction?' (2009–10) 33 *Fordham International Law Journal* 1449.

[52] The language used ('measures applying without distinction' rather than non-discriminatory measures) in the cases cited above (see n 49) has meant that the Court considered indirectly discriminatory measures to be indistinctly applicable and subjected them to imperative requirements; see somewhat more recently Case C-309/02 *Radlberger Getränkegesellschaft mbH & Co and S Spitz KG v Land Baden-Württemberg* [2004] ECR I-11763 [73]–[75]; and Case C-441/04 *A-Punkt Schmuckhandels GmbH v Claudia Schmidt* [2006] ECR I-2093 [26]. The matter as to whether direct discrimination can potentially be justified by reference to imperative requirements is not settled in law; see Case C-379/98 *PreussenElektra AG v Schleswag AG* [2001] ECR I-2099, Opinion of AG Jacobs [228]–[229]. However, the Court has, at least in the sphere of imperative requirements in relation to environmental protection, accepted the availability of such a justification for prima facie direct discrimination; see Case C-2/90 *Commission v Kingdom of Belgium* [1992] ECR I-4431 [29]–[36] and later on, by avoiding explicitly tackling the question of discrimination; see Case C-203/96 *Chemische Afvalstoffen Dusseldorp BV and others v Minister van Volkshuisvesting, Ruimtelijke Ordening en Milieubeheer* [1998] ECR I-4075 [42]–[44]; and Case C-379/98 *PreussenElektra AG v Schhleswag AG* [2001] ECR I-2099 [72]–[81]. Contra Case C-153/08 *Commission v Kingdom of Spain* [2009] ECR I-9735 [36]–[38]; and Case 341/05 *Laval un Partneri Ltd v Svenska Byggnadsarbetareförbundet and others* [2007] ECR I-11767 [117]–[119], in which the Court explicitly rejected non-Treaty-based justifications to directly discriminatory measures. A test case is pending before the Court of Justice. In Joined Cases C-204–208/12 *Essent Belgium*, Opinion of AG Bot, of 8 May 2013 [92]–[95], AG Bot invited the Court to revisit its case law as regards the availability of environmental protection as a justification to a directly discriminatory measure, namely the Belgian law that required electricity suppliers in Belgium to surrender a certain quota of green certificates, which were only granted to Belgian producers of green electricity.

[53] In Case C-110/05 *Commission v Italian Republic* [2009] ECR I-519 [58]–[59], the Court held that rules on the use of goods that hinder market access for imported products constitute MEQR, unless they could be objectively justified based on either one of the public interest grounds set out in Article 36 TFEU or imperative requirements (interchangeably). Similarly, see Case C-142/05 *Åklagaren v Percy Mickelsson and Joakim Roos* [2009] ECR I-4273 [28], [31]–[33], where the Court explicitly merged, at the qualification stage, the examination of environmental protection as general justification and the protection of the health and life of humans, animals and plants set out in Article 36 TFEU. In Case C-265/06 *Commission v Portuguese Republic* [2008] ECR I-2245 [37], the Court held that mandatory requirements and Treaty-based justifications apply interchangeably at the justification level. The issue of using mandatory requirements for justifying directly discriminatory measures did not arise in those cases.

A second, substantive, challenge to the correspondence of concepts adopted above could be the Court's actual practice which, under specific circumstances, is more permissive concerning economic justifications.[54] However, this does not rule out the link between economic values and trade barriers; it only limits the link between non-economic values and justified trade barriers.

In *Campus Oil*, in particular, the Court created an opening for economic interests to be taken into account as justifications, by holding that:

> [Article 36 TFEU] refers to matters of a non-economic nature. A Member State cannot be allowed to avoid the effects of measures provided for in the Treaty by pleading the economic difficulties caused by the elimination of barriers to intra-community trade. However, in the light of the seriousness of the consequence that an interruption in supplies of petroleum products may have for a country's existence, the aim of ensuring a minimum supply of petroleum products at all times is to be regarded as transcending purely economic considerations and thus as capable of constituting an objective covered by the concept of public security.[55]

It seems from *Campus Oil* that the 'purely economic considerations' precluded by Article 36 TFEU (or by mandatory requirements) are identified with the effects of the measures under consideration on *intra*-EU trade.[56] In other words, the Court itself draws a distinction between economic and non-economic values based on the notion of discrimination or (more recently) hindrances to market access as trade barriers. Therefore, *Campus Oil* could only support a partial breakdown of the link between economic/non-economic values and trade barriers/justifications:[57] it does not provide an argument against the link between

[54] See K Mortelmans, 'Towards Convergence in the Application of the Rules on Free Movement and on Competition?' (2001) 38 *Common Market Law Review* 637; J Snell, 'Economic Aims as Justification for Restrictions on Free Movement' in A Schrauwen (eds), *Rule of Reason: Rethinking Another Classic of European Legal Doctrine* (Europa Law, 2005) 35, 39–47.

[55] Case 72/83 *Campus Oil Ltd and others v Minister for Industry and Energy and others* [1984] ECR 2727 [35].

[56] Similarly, see the more recent Case C-456/10 *ANETT v Administración del Estado*, Judgment of 26 April 2012 (NYR) [53], in which the Court of Justice rejected the claim that a national law prohibiting tobacco retailers from importing manufactured tobacco products from other Member States might be justified on the ground that the possibility of importing tobacco products would create an excessive competitive advantage for tobacco retailers. Earlier, the Court ruled that the national law was capable of having a negative effect on the choice of products that the tobacco retailers include in their range of products and, ultimately, on the access of various products coming from other Member States to the Spanish market; ibid [42].

[57] As to the link between non-economic values and justifications, it could be argued that the case law in n 50 supports the view that economic considerations could, at the most, be potentially accepted as a means for the achievement of a non-economic objective. In the context of services, Case C-384/93 *Alpine Investments BV v Minister van Financiën* [1995] ECR I-1141 [44] ('good reputation of national financial sector') presents a similar example. Even some Treaty-based justifications, such as protection of intellectual property rights, share elements of economic rationales; see, eg, P Regibeau and K Rockett, 'The Relationship between Intellectual Property Law and Competition Law: An Economic Approach' in S Anderman (ed), *The Interface between Intellectual Property Rights and Competition Policy* (Cambridge University Press, 2007) 506–21. See also S Enchelmaier, 'Mandatory Requirements under Art 101(3) TFEU? The Complementary Relationship between EU Competition and Free

economic values and trade barriers. On the contrary, by explicitly excluding, at the justification stage, only the economic effect of a trade barrier from the non-economic values, the judgment indicates that there is a link between the promotion of certain economic values and trade barriers, whose analytical core cannot be further diminished and shrunk. This view is also supported by the reference in Article 36 TFEU to a 'disguised restriction on trade'.[58]

Another category of cases in which the Court has been prepared to accept economic aims as justifications are those cases involving an economic evaluation of the provision of a service of a non-economic nature. In that sense, this is not an exception to the principle that aims of a purely economic character cannot serve as general justifications, but, rather, it resembles the exception in Article 106(2) TFEU.[59] More recently, after *Viking*, trade unions, as addressees of the fundamental freedoms, are able to justify their actions by reference to the economic interests of their members.[60] Roth interprets this as introducing the protection of domestic working places as an economic objective for justifying the actions of trade unions, but not of states.[61] However, first, the Court expressly associates the protection of workers with social protection by reference to ex-Article 2 TEC[62] and, second, even if it is considered to be an economic objective, it cannot be used as a justification to the extent that such 'a policy results in ship-owners being prevented from

Movement Law' [2012] *Competition Law Journal* 192–93, who argues that almost 'anything goes' as a ground for justification, because all legislation entails, inevitably, some unequal treatment. Thus, that same reason for the adoption of the legislation (the policy pursued) should double as the ground for justification of the unavoidable inequality; hence, the real hurdle, at the justification stage, is the proportionality test. The issue of the conceptual foundation of the process at the justification stage and, therefore, the question as to whether this correspondence breakdown between non-economic values and justified trade barriers is important is addressed in ch 4, section II.A.

[58] W-H Roth, 'Economic Justifications and the Internal Market' in M Bulterman, L Hancher, A McDonnell and H Sevenster (eds), *Views of European Law from the Mountain: Liber Amicorum Piet Jan Slot* (Kluwer Law International, 2009) 75–76. Roth describes the notion of economic considerations as having the objective of the protection of the national economy vis-a-vis the competitive forces from other Member States, but this is just giving specific definition to the broader notion of trade barrier. Similarly, Snell (n 54) 52 poses the question whether the Court should use the term 'protectionist' rather than 'economic aims' and gives a negative answer.

[59] In Case C-158/96 *Raymond Kohll v Union des caisses de maladie* [1998] ECR I-1931 [41], the Court repeated that 'aims of a purely economic nature cannot justify a barrier to the fundamental principle of freedom to provide services', but 'it cannot be excluded that the risk of seriously undermining the financial balance of the social security system may constitute an overriding reason in the general interest capable of justifying a barrier of that kind'. This is reflected to some extent in Article 153(4) TFEU, following the Treaty of Nice; see Mortelmans (n 54) 638. See also the analysis by N Nic Shuibhne and M Maci, 'Proving Public Interest: The Growing Importance of Evidence in Free Movement Case Law' (2013) 50 *Common Market Law Review* 997–1004, who discuss the establishment of a justification on the basis of economic rationales—that is, public spending issues—as a problem of standard of proof of public interest claims—that is, healthcare services, the funding of education or social benefits.

[60] See Case C-438/05 *International Transport Workers' Federation and Finnish Seamen's Union v Viking Line ABP and OÜ Viking Line Eesti* [2007] ECR I-10779 [81] (*Viking Line ABP*).

[61] Roth (n 58) 87.

[62] *Viking Line ABP* (n 60) [78]–[79].

registering their vessels in a State other than that of which the beneficial owners of those vessels are nationals'.[63] Therefore, even considered as a justification of an economic nature, it can never be considered to be a trade barrier.[64]

To conclude, the conceptual foundation of the first step analysis under the Treaty provisions for free movement is the promotion of certain economic values. These economic values constitute the minimum analytical core of the 'internal' element of the Internal Market because they trigger the application of the Treaty mechanism under the free movement provisions. The next sub-section examines the specific content given to these economic values by the Court's case law.

B. Economic Values Promoted by the Free Movement Provisions: A Discrimination Test, a Market Access Test or Both?

This section identifies the conceptual basis of the economic values promoted by the free movement provisions. If this is just non-discrimination against foreigners (anti-protectionism), the important factor is the disparate impact of the measure. Alternatively, it may also be a restriction of market access in absolute terms that is prohibited.[65] If the conceptual basis of the prohibited effect under the free movement provisions is identified, then it can be used as an indicator of the actual integrationist thrust of the market separation cases under Article 102 TFEU.

One alleged limitation to this approach is the interplay between the two steps of the analysis under the Treaty provisions on free movement, namely between what has been described in the previous section as restrictions and justifications. Commentators often refer to the political bargaining that actually takes place in every Court judgment. The broader the definition of trade barriers which brings national measures within the scope of the Treaty mechanism, the more assessment takes place at the level of justifications advanced by Member States. It could be argued that it would be more convincing to draw conclusions as to the conceptual basis of the prohibited effect by using cases in which the national measure

[63] ibid [88].

[64] Particularly after *Viking*, there has been extensive debate and copious academic literature on the scope of non-economic values that are recognised as justifications to restrictions on the freedoms. However, this discussion is not relevant for the research presented in this chapter. Discussion of the justifications being accepted in *Viking* is only relevant to the extent that it considers the question whether the link between economic values and restrictions has been corroded.

[65] There has been extensive academic literature on the interpretation of the case law on the free movement provisions over the years, since the development of (what has been for many years) Community law has primarily rested on the application of free movement provisions. See, for example, the leading books on the subject: C Barnard, *The Substantive Law of the EU: The Four Freedoms* (Oxford University Press, 2010); P Oliver (ed), *Oliver on Free Movement of Goods in the European Union* (Hart Publishing, 2010); L Gormley, *EU Law of Free Movement of Goods and Customs Union* (Oxford University Press, 2009); G Davies, *Nationality Discrimination in the European Internal Market* (Kluwer Law International, 2003); J Snell, *Goods and Services in EC Law: A Study of the Relationship Between the Freedoms* (Oxford University Press, 2002).

is actually prohibited at the stage of justification; namely, it is illegal overall.[66] However, even in that case, the outer limit of the scope of the prohibitions provided for in the free movement provisions is defined by what constitutes a trade barrier, or a restriction, under the freedoms, rather than by what constitutes a justified, and therefore overall legal, trade barrier. The fact that a trade barrier is only potentially unlawful overall does not detract from its function of qualifying the measure as a trade barrier in the first place, nor do trade-restricting effects cease to exist if the trade barrier is, after all, justified.[67]

Judgments concerning rules on the use of goods will be the point of reference for the development of the case law in recent years. In *Commission v Italy*, the Court summarised the principles governing the scope of Article 34 TFEU. After repeating the three main pillars of the relevant case law (*Dassonville*, *Cassis de Dijon* and *Keck and Mithouard*),[68] the Court, in paragraph [37], defined MEQR as falling into three categories. First, MEQR include measures which have as their object or effect to treat products coming from other Member States less favourably; in other words, measures which discriminate against imports. Second, MEQR include rules that lay down requirements to be met by goods which have been lawfully manufactured and marketed in other Member States, even if those rules apply without distinction to all products alike. Third, any other measure which hinders access of products originating in other Member States is included. The first two categories hinge upon the well-established principles of non-discrimination (direct or indirect) against imports and of mutual recognition.[69] Mutual recognition is also considered to be an expression of regulatory equivalence,[70] and therefore product-related rules are presumed to have a disparate impact and discriminate against imports because of the so-called dual burden that they impose.[71]

[66] See Davies (n 65) 89, in the context of non-discriminatory measures. However, Davies defines (indirect) 'discrimination' as unjustified disparate impact; see ibid 11–14. See also L Gormley, 'Free Movement of Goods and their Use: What is the Use of it?' (2009–10) 33 *Fordham International Law Journal* 1613–14, 1616, in relation to the Court's judgment in Case C-110/05 *Commission v Italian Republic* (n 53), in which he states that the rejection of the argument that rules on the use of goods should be taken outside the scope of Article 34 TFEU came at the price of accepting the necessity of the rule for the attainment of the legitimate objective advanced by Italy; *cf* Oliver (n 51) 1465.

[67] This also seems to be accepted by Gormley (n 66) 1614, 1617, even though he is critical of the use of general and Treaty-based justifications interchangeably.

[68] *Commission v Italian Republic* (n 53) [33]–[36].

[69] For an enumeration of the principles, see also ibid [34].

[70] See the distinction put forward in Case C-145/88 *Torfaen Borough Council v B & Q plc* [1989] ECR 3851, Opinion of AG Van Gerven [13] in regard to trade barriers that arise from the disparities between the various national rules and barriers created by the very existence of the rules. In the latter category of barriers there is no regulatory equivalence in the first place.

[71] See Davies (n 65) 65–67 for a view on the shifting role of discrimination in the construction of the Internal Market over time. See G De Búrca, 'Unpacking the Concept of Discrimination in the EC and International Trade Law' in C Barnard and J Scott (eds), *The Law of the Single European Market: Unpacking the Premises* (Hart Publishing, 2002) 181 for a view that discrimination (or selectivity) remains the key concept of the free movement provisions. See also N Bernard, 'Discrimination and Free Movement in EC Law' (1996) 45 *International and Comparative Law Quarterly* 82; and, more recently, G Davies, 'Understanding Market Access: Exploring the Economic Rationality of Different Conceptions of Free Movement Law' (2010) 11 *German Law Journal* 671.

However, the third category of MEQR has provoked considerable debate because it seems to define in an affirmative way for the first time the principle of 'free access of [European] products to national markets'.[72] Until *Commission v Italy*, the principle of free access to national markets within the EU in the context of goods had been inferred from the negative presumption established by *Keck and Mithouard*, namely that selling arrangements are outside the scope of Article 34 TFEU precisely because it is presumed that 'they are not by nature such as to prevent their access to the market or to impede access any more than they impede the access of domestic products'.[73] The Court's pronouncement in *Commission v Italy* has provoked considerable discussion, particularly as to whether it signals abandonment of the *Keck and Mithouard* presumption *in globo*.[74] From the Court's ruling, it is only clear that rules on the use of goods do not fall under the same negative presumption as selling arrangements, presumably because they directly affect the consumer (rather than the producer, importer or retailer). Instead, they are subject to an intensity-based market access test. It cannot be safely concluded from the judgment whether the selling arrangements presumption is still valid or whether the category of 'any other measures that hinder market access' also covers selling arrangements.[75] The measures in question amounted to total or semi-total banning rather than regulating use, and therefore the Court did not need to rule on the intensity of hindrances to market access. However, the fact remains that the Court chose not to treat explicitly the

[72] *Commission v Italian Republic* (n 53) [34].

[73] Joined Cases C-267/91 and C-268/91 *Keck and Mithouard* [1993] ECR I-6097 [17], to the extent that the conditions set out in para [16] of the judgment are fulfilled, namely that the national provisions apply to all relevant traders operating within the national territory and that they affect in the same manner, in law and in fact, the marketing of domestic products and those from other Member States. It was not clear until the judgment in *Commission v Italy* whether the reference to market access in para [17] of *Keck and Mithouard* was simply a failure to discharge the burden of proof for indirect discrimination in para [16] or a distinct substantive test. Subsequent cases, such as Joined Cases C-34/95, C-35/95 and C-36/95 *Konsumentombudsmannen (KO) v De Agostini (Svenska) Förlag AB and TV-Shop i Sverige AB* [1997] ECR I-3843 [42]–[44] and Case C-405/98 *Konsumentombudsmannen (KO) v Gourmet International Products AB* [2001] ECR I-1795 [20]–[25], seem to confirm the view that the reference to market access in *Keck and Mithouard* is closely connected to indirect discrimination, with a reversed burden of proof.

[74] The issue was first raised in *Åklagaren v Percy Mickelsson and Joakim Roos* (n 53), Opinion of AG Kokott [51], even though there was actually no need to address it in that case since, according to her, the rules resulted in complete exclusion; ibid [64]. In light of the Opinion of AG Kokott, the Chamber hearing *Commission v Italy* referred the case to the Grand Chamber, which reopened the hearing proceedings and invited Member States to submit their observations on the issue.

[75] In favour of the view that the Court did not intend to revise and has not revised the *Keck* exception, see Oliver (n 51) 1462–63, 1470; Gormley (n 66) 1626–27; Pecho (n 51) 262–64; and P Wenneras and K Boe Moen, 'Selling Arrangements, Keeping *Keck*' (2010) 35 *European Law Review* 393–94. In favour of the view that the Court's ruling is narrow and did not analyse the *Keck* exception, see S Weatherill, 'I. Free Movement of Goods' in J McMahon (ed), *Current Developments: European Union Law* (2009) 58 *International and Comparative Law Quarterly* 987. In favour of the view that the Court overruled *Keck*, regardless of whether they agree or disagree with the ruling at a normative level, see E Spaventa, 'Leaving *Keck* Behind? The Free Movement of Goods after the Rulings in *Commission v Italy* and *Mickelsson and Roos*' (2009) 34 *European Law Review* 922–23; and T Horsley, 'Anyone for *Keck*?' (2009) 46 *Common Market Law Review* 2015–16.

measures in question under the traditional *Dassonville* formula, even though it could have done so based on the *Toolex Alpha* precedent.[76] Instead, it formulated a unified market access test and subjected the rules under examination to that test. Based on the observation made above, one would be more inclined to interpret paragraph [37] of the judgment in *Commission v Italy* as distinguishing between 'product-bound measures' and 'all other measures' that apply to all products alike, rather than as distinguishing between 'selling arrangements' and 'all other measures'. 'Selling arrangements' remains a distinct sub-division within the broader category of either hindrances to market access or (indirectly) discriminatory trade barriers with a reversed burden of proof, which was beyond the facts before the Court in *Commission v Italy*.[77] Subsequent cases include *LIBRO*, which concerned directly discriminatory minimum retail prices for imported German language books imposed by the Austrian legislation,[78] and *Ker Optika*, which concerned Hungarian legislation prohibiting the selling of contact lenses via the Internet.[79] The latter judgment is more important because it appears to assess certain selling arrangements under the (indirect) discrimination test with a reversed burden of proof, while citing *Commission v Italy*.[80] In other words, it seems to keep 'certain selling arrangements' as outside the broader category of measures assessed under the 'market access' test established in *Commission v Italy*.[81]

Therefore, in *Commission v Italy*, it appears that the Court intended to reformulate rather than return to the narrow understanding of the *Dassonville* formula,[82]

[76] Case C-473/98 *Kemikalieinspektionen v Toolex Alpha AB* [2000] ECR I-5681, where the Court held that a general prohibition on the industrial use of a chemical falls within the scope of Article 34 TFEU because 'it is likely to bring about a reduction in the volume of trichloroethylene imported'; ibid [36]. It could be argued that *Toolex Alpha* is not comparable because it concerns the industrial use of a product rather than use by final consumers; hence, it concerns a *Cassis de Dijon* type of measure imposing a dual burden on imports. However, this does not challenge the argument that if the Court were to retain the status quo, the most appropriate available formula to assess the rules on the use of goods by final consumers would be the *Dassonville* formula.

[77] The same is true about *Åklagaren v Percy Mickelsson and Joakim Roos* (n 53). The lack of any reference to *Keck* is not conclusive as to whether a measure that fulfils the *Keck* conditions is presumed to be outside the scope of Article 34 TFEU or assessed under the market access test.

[78] Case C-531/07 *Fachverband der Buch- und Medienwirtschaft v LIBRO Handelsgesellschaft mbH* [2009] ECR I-3717 [22].

[79] Case C-108/09 *Ker-Optika bt v ÀNTSZ Dél-dunántúli Regionális Intézete* [2011] 2 CMLR 15 [47]–[52].

[80] ibid [51].

[81] However, it should be noted that it is a Second Chamber judgment. A rather odd case, decided on the basis of both *Commission v Italy* and *Ker Optika*, is *ANETT v Administración del Estado* (n 56) [34]–[37], in which the Court explicitly subjects to the market access test a seemingly (directly) discriminatory measure, namely a national law prohibiting tobacco retailers from importing manufactured tobacco products from other Member States.

[82] This view rejects the opinion that *Dassonville* overshot its target, in the sense that non-discriminatory measures were already within the *Dassonville* formulation of trade barriers. This is because the subsequent application of the *Dassonville* formula was guided by the principle of non-discrimination, either direct or indirect, on the facts of the cases that came before the Court. The *Sunday Trading* litigation, in which the Court found restrictive effects on European trade to exist despite the fact that the rules applied to and affected imported and domestic products alike, was

to the extent that the formula now appears to apply to non-discriminatory measures. Discrimination appears, at the moment, to be a sufficient but not necessary conceptual basis for finding a trade barrier. Based on the above, if one wishes to look for the broader distinction that underlies the revised definition of MEQR, this lies between discrimination and market access. Discrimination, as formulated in the years between *Dassonville* and *Cassis de Dijon*, was based on market equivalence, namely goods that could be substituted according to their characteristics or uses from the perspective of economic actors.[83] Wilsher has shown that those cases relate to a very narrow situation in which an identical domestic product exists and the rules have a disparate impact upon the imported version.[84] This is why the case law under Article 34 TFEU on national rules aimed at restricting the freedom to compete did not actually present a challenge to the discrimination analysis under Article 34 TFEU. This includes national laws regulating prices, when they result in a loss of a competitive advantage enjoyed by imports.[85] The *LIBRO* case cited above, decided after *Commission v Italy*, confirms that this is still the situation with directly discriminatory measures. The Court rejected the German government's argument that the Austrian market for German-language books cannot be considered independently of the German market, by holding that 'such considerations do not allow it to be ruled out that the provisions … have the effect of restricting the ability of Austrian importers to compete, as the latter cannot act freely on their market unlike the Austrian publishers who are their direct competitors'.[86]

To the extent that it also covers non-discriminatory measures that hinder market access, the question is: what is the rationale behind the reformed definition of MEQR?[87] AG Jacobs in *Leclerc-Siplec* based his Opinion on the inadequacy of a

exceptional and this status is confirmed by the Court's own attempt to remedy the shift from the principle of non-discrimination in *Keck and Mithouard*; see *Torfaen Borough Council v B & Q plc* (n 70); and Case C-169/91 *Council of the City of Stoke-on-Trent and Norwich City Council v B & Q plc* [1992] ECR I-6635; similarly, see Wenneras and Boe Moen (n 75) 388–89.

[83] D Wilsher, 'Does *Keck* Discrimination Make Any Sense? An Assessment of the Non-Discrimination Principle within the European Single Market' (2008) 33 *European Law Review* 5–6.

[84] ibid 10-11. See Case 82/77 *Openbaar Ministerie of the Kingdom of the Netherlands v Jacobus Philippus van Tiggele* [1978] ECR 25 [14].

[85] This is either because the minimum fixed price does not allow the lower cost price of imports to be reflected or because the maximum fixed price only allows imports to be marketed at a loss. See further references to the case law in ch 1, text to n 83.

[86] *LIBRO Handelsgesellschaft mbH* (n 78) [23]–[24]. See also *ANETT v Administración del Estado* (n 56) [41]: 'the tobacco retailers are prevented from procuring supplies in other Member States, even if the manufacturers and wholesalers located there could offer more advantageous procurement conditions, particularly in border areas, either because of their geographic proximity or because of the specific delivery methods they offer'.

[87] These measures have no connection to regulatory equivalence, which is at the heart of the principle of mutual recognition. In this book they are treated as two conceptually different categories of effects, to the extent that mutual recognition refers to regulatory competition, whereas non-discriminatory MEQR refers to market competition. For two opposing views as to whether there is conflict between the two, see Davies (n 65) 107–12; and C Barnard and S Deakin, 'Market Access and Regulatory Competition' in C Barnard and J Scott (eds), *The Law of the Single European Market:*

test solely grounded on discrimination and market equivalence, 'since restrictions on trade should not be tested against local conditions which happen to prevail in each Member State, but against the aim of access to the entire [EU]'.[88] It could be argued that the newly formulated market access test embraces such a view, to the extent that it applies to measures that have a direct impact upon the consumer only.[89] In that regard, an examination of how the new test has been applied in the cases concerning rules on use, even though the test seems unqualified, identifies three elements. First, in all these judgments, the Court has emphasised the position of consumers, either final or intermediate, in relation to market access. The point is that if the use of a product is prohibited or restricted, there will be no purchasers and no product market.[90]

Second, as most clearly reflected in *Mickelsson and Roos*, the Court has seemed to adopt an intensity requirement for a measure to fall foul of the market access test. The Court, citing *Commission v Italy*, stated that 'the restriction which they impose on the use of a product in the territory of a Member State may, *depending on its scope*, have a *considerable* influence on the behaviour of consumers'[91] and, in addition, that:

> [W]here national regulations have the effect of preventing users of personal watercraft from using them for the specific and inherent purposes for which they were intended or of *greatly restricting* their use, which is for the national court to ascertain, such regulations have the effect of hindering the access to the domestic market in question for those goods.[92]

Third, the most important element common to the three judgments applying the new market access test on rules on use is the shift to potential rather than actual *inter*-state trade and, consequently, to the effect thereupon. In neither case did the

Unpacking the Premises (Hart Publishing, 2002) 197. See ch 4, text to nn 21–24 for a revised view of mutual recognition, which functionally associates mutual recognition with the justification stage under the free movement provisions.

[88] Case C-412/93 *Leclerc-Siplec v TF1 and M6* [1995] ECR I-179, Opinion of AG Jacobs [40]. See also ibid [39]: 'if an obstacle to inter-State trade exists, it cannot cease to exist simply because an identical obstacle affects domestic trade'.

[89] In that sense, rules on the use of goods are different from selling arrangements such as advertising or rules regulating when and where goods are sold. Selling arrangements do not only directly affect consumers' choices; their predominant impacts are directly on the importer or retailer.

[90] *Commission v Portuguese Republic* (n 53) [33]; *Commission v Italian Republic* (n 53) [56]–[57]; *Åklagaren v Percy Mickelsson and Joakim Roos* (n 53) [26]–[27].

[91] *Åklagaren v Percy Mickelsson and Joakim Roos* (n 53) [26].

[92] ibid [28], emphasis added. However, *cf* Case C-443/10 *Philippe Bonnarde v Agence de Services et de Paiement* [2012] 1 CMLR 37 [30], citing *Commission v Italy* but not adopting an intensity requirement. It should be noted, though, that the national legislation required the registration document for all demonstration motor vehicles, irrespective of their origin, to state that it was a 'demonstration vehicle' in order for those vehicles to be granted the ecological subsidy. Therefore, it was not a rule on the use of products directly affecting the consumer, but, rather, a discriminatory rule imposing a 'dual burden' upon the importer or retailer. See, the scepticism expressed by S Weatherill, 'The Road to Ruin: "Restrictions on Use" and the Circular Lifecycle of Article 34 TFEU' (2012) Oxford University Legal Research Paper Series, Paper No 58/2012 [7].

Court examine whether there was indeed an existing demand for the product in question.[93] It was sufficient that the importer would be dissuaded from entering that market.

It is not clear whether by adopting an intensity requirement, the Court intended to subject the market access test to a de minimis rule as to the proportion of import volumes that are affected[94] or to a remoteness rule based on excluding restrictive effects on trade that are 'too uncertain and indirect'.[95] It would be more consistent, however, with the Court's intention to reformulate the *Dassonville* formula to consider that it is not a remoteness test, given that such a test is the 'flip side' of the *Dassonville* formula.[96] A more plausible interpretation of this requirement is to find that rules which are equally applicable constitute MEQR, when their effect upon market size is so striking, to the extent that the market ceases to exist or to be profitable as a whole.[97] In that sense, the rationale behind the finding of a trade barrier is not that trade barriers impede market access, but rather that they impede the enlargement of the market as such.[98] The 'size' of the market is used as shorthand for the potential static and dynamic efficiency gains of an enlarged (integrated) market.[99] This reorientation is also in line with the more general policy discussion about taking measures to boost growth and reinforce the

[93] For such an approach, see *Åklagaren v Percy Mickelsson and Joakim Roos* (n 53), Opinion of AG Kokott [60]–[64], but in the context of further assessment if the domestic products are less affected than the imported ones.

[94] See particularly *Leclerc-Siplec v TF1 and M6* (n 88), Opinion of AG Jacobs [38]–[49], who suggests a test for non-discriminatory measures based on whether they substantially restrict market access. For academic support, see S Weatherill, 'After *Keck*: Some Thoughts on How to Clarify the Clarification' (1996) 33 *Common Market Law Review* 897; and C Barnard, 'Fitting the Remaining Pieces into the Goods and Services Jigsaw' (2001) 26 *European Law Review* 44–52.

[95] Case C-379/92 *Criminal proceedings against Matteo Peralta* [1994] ECR I-3453 [24]; Joined Cases C-140/94, C-141/94 and C-142/94 *DIP SpA v Comune di Bassano del Grappa, LIDL Italia Srl v Comune di Chioggia and Lingral Srl v Comune di Chiogga* [1995] ECR I-3257 [29].

[96] Support for a de minimis interpretation is provided by J Snell, 'The Notion of Market Access: A Concept or a Slogan?' (2010) 47 *Common Market Law Review* 457–58, on the basis that the hindrance need not be direct, but can be felt through reduction in demand. See also P Lindh, 'The Influence of Competition Law on Free Movement Rules' in H Kanninen, N Korjus and A Rosas (eds), *EU Competition Law in Context: Essays in Honour of Virpi Tiili* (Hart Publishing, 2009) 23–25; and G Straetmans, 'Market Access, The Outer Limits of the Free Movement of Goods and … The Law?' in Bulterman et al (n 58) 101–05.

[97] See Davies (n 71) 683–84, 696–97; however, Davies places this exceptional category of measures in the context of 'selectivity' and argues that overall non-discriminatory measures which, as a matter of economic fact, impede market access are 'more mythical than real'. Similarly, Wenneras and Boe Moen (n 75) 396–98 point out that 'the qualified nature of the market hindrance test suggests, therefore, that it will have limited complementary value next to the prohibition on discriminatory restrictions of market access'. See also I Lianos, 'Shifting the Narratives in the European Internal Market: Efficient Restrictions of Trade and the Nature of "Economic" Integration' [2010] *European Business Law Review* 734–36, who uses the criterion of 'protectionist manipulation of the behaviour of the consumers' for situations in which there is no similar or competing domestic production. He thereby also incorporates the (consumer) demand-oriented test into discrimination analysis.

[98] See in favour of such an interpretation at a normative level Spaventa (n 75) 924–25, and against it, see Horsley (n 75) 2012–19.

[99] See the extensive discussion in ch 1, section III.B.i.

citizens' confidence in the Internal Market. At a policy level, the Commission in its 'Single Market Act' has very recently confirmed the aim to boost growth in the EU by identifying 12 specific sectors where measures need to be taken, in accordance with the 'Europe 2020' strategy.[100] This initiative followed a report by M Monti, which outlined a strategy for making the relaunching of the Single Market politically successful and economically and socially viable. The underlying assumption of the report in relation to 'building a *stronger* Internal Market' appears to be that 'achieving a deep and efficient single market is a key factor in determining the EU's overall macroeconomic performance'.[101]

Finally, the reorientation of the application of the free movement provisions towards efficiency displays similarities to, and further develops, the analysis of AG Van Gerven in *Torfaen*. AG Van Gerven suggested that a non-discriminatory rule should fall under Article 34 TFEU automatically if it rules out a national market and should be supported by quantitative factors if it merely increases the difficulty in penetrating the national market. To that end, he employed an argument based on the effect of vertical agreements caught by Article 101 TFEU to compartmentalise the market.[102] This Opinion could be read with the hindsight provided by the now well-established reorientation of the law on vertical restraints towards an economics-based approach,[103] while acknowledging that the case law in the field of free movement of goods is not settled. In particular, it could be argued that discrimination, either direct or indirect, now appears not to be a necessary element for finding a trade barrier, but is, rather, merely the most blatant manifestation of a restriction to market access. By contrast, measures that directly affect the consumer, such as rules on the use of goods, may be outlawed as MEQR if the impact they have upon an enlarged market can be supported by quantitative factors.

IV. ESTABLISHING MARKET SEPARATION AS AN ABUSE OF THE DOMINANT POSITION

The survey of the case law in this section assesses the actual integrationist thrust of the cases identified in chapter two, section II as involving market separation under Article 102 TFEU. These are cases of either geographic price

[100] Commission (EU), 'Europe 2020: A strategy for smart, sustainable and inclusive growth' (Communication) COM(2010) 2020 final; Commission (EU), 'Single Market Act: Twelve levers to boost growth and strengthen confidence: "Working together to create new growth"' (Communication) COM(2011) 206 final.

[101] M Monti, 'A New Strategy for the Single Market: At the Service of Europe's Economy and Society' (Report to the President of the European Commission JM Barroso) 9 May 2010, available at http://ec.europa.eu/commission_2010-2014/president/news/press-releases/pdf/20100510_1_en.pdf [7].

[102] *Torfaen Borough Council v B & Q plc* (n 70), Opinion of AG Van Gerven [21]–[24].

[103] Ie, Commission Regulation (EC) 2790/1999 on the application of Article 81(3) of the Treaty to categories of vertical agreements and concerted practices [1999] OJ L336/21; and Commission (EC), 'Guidelines on Vertical Restraints' [2000] OJ C291/1.

discrimination or exclusionary abuses hindering competition across national borders.[104] The distinction between horizontal and vertical market power of the undertakings involved is not relevant in the context of Article 102 TFEU, as opposed to the approach under Article 101 TFEU in which horizontal agreements involving market partitioning by territory are in general considered to be a hard-core restriction of competition.[105] The reason is that the conduct under examination is a 'qualified' unilateral conduct, as explained in section II.B above. Therefore, market separation under Article 102 TFEU has always in practice arisen either out of conduct by vertically integrated undertakings or out of vertical agreements, usually in the context of an independent distribution system.

In particular, as was shown in section III above, two tests can be said to underlie the notion of trade barriers: a discrimination test and a market access test. Similarly, under Article 102 TFEU, market separation as an abuse of dominance can be established by two tests: an intent-based test and an effects-based test. Analogies between the two sets of tests are provided, namely it is suggested that tests based on discrimination and market access in free movement law run in parallel to those governed by intent and effects in competition law. Interestingly, the benchmarks for assessing the legality of the conduct are the same only in the second set of comparators (market access and effects-based market separation). In the first set of comparators (discrimination and intent), the individual tests compared differ in terms of substance. However, they perform the same function. They manifest the illegal conduct in such a way that there is no need for the second-phase tests to apply. They are sufficient but not necessary elements for establishing a trade barrier and an abuse of the dominant position. In other words, whereas discrimination and market access are sliding scales of one and the same effect under the provision of the free movement of goods, there is a qualitative difference between intent-based and effects-based abusive market separation.

A. The Role of Intent: An Analogy with Discriminatory Trade Barriers?

The notion of abuse is an objective concept, as commonly cited by reference to the definition of abuse in *Hoffmann-La Roche*.[106] However, the Court's ruling in regard to abuse as an objective concept is made for the purpose of rejecting the parties' argument that there needs to be a causal relationship between dominance and abuse.[107] Therefore, this has less to do with the relationship between the subjective

[104] See ch 2, sections II.A and II.B.

[105] See Commission (EC), 'Guidelines on the application of Article 81 (3) of the Treaty' [2004] OJ C101/97 [23] on the different treatment of horizontal and vertical restraints including market partitioning under Article 101 TFEU.

[106] See n 3.

[107] See ch 2, text to nn 99–102.

intent of the dominant undertaking and its conduct. The orthodox position in relation to the subjective intent of the dominant undertaking is that fault is neither a sufficient nor a necessary element for establishing an abuse of dominance. In this section, only the first limb of the orthodox position is critically examined. The second limb—that fault is not a necessary element—is not disputed.[108]

The establishment of the subjective intent of the dominant undertaking to separate the internal market along national lines only when proved is sufficient to substantiate market separation as an abuse of dominance. It can reliably be presumed that the negative effects on competition are likely to occur by proving the existence of the undertaking's conduct and its intent, which is externalised as an attempt.[109] The reason is that market analysis has already been carried out for the purpose of defining the relevant market and establishing dominance.[110] Equally, this is the reason why the General Court has held that 'where an undertaking in a dominant position actually implements a practice whose object is to oust a competitor, the fact that the result hoped for is not achieved is not sufficient to prevent that being an abuse of a dominant position'.[111] In that sense, intent in market separation cases under Article 102 TFEU can only be proved, not presumed, and the conduct is not then capable of being objectively justified. In other words, under Article 102 TFEU, intent can point to the likely anti-competitive effects of the undertaking's conduct. However, the reverse proposition is not valid: intent cannot be presumed by the undertaking's conduct alone.

The situation under Article 102 TFEU is thus different compared with a restriction of competition 'by object' under Article 101 TFEU, which can be established by reference to the necessary consequences of the agreement according to the case law: ie, it can be deduced rather than only proved.[112] Then, if a plausible

[108] *BPB Industries plc and British Gypsum Ltd v Commission* (n 24) [70]; Case T-301/04 *Clearstream Banking AG and Clearstream International SA v Commission* [2009] ECR II-3155 [141]–[143]; Case T-321/05 *AstraZeneca AB and AstraZeneca plc v Commission* [2010] ECR II-02805 [359], [493], in relation to the first abuse (misleading representations made to public authorities for the purpose of improperly obtaining exclusive rights); the General Court ruled that proof of the deliberate nature of the conduct is not necessary for finding an abuse. In other words, the absence of evidence of intent is not conclusive of the absence of effects. Similarly, see *Post Danmark A/S* (n 9) [28]–[29], in which anti-competitive effect was not established; however, the Court of Justice clearly examined it as a second-phase test, distinct from the intent-based test and only after the latter was failed.

[109] This is why the General Court has stated that 'showing an anti-competitive object and an anti-competitive effect may, in some cases, be one and the same thing. If it is shown that the object pursued by the conduct of an undertaking in a dominant position is to restrict competition, that conduct will also be liable to have such an effect'; see *France Télécom SA v Commission* (n 8) [195]; Case T-203/01 *Michelin v Commission* [2003] ECR II 4071 [241].

[110] This applies to the extent that any kind of market share-based presumption of dominance is open to rebuttal.

[111] *France Télécom SA v Commission* (n 8) [196]; *Irish Sugar v Commission* (n 23) [191].

[112] For the rationale behind this, see Case C-209/07 *Competition Authority v Beef Industry Development Society Ltd and Barry Brothers (Carrigmore) Meats Ltd* [2008] ECR I-8637, Opinion of AG Trstenjak [45]: 'when acting rationally undertakings will expect the agreement to have the effects which can reasonably be assumed according to the circumstances, with the result that they intended those effects at least to some extent'.

explanation exists as to why the necessary consequence is not the intended one, the legal presumption under Article 101(1) TFEU is rebutted and the burden of proof is shifted to showing either lack of anti-competitive effects under Article 101(1) TFEU or a pro-competitive effect under Article 101(3) TFEU.[113] This is why, at a normative level, the case law under Article 101 TFEU, according to which agreements aimed at preventing or restricting parallel exports are considered to be agreements whose object is to restrict competition, should not in principle be followed and cited in Article 102 TFEU cases when market separation issues arise.[114]

In particular, under Article 102 TFEU, intent cannot be presumed from the undertaking's conduct alone. The reason for this is that presumptions of intent are deduced based on prior experience, namely that a conduct in fact brings about the restriction of competition effects.[115] However, in Article 102 TFEU cases, there is no such prior experience: first, because there are very few Article 102 TFEU cases; and, second, because there has been no notification system operating in practice under Article 102 TFEU. The experience gained from the notification procedure under Article 101 TFEU has essentially led to the adoption of specific market power thresholds for Block Exemption Regulation to apply under that provision. The lack of equivalent experience under Article 102 TFEU explains why intent, under that Article, should not be deduced from conduct.[116] It is only in relation to intent-based, as opposed to presumption-based, 'by object' restrictions under Article 101 TFEU that one is able to draw an analogy with the intent to

[113] See, in particular, O Odudu, 'Interpreting Article 81(1): Object as Subjective Intention' (2001) 26 *European Law Review* 60; and O Odudu, 'Interpreting Article 81(1): The Object Requirement Revisited' (2001) 26 *European Law Review* 381–83, who points to the fact that making a reliable prediction of effects requires an assessment of market power, which removes the key advantage of the object category under Article 101 TFEU. See, more recently, O Odudu, 'Restrictions of Competition by Object: What's the Beef?' [2009] *Competition Law Journal* 14–17. This is also confirmed by recent case law on the restrictions 'by object' under Article 101 TFEU, eg, Case C-551/03 P *General Motors BV v Commission* [2006] ECR I-3173 [64], [66]; Joined Cases C-501/06 P, C-513/06 P, C-515/06 P and C-519/06 P *GlaxoSmithKline Services Unlimited v Commission* [2009] ECR I-9291 [55], [58]; most clearly articulated in *Beef Industry Development Society Ltd* (n 112) [17], [19], [21], in which the Court, for the purpose of substantiating the 'object' of the arrangements, rejected the Society's arguments contesting the intent as such of the arrangements, as well as arguments relating to pro-competitive effects that would otherwise be assessed under Article 101(3) TFEU. See, however, the odd case C-32/11 *Allianz Hungária Biztosító Zrt and others v Gazdasági Versenyhivatal*, Judgment of 14 March 2013 (NYR) [36], [46], [48]. The Court of Justice seems to blur the distinction between a restriction under Article 101(1) TFEU by object and a restriction by effect, by essentially requiring full market analysis for assessing a restriction by object, which is similar to the one conducted for assessing a restriction by effect.

[114] See, for example, the case law under Article 101 TFEU cited in *Sotirios Lélos kai Sia EE and others* (n 27) [65], which is then cited in *GlaxoSmithKline Services Unlimited v Commission* (n 113) [61].

[115] See D Bailey, 'Presumptions in EU Competition Law' (2010) 31(9) *European Competition Law Review* 362, 367–68, who states that the reason for presumptions is, inter alia, a common sense approach derived from experience to the assessment of the effect of evidence in certain circumstances.

[116] In addition, this would mean that dominance itself is prohibited under Article 102 TFEU, since behavioural criteria are taken into consideration as strategic entry barriers when assessing dominance. See ch 2, text to nn 117–18.

separate markets under Article 102 TFEU. However, this category of criterion for establishing 'object' does not seem to be used by the Court of Justice.[117]

This is not contradicted by the General Court judgment in *AstraZeneca*.[118] Documentary evidence was found to show AstraZeneca's intent to exclude parallel imports by deregistering the Losec capsule marketing authorisation. However, at the same time, the General Court held that the conduct in question was not objectively capable of restricting competition.[119] The reason was that the exclusion of parallel imports was dependent upon additional conduct, namely the withdrawal of the parallel imports licences by the public authorities. Therefore, there was a mismatch between the conduct of the undertaking and the presumed effect in the first place, rather than between the intent and the undertaking's conduct.

Based on the above, the distinction drawn by AG Jacobs in *Syfait* between primary intent to limit parallel trade and the inevitable consequence of a legitimate intention makes little sense.[120] The dominant undertaking either possesses or does not possess the subjective intent of restricting competition by separating markets along national lines. In this case, it was not shown that Glaxo did have the subjective intent to restrict competition.

The method by which the subjective intent is to be proved is a conceptually distinct question. Indeed, this could be difficult, and such difficulty precisely explains why intent is rarely invoked in practice, as well as why commentators have been generally critical with regard to its use.[121] However, this does not preclude in principle the conceptualisation of instances in which evidence of direct intent to separate the markets along national lines may be furnished, and then objective or

[117] The first case that seems to point to 'intent' as a stand-alone criterion for establishing 'object' under Article 101 TFEU is *Beef Industry Development Society Ltd* (n 112) [19], in which the Court distinguished between two categories of arguments. First, there is an argument that the arrangements are not anti-competitive in purpose and, second, an argument is presented that they do not entail injurious consequences for competition. See also *Beef Industry Development Society Ltd*, Opinion of AG Trstenjak [44]–[46]; and *General Motors BV v Commission* (n 113), Opinion of AG Tizzano [77]–[79].

[118] *AstraZeneca AB and AstraZeneca plc v Commission* (n 108).

[119] ibid [849].

[120] *Syfait* (n 2), Opinion of AG Jacobs [71]. For the opposite view, see L Gormsen, *A Principled Approach to Abuse of Dominance in European Competition Law* (Cambridge University Press, 2010) 137–42, who argues that reliance on intent is acceptable only if pursuing an objective of economic freedom, but not if the focus is consumer welfare.

[121] Precisely because in most cases intent is presumed (rather than proved) from the undertaking's conduct, it cannot then support a presumption of effects. For criticism in regard to the use of induction-based intent in a way that effects are being ignored, see A Bavasso, 'The Role of Intent under Article 82 EC: From "Flushing the Turkeys" to "Spotting Lionesses in Regent's Park"' (2005) 26 *European Competition Law Review* 621–23; R Moisejevas, 'The Importance of Intent in Predatory Pricing Cases' (2010) 4 (122) *Jurisprudencija* 326–28. O'Donoghue and Padilla (n 13) 250–51 provide more focused criticism on the use of direct intent evidence. So too do R Cass and K Hylton, 'Antitrust Intent' (2010) Boston University School of Law, Working Paper Series Public Law and Legal Theory WP No 00-02 [22]–[23], even though they are in favour of a specific intent (objective) test, on the basis of a theory of minimising the costs of legal errors.

efficiency justifications should not be available to the dominant undertaking.[122] This seems to be supported by the General Court judgment in *France Télécom*, where cost-saving justifications based on economies of scale and learning effects were rejected,[123] arguably because, in that case, direct intent evidence was furnished.[124]

Intent has not been thoroughly analysed by the EU courts in market separation cases. The only explicit reference was made by AG Jacobs in his Opinion in *Syfait*. In principle, the Court of Justice seems to accept in *United Brands* the proposition made above, namely that 'such behaviour cannot be countenanced if its actual purpose is to strengthen this dominant position and abuse it' (regarding a refusal to supply by the dominant undertaking in order to protect its own commercial interests).[125] However, such actual purpose was not proved in that case. The only reference to direct intent evidence in the judgment is the wording of the 'green bananas' clause. According to the Court, this clause 'implies that UBC, far from rejecting the idea of imposing sanctions on duly appointed distributors which do not comply with its directions, held out this possibility as a threat'.[126] However, there was no direct evidence of intent that the dominant undertaking segregated the market along national lines from the outset through contractual clauses prohibiting exports, which would permit it to charge artificially different prices in each Member State. On the contrary, it could have equally, first, constructed a pricing scheme with differentiated prices among the Member States according to the local market conditions and, then, imposed the 'green bananas' clause to prevent this pricing scheme from being bypassed.

[122] See also Loewenthal (n 16) 472. In addition, see Nazzini (n 13) 59–65, who suggests that the intent test can be perceived, inter alia, as the test for 'naked abuse'.

[123] *France Télécom SA v Commission* (n 8) [216]–[217]. See also the more ambiguous Case T-24-26 and 28/93 *Compagnie Maritime Belge Transports SA and others v Commission* (1996) ECR II-1201 [147]–[148], in which it is not clear if 'meeting competition defence' when eliminatory intent has been proved was rejected as a matter of principle or on the facts of the case.

[124] In general, in Article 102 TFEU jurisprudence, the Court has had explicit recourse to direct intent evidence only in predation cases in relation to prices above Average Variable Costs but below Average Total Cost, which are considered to be abusive if they are determined as part of a plan for eliminating a competitor. By direct intent evidence, the Court of Justice has accepted documentary evidence of direct threats to a particular competitor made during meetings that the competitor would face retaliation if it did not withdraw from the relevant market: Case C-62/86 *AKZO Chemie BV v Commission* [1991] ECR I-3359 [75]–[82]. The General Court has accepted both the reports of the board of directors referring to the need to make major financial sacrifices in the area of prices and supply terms in order to fight competition as direct intent evidence and a series of factors providing indirect evidence of intent, such as duration and scale of sales at a loss or importation for the purpose of reselling at a loss or lower prices in one Member State as opposed to all other Member States, as in *Tetra Pak International SA v Commission* (n 26) [151]. Finally, the Commission has relied on a number of internal documents originating with management-level staff within the undertaking and expressed in the context of formal presentations for the purpose of taking a decision, which attest to the existence of a strategy of 'pre-emption' for the relevant market, as in *France Télécom SA v Commission* (n 8) [199]–[215], in which the undertaking's claims as to the binding force of those internal documents and their integrity were rejected.

[125] *United Brands Company* (n 25) [189].

[126] ibid [155].

Tetra Pak II is the only market separation case in which direct intent evidence could be considered to have played an important role. The Court seems to have based its finding regarding the existence of an overall strategy of partitioning markets on various documents exchanged between Tetra Pak and its subsidiaries, showing that the commercial policy was determined at the group level.[127]

The analogy between intended market separation by dominant undertakings and discriminatory trade barriers under the free movement provisions is present here. The analogy is drawn to the extent that discrimination, either direct or indirect, is a sufficient but not a necessary element of a trade barrier, as explained previously. In both cases, the effect of the undertaking's conduct or the state conduct is manifested in such a way that there is no need to show any further actual effect. On the one hand, the effect of the conduct is manifested by proven intent externalised as an attempt to separate markets and after market analysis has been carried out for the purpose of establishing dominance in the case of dominant undertakings. On the other hand, it is manifested by discriminatory action in the case of states.[128] The additional element in both cases substitutes for the need to show actual effect and, in that sense, it seems that the threshold of degree of market distortion required for establishing abuse or a trade barrier is explicitly lowered to potential market distortions.[129] However, intent and discrimination, respectively, are sufficient elements to establish the notion of abuse and a trade barrier, since the Court is also adopting this lowered threshold of proof of potential effects, even in cases of market separation in which intent is not proved, or in cases of hindrance to market access.[130]

B. 'Efficiency' and 'Objective' Justifications: Is Uniformity within the Internal Market an End in itself?

Chapter two showed that market separation cases under Article 102 TFEU cover conduct that has the effect of hindering cross-border trade, regardless of the

[127] *Tetra Pak International SA v Commission* (n 26) [92], [171].

[128] Discrimination in the context of the free movement provisions is effects-based rather than intention- or form-based. However, this does not influence the analogy drawn here, to the extent that discrimination is opposed to market access.

[129] See, eg, *Konkurrensverket v TeliaSonera Sverige AB* (n 9) [64]–[65], in which the Court held that '[it] is sufficient to demonstrate that there is an anti-competitive effect which *may potentially* exclude competitors who are at least as efficient as the dominant undertaking' (emphasis added); and, immediately afterwards, the Court went on to rule that in principle, 'where a dominant undertaking actually implements a pricing practice resulting in a margin squeeze on its equally efficient competitors, with the purpose of driving them from the relevant market, the fact that the desired result, namely the exclusion of those competitors, is not ultimately achieved does not alter its categorisation as abuse within the meaning of Article 102 TFEU'.

[130] For the shift to potential, rather than actual, *inter*-state trade in the context of rules on the use of goods, see text to n 93. The anti-competitive effect of market separation cases under Article 102 TFEU is the subject matter of section IV.B.

form it takes. In cases of allegedly abusive market separation, price uniformity throughout the EU is what is essentially being endangered. This is done either directly, through (retail) price differentiation on a geographic basis, or indirectly, through exclusionary abuses (refusal to supply, rebates or margin squeeze practices) that limit the sources of supply within one Member State, thereby leading to price increases in that Member State. However, it was explained in chapter one that this price uniformity, from an economic point of view, is in conformity with the purpose of increasing the allocative efficiency of the economies of the Member States, such that the markets concerned are characterised by equivalent supply–demand situations and other market conditions which are beyond the control of the dominant undertakings. In that case, prevention of market separation prevents the redistribution of consumer benefits from high-price countries to consumers in low-price countries, and the redistribution from consumers in high-price countries that are net importers to producers in countries that are net exporters.[131]

However, if direct or indirect price differentiation is instead a response to different market conditions across the EU for which the dominant undertaking is not responsible, condemning such practices actually means that the dominant undertaking will either withdraw its products from the low-price Member State or will charge a uniform higher price, thereby making consumers in some countries at least worse off. Therefore, in those cases, there is no conflict between 'market integration' and 'competition'. Rather, first, the trade-off between the various classes of consumers within the EU whose interests may clash is internal to the policy decision as to what is the desirable form of the Internal Market. Section III showed that embracing the market access test guides this decision, particularly in relation to measures that affect final consumers. Second, given the choice on the first policy question, the varying consumer preferences across the EU and, more generally, the fluctuating market conditions for which the dominant undertaking is not responsible represent the inherent limit of economic integration which should also be respected under competition law enforcement. Otherwise, the use of Article 102 TFEU to foster market integration does not make economic sense and is somewhat self-defeating.

This is partly confirmed by the Court's case law on market separation under Article 102 TFEU, which indicates that fluctuating market factors beyond the control of the dominant undertaking can in principle serve as objective justifications for conduct that would otherwise constitute an abuse.

In *United Brands*, the dominant undertaking argued that it charged different prices based on the competitive context in which distributors in the various countries were operating so as to reflect the anticipated yellow (ie, banana) market price in the following week for each national market. Therefore, according to the applicant, price differences were in fact 'due to fluctuating market factors

[131] See ch 1, text to n 77.

such as the *weather, different availability of seasonal competing fruit, holidays, strikes, government measures, currency denominations*'.[132] The Court in principle accepted that 'differences in *transport costs, taxation, customs duties, the wages of the labour force, the conditions of marketing, the differences in the parity of currencies, the density of competition* may eventually culminate in different retail selling price levels according to the Member States'.[133] However, it held that UBC (the wholesaler) could rely upon those factors only to a limited extent, since it was the distributors alone who bore the risk of the consumers' markets.[134] There are two main economic interpretations of the Court's ruling. Bishop has accepted that the dominant undertaking can rely upon those factors as long as they impact upon its actual, individual costs.[135] A second interpretation provided by Siragusa is that the Court accepted those costs as a justification to the extent that they refer to general or average cost differences among the Member States (by comparison with the traditional economic indicators such as national income per capita), even if the undertaking's own costs are the same in the different countries.[136] However, in either case, ignoring what each geographic part of the market can bear does not make economic sense, even from a market integration perspective. Bananas are a final product rather than an input, and the natural circumstances that influence consumer behaviour across the EU are not identical.[137]

In *Tetra Pak II*, the Court examined the existence of local markets characterised by objectively different conditions of competition at two stages: first, in the context of defining the geographic market as comprising the whole of the EU; and, second, as a justification for the price differences between Italy and all other Member States. Regarding geographic market definition, the Court relied particularly upon the very low *cost of transport* that made cartons and machines easily and rapidly tradable across Europe and dismissed differences in *consumption patterns* by stating that 'the alleged differences in *consumer tastes* concerning the type of milk or the form of packaging affected only the overall size of the markets in the relevant products in each Member State and had no effect on the conditions of competition within those markets between the manufacturers of those specific products, who were subject *vis-a-vis* one to another to conditions of competition which were the same for all such manufacturers throughout the Community'.[138]

132 *United Brands Company* (n 25) [220], emphasis added.

133 ibid [228], emphasis added.

134 ibid.

135 W Bishop, 'Price Discrimination under Article 86: Political Economy in the European Court' (1981) 44 *Modern Law Review* 292.

136 M Siragusa, 'The Application of Article 86 to the Pricing Policy of Dominant Companies: Discriminatory and Unfair Prices' (1979) 16 *Common Market Law Review* 185.

137 As Bishop (n 135) 290 notes, 'the fact that one firm must pay more for some input in Germany than its competitor in England is no more a violation of the Single Market principle than is the existence of greater sunshine in Sicily a violation because it makes growing oranges cheaper there than in Denmark'. See also L Zanon di Valgiurata, 'Primary Discrimination under Article 86 of the EEC Treaty: The *United Brands* Case' (1982) 31 *International and Comparative Law Quarterly* 45–47, 52–55.

138 *Tetra Pak v Commission* (n 26) [94]–[95], emphasis added.

In relation to the justifications for the different prices between the Member States, the Court seems to reject in principle the existence of local markets as a justification by making a cross-reference to the geographic market definition, to the extent that the various Member States have already been found to belong to the same geographic market.[139] This may seem at first sight to contradict the Court judgment in *United Brands*, in which the geographic market also comprised more than one Member State; nevertheless, fluctuating market conditions were in principle accepted as justifications. However, as mentioned above, in *Tetra Pak II*, the Court partly relied upon direct intent evidence that there was an overall strategy of partitioning the markets.[140] Therefore, the case is not a precedent for accepting that, once fluctuating market conditions have been taken into account in the context of geographic market definition, they are 'exhausted' and cannot justify a varying pricing policy across the Member States. On the contrary, consumer tastes may differ within the Internal Market, just as they do within a single state.[141]

In the remaining market separation cases, the geographic market comprised a single Member State. In *British Leyland*, no justifications based on market conditions beyond the control of the dominant undertaking or on efficiencies were advanced. On the contrary, the parallel trade came as a result of the dominant undertaking's own pricing policy, charging in the first place different prices in the UK for right-hand-drive vehicles from prices in the continental EU Member States for left-hand-drive vehicles. British Leyland claimed no objective or efficiency justification for such price discrimination. This resulted in the subsequent conduct of the undertaking in the ancillary market of issuing certificates of conformity for vehicles in the UK[142] being the means for preserving the undertaking's discriminatory pricing policy in the market for sales of vehicles.[143] Therefore, it is legitimate to assume that British Leyland was facing competition in the

139 ibid [164]–[165], [170]–[171].

140 See text to n 127.

141 Similarly, in Case T-229/94 *Deutsche Bahn AG v Commission* [1997] ECR II-1689 [65]–[93], the General Court ruled that the definition of the geographic market for the purposes of applying Article 102 TFEU does not require the objective conditions of competition between traders to be perfectly homogeneous. However, it agreed to examine in principle the appellant's allegations that the varying costs for providing railway services, as well as the variations in intensity of competition from other transportation means in the western and northern journeys, could justify different tariffs for the provision of railway services. Therefore, geographic market definition does not 'pre-empt' the finding that two services are 'equivalent' for the purposes of establishing price discrimination as an abuse of dominance under Article 102(c) TFEU.

142 The conduct was the non-renewal of the conformity certificate for reimported left-hand-drive vehicles, as well as the charging of higher fees for the grant of conformity certificates for such vehicles.

143 On the contrary, in the more recent judgment in *AstraZeneca*, the General Court examined whether AstraZeneca's deregistration of product marketing authorisations in regard to Losec capsules from certain Member States constituted an abuse insofar as it restricted parallel trade of that product. The General Court held that a causal link between the two could be upheld only to the extent that the national authorities were liable to withdraw, or usually did withdraw, parallel import licences following the deregistration, at the request of their holder, of the marketing authorisations for the relevant product, which, in itself, was potentially in violation of Articles 34 and 36 TFEU: *AstraZeneca AB and AstraZeneca plc v Commission* (n 108) [838]–[863].

continental EU Member States, so could not have raised prices there. Consequently, the parallel trade in reimported left-hand-drive vehicles in the UK was operating to the benefit of price competition and of the consumers there, leading to price uniformity in the EU. In addition, the means used by British Leyland to attain its objective, namely the misuse of its regulatory control powers, could not, in itself, be justified by reference to administrative cost savings.[144]

This is contrasted with refusals to supply, which can be justified, as a means of restricting parallel imports, by reference to '*the commercial interests of the dominant undertaking*', to the extent that '*the order is out of the ordinary in terms of quantity based on the prior business relations between the dominant undertaking and the wholesaler and on domestic consumption*'.[145] This interpretation was given by the Court in *Sotirios Lélos* and represents a remarkable shift in the Court's approach to parallel trade. In earlier cases on refusal to supply as a means of restricting parallel trade, the Commission had rejected the dominant undertaking's arguments that the quantity ordered was far too great for the national market concerned.[146] On the contrary, in *Sotirios Lélos*, the Court essentially upheld the aggregate amount supplied to satisfy domestic demand as an upper limit to the obligation of the dominant undertaking to supply wholesalers.[147]

[144] Case 226/84 *British Leyland plc v Commission* [1986] ECR 3263 [28].

[145] *Sotirios Lélos kai Sia EE and others* (n 27) [70]–[73], emphasis added. For an analysis of the case, see also ch 4, section 3.4 and ch 5, text to nn 152–53.

[146] In *Polaroid/SSI Europe*, Polaroid Netherlands refused to provide a quotation to SSI Europe for a larger than previous order, on the grounds that the quantities were far too great for the Netherlands and even the European market. The Commission initiated an investigation, Polaroid agreed to provide the quotation and the case was closed; see Commission (EEC), 'Thirteenth Report on Competition Policy' (published in conjunction with 'Seventeenth General Report on the Activities of the Communities 1983') 1984 [155]–[157]. Similarly, in *Eurofix-Bauco v Hilti* (Cases IV/30.787 and 31.488) Commission Decision 88/138/EEC [1988] OJ L65/19 [35]–[37], [76], Hilti induced its independent distributors in the Netherlands not to fulfil export orders for cartridges for Hilti nail guns to two UK companies, which would have enabled those two companies to supply their own nails together with cartridges for Hilti nail guns. This was found to be abusive and it was not challenged on appeal; see Case T-30/89 *Hilti AG v Commission* [1991] ECR II-1439 [27], [40].

[147] In favour of this interpretation of the criterion for 'ordinary', see O'Donoghue and Macnab (n 6) 159. T Nguyen, T Minssen and X Groussot, 'The Rule of Reason under Article 82 EC after Sot Lélos kai Sia' (2009) Working Paper [16] (available at www.researchgate.net/publication/228250379_The_Rule_of_Reason_under_Article_82_EC_after_Sot_Lelos_Kai_Sia) and S Kingston, 'Joined Cases C-468/06 to C-478/06 *Sotirios Lélos kai Sia EE and Others v GlaxoSmithKline AEVE Farmakeftikon Proïonton, formerly Glaxowellcome AEVE* (Case Comment)' (2009) 46 *Common Market Law Review* 698 point to the uncertainty that persists, given that it is for the national courts to apply those criteria on an ad hoc basis. The Greek administrative Court of Appeal applied those criteria and annulled the Greek Competition Authority's decision finding that Glaxo had not violated Article 102 TFEU. However, Glaxo's refusal to supply was unqualified, in the sense that it did not provide wholesalers with the products involved at all; see Athens Administrative Court of Appeal, Judgment No 1983/2010 [17] (text in Greek). The Athens First Instance Court in a string of judgments, which culminated in *Sotirios Lélos*, successfully delved into the details in ascertaining the domestic demand. The domestic demand was estimated based on the total pharmacy sales of the preceding month, with an additional 10 per cent to cover a potential increase in demand, and to create stock as well as fully cover hospitals' needs. See, eg, Athens First Instance Court, Judgments No 6440/2003, 4094/2003, 4084/2003, 4016/2003 and 4014/2003 (text in Greek). These cases are remarkable inasmuch as they preceded *Sotirios Lélos*, yet

Similarly, in the relatively more recent *Swedish Interconnectors*, the Commission's analysis of the proposed commitments reveals a concern about treating the local trade (from north to south Sweden) and the international trade (from north Sweden to Denmark) of electricity in a non-discriminatory manner, on the basis of the equivalence of the day-ahead prices as well as of regulating resources for counter-trade. Besides the main proposed commitment, namely that of splitting the transmission system into separate bidding (price) zones, on both sides of the bottleneck, to give price signals to increase production and decrease consumption in the higher priced side of the bottleneck, SvK also proposed an increased use of counter-trade to limit curtailments as an interim measure.[148] In that regard, the Commission accepted modified commitments by SvK, namely taking into account not only Swedish but also non-Swedish regulatory resources for counter-trade.[149]

In the discriminatory rebates cases based on the geographic location of the customer or of the customer's buyers, the geographic market concerned comprised a single Member State. In *Irish Sugar*, both the system of 'export rebates' and its allegedly abusive effect were present in the market for industrial sugar in Ireland. Similarly, in *British Gypsum*, the geographic market concerned was that of Ireland alone in relation to the rebates granted and the UK alone in relation to the policy of priority deliveries. However, in those cases (as opposed to geographic price discrimination cases), the condemned market separation effect was equated with preventing the dominant undertaking's competitors established in another Member State from entering the national market concerned. Therefore, it is more a potential exclusionary effect, to the extent that the competitors established outside Ireland and the UK could not enter the national markets without entering into contracts with the tied customers (ie, with the exporting customers of Irish Sugar and with the merchants which intended to import plasterboard from Spain or agreed to obtain their supplies exclusively from British Gypsum). In this regard, the application of Article 102 TFEU in those cases could, in principle, be in conformity with the market integration objective, since hindering market access to out-of-state competitors means that consumers in the Member State concerned might be denied the lower-cost price of imports. Thus, in *British Gypsum*, the dominant undertaking unsuccessfully argued that the introduction of the rebates was not an initiative to counter competition from imported plasterboard as such,

the analysis is consistent with the Court of Justice's criterion of domestic demand as an upper limit for the dominant pharmaceutical undertaking's obligation to supply parallel traders. The cases are still pending before the Greek civil courts, after the Court of Justice judgment in *Sotirios Lélos*.

[148] Counter-trade is essentially a procedure by which SvK can pay generators (or large consumers) on both sides of the bottleneck to change their planned production (or consumption), which effectively reduces the transmission flow to the bottleneck. The costs of such counter-trade are paid by all network users of the Transmission System Operator, which carries out counter-trading. See *Swedish Interconnectors* (Case 39351), Commission Decision of 14 April 2010 (NYR) [37].

[149] ibid [73]–[74]. See M Sadowska and B Willems, 'Market Integration and Economic Efficiency at Conflict? Commitments at the Swedish Interconnectors Case' (2013) 36 *World Competition* 99 for an economic analysis of the optimal solution to the internal congestion problem.

but a response to a threat from a group of four merchants in Northern Ireland to sell imported plasterboard from Spain at 'appeal' prices.[150] However, the difference between the two cases is that while in *British Gypsum*, conformity with the market integration objective only depended upon the efficiency of those competitors and their ability to match British Gypsum's unit price offered to the tied customers, in *Irish Sugar*, the potential exclusionary effect also involved the validity of the assumption that the tied customers were more likely to engage in *inter*-state trade at the input level, precisely because they exported their own processed products. Thus, Irish Sugar argued that the competitive position of its exporting customers was not commercially comparable to the competitive position of its non-exporting customers. However, the Court rejected the argument by reference to the fact that non-exporting customers also faced competition at the retail level by traders established in other Member States.[151]

With regard to the policy of priority delivery of plaster to customers in the UK which did not handle imported plasterboard in *British Gypsum*, the Court held that, in principle, 'it is open to an undertaking in a dominant position and is also a matter of normal commercial policy, in times of shortage, to lay down criteria for according priority in meeting orders, those criteria must be objective and must not be discriminatory in any way'.[152] However, the 'loyalty' of its customers vis-a-vis its out-of-state competitors in the market for plasterboard was not accepted by the Court as a factor that could justify the priority delivery of plaster to its customers that did not market imported plasterboard. This is in contrast with the case law regarding refusal to supply in times of shortage. In particular, in *BP and others v Commission*, the Court accepted that the distinction between regular and occasional customers during times of petrol shortage could justify a differential treatment in the delivery of supplies to the two categories of customers.[153] A comparison of the two cases seems to suggest that, in *British Gypsum*, there was an additional element, namely that the 'disloyal' customers were marketing imported plasterboard. In that sense, unqualified market integration seems to have been used incorrectly to tip the balance between whether or not a violation has occurred.

Finally, in *Irish Sugar*, the dominant undertaking argued that the discriminatory rebates granted to its retailers established in the border area between Ireland and Northern Ireland were objectively justified by a defence of meeting competition—namely that it was responding, in the context of its market,

[150] *BPB Industries plc and British Gypsum Ltd v Commission* (n 24) [110].

[151] *Irish Sugar plc v Commission* (n 23) [142]–[144].

[152] Case T-65/89 *BPB Industries plc and British Gypsum Ltd v Commission* [1993] ECR II-389 [94].

[153] Case 77/77 *Benzine en Petroleum Handelsmaatschappij BV and others v Commission* [1978] ECR 1513 [22], [32]–[33]. E Buttigieg, *Competition Law: Safeguarding the Consumer Interest: A Comparative Analysis of US Antitrust Law and EC Competition Law* (Kluwer Law International, 2009) 194–96 argues that the same distinction should be accepted in price discrimination cases in times of shortage, but not in all price discrimination cases.

to attacks by competitors, particularly foreigners.[154] The pricing practice was condemned under Article 102(c) TFEU, given that the prices charged by Irish Sugar were not predatory within the meaning of the case law. The Court seems to accept, in theory, that the dominant undertaking can protect its own commercial interests when being threatened, and that such protection, in order to be lawful, must 'be based on criteria of *economic efficiency* and consistent with the *interests of consumers*'.[155] However, in that case, the Court rejected the dominant undertaking's claim on the basis that the price alignment was selective and was enabled precisely because of the price stability in the rest of the Irish market, which allowed Irish Sugar to finance those rebates.[156] Therefore, it seems that selectivity itself was condemned, arguably in light of the fact that the competitors attacking Irish Sugar were established in another Member State.[157]

To sum up, section III revealed that the economic values promoted and protected under the free movement provisions through a 'market access' test guarantee uniformity in the treatment of the interests of the various classes of consumers across the EU, but only as far as such uniformity promotes the efficiency of the economies of the Member States of the EU. The same rationale should underpin the condemnation as abuse of conduct that has the potential effect of hindering cross-border trade. In cases in which the geographic market involves more than one Member State, such conduct usually takes the form of geographic price discrimination. In cases in which the geographic market concerned consists of just one Member State, it takes the form of exclusionary conduct for out-of-state competitors. However, in either case, fluctuating market conditions and factors that are beyond the control of the dominant undertaking should be capable of justifying differential treatment among the various categories of consumers in the different Member States. Otherwise, an attempt to achieve uniformity and integrate the markets does not make economic sense; rather, it goes against the aim of boosting the efficiency of the Member States' economies, because the market conditions across the EU are not comparable. In that sense, there is full substantive alliance between the second-phase tests under both the free movement provisions and Article 102 TFEU, namely the market access test and the effects-based test, respectively.

[154] *Irish Sugar plc v Commission* (n 23) [181], [182], [184].

[155] ibid [189], emphasis added.

[156] ibid [188].

[157] P Andrews, 'Is Meeting Competition a Defence to Predatory Pricing? The Irish Sugar Decision Suggests a New Approach' (1998) 19 *European Competition Law Review* 49 seems to disregard this element and wrongly argues that, after *Irish Sugar*, selectivity itself is indicative of predatory intent, to the extent that previously, in *Hilti*, the Court had condemned selective price cuts as specific attempts to attract the customers of the dominant undertaking's competitors, hence requiring an additional element of eliminatory intent. However, first, Hilti's selective and discriminatory pricing policies were directed against its competitors and their customers only in the UK, and also there was direct intent evidence; see *Eurofix-Bauco v Hilti* (Cases IV/30.787 and 31.488) Commission Decision 88/138/EEC [1988] OJ L65/19 [45]–[47], [80]–[83] and Case T-30/89 *Hilti AG v Commission* [1991] ECR II-1439 [100]; second, as has been argued forcefully above, in Article 102 TFEU cases, conduct-based presumptions about intent do not make any sense and should not be used.

V. THE CONSTITUTIONAL BASIS FOR ALIGNING THE NOTIONS OF TRADE BARRIER AND ABUSE OF THE DOMINANT POSITION

In sections III and IV, it was argued that the rationale of finding a trade barrier and an abuse of the dominant position should be, and to some extent is, aligned according to the case law. Subsequently, this section first highlights the different use of economics under the provisions of the free movement and under Article 102 TFEU for the purpose of promoting efficiency. Second, it is argued that the concordance between the aims of market integration and abuse of the dominant position, as well as the different use of economics, is explained at the constitutional level of the Treaty, even after the relocation of ex-Article 3(1)(g)TEC to Protocol No 27 TFEU when the Lisbon Treaty entered into force.

A. The Different Use of Economics to Establish a Trade Barrier versus an Abuse of the Dominant Position

The rationale behind addressing trade barriers originating in the state sphere under the free movement provisions and behind addressing abuses hindering *inter*-state trade conducted by dominant undertakings should be aligned. However, the economic values promoted under the notion of trade barriers, under either the discrimination test or the market access test, are framed on the basis of the regulatory equivalence of the products involved rather than market equivalence. For example, in *Commission v Italy*, which dealt with a prohibition, pursuant to Article 56 of the Italian Highway Code on using a motorcycle and a trailer together in Italy, the Court distinguished between two types of trailers when assessing the conformity of Article 56 of the Highway Code with Article 34 TFEU: namely, trailers specifically designed for motorcycles and trailers intended to be towed by automobiles or other types of vehicles.[158] Arguably, the distinction is based on the perception of the Italian regulator, as reflected in Article 56 of the Highway Code, that road safety was being endangered by the use of trailers with motorcycles. Therefore, the Court focused on the effect of the prohibition on market access for trailers specifically designed for motorcycles only,[159] even if that product could be considered to be part of the same product market, from a market equivalence perspective, as trailers intended for other vehicles.

In contrast, Article 102 TFEU is applied within a specific product market, defined on the basis of demand and supply substitution as measured by economic

[158] See *Commission v Italian Republic* (n 53) [49]–[51].
[159] ibid [52]–[54].

theory[160] or the perception of the dominant undertaking itself as to the product market in which it operates.[161] In any case, the effects of the dominant undertaking's conduct are measured on products, which are equivalent from the economic actors' perspective. Therefore, one cannot dismiss the high relevance of economics for fact-imperative purposes when applying Article 102 TFEU in individual cases.[162] This is so, even if one does not agree with the use of economics in the sphere of EU competition law for the purposes of providing the standard of legality of the dominant undertaking's conduct.[163]

In addition, there are institutional differences that warrant the use of economics in an alternative manner in the application of either rule. Economics are institutionally embedded in competition law enforcement because of the enhanced economic know-how and the capabilities of the Commission as an enforcer.[164] This has been particularly the case since the Commission's launch of an 'effects-based' approach to competition law. After decentralisation of EU competition law enforcement, it may be the case that procedural rules concerning data access and control in Europe allow a more limited use of economics compared with antitrust litigation in the US.[165] However, compared with preliminary references in the area of free movement rules, private enforcement of Article 102 TFEU still allows for a more extensive use of economics. This is because it is the dominant undertaking which bears the evidential burden of objective or efficiency justifications for its conduct in Article 102 TFEU proceedings. By contrast, in free movement proceedings before the national courts, it falls upon the individual trader to prove the existence of a trade barrier.[166]

160 See particularly Commission (EC), Notice on the Definition of Relevant Markets for the Purposes of Community Competition Law [1997] OJ C372/5 [13]–[27], [33]–[43]. Evidence may be acquired by the Commission by contacting consumers, undertakings in the industry, professional associations or undertakings in upstream markets, in order to identify their views on consumers' behaviour; see, eg, D Hildebrand, 'Using Conjoint Analysis for Market Definition: Application of Modern Market Research Tools to Implement the Hypothetical Monopolist Test' (2006) 29 *World Competition Law and Economics Review* 315.

161 See, eg, *Aberdeen Journals Ltd v OFT* [2003] CAT 11, [2003] CompAR 67 [235]: 'documents emanating from the undertaking concerned showing how that undertaking saw the market, and the commercial strategy it had adopted in that market, may be decisive evidence of what the market is'.

162 The distinction between the normative and the fact-imperative role of economics in the sphere of EU competition law is drawn by D Gerber, 'The Future of Article 82: Dissecting the Conflict' in C-D Ehlermann and M Marquis (eds), *European Competition Law Annual 2007: A Reformed Approach to Article 82 TEC* (Hart Publishing, 2008) 47–48. See also D Zimmer, 'Competition Law *De Lege Ferenda*' in R Zach, A Heinemann and A Kallerhals (eds), *The Development of Competition Law: Global Perspectives* (Edward Elgar, 2010) 324–29.

163 See ch 1, section II.A on the relationship between competition and efficiency.

164 H Friederiszick, 'Economic Analysis in EU Competition Cases' in J Drexl, L Idot and J Moneger (eds), *Economic Theory and Competition Law* (Edward Elgar, 2009) 4 refers to the ratio of economists to lawyers at DG Comp, which was around one to seven in the early 1990s and had increased to one to two by 2007.

165 See G Gerber, 'Competition Law and Institutional Embeddedness of Economics' in J Drexl, L Idot and J Moneger (eds), *Economic Theory and Competition Law* (Edward Elgar, 2009) 20–44.

166 See Davies (n 65) 96–98, who is in favour of this lack of empiricism in the application of free movement provisions. See also G Davies, 'The Court's Jurisprudence on Free Movement of

B. From Article 3(1)(g) TEC to Protocol No 27 TFEU: No Conflict in Substantive Values between Competition and Market Integration

The historical link between Article 102 TFEU and market integration at the level of objectives has been achieved through the teleological interpretation of the concept of abuse by reference to ex-Article 3(1)(g) TEC.[167] The question that arises relates to the relevance of the clause on 'a system ensuring that competition in the Internal Market is not distorted' in the cases of market separation under Article 102 TFEU.

On the one hand, the answer to this question is dictated by the fact that in none of the cases of market separation under Article 102 TFEU analysed above did the European courts feel obliged to have recourse to Article 3(1)(g) TEC for the purposes of substantiating an abuse of the dominant position.[168] This is indicative of the lack of conflict in substantive values between market integration and Article 102 TFEU once Article 102 TFEU is used to address barriers to *inter*-state trade stemming from the conduct of dominant undertakings. By contrast, in chapter five, it is argued that, whenever the Court uses Article 102 TFEU to address market distortions arguably stemming, in part, from the state sphere, it has recourse to Article 3(1)(g) TEC as an additional instrument to overcome potential conflicts in substantive values and justify the enforcement of Article 102 TFEU. For example, this is the case in *Sotirios Lélos* and *Deutsche Telekom*.[169] Therefore, the case law on market separation as an abuse of dominance confirms the view that competition law is one of the cornerstones of the internal market, on which the Court of Justice has pronounced judgment on other occasions in the field of applying the competition provisions against private undertakings, rather than against the state.[170]

On the other hand, after the entry into force of the Lisbon Treaty, the clause on 'a system ensuring that competition in the Internal Market is not distorted' has been relocated from Article 3(1)(g) TEC to Protocol No 27 TFEU. Article 3 TEC set out the activities of the then Community for the purposes of achieving

Goods: Pragmatic Presumptions, Not Philosophical Principles' (2012) 2 *European Journal of Consumer Law* 30–31.

[167] See the extensive analysis provided in ch 1, section III.C.

[168] Reference to the clause provided for in Article 3(1)(g) TEC is made in *United Brands*, but this is for the purposes of establishing the dominant position and the refusal to supply a long-standing customer: *United Brands Company* (n 25) [63], [183].

[169] *Sotirios Lélos kai Sia EE and others* (n 27) [66]; Case C-280/08 P *Deutsche Telekom v Commission* [2010] ECR I-09555 [180], [230], [234]. Similarly, Article 3(1)(g) TEC has been the cornerstone of the principle that Member States should not introduce measures which render EU competition rules ineffective (*effet utile*); see ch 5, section IV.A.

[170] See, eg, Case C-126/97 *Eco Swiss China Time Ltd v Benetton International NV* [1999] ECR I-3055 [36] in order to establish that the competition provisions are considered rules of public policy, the breach of which could, according to national law, justify annulment of an arbitration award. See also *Courage Ltd v Bernard Crehan* (n 40) [20] in order to establish the right of a party to a contract in breach of the competition provisions to claim damages from the other contracting party.

the objectives (or tasks) set out in Article 2 TEC. Article I-3(2) of the Treaty establishing a Constitution for Europe promoted in a positive way the 'Internal Market where competition is free and undistorted' as one of the aims of the EU.[171] However, in the run-up to the 2007 French presidential elections and after the French referendum on the Constitution, Nicolas Sarkozy picked up on this issue and insisted on the suppression of the reference to the aim of 'free and undistorted competition'.[172] As a result, in Article 3(2) TEU-L, the final clause on 'free and undistorted competition' is not included, and Article 3(1)(g) TEC has been deleted. More generally, the 'activities' of the then Community set out in Article 3 TEC have, instead, been transformed into 'competences', including that to 'establish the competition rules necessary for the functioning of the Internal Market' amongst the enumerated exclusive EU competences.[173] As a political compromise and a response to those who feared the downgrading of the status quo of competition in the EU, Protocol No 27 on the Internal Market and Competition was adopted, including, inter alia, the clause on 'a system ensuring that competition in the Internal Market is not distorted'.[174] The question is whether these changes could have an impact upon the identified concordance between the aims of Article 102 TFEU and market integration.

From a legal perspective, according to Article 51 TEU-L, 'the Protocols and Annexes to the Treaties shall form an integral part thereof', and so they have the same normative value as any other Treaty article. The relocation of the clause on 'a system ensuring that competition in the Internal Market is not distorted' from Article 3(1)(g) TEC to the Protocol brings about no formal, legal change in the hierarchy of the competition provisions as fundamental provisions for the functioning of the Internal Market. However, one could argue that its relocation from the head to the tail end of the Treaty has a symbolic meaning. It could be regarded as a sign of the 'emancipation' of competition law and policy from the establishment and functioning of the Internal Market, in the sense of integrating the more economic approach to competition law into the European constitutional

[171] [2004] OJ C310/1.

[172] See European Council Statements made by Nicolas Sarkozy, President of the Republic, during his final joint press conference with Bernard Kouchner, Minister of Foreign and European Affairs (Brussels, 23 June 2007) https://pastel.diplomatie.gouv.fr/editorial/actual/ael2/bulletin.gb.asp?liste=20070626.gb.html.

[173] Article 3(1)(b) TFEU. For the meaningless initial debate between Wolfgang Munchau, commentator at the *Financial Times*, and Michel Petite, the then Director General of the Legal Service of the Commission, on the distinction between 'aims' and 'activities', see A Riley, 'The EU Reform Treaty and the Competition Protocol: Undermining EC Competition Law' [2007] *European Competition Law Review* 703–04.

[174] For a detailed examination of the wording of the Protocol, see R Barents, 'Constitutional Horse Riding: Some Comments on the Protocol on the Internal Market and Competition' in Bulterman et al (n 58) 124; and R Lane, 'EC Competition Law Post-Lisbon: A Matter of Protocol' in Bulterman et al (n 58) 172.

order.[175] Such an interpretation can be supported by the fact that the substantive competition provisions remain unchanged, while they do not inform the definition of the Internal Market, which is only informed by reference to the free movement provisions in Article 26(2) TFEU.

In the market separation cases under Article 102 TFEU considered in this chapter, such separation of the competition provisions from the Internal Market has no practical significance, to the extent that there is no conflict in substantive values between the two. According to the analysis of the case law carried out in this chapter, both Article 102 TFEU and the provisions on free movement aim at increasing the efficiency of the economies of the Member States, and no reference is made in those cases to Article 3(1)(g) TEC. Consequently, there is no margin for any kind of differentiation in the Commission's and Courts' future reasoning or economic analysis conducted to establish market separation as an abuse of dominance. This is implicitly confirmed in *TeliaSonera*, the first judgment of the Court of Justice after the entry into force of the Lisbon Treaty.[176] The Court of Justice interpreted Article 102 TFEU with explicit reference to Protocol No 27 TFEU so as precisely to 'prevent competition from being distorted to the detriment of the public interest, individual undertakings and consumers, thereby ensuring the well-being of the European Union'.[177] Indeed, *TeliaSonera* is a case of an abusive margin squeeze by a dominant undertaking with no regulatory obligation to supply the input to its downstream competitors. Therefore, it is not a case of conflict in substantive values, and not even a case of unclear attribution of the alleged market distortion to the undertaking and/or the state. This is why the Court's reference to Protocol No 27 TFEU is anodyne; it would have been rather absurd to ignore decades of case law on exclusionary abuses based on ex-Article 3(1)(g) TEC as established in *Continental Can*.[178]

The only change brought about by the alleged 'emancipation' of the competition provisions from the Internal Market by virtue of the relocation of the clause would be to put into constitutional perspective the different use of economics in Article 102 TFEU and the free movement provisions, as explained above.

[175] The word 'emancipation' is used by A Komnimos, 'Continuity and Change in EU Competition Policy' (2010) 1 *Competition Policy International* 6. For arguments against such an interpretation, see J Drexl, 'Competition Law as Part of the European Constitution' in A von Bogdandy and J Bast (eds), *Principles of European Constitutional Law* (2nd rev edn, Hart Publishing, 2010) 659. For the opposite side of such 'emancipation', see Weatherill (n 75) 990, who highlights the potential for 're-orienteering the free movement law towards socially motivated regulation'.

[176] *Konkurrensverket v TeliaSonera Sverige AB* (n 9).

[177] ibid [20]–[22].

[178] See the analysis in ch 1, section III.C. However, one could criticise the Court of Justice's economic analysis of margin squeeze, particularly in regard to whether it requires the fulfilment of the conditions for a competition law duty to supply; however, this aspect of the economic analysis of margin squeeze is not related to the exclusion of out-of-state competitors any more than it is related to Swedish competitors. In any case, it is, as explained in ch 4, section III.C, an illustrative example of how regular competition law analysis can be distorted by endorsing regulatory standards even exceptionally, as has happened in relation to the test governing margin squeeze abuses first established in *Deutsche Telekom*.

However, this consequence would be of marginal significance for the purpose of this book, which is to understand the enforcement of Article 102 TFEU against market separation, since economic analysis has already been shown to constitute an integral part of applying Article 102 TFEU. Rather, it could be of great importance to the development of the principles governing the application of the free movement provisions by providing a legal basis for a reorientation of their application towards economic efficiency, without necessarily imitating the specifics of the use of economics under competition law.

VI. CONCLUSIONS

This chapter has addressed the interface between market separation as an abuse of the dominant position and market integration as reflected in the notion of trade barriers.

It is argued that alleged market separation by dominant undertakings should be exclusively assessed under Article 102 TFEU rather than under both Articles 101 and Article 102 TFEU, the reason being that there is a qualitative difference between genuinely unilateral conduct and agreements. Therefore, precedents of market separation under Article 101 TFEU should not be mechanically cited to establish a violation of Article 102 TFEU, when market separation takes the form of genuinely unilateral conduct such as geographic price discrimination or refusal to supply. Similarly, in the grey area of contractual abuses, such as border rebates, the dominant undertaking's conduct should be assessed as a unilateral activity, exclusively under Article 102 TFEU, when the market position of the undertaking (dominant position) constitutes the centre of gravity and manifests itself over the form of the conduct (agreement). This delimitation of the scope of Article 102 TFEU in relation to the scope of Article 101 TFEU has consequences for the allocation of the burden of proving 'efficiency' justifications, or 'objective' justifications, for conduct that would otherwise constitute abusive market separation. In particular, balancing interests under Article 102 TFEU in a manner similar to that used under Article 101(3) TFEU cannot be put into practice. Instead, it is suggested that the lack of efficiency or objective justifications should be a necessary condition for establishing market separation as an abuse of the dominant position.

The chapter then moved on to identify the guiding principle in assessing the integrationist thrust of market separation cases under Article 102 TFEU. This guiding principle is the distinction between economic and non-economic values, as reflected in the distinction between the notions of trade barriers and justified trade barriers. Two challenges to this connection of concepts have been examined and dismissed. The first is that non-economic values incorporated in the mandatory requirements concept operate as a negative qualification to the finding of a trade barrier. The second is the Court's actual practice, which, under specific circumstances, is permissive regarding economic justifications to trade barriers.

Subsequently, the chapter has shed light on the conceptual foundation of trade barriers under the provisions on free movement of goods by examining the recent cases on rules on the use of goods. It is argued that discrimination is a sufficient but not necessary element for establishing a trade barrier, as it is the most blatant form of a restriction to market access. Therefore, the conceptual foundation of the economic values promoted by the establishment of a trade barrier is the efficiency of the economies of the Member States as a whole: it is the efficiency of the enlarged market.

Discrimination and market access, as the two tests for establishing a trade barrier, have been compared with the intent-based and the effects-based tests for establishing market separation as an abuse of the dominant position under Article 102 TFEU. It is argued that the intent to separate the market must be proved and cannot be presumed. Therefore, induction-based presumptions under Article 101 TFEU about 'by object' restrictions of competition do not apply under Article 102 TFEU. Once proved, intent is sufficient to establish an abuse of dominant position. The reason is that market analysis has already been carried out for the purposes of defining the relevant market and establishing dominance. In that sense, there is an analogy between the intent-based test under Article 102 TFEU and discrimination under the provisions of the free movement, since they perform the same function. They manifest the illegal conduct in such a manner that there is no need for the second-phase tests to be applied.

With regard to the second-phase tests, it is argued that there is no conflict in substantive values between market separation as an abuse of the dominant position and trade barriers. Analysis of the case law under Article 102 TFEU confirms that the varying consumer preferences across the EU and, more generally, the fluctuating market conditions for which the dominant undertaking is not responsible represent the inherent limit of economic integration. They can in principle serve as objective justifications for conduct that would otherwise constitute an abuse. Otherwise, enforcement of Article 102 TFEU against conduct that hinders cross-border trade does not make sense from an economic perspective.

In the final section of this chapter, it has been argued that economic efficiency is substantiated differently under Article 102 TFEU compared with the free movement provisions. In particular, the use of economics is of central importance under Article 102 TFEU because 'uniformity' across the EU is assessed on the basis of the market equivalence of products, whereas, under the free movement provisions, it is assessed on the basis of the regulatory equivalence of products. Both the concordance of objectives and the different use of economics in market separation under Article 102 TFEU and trade barriers failing the market access test are justified at the constitutional level of the TFEU. A fortiori, this is the case after the relocation of the clause on a 'system of undistorted competition within the Internal Market' from Article 3(1)(g) TEC to Protocol No 27 TFEU. It is argued that, in the market separation cases under Article 102 TFEU considered in this chapter, the 'emancipation' of the competition provisions from the Internal Market has no practical significance, to the extent that there is no conflict in substantive values between the two and the case law is, so far, principled.

4

Market Separation under Article 102 TFEU and the Role of Non-economic Justifications: A Question of Attribution

I. INTRODUCTION

This chapter addresses the link between market separation under Article 102 TFEU and the non-economic values underpinning market integration, as reflected in the notion of justified trade barriers under the free movement provisions.

It is argued that the question of attribution of market separation to the dominant undertaking or the state, rather than conflicts in substantive values, represents the analytical core of this link. Conflicts in substantive values come to the surface whenever attribution of the anti-competitive effect is not principled. Therefore, academic debate and more reasoned court judgments should place the emphasis on formulating the test for attribution to the undertaking and/or the state.

The purpose of this chapter is to show that the analytical core of the interface between market separation under Article 102 TFEU and non-economic values is attribution. Subsequent chapters (five and six) will address the actual test of attribution.

The present chapter is structured in two main sections, one laying down Treaty-based arguments (section II) and one providing an interpretation of the case law in accordance with those arguments (section III).

The conceptual foundation of finding a justified trade barrier under the free movement provisions is identified in section II. This is the allocation of competences between the EU and the Member States to regulate the Internal Market. Subsequently, the concept of distribution of competence for market regulation is used to question the setting of such regulations by, otherwise, abusive conduct by dominant undertakings. It is argued that the constitutional distribution of competence between the EU and the Member States is ignored by permitting public policy considerations to operate as a justification under Article 102 TFEU.[1] Furthermore, the exclusion from the outset of public policy considerations from the scope of Article 102 TFEU is tested against the structure of the analysis under this Article, which is not susceptible to balancing. It is also tested against related arguments common to both Articles 101 and 102 TFEU.

Section III provides an interpretation of the case law under Article 102 TFEU, which rejects public policy justifications, in conjunction with case law under Article 102 TFEU, which upholds the right of the dominant undertaking to approach public authorities and 'lobby' in favour of setting specific regulations in the public interest.

In particular, it is argued that the express rejection by the European courts of public policy justifications under Article 102 TFEU on the basis that there are other legal routes by which the undertaking can achieve such policy objectives is, at a descriptive level, an indication that conduct by the undertaking and genuine public policy justifications are, as an evidentiary matter, mutually exclusive. Instead, 'lobbying' by the dominant undertakings is more likely to be genuinely in the public interest than to be an abuse of rights, as is confirmed by the relevant case law. Therefore, purely private actions that are genuinely in the public interest are more mythical than real, because there is always the potential for state involvement.

Finally, permitting in principle the public policy justifications advanced by dominant undertakings, which have not been proved by the facts to date, may potentially have added costs in terms of distorting the subsequent competition law analysis in cases in which no public policy issues arise. Therefore, excluding public policy considerations, as a matter of principle, from the scope of Article 102 TFEU presents the optimal means of analysis and allows the focus to shift to state action defence, which explicitly addresses the question of attribution.

II. ABUSE AND PUBLIC POLICY JUSTIFICATIONS: TREATY-BASED ARGUMENTS

In this section, the question explored is whether non-economic values can serve as objective justifications in market separation cases under Article 102 TFEU. The imperfect link between non-economic values and justified trade barriers under the free movement provisions is employed as the starting point of this inquiry. It is argued that the analytical core of the interface between market separation and justified trade barriers lies beyond the substantive values promoted by finding a

[1] 'Public policy considerations' is the predominant term which is used for non-economic values in the competition law discourse. However, a comprehensive definition, in particular by those who support the inclusion of public policy considerations, is nowhere to be found; see also n 59. In this book the line is drawn between economic and non-economic values under the free movement provisions, as explained in ch 3, section III.A.

justified trade barrier. Rather, there is no 'stateless market' and market integration (or deregulation) necessarily needs to be backed up by policy integration (or regulation). The other side of accepting this proposition is that the conceptual foundation of finding a justified trade barrier is the level at which such policy integration takes place: the national or the European level. Subsequently, it is argued that by permitting public policy considerations to operate within Article 102 TFEU, the outcome of competence distribution for market regulation is being pre-empted, inasmuch as the establishment of the rules on competition falls under the exclusive competence of the EU. Therefore, justifications on the basis of public policy considerations cannot be accepted under Article 102 TFEU.

A. The Conceptual Foundation of Justified Trade Barriers: Distribution of Competences for Market Regulation

The conceptual foundation for finding a justified trade barrier is not the substance of the non-economic values that operate as justifications. It has been shown in chapter three, section III.A, that almost 'anything' can serve as a ground for justification, except for the economic values underlying the finding of a trade barrier, since the link between the justified trade barrier and non-economic values that operate as justifications is not a perfect one. This is well reflected in the Court of Justice's permissive approach towards economic justifications, despite the fact that it consistently repeats the dictum that purely economic grounds can never serve as a justification.[2] Therefore, the second step under the Treaty mechanism to assess whether or not the trade barrier is justified refers necessarily to 'trade/market plus'.

At the same time, the importance of any non-economic value is undeniable and inextricably linked to a 'market'. The purpose of this section is to explain this proposition, which would permit our focus to shift from the substance of the non-economic values and to look for the conceptual foundation of this second-step inquiry beyond the substance of the non-economic values.

In particular, policy integration that backs up market integration is an integral part of the process of constructing a market. This was explained by Karl Polanyi's well-known concept of 'embeddedness', on the basis of economic history (or economic sociology).[3] In *The Great Transformation*, Polanyi argued that markets are always socially embedded and that once a disembedding stage of market soci-

[2] See ch 3, text to nn 48, 50 and 54.

[3] In *The Great Transformation* (Beacon Press, 1957), K Polanyi told the story of nineteenth-century English industrial capitalism, also looking at what he called 'primitive' (pre-industrial) man, societies and economies.

ety has been constructed, a re-embedding counter-movement becomes visible.[4] This re-embedding stage of the market society is distinguished by regulations, which reinforce the layers of social protection and slow down the rate of change.[5] The contemporary relevance of Polanyi's storytelling is emphasised in relation to building the European Internal Market[6] because of the perceived mismatch between a European market and a European state.[7] A Polanyian interpretation of the process of building the Internal Market inevitably involves regulation beyond efficiency, precisely because there is no such a thing as a 'stateless market', and in that sense the orthodox position of the EU as a 'regulatory state' is 'not so much wrong as incomplete'.[8]

[4] It seems that, according to Polanyi, the movement and the counter-movement occur simultaneously, even though they are not balanced; see, eg, his reference to the policy of the Tudor and early Stuart statesmen who 'used the powers of the Crown to slow down the process of economic improvement until it became socially bearable': ibid, 38.

[5] Here, the opposition between Polanyi's 'dis-embedding' stage of market society and economic liberalism in terms of what is spontaneous and what is artificial—market institutions or social movements—is not endorsed or even examined; see, eg, S Frerichs, 'Re-embedding Neo-liberal Constitutionalism: A Polanyian Case for the Economic Sociology of Law' in C Joerges and J Falke (eds), *Karl Polanyi, Globalisation and the Potential of Law in Transnational Markets* (Hart Publishing, 2011) 65–84. Polanyi's storytelling is endorsed here only in relation to the re-embedding stage of market societies and as an 'ontological reality', namely once a 'self-regulating market' has already been shown to exist. For the competing view, namely that Polanyi's storytelling is not about an impossibility as an 'ontological reality' but as an ideal type, see G Dale, *Karl Polanyi—The Limits of the Market* (Polity Press, 2010) 72–79 with further references.

[6] See, eg, M Egan, *Constructing a European Market: Standards, Regulations, and Governance* (Oxford University Press, 2001) 1–11; C Joerges, 'Democracy and European Integration: A Legacy of Tensions, a Re-conceptualisation and Recent True Conflicts' (2007) European University Institute Working Papers Law 2007/25 8–9; J Caporaso and S Tarrow, 'Polanyi in Brussels: European Institutions and the Embedding of Markets in Society' (2008) RECON Online Working Paper 2008/01 9–19; C Joerges and F Rödl, 'Informal Politics, Formalised Law and the "Social Deficit" of European Integration: Reflections after the Judgments of the ECJ in Viking and Laval' (2009) 15 *European Law Journal* 6–7; D Schiek, 'Re-embedding Economic and Social Constitutionalism: Normative Perspectives for the EU' in D Schiek, U Liebert and H Schneider (eds), *European Economic and Social Constitutionalism after the Treaty of Lisbon* (Cambridge University Press, 2011) 17–46; N Lindstrom, 'Constitutionalism between Normative Frameworks and the Socio-legal Frameworks of Societies' in Schiek, Liebert and Schneider, *European Economic and Social Constitutionalism*, 74–94.

[7] See, eg, C Scott, 'Governing without Law or Governing without Government? New-ish Governance and the Legitimacy of the EU' (2009) 15 *European Law Journal* 166–70, who uses the example of governance and argues that the EU is 'governing without law' rather than 'governing without government'. See more generally N Nic Shuibne, 'The Resilience of EU Market Citizenship' (2010) 47 *Common Market Law Review* 1601–05 on the weak political dimension of the EU polity, with reference to its law-making institutional structure.

[8] Caporaso and Tarrow (n 6) 10, in response to Majone's work on the EU as 'a regulatory state'. They use the free movement of workers as a case study. J Snell, '"European Constitutional Settlement", an Ever Closer Union, and the Treaty of Lisbon: Democracy or Relevance?' (2008) 33 *European Law Review* 624–31, 631 argues that the orthodox position is 'paying insufficient regard to the fundamentally dynamic nature of European integration, which is defined by an urge to create an ever closer union'; similarly, Nic Shuibne (n 7) 1605–10 labels a more nuanced EU market, in terms of economic virtues or vices, as the EU 'constitutional market'. See also G Busschaert, 'Revisiting the Fundamentals of Internal Market Law: Civil Society as a Third Sector between the State and the Market' [2011] *European Business Law Review* 725–39, who uses the examples of the freedom of establishment and the freedom to provide services to assess whether civil solidarity, defined as

Adopting such a Polanyian grand design of the EU free movement provisions supports the argument that demand for regulations driven by non-economic values is inevitable and that the critical question is a different one: who will enact such regulations, the EU or the Member States? This was the initial conception of the Internal Market, since the creation of the then Common Market was perceived to be a means to a non-economic end, namely 'an ever closer union among the peoples of Europe', 'to preserve and strengthen peace and liberty'.[9] However, the policy integration aspect of the Internal Market was largely considered to be in the hands of the Member States, which, in legal terms, translated into the constitutional principles of supremacy and direct effect of the Treaty free movement provisions *pre*-1992.[10]

The successive Treaty revisions have, however, explicitly changed that assumption by enhancing the social element at the EU level. In that regard, the insertion of a legal basis for the adoption of legislation at the EU level in sectors such as environmental protection or consumer protection,[11] or for the adoption of measures supplementing national measures (for example, in the field of public health or culture),[12] the insertion of the horizontal, policy-linking (or flanking) clauses,[13] as well as the strengthening of the re-regulatory function of harmonisation legislation once the EU competence is established,[14] are all very significant. An extended social policy-linking clause was added after the enactment of the

redistribution by the demands of civil society, is part of Internal Market law. *Cf* Lindstrom (n 6) 82–94, who uses the examples of *Viking* and *Laval* to cast doubts on whether societal counter-movements at the national level can be waged at the transnational market level.

[9] See the Preamble of the 1992 consolidated version of the Treaty establishing the European Community. The same ideal was reflected in the Schuman Declaration of 1950, which was the foundation of the European project.

[10] See ch 1, text to nn 48–49. See also F Scharpf, *Governing in Europe: Effective and Democratic?* (Oxford University Press, 1999) 43–83; and F Scharpf, 'The European Social Model: Coping with the Challenges of Diversity' (2002) 40 *Journal of Common Market Studies* 645–48 for an accurate description of the 'political decoupling of economic integration and social protection issues' before the Treaty of Maastricht. This political decoupling has also given rise to criticism of social dumping and race to the bottom amongst the competing jurisdictions; see J Snell, 'Who's Got the Power? Free Movement and Allocation of Competences in EC Law' (2003) 22 *Yearbook of European Law* 334–35 for a comprehensive rejection of such critiques in the EU context with further references to the literature.

[11] Now Article 192 TFEU; Article 169(2) TFEU.

[12] Article 168 TFEU; Article 167(2) TFEU.

[13] Article 11 TFEU; Article 12 TFEU; Article 168(1) TFEU; Article 167(4) TFEU. See S de Vries, *Tensions within the Internal Market: The Functioning of the Internal Market and the Development of Horizontal and Flanking Policies* (Europa Law, 2006) for a detailed account of the policy-linking clauses.

[14] See Article 114(3) TFEU. See also S Weatherill, 'Supply and Demand for Internal Market Regulation: Strategies, Preferences and Interpretation' in N Nic Shuibhne (ed), *Regulating the Internal Market* (Edward Elgar, 2006) 52, where it is pointed out that 'the quality of a harmonised regime is constitutionally relevant'; similarly, see B de Witte, 'Non-market Values in Internal Market Legislation' in Nic Shuibhne, *Regulating the Internal Market*, 68–77.

Lisbon Treaty[15] and Article 3(3) TEU-L provides for 'a competitive social market economy' as one of the objectives of the EU.[16]

At the same time, diversity at the Member State level continues to persist in relation to non-economic values and this is not only acceptable, but often the desirable form of market regulation. The reason for this is not only the practical difficulty of achieving consensus at a political level. For example, in the 2012 Monti Report for the relaunching of the Single Market, the Member States are grouped into four categories of different views on the balance between market and policy integration.[17] In addition, in 'realms remote from the orthodox core of market-building … space for local preferences and for regulatory experimentation' is considered to be beneficial.[18] In legal terms, this is the case where justified trade barriers do not trigger (or trigger only partial) EU harmonisation initiatives or trigger *minimum* harmonisation.[19] This legislative space left to the national level regulator is arguably subject again to the free movement provisions.[20]

Similarly, recent theoretical work shows that the principle of mutual recognition in the EU, which is conditional on the functional equivalence of the effects of the regulations,[21] is better understood as a kind of test that triggers a dynamic

[15] See Article 9 TFEU. See also the Commission rhetoric on relaunching the Single Market, namely that 'the responses to the challenges concerning growth, social cohesion and employment, security and climate change, will be more likely to succeed if the Single Market works as it should'; Commission (EU): 'Towards a Single Market Act—For a highly competitive social market economy—50 proposals for improving our work, business and exchanges with one another' (Communication) COM(2010) 608 final/2 [4].

[16] See R Nazzini, *The Foundations of European Union Competition Law: The Objective and Principle of Article 102* (Oxford University Press, 2011) 116–19, who reads the clause on a 'competitive social market economy' in Article 3(3) TEU-L as prescribing the long-term social welfare of the EU as the objective of the Internal Market. And see also I Lianos, 'Shifting the Narratives in the European Internal Market: Efficient Restrictions of Trade and the Nature of "Economic" Integration' [2010] *European Business Law Review* 755–57, who advocates a more holistic approach to the Internal Market that integrates consumers'/citizens' interests, based on the Commission policy documents as regards the Single Market.

[17] M Monti, 'A New Strategy for the Single Market—At the Service of Europe's Economy and Society' (Report to the President of the European Commission J M Barroso) 9 May 2010, available at http://ec.europa.eu/commission_2010-2014/president/news/press-releases/pdf/20100510_1_en.pdf [28]–[30]. The Member States are grouped into the Continental social-market economy countries, the Anglo-Saxon countries, the new Member States and the Nordic countries.

[18] Weatherill (n 14) 40.

[19] These are aspects of the two main dimensions of the pre-emptive capacity of the EU legislation, namely the scope and the intensity of the legislative act, as described by R Schutze, *From Dual to Cooperative Federalism: The Changing Structure of European Law* (Oxford University Press, 2009) 194–99. See also S Weatherill, 'Pre-emption, Harmonisation and the Distribution of Competence to Regulate the Internal Market' in C Barnard and J Scott (eds), *The Law of the Single European Market: Unpacking the Premises* (Hart Publishing, 2002) 52–57 on the scope and intensity of market regulation.

[20] See S Weatherill, 'Beyond Pre-emption? Shared Competence and Constitutional Change in the European Community' in D O'Keefe and P Twomey (eds), *Legal Issues of the Maastricht Treaty* (Chancery Law, 1994) 25. See also M Dougan, 'Minimum Harmonisation and the Internal Market' (2000) 37 *Common Market Law Review* 866–78 on the controversy as to whether the more stringent national rules apply only to domestic goods or to domestic and imported goods alike.

[21] See J Weiler, 'Mutual Recognition, Functional Equivalence and Harmonization in the Evolution of the European Common Market and the WTO' in F Padoa-Schioppa (ed), *The Principle of Mutual*

process of reallocation of regulatory competences.[22] In essence, this allows for the balancing between the advantages of national regulatory autonomy and the disadvantages of the non-removal of trade barriers, without prescribing whether the new allocation of competences should be made through harmonisation, free choice of (national) regulations or a combination of these.[23] Therefore, mutual recognition is functionally associated with the second stage of the application of the free movement provisions, namely that of finding a justified trade barrier, rather than with the trade-restricting effects of trade barriers, which refer to market competition and economic values.[24]

Confirmation of the link between the free movement provisions and policy integration, which is achieved by market regulation at either the EU or the national level, is found in Article 4(2)(a) TFEU. In this Article, the Internal Market, which is defined by reference to the free movement provisions, is listed as an area of shared competence between the EU and the Member States. According to Craig, the original text produced for the Treaty establishing a Constitution for Europe included the four freedoms within the category of exclusive competence, but they were then moved to the shared competence category. The reason for including the Internal Market within the category of shared competences is that, otherwise, Member State action that is ahead of EU action would be precluded, even if it might supply the catalyst for EU action.[25] It is national legislation acceptable under the free movement provisions, namely a justified trade barrier, which provides the impetus for harmonisation legislation at the EU level.[26]

The link between the application of the free movement provisions and the subsequent exercise of law-making powers by either the EU, for the first time, or the Member States is the essence of the shared competence to build the Internal Market. This division of powers largely depends on the application of the proportionality principle by the Court of Justice under the free movement provisions

Recognition in the European Integration Process (Palgrave Macmillan, 2005) 25–84; and K Nicolaidis, 'Kir Forever? The Journey of a Political Scientist in the Landscape of Mutual Recognition' in M Maduro and L Azoulai (eds), *The Past and Future of EU Law: The Classics of EU Law Revisited on the 50th Anniversary of the Rome Treaty* (Hart Publishing, 2010) 447–55 for a historical account of the evolution of the principle in the EU.

22 See W Kerber and R van den Bergh, 'Mutual Recognition in the Global Trade Regime: Lessons from the EU Experience' in I Lianos and O Odudu (eds), *Regulating Trade in Services in the EU and the WTO: Trust, Distrust and Economic Integration* (Cambridge University Press, 2012) 138–42.

23 ibid 139–40. The reconceptualisation of the principle of mutual recognition is based on a critique of the orthodox view that mutual recognition necessarily permits the removal of trade barriers without leading to centralisation or harmonisation. See W Kerber and R van den Bergh, 'Mutual Recognition Revisited: Misunderstandings, Inconsistencies, and a Suggested Reinterpretation' (2008) 61 *Kyklos* 447 for this critique. See also J Pelkmans, 'Mutual Recognition in Goods and Services: An Economic Perspective' in F Padoa-Schioppa (ed), *The Principle of Mutual Recognition in the European Integration Process* (Palgrave Macmillan, 2005) 97–107.

24 See also ch 3, n 87.

25 P Craig, *The Lisbon Treaty: Law, Politics, and Treaty Reform* (Oxford University Press, 2010) 160.

26 See the seminal article on harmonisation by P-J Slot, 'Harmonisation' (1996) 21 *European Law Review* 380–82.

as well as by national courts.[27] However, this does not make the establishment and the functioning of the Internal Market an exclusive competence. As noted by de Búrca and de Witte, building the Internal Market is 'a broad functional power which, by definition, belongs to the [European] institutions and not to the Member States', but 'the concrete policy content of an Internal Market measure can rarely, if ever, be said to fall within the [Union's] exclusive competence'.[28] In fact, the Court of Justice is prepared to apply the third limb of the proportionality principle, proportionality *stricto sensu*, with varied intensity, depending on whether the subject matter of the measure falls under the competence of the EU or the Member States.[29] Even in the former case, the Court recognises that national regulation carries a legitimate value ascribed to it by national preferences and is therefore willing to abstain with increasing frequency from determining the outcome of the final assessment for the benefit of the national courts.[30] This is also the underlying political importance of the Court of Justice deciding, in preliminary references, whether the proportionality assessment is a question of interpretation (law) or application (facts).[31] The same constitutional considerations and sensitivities underlie the absence of detailed and clear guidance as to what is, and how to reach, the standard of proof for public interest justifications in free movement law, in particular with regard to the appropriateness and necessity of the national rules that constitute trade barriers.[32]

[27] See P-H Jans, R de Lange, S Prechal and R Widdershoven, *Europeanisation of Public Law* (Europa Law, 2007) 151–53; M Jarvis, *The Application of EC Law by National Courts—The Free Movement of Goods* (Clarendon Press, 1998) 227–30. See also the analysis provided by Snell (n 10) 337–45, who focuses on the impact of the application of the proportionality principle under the free movement provisions on the vertical division of powers within the EU.

[28] G de Búrca and B de Witte, 'The Delimitation of Powers between the EU and the Member States' in A Arnull and D Wincott (eds), *Accountability and Legitimacy in the European Union* (Oxford University Press, 2002) 209. Similarly, see T Tridimas, 'Competence after Lisbon: The Elusive Search for Bright Lines' in D Ashiagbor, N Countouris and I Lianos (eds), *The European Union after the Treaty of Lisbon* (Cambridge University Press, 2012) 66.

[29] Snell (n 10) 342–45; T Tridimas, *The General Principles of EU Law* (2nd edn, Oxford University Press, 2006) 209–34. See also N Nic Shuibne, 'Margins of Appreciation: National Values, Fundamental Rights and EC Free Movement Law' (2009) 34 *European Law Review* 230 for the specific case of fundamental rights and free movement law. I Lianos and D Gerard, 'Shifting Narratives in European Economic Integration: Trade in Services, Pluralism and Trust' in I Lianos and O Odudu (eds), *Regulating Trade in Services in the EU and the WTO: Trust, Distrust and Economic Integration* (Cambridge University Press, 2012) 197–206 emphasise that the Court displays great flexibility in adjusting the width of the 'margin of appreciation' granted to Member States from case to case and the Court thereby discloses a pluralistic approach to the management of regulatory diversity.

[30] Tridimas (n 29) 238–41. See also Jarvis (n 27) 231–94 for a review of the application of the proportionality principle under the free movement provisions by national courts.

[31] See G Davies, 'Abstractness and Correctness in the Preliminary Reference Procedure: Implications for the Division of Powers and Effective Market Regulation' in Nic Shuibhne (n 14) 218–24; T Tridimas, 'Proportionality in Community Law: Searching for the Appropriate Standard of Scrutiny' in E Ellis (ed), *The Principle of Proportionality in the Laws of Europe* (Hart Publishing, 1999) 77–80; G Beck, *The Legal Reasoning of the Court of Justice of the EU* (Hart Publishing, 2013) 225–28 .

[32] See the analysis by N Nic Shuibhne and M Maci, 'Proving Public Interest: The Growing Importance of Evidence in Free Movement Case Law' (2013) 50 *Common Market Law Review* 969–74 and 991–97.

In short, if the trade barriers are not justified, the national perception of public policy is set aside. Policy integration can then be pursued at the EU level on the basis of sector-specific Treaty provisions (or preventive harmonisation). Alternatively, policy integration at the national level should be modified to respect the free movement provisions, precisely because the problem is more often the proportionality *stricto sensu* of the measure promoting such justification than the lack of a valid and recognised public interest justification. If the trade barrier is justified, the divergent national perceptions concerning policy integration are permitted to prevail. Furthermore, this can trigger the process of harmonisation at the EU level. Harmonisation legislation has a dual function: namely a deregulatory function and, at the same time, a regulatory function, since it replaces national regulations which constitute justified trade barriers.[33]

In light of this shared competence between the EU and the Member States for market regulation, the key question is how to shape the policy aspect of market integration, in the absence of comprehensive legislative powers.[34] Therefore, the content of justified trade barriers is not, in itself, important. It is, rather, the process of deciding who will shape the policy aspect of the Internal Market and how it will be shaped that further dictates the substantive choice over potentially conflicting values.[35] Kallaugher, writing in relation to the protection of national IP rights as provided for in Article 36 TFEU, has put forward that this second stage of applying the free movement provisions 'is in essence a device for determining regulatory competence'.[36] This is, in fact, true with regard to all substantive values underpinning potentially justified trade barriers, and not only IP rights.

Therefore, finding a justified trade barrier has nothing to do with the economic analysis of the effect of the measure in question, as under the competition law provisions. In chapter three, it was shown that the specific economic values that determine the minimum scope of what is 'internal' in the Internal Market are important, because they trigger the application of the Treaty provisions of the free movement. Once a trade barrier is shown to exist based on this core of substantive

[33] Legislation at the EU level should comply with the free movement provisions. However, the Court of Justice adopts a softer approach at judicial review, arguably because all affected parties are represented in the political process at the EU level and therefore the outcome is in the general interest. See Snell (n 10) 345–50; K Mortelmans, 'The Relationship between the Treaty Rules and Community Measures for the Establishment and Functioning of the Internal Market—Towards a Concordance Rule' (2002) 39 *Common Market Law Review* 1336; Jarvis (n 27) 345–58.

[34] This paraphrases C Semmelmann, 'The European Union's Economic Constitution under the Lisbon Treaty: Soul-Searching among Lawyers Shifts the Focus to Procedure' (2010) 35 *European Law Review* 521, who poses the question as to how to shape the social element in the absence of comprehensive legislative powers.

[35] See ibid 531–34 on the change of focus to proceduralisation and procedure. Similarly, on the shift from hierarchy and conflicts to coherence and pluralism, see L Azoulai, 'The Court of Justice and the Social Market Economy: The Emergence of an Ideal and the Conditions for its Realisation' (2008) 45 *Common Market Law Review* 1336–37.

[36] J Kallaugher, 'Existence, Exercise and Exceptional Circumstances: The Limited Scope for a More Economic Approach to IP Issues under Article 102 TFEU' in S Anderman and A Ezrachi (eds), *Intellectual Property and Competition Law—New Frontiers* (Oxford University Press, 2011) 121.

values, anything apart from these substantive market values can be called upon by the Member State to justify the adoption of such a restriction. This means that the regulatory views of either a Member State or the EU legislature are, at this stage, permitted to modify the core of the internal element of the Internal Market. The fact that the economic values will be modified in any case is not questioned; the only question is at which level of governance this will occur. The narrative provided in this section shows that this process of competence distribution for market regulation, as well as its exercise, is dynamic and is based on constantly discursive interaction between the EU and national institutions, both legislative and judicial.

B. 'Pre-emption' and the Exclusive Competence to Establish the Rules on Competition

The conceptual foundation of finding justified trade barriers is not the substantive values that underpin policy integration. Rather, this second stage of the application of the free movement provisions is concerned with the allocation of competences between the EU and the Member States as regards the level at which policy integration takes place. In this section, it is argued that this function of competence allocation cannot be performed in an equivalent manner under Article 102 TFEU. Article 102 TFEU is linked with the implementation, either centralised or decentralised, of the rules on competition, and the establishment of these rules falls under the exclusive competence of the EU.

A link between the competition law provisions, including Article 102 TFEU, and subsequent legislative action, equivalent to the link described above in the area of the Internal Market, is not to be found in the scheme of the Treaty. Rather, the reverse relationship exists. Legislative action 'establishing rules on competition' precedes their implementation. Confirmation of the existence of this reverse relationship is found by considering that 'competition law is a tall order', as pointed out by Slot, since it has always been an area of exclusive competence of the EU.[37] Therefore, inasmuch as the link between the finding of a justified trade barrier and subsequent legislative action is the essence of a shared competence for

[37] P-J Slot, 'The Past, Present and Future of Competition Law in the European Union' in A Arnul, C Barnard, M Dougan and E Spaventa (eds), *A Constitutional Order of States? Essays in EU Law in Honour of Alan Dashwood* (Hart Publishing, 2011) 375. Article 3(2) of Regulation 1/2003, which allows Member States to adopt more strict national rules for unilateral conduct by undertakings, also confirms the exclusive nature of the competence. This deviation is authorised not only by Regulation 1/2003, but a fortiori by the Treaty itself which, in Article 103(2)(e) TFEU, provides for the legal basis of Regulation 1/2003. However, *cf* M Dougan, *National Remedies before the Court of Justice: Issues of Harmonisation and Differentiation* (Hart Publishing, 2004) 120–23, who argues that the competence of the then Community as regards the establishment of competition rules was a shared one, before the entry into force of the Lisbon Treaty. However, this shared competence was exercised de facto as exclusive, even before the adoption of Regulation 1/2003, inasmuch as conflicts between European and

market regulation,[38] the exclusive competence of the EU to establish the rules on competition confirms the absence of a similar link in relation to Article 102 TFEU.

A fortiori since the Lisbon Treaty came into force, competition became expressly listed in Article 3(1)(b) TFEU as an area in which the EU is to have exclusive competence. The category of exclusive competence refers to areas in which 'only the Union can legislate and adopt legally binding acts, the Member States being able to do so themselves only if so empowered by the Union or for the implementation of Union acts'.[39] Article 3(1)(b) TFEU and the exclusive competence of the EU referred to therein are clearly associated with the 'establishment of the competition rules necessary for the functioning of the Internal Market' and not with their application.[40] Therefore, the decentralised enforcement system established by Regulation 1/2003 did not bring about any change in relation to the exclusive nature of the EU's competence as regards competition rules. The EU institutions are exclusively empowered to provide content for the competition law provisions and define the reach of application of those provisions by adopting legally binding acts. One might be tempted to assume that competition law is 'legislated through directly applicable Treaty provisions'.[41] Even in this case, the exclusive nature of the EU competence to establish rules on competition would increasingly mean that there should be a unitary framework for assessing, in a consistent manner, whether public policy considerations are suitable and necessary justifications, given the possibility of private enforcement of competition law. This also holds true for the discretionary powers of the National Competition Authorities, as well as of the Commission itself, to apply varying degrees of priority to the complaints submitted to them in the context of decentralised public enforcement. By contrast, the true concern as regards the enforcement of the free movement provisions is the proportionality of the national measure *stricto sensu*, which is why it is problematic when the Court of Justice dictates the outcome of the assessment rather than engages in a discursive interaction with national courts.[42]

Let us consider a hypothetical question to demonstrate the argument based on the distinction between the exclusive competence to establish rules on competition and the shared competence to establish rules regarding the Internal Market. Could the Council, on a proposal from the Commission and after consulting the European Parliament, adopt a valid regulation or directive on the basis of Article 103(1) TFEU? The legislation would provide for the obligations of the

national competition rules were to be solved by the principle of supremacy of European law as in Case 14/68 *Walt Wilhelm and others v Bundeskartellamt* [1969] ECR 1 [6], [9].

[38] See section II.A above.

[39] Article 2(1) TFEU.

[40] Craig (n 25) 160.

[41] Eg, K Cseres, 'Comparing Laws in the Enforcement of EU and National Competition Law' (2010) 3 *European Journal of Legal Studies* 10. This is not true, however, since the competition law provisions apply only inasmuch as the conduct in question 'affects trade'. See ch 1, section IV.C on the jurisdictional function of this requirement and its comparator under the free movement provisions.

[42] See text to nn 30–31 above.

Commission, National Competition Authorities and national courts to allow for allegedly exclusionary tying by a dominant undertaking if such conduct also promotes a specific eco-friendly (tied) product over less eco-friendly products or because the environment would thereby be generally less polluted. For example, the dominant manufacturer of energy-efficient washing machines in a Member State ties a specific washing powder to that machine, the consequence being that manufacturers of competing washing powders, which are less eco-friendly, exit the market. Had the obligation to buy the tied washing powder been imposed upon consumers by state regulation, this regulation would have been found to be a trade barrier. If it were further found to be justified by the Court of Justice, it would possibly trigger harmonisation legislation at the EU level based on Article 114 TFEU. This also involves adapting the content of the measure to conform to the principle of proportionality. Both the courts (European and national) and the Member States and institutions involved in the harmonisation process design the framework which governs environmental protection in the washing powder sector. By contrast, under Article 102 TFEU, the tying conduct will either be upheld or not upheld, regardless of whether Article 102 TFEU is applied in the context of public or private enforcement. There is no margin for adjusting the content of the 'conduct'/measure, even if one accepts that the proportionality principle applies with regard to the fines or the remedies imposed. The environmental protection, if upheld, will invariably take the form of excluding less eco-friendly washing powders from the market and allowing the more eco-friendly washing powder to prevail in the market. This is how 'the effectiveness of the European rules on competition would not be jeopardized'. Therefore, a distinction can be drawn between the establishment and implementation of competition law for the purposes of defining the scope of the exclusive competence of the EU provided for in Article 3(1)(b) TFEU. To the extent that such a regulation has not been adopted, it cannot be further assumed that the already established 'rules on competition', including Article 102 TFEU, accommodate, for example, environmental considerations, unless it can be shown to be the case.[43]

This is the 'flip side' of the legal arguments in relation to the use of policy-linking clauses, which are advanced by scholars against assessing public policy considerations within the competition law provisions, notably Article 101 TFEU.[44] It is

[43] See section III.A below for a description of the current state of the case law.

[44] There is fierce academic discussion surrounding the context of Article 101 TFEU because of its bifurcated structure, which led to cases such as *CECD* (Case IV.F.1/36.718) Commission Decision 2000/475/EC [2000] OJ L187/47, prior to the enactment of Regulation 1/2003 abolishing the notification procedure. See the contributions by G Monti, 'Article 81 EC and Public Policy' (2002) 39 *Common Market Law Review* 1057; De Vries (n 13) 198–221; O Odudu, *The Boundaries of EC Competition Law: The Scope of Article 81* (Oxford University Press, 2006) 159–80; H Schweitzer, 'Competition Law and Public Policy: Reconsidering an Uneasy Relationship. The Example of Art. 81' (2007) EUI Working Papers—Law 2007/30; C Townley, *Article 81 EC and Public Policy* (Hart Publishing, 2009) 46–103. See also the recent paper by the OFT, 'Article 101(3)—A Discussion of Narrow versus Broad Definition of Benefits' (Discussion Note for OFT Breakfast Roundtable) 2010, available at www.oft.gov.uk/shared_oft/events/Article101(3)-discussionnote.pdf.

worth mentioning this here, since the relevant debate is common to both Article 101 TFEU and Article 102 TFEU *mutatis mutandis*. Odudu has argued that the reading of public policy justifications into the competition law provisions creates horizontal direct effect for provisions incapable of direct effect, such as Articles 11, 12 and 168(1) TFEU on environmental, consumer and human health protection.[45] In particular, Odudu objects to the generation of positive legal obligations by the operation of such policy-linking clauses, when the EU legislation is simply enforced rather than adopted.[46] This is similarly confirmed by the observation that the subject matter of the policy-linking clauses falls under areas of shared competence between the EU and the Member States. Therefore, one can arguably read these clauses into Treaty provisions addressed to Member States only inasmuch as an EU measure has not pre-empted the field.[47] An alternative approach would be to use the policy-linking clauses as rules of interpretation with regard to the application of the competition provisions.[48] However, such use would necessarily turn the policy-linking clauses into instruments used to inform and generate legal tests, namely the tests under Articles 101 and 102 TFEU.[49] This stems from the particularity of the competition law provisions, which are expressly addressed to undertakings and not to Member States, and is confirmed by the comparable use of the clause provided for in ex-Article 3(1)(g) TEC, which has, in fact, been used judicially to generate the legal test governing exclusionary abuses.[50] Therefore, at a

[45] Odudu (n 44) 166–67.

[46] More recently, see O Odudu, 'The Wider Concerns of EU Competition Law' [2010] *Oxford Journal of Legal Studies* 8–9, with references to case law and, in particular, to Case C-221/08 *Commission v Ireland* [2010] ECR I-01669 [51]–[54], in response to Townley's (n 44) criticism. Odudu's argument does not dismiss the usefulness of the flanking clauses *in globo*; it properly delimits their scope of application to instances when the EU legislates (or takes enforcement action against the legislation of Member States). Therefore, the issue is not, as presented by Townley, 'a chicken or egg dilemma', ie, either ignoring public policy considerations within Article 101 TFEU or suggesting that this provision is not directly effective; see Townley (n 44) 96. The question is whether the policy-linking clauses are directly effective Treaty provisions in the first place.

[47] This is not challenged by Townley in principle, but only as being irrelevant for the interpretation and application of a Treaty provision like Article 101(3) TFEU. See C Townley, 'Which Goals Count in Article 101 TFEU? Public Policy and its Discontents: The OFT's Roundtable Discussion on Article 101(3) of the Treaty on the Functioning of the European Union' (2011) 32 (9) *European Competition Law Review* 442, in particular n 17.

[48] See I Lianos, 'Competition Law in the European Union after the Treaty of Lisbon' in Ashiagbor, Countouris and Lianos (n 28) 269. See also M Wasmeier, 'The Integration of Environmental Protection as a General Rule for Interpreting Community Law' (2001) 38 *Common Market Law Review* 159; and S Kingston, *Greening EU Competition Law and Policy* (Cambridge University Press, 2012) 106–19 on the use of the environmental integration principle, in particular, as a rule for interpretation.

[49] The function of the flanking clauses in relation to the competition law provisions is inspired by E Scotford, 'Mapping the Article 174(2) Case Law: A First Step to Analysis Community Environmental Principles' (2008) 8 *Yearbook of European Environmental Law* 1, who places the judicial treatment of the environmental law principles provided for in Article 191(2) TFEU into four categories: policy cases, interpretative cases, cases informing and cases generating legal tests.

[50] See ch 1, text to nn 96–97. This is so, even though the Court has often proclaimed that the provision cannot produce legal obligations for the Member States; see, eg, Case C-484/08 *Caja de Ahorros y Monte de Piedad de Madrid v Asociación de Usuarios de Servicios Bancarios (Ausbanc)* [2010] ECR I-04785 [46]–[47]; and Case C-181/06 *Deutsche Lufthansa AG v ANA - Aeroportos de Portugal SA* [2007] ECR I-5903 [31].

descriptive level, it cannot be said that policy-linking clauses have a binding legal effect vis-a-vis undertakings until there is a case positively citing a policy-linking clause as a basis for taking public policy considerations under Article 101 or 102 TFEU into account.

Article 3(3) of Regulation 1/2003 provides further confirmation of the argument that public policy considerations cannot inform the legal test under Article 102 TFEU. Article 3(3) provides for an exemption of the primacy of EU competition provisions, for 'provisions of national law that predominantly pursue an objective different from that pursued by [Articles 101 and 102 TFEU] ... provided that such [national] legislation is compatible with the general principles and other provisions of [EU] law'.[51] Here, 'other provisions' arguably refers to the free movement provisions. Therefore, Article 3(3) of Regulation 1/2003 confirms that what seems to be an issue of conflicting substantive values beyond the scope of 'rules on competition' is instead a problem of division of competence between the EU and the Member States in regard to their legislation.

Schmid, writing from the perspective of conflict of laws, qualifies such conflicts between norms with different subject matters that are also situated at different hierarchical levels as *diagonal* conflicts. He then advances a justification-based approach within the scope of the competition provisions for procedural, discursive, reasons,[52] but, at the same time, he assimilates the test in terms of burden of proof and the enforcement agency's discretion to the test under the free movement provisions for normative consistency purposes.[53] However, if the implicated undertakings and the Commission are placed on a level playing field in terms of the margin of discretion and the burden of proof within the competition

[51] This is elaborated in Council Regulation (EC) 1/2003 on the implementation of the rules on competition laid down in Articles 81 and 82 of the Treaty [2003] OJ L1/1 (Recital 9): '[Articles 101 and 102 TFEU] have as their objective the protection of competition on the market. This Regulation, which is adopted for the implementation of these Treaty provisions, does not preclude Member States from implementing on their territory national legislation, which protects other legitimate interests *provided that such legislation is compatible with general principles and other provisions of Community law*. In so far as such national legislation pursues predominantly an objective different from that of protecting competition on the market, the competition authorities and courts of the Member States may apply such legislation on their territory' (emphasis added). See H Ullrich, 'Anti-unfair Competition Law and Anti-trust Law: A Continental Conundrum?' (2005) EUI Working Paper LAW No 2005/01 6–9 for an analysis in relation to national law on unfair competition.

[52] This is prior to the enactment of Regulation 1/2003, which established the decentralised enforcement of the competition provisions.

[53] C Schmid, 'Diagonal Competence Conflicts between European Competition Law and National Regulation—A Conflict of Laws Reconstruction of the Dispute on Book Price Fixing' (2000) 1 *European Review of Private Law* 166–71; similarly, see K Mortelmans, 'Towards Convergence in the Application of the Rules on Free Movement and on Competition?' (2001) 38 *Common Market Law Review* 638–42, 644–45; W van de Gronden, 'Rule of Reason and Convergence in Internal Market Law and Competition Law' in A Schrauwen (ed), *Rule of Reason: Rethinking Another Classic of European Legal Doctrine* (Europa Law, 2005) 90–92; W van de Gronden, 'The Internal Market, the State and Private Initiative' (2006) 33 *Legal Issues of Economic Integration* 107, 127–37. These authors all recognise that the judicial review of the undertaking's action cannot allow deference to the judges, inasmuch as the judicial review of state action allows it.

provisions,[54] the alleged procedural advantage of the discursive solution is, in practice, being withdrawn and the solution is no different from an 'all or nothing' approach of delimiting the scope of the competition law provisions.[55]

This 'all or nothing' jurisdictional approach, which excludes public policy considerations from the scope of Article 102 TFEU, is also consistent with the structure of Article 102 TFEU, as advanced in chapter three, with regard to efficiency justifications. In particular, it has been argued that balancing the anti- and pro-competitive effects of the conduct in a similar way to Article 101(3) TFEU should be rejected under Article 102 TFEU. Instead, the lack of any efficiency justification should operate as an affirmative defence.[56] Using the language of proportionality, such a defence would only involve a suitability/necessity test, excluding any form of balancing.[57] Applying such a test to public policy considerations under Article 102 TFEU does not make much sense, since for any benefits which cannot be translated into economic benefits, there are arguably other suitable ways of attaining them than exclusion of a competitor from the market (see section III.A below).[58] This already makes suitability and necessity control by the enforcement authorities or the national courts largely redundant.

III. ABUSE AND PUBLIC POLICY JUSTIFICATIONS: INTERPRETATION OF THE CASE LAW

The interface between market separation as an abuse of dominance and justified trade barriers was analysed in section II. There it was argued that non-economic justifications should be excluded from Article 102 TFEU at the outset, inasmuch as the EU legislature has not established rules on competition by integrating public policy considerations. Given the current status of the law, the distribution of

[54] As opposed to the 'margin of appreciation' that the defendant state has under the free movement provisions.

[55] However, the outright, general exemption from the scope of the competition provisions of collective labour agreements in the Court's case law has been criticised from a 'law and economics' perspective by competition law scholars; see P Camesasca and R Van den Bergh, 'Irreconcilable Principles? The Court of Justice Exempts Collective Labour Agreements from the Wrath of Antitrust' (2000) 25 *European Law Review* 505–07. This criticism, though, followed the judgment of the Court of Justice in *Albany* and disregards the fact that this case is a state action case: there are inherent problems with the state action doctrine (see the comprehensive analysis in ch 5), which are particularly evidenced by the fact that collective labour agreements, which were exempted from the scope of the state action doctrine, were subjected to the free movement provisions in *Viking* (see ch 5, text to nn 142–43).

[56] See ch 3, section II.A.

[57] See J Steenbergen, 'Proportionality in Competition Law and Policy' (2008) 35 *Legal Issues of Economic Integration* 259 on the notion of proportionality in competition law and policy. However, he seems to suggest that the standard of scrutiny under the proportionality principle in Article 102 TFEU is higher than indispensability; ibid 266.

[58] See, in particular, section III.A.ii on the right of the dominant undertakings to influence and incite public authorities to act (the right to 'lobby').

competence between the EU and the Member States for market regulation would be sidestepped if public policy considerations had been permitted as justifications under Article 102 TFEU. Therefore, it falls upon academics who advocate that public policy considerations should be brought within the scope of Article 102 TFEU, when it is enforced against dominant undertakings, to provide normative arguments to that end. This also involves the additional question of providing a substantive definition of public policy considerations that can positively be taken into account under Article 102 TFEU, since this definition is not provided by EU legislation.

In turn, this section examines the existing case law under Article 102 TFEU, all of which has rejected alleged public policy justifications at a descriptive level. An alternative interpretation of the case law is provided. In particular, it is argued that conduct by dominant undertakings and public policy justifications are mutually exclusive because whenever public policy considerations come into play, there is at least the potential for state involvement to occur. Therefore, the focus should predominantly shift to the question of attribution of the market-distorting effect to the undertaking or the state.[59] Nevertheless, in order to be able to reflect upon and articulate a principled test for attribution, the first step is to expressly recognise that there is a question of attribution. Answering this question makes it possible to determine whose conduct is being assessed, prior to formulating or blurring the substantive legality test applicable to the conduct under assessment. This section identifies the analytical core of the interface between abuse of dominance and public policy considerations as being a question of attribution. Chapters five and six provide an answer to this question.

A. Interpretation of the Case Law at a Descriptive Level

The first stage of the analysis concerns a conjoint reading of the cases under Article 102 TFEU that treat abusive market participation on the one hand and

[59] In the academic discussion on Article 101(3) TFEU, taking into account non-economic benefits is very often presented as desirable, without those non-economic benefits first being defined or without an express acknowledgment that any definition necessarily centres around the link with state action. For example, the 2010 OFT discussion paper concerning Article 101(3) TFEU (n 44) is, in itself, an attempt to define the benefits that should be taken into consideration under Article 101(3) TFEU. In paragraph [3.28] indirect economic benefits (such as reductions in cleaning and disposal costs for local councils) as well as non-economic benefits (such as a less polluted environment) of an agreement between food retailers to charge an agreed amount for the use of plastic bags are presented as part of the government's encouragement of self-regulation for the purpose of reducing environmental pollution; hence, permitting such an agreement would not block government policy. This means that the non-economic benefits suitable for consideration under Article 101(3) TFEU are somehow linked to government action, which confirms the view endorsed here. The *decisive* element is the attribution of the conduct and effect to the undertaking and the remoteness or intensity of its link with state action.

the exercise of the right of dominant undertaking to 'lobby' on the other hand as alternative means for the achievement of public policy. According to the European courts, the two sets of cases constitute two sides of the same coin: to the extent that the dominant undertaking is not allowed to pre-empt with its 'anti-competitive' behaviour the setting of regulations, the other side is, naturally, the right of the undertakings to incite the public authorities to act as part of the democratic process. The exercise of this right should be and is, according to case law, neutral in regard to its assessment under Article 102 TFEU.

i. *Market Participation*

A review of the case law under Article 102 TFEU reveals that the European courts have never allowed justifications advanced by the dominant undertaking on the basis that the abusive conduct is in the public interest. Such, for example, was the case in *Hilti*, in which the applicant claimed that its tying practice was justified by its 'duty of care under product-liability law' as a manufacturer, in light of the misleading advertisement of the competitor's product as being compatible with Hilti's products.[60] The General Court rejected the argument on the basis that:

> [T]here are laws in the United Kingdom attaching penalties to the sale of dangerous products and to the use of misleading claims as to the characteristics of any product. There are also authorities vested with powers to enforce those laws. In those circumstances it is clearly not the task of an undertaking in a dominant position to take steps on its own initiative to eliminate products which, rightly or wrongly, it regards as dangerous or at least as inferior in quality to its own products.[61]

Similarly, in *Tetra Pak II*, the General Court, in a decision affirmed by the Court of Justice, rejected the applicant's claim that the tied sales of machines and cartons were justified by requirements for the protection of public health and the interests of consumers.[62] It held that:

> [T]he protection of public health may be guaranteed by other means ... the remedy must lie in appropriate legislation or regulations, and not in rules adopted unilaterally by manufacturers, which would amount to prohibiting independent manufacturers from conducting the essential part of their business.[63]

Somewhat more recently, in *Sotirios Lélos*, the dominant pharmaceutical undertaking advanced a defence to its refusal to supply wholesalers engaged in parallel exports which was based on public health considerations, namely to prevent

[60] Case T-30/89 *Hilti AG v Commission* [1991] ECR II-1439 [105]–[107].

[61] ibid [118].

[62] See Case T-83/91 *Tetra Pak International SA v Commission* [1994] ECR II-755 [82]–[85] in relation to product market definition, but with cross-reference in relation to the finding of an abuse, ibid [138]–[139]; affirmed by the Court of Justice in Case C-333/94 P *Tetra Pak International SA v Commission* [1996] ECR I-5951 [36]–[37].

[63] Case T-83/91 *Tetra Pak International SA v Commission* (n 62) [84].

shortage of medicines on a given national market. The Court of Justice rejected the claim and held that:

> [I]n cases where parallel trade would effectively lead to a shortage of medicines on a given national market, it would not be for the undertakings holding a dominant position but for the national authorities to resolve the situation, by taking appropriate and proportionate steps that were consistent with national legislation as well as with the obligations flowing from Article 81 of Directive 2001/83.[64]

All cases seem to demonstrate that, when there are other means available for achieving public policy considerations outside the scope of Article 102 TFEU, namely either the adoption or the enforcement of appropriate legislation, public policy considerations do not form objective justifications. In all cases, the Court seems sceptical of private undertakings unilaterally shaping public policy objectives and treats market participation and recourse to democratic processes as true alternatives with regard to achieving public policy objectives. Therefore, the observation made—that it is not clear from those cases if the defence failed on the merits or as a matter of principle[65]—is not valid, since the option of adopting legislation or enforcing the already existing legislation will always be open as an alternative means for the attainment of those objectives and as part of the democratic process. The dictum that private conduct is inappropriate for the attainment of regulatory objectives was also repeated by the General Court in *Irish Sugar* and in *British Gypsum* in relation to ensuring compliance with legal standards at the national level, with reference to its judgment in *Hilti*.[66]

However, for the purposes of strengthening the argument advanced, it will be assumed that, in the cases mentioned above, the public policy justifications failed on the facts, as an evidentiary matter. Thus, the minimum interpretation of the case law under Article 102 TFEU for rejecting public policy justifications

[64] Joined Cases C-468–478/06 *Sotirios Lélos kai Sia EE and others v GlaxoSmithKline AEVE Farmakeftikon Proïonton, formerly Glaxowellcome AEVE* [2008] ECR I-7139 [75].

[65] See, eg, E Rousseva, *Rethinking Exclusionary Abuses in EU Competition Law: Rethinking Article 82 of the EC Treaty* (Hart Publishing, 2010) 267. Similarly, see A Albors-Llorens, 'The Role of Objective Justification and Efficiencies in the Application of Article 82 EC' (2007) 44 *Common Market Law Review* 1740, who points to the fact that the Commission's decision in *Hilti* was very comprehensive in demonstrating that the undertaking's actions were not rooted in a genuine concern for safety. However, this was not decisive, as the Court based the rejection of the undertaking's arguments on a principled reason, namely that it is inappropriate to use private conduct for the purpose of defining public policy considerations. G Davies, 'Article 86 EC, the EC's Economic Approach to Competition Law, and the General Interest' (2009) 5 *European Competition Journal* 564–65 states that in *Hilti* and *Tetra Pak*, the undertakings lost their argument on the facts, even though he acknowledges that private undertakings should not be allowed to define the public interest on their own initiative.

[66] Case T-228/97 *Irish Sugar plc v Commission* [1999] ECR II-2969 [192]; Case T-65/89 *BPB Industries plc and British Gypsum Ltd v Commission* [1993] ECR II-389 [47], [58], [69]. Similarly, in relation to ensuring compliance with EU rules, see *Cement* (Cases IV/33.126 and 33.322) Commission Decision 94/815/EC [1994] OJ L343/1 [53 (8)]: 'The Commission would point out first that it is not for undertakings to substitute themselves for the [EU] authorities, which are responsible for the implementation of [Articles 107 and 108 TFEU], and to prevent the movement within the [EU] of products which they believe, rightly or wrongly, are receiving government aid.'

is adopted to fortify the argument against allegations that the depiction of the case law is not accurate. All the cases show that public policy justifications have been used strategically in litigation by dominant undertakings, and the standard required by the European courts to prove that such justifications are genuine is high. Once again, the difficulty of actually proving genuine public policy justifications for allegedly abusive conduct indicates that the European courts are sceptical of private conduct shaping the public interest.

A counter-argument to this facts-based approach to the case law is that the Commission has been 'self-policing' when deciding which cases to take up, so as to pursue only cases of outright abuse. This counter-argument would only make sense in the context of public enforcement of competition law, since it is indeed unlikely that the Commission would begin an investigation in the first place if a viable objective justification were evidenced. However, *Sotirios Lélos* is a case that reached the Court of Justice as a preliminary reference from a national court in the context of private competition law enforcement.[67] Despite the lack of initial screening, the Court of Justice decisively confirmed that there are other legal routes open for achieving public policy objectives.[68] This point is further reinforced by contrasting the differentiated stance of the Court of Justice in regard to efficiency justifications under Article 102 TFEU in (older) public enforcement cases and (more recent) private enforcement cases.[69] The receptiveness of the Court to efficiency justifications in a private enforcement case indicates that the 'self-policing' argument cannot provide an adequate explanation of the unaltered stance of the Court of Justice in regard to the rejection of public policy justifications.

Besides, the fact that all cases in which a public policy justification was advanced failed on the facts may be considered a weak proxy for arguing in absolute terms that genuine public policy considerations and conduct by dominant undertakings are mutually exclusive. However, it can be considered one indication, in comparative terms, when juxtaposed to the contrary view that regulation genuinely in the public interest by market participation is, hypothetically, possible.

[67] This point is not invalidated by the fact that the Hellenic Competition Commission (HCC) was the first to send the same preliminary reference to the Court of Justice, which was rejected as inadmissible, in Case C-53/03 *SYFAIT and others v GlaxoSmithKline plc and GlaxoSmithKline AEVE* [2005] ECR I- 4609. The reason for this is that the litigation before the Greek Civil Courts, namely the actions for damages for violation of Article 102 TFEU, pre-dated the complaint to the HCC. The relevant judgments by the Athens First Instance Court are remarkable inasmuch as they form the basis of the reasoning of both the HCC decision and the Court of Justice judgment in *Sotirios Lélos*; see also ch 3, n 147.

[68] This is also confirmed in a relatively more recent case under Article 101 TFEU, which reached the Court as a preliminary reference in the context of private enforcement of competition law. In Case C-68/12 *Protimonopolný úrad Slovenskej republiky v Slovenská sporiteľňa*, Judgment of 7 February 2013 (NYR) [19]–[20], the Court of Justice held that a restriction of competition by object may not be justified by the fact the affected competitor operated on the market illegally, namely, in that case, that the affected bank was operating in Slovakia without a licence from the National Slovakian Bank. The Court repeated the dictum that it is for public authorities and not private undertakings to ensure compliance with statutory requirements, which may require complex assessments.

[69] See ch 3, text to nn 20–21.

ii. 'Lobbying' and Incitement to Public Authorities to Act

According to the courts, the alternative to not allowing the dominant undertaking to shape public interest by otherwise 'abusive' market participation is to uphold the undertaking's right to approach the public authorities and either negotiate or lobby in favour of setting or enforcing specific regulations that may be considered to be anti-competitive.[70] The rationale for upholding the right of undertakings to influence public authorities was pointed out by AG Jacobs in *Albany*, with regard to the joint application by the employers and trade unions to the government to make affiliation to a sectoral pension fund compulsory for all undertakings belonging to the sector:

> Coordinated application to the State authorities is part of our democratic societies. Natural or legal persons are entitled to organise themselves and to submit jointly their requests to the government or the legislature. The public authorities then have to decide whether the proposed action is in the public interest. They have sole power, but also sole responsibility for their decision.[71]

This proposition itself may seem obvious. However, what is advanced here is a conjoint reading of the cases on the right of undertakings to 'lobby' under Article 102 TFEU as the reverse side of the cases that reject public policy justifications under Article 102 TFEU.

Indeed, the Commission and the General Court have held that mere efforts by undertakings to approach and influence public authorities at the national level are not, as such, infringements of the competition law provisions.[72] Similarly, with regard to the use of institutional channels at the EU level, the Commission found in *Industrie des Poudres Sphériques* that 'having recourse to a legitimate

[70] The issue has not been dealt with extensively from the perspective of the undertaking's conduct, even though there is a plethora of academic literature on 'regulatory capture' which is always internalised in the analysis of the conformity of the regulations with the competition provisions. For example, see H Vedder, 'Of Jurisdiction and Justification: Why Competition is Good for 'Non-Economic' Goals, But May Need to be Restricted' (2009) 6 *Competition Law Review* 55; and M Gal and I Faibish, 'Six Principles for Limiting Government-Facilitated Restraints on Competition' (2007) 44 *Common Market Law Review* 73–75. See also R Wainwright and A Bouquet, 'State Intervention and Action in EC Competition Law' [2003] *Fordham Corporate Law Institute* 560–62; and A Vossesstein, 'Corporate Efforts to Influence Public Authorities, and the EC Rules on Competition' (2000) 37 *Common Market Law Review* 1383–402, who, exceptionally, consider the right of the undertaking to approach government and its conformity with the competition provisions.

[71] Case C-67/96 *Albany International BV v Stichting Bedrijfspensioenfonds Textielindustrie* [1999] ECR I-5751, Opinion of AG Jacobs [293]. The Court of Justice did not rule on the issue because it held that agreements concluded in the context of collective negotiations between management and labour, in pursuit of social policy objectives, must, by virtue of their nature and purpose, be regarded as falling outside the scope of the competition provisions.

[72] *French-West African Shipowners' Committees* (Case IV/32.450) Commission Decision 92/262/EEC [1992] OJ L134/1 [68], on jointly approaching public authorities, in their own common interests; *Cement* (n 66) on jointly notifying public authorities about infringements and, to that end, holding preparatory discussions; and Case T-111/96 *ITT Promedia NV v Commission* [1998] ECR II-2937 [60] on bringing legal proceedings, which can be considered abusive in wholly exceptional circumstances.

instrument of [EU] law such as the anti-dumping procedure did not, in itself, constitute an abuse, even were a dominant position is to be demonstrated'.[73] The legality of the undertakings' conduct is consistent with the case law rejecting public policy considerations as objective justifications,[74] and confirms the argument that has been raised above. There are other means than exclusionary conduct by dominant undertakings for achieving public policy objectives, which decisively lie in the hands of the competent authorities, but which can be triggered, in part, by the undertakings themselves in the form of a genuine 'lobbying' effort to promote their own interest.

There is a question as to whether genuine 'lobbying' efforts by dominant undertakings to achieve changes in public policy and otherwise abusive conduct in the market genuinely in the public interest are in fact true alternatives from the perspective of the undertaking, as suggested by the courts. From the perspective of the undertaking, there is definitely a time gap, since otherwise exclusionary conduct in the market provides an 'instant' remedy to the undertaking's concerns about, eg, unsafe products or a shortage in medicines, whereas 'lobbying' can take considerable time and effort, particularly with regard to bringing in new regulations, rather than incitement to the public authorities to enforce the already existing regulations. Given the above-mentioned caveat, the following sections will explain why it is still normatively desirable not to allow public policy justifications under Article 102 TFEU. However, from the perspective of the public authorities, the European courts' firm position, at the descriptive level, that genuine 'lobbying' efforts by the dominant undertakings are neutral with regard to competition law assessment would also provide dominant undertakings with an incentive to invest more in 'lobbying'. Therefore, by showing that public policy considerations should not be allowed to operate as objective justifications under Article 102 TFEU, this jigsaw of incentives is being reinforced and allowed to fully unfold its potential.

B. The Potential for Abusive Conduct Genuinely in the Public Interest versus the Potential for Genuine 'Lobbying' Efforts

Section III.A described two alternative routes open to dominant undertakings for advancing public policy objectives. The first route is market participation which would otherwise constitute an abuse of dominance, but which is genuinely in the public interest. The second route is genuine 'lobbying' efforts for the adoption or enforcement of anti-competitive regulations by the competent authorities. The

[73] Commission (EC), 'XXVIth Report on Competition Policy-1996 (Published in Conjunction with the General Report on the Activities of the European Union-1996)' 1997 [138]–[139].

[74] This is pointed out by AG Jacobs in *Albany International BV* (n 71) [289], who distinguishes between mere efforts to convince public authorities and direct action against competing undertakings by citing *Cement* and *Hilti*, respectively.

first route should not be available, based on an examination of the potential for the genuine versus the corrupted form of each route to occur. There are no cases in which public policy justifications to otherwise abusive conduct are accepted on the facts; all the cases are about the corrupted form of that first route, namely meritless claims tactically used in litigation. In contrast, there is exceptionally little case law finding that the exercise of the right of the dominant undertaking to 'lobby' is not genuine, but, rather, constitutes an abuse of law. By showing the rarity of the latter instance in the European courts' case law, it is argued that there is no correlation between the potential for the two forms of each route to occur.

Private conduct that is an expression of the right of undertakings to approach and influence public authorities has been distinguished de facto from instances in which the preceding private conduct is not merely an incitement to public authorities to act, but a strategic use of regulatory rights, and the state conduct is merely a consolidation of the undertaking's expressed will.[75] These are instances in which the dominant undertaking unilaterally changes the regulatory situation and any subsequent state conduct exclusively relies upon the private conduct without examining its merits. This has been shown to be a very narrow issue and is dependent upon the factual instances of the litigation. So far, it has arisen under EU competition law provisions in only two cases, *CMB* and *AstraZeneca*, and the assessment of the undertaking's conduct is pinpointed by the context of the litigation.[76]

In *CMB*, a shipping conference was granted, by a non-Member State, the exclusive right to transport all cargoes, with the entitlement to agree to waive that right, and it was found that the conference's insistence on the government complying with their agreement as to the third parties' right to access the transport market was an abuse of a dominant position. The shipping conference's claim that its conduct was 'mere inducement of governmental action', namely of compliance with an agreement, was rejected by the General Court in a judgment which was affirmed by the Court of Justice.[77] According to Vossesstein, the reasoning of the European courts is misleading because it seems to be based on a distinction between a request to the public authorities to exercise discretionary powers

[75] Both E Blomme, 'State Action as a Defence against 81 and 82 EC' (2007) 30 *World Competition Law and Economics Review* 259 and Wainwright and Bouquet (n 70) 562 assume the distinction without providing any criteria for it.

[76] However, it should be noted that both cases could be used as examples of general principles of abuse of EU rights/law, regardless of the degree of market power of the undertaking involved and of Article 102 TFEU enforcement. On the emerging doctrine of 'abuse of EU rights/law', see E Sorensen, 'Abuse of Rights in Community Law: A Principle of Substance or Merely Rhetoric?' (2006) 43 *Common Market Law Review* 423–59; P Schammo, 'Arbitrage and Abuse of Rights in the EC Legal System' (2008) 14 *European Law Journal* 351–76; and the contributions in R de la Feria and S Vogenauer (eds), *Prohibition of Abuse of Law: A New General Principle of EU Law?* (Hart Publishing, 2011).

[77] Joined Cases T-24/93, T-25/93, T-26/93 and T-28/93 *Compagnie Maritime Belge Transports SA and Compagnie Maritime Belge SA and others v Commission* [1996] ECR II-1201 [88], [108]–[109]; Joined Cases C-395/96 P and C-396/96 P *Compagnie Maritime Belge Transports SA and others v Commission* [2000] ECR I-1365 [81]–[84].

and a request to comply with a specific contractual obligation.[78] Indeed, a more principled reasoning would be based upon the inverse order of succession of the private and state conduct in light of the facts of the case, as well as the exclusive reliance of the state conduct on the private conduct without any further examination of its merits. In *CMB*, it seems that the dominant undertaking first decided not to exercise its right to veto granted to it by an agreement with the government, and the government simply adhered to the latter agreement and consolidated the undertaking's will, although there had been no private conduct implementing the government's adherence to the agreement. More importantly, the conferral of exclusivity by the Zairian government could not be subject to EU rules, for example, on free movement, as would have been the case with a Member State.[79]

The facts- and evidence-specific nature of finding an abuse of rights is well illustrated in *AstraZeneca*. The General Court annulled part of the Commission decision that found the deregistration of the marketing authorisations for Losec capsules in Denmark to be an abuse of a dominant position because:

> [The Commission] did not establish that the Danish authorities were actually inclined to withdraw, potentially in violation of [Articles 34 and 36 TFEU], the parallel import licences as a result of AstraZeneca's deregistration of its marketing authorisation for reasons unrelated to public health.

Therefore, the Commission did not establish the causal order of succession of the private conduct and state conduct.[80] However, in principle the use of regulatory procedures by the dominant undertaking can qualify as an abuse of the dominant position, rather than mere inducement of the public authorities' conduct, if tangible evidence is adduced that:

> [T]he national authorities were liable to withdraw or did usually withdraw parallel import licences following the deregistration, at the request of their holder, of the marketing authorisations for the relevant product.[81]

[78] Vossesstein (n 70) 1397–98. See Joined Cases C-395/96 P and C-396/96 P *Compagnie Maritime Belge Transports SA and others v Commission* (n 77) [82], 'there is a difference between a request to a public authority to comply with a specific contractual obligation and mere incitement or inducement of the authority to take action. In the latter case, there is a simple attempt to influence the authority concerned in the exercise of its discretion. The purpose of a request to comply with a specific contractual obligation, by contrast, is to enforce legal rights which the authority concerned is, by definition, bound to observe'.

[79] In any case, the Court of Justice observed that 'Cewal sought to rely on the contractual exclusivity provided for in the Ogefrem Agreement in order to remove its only competitor from the market. Such conduct was in no way required by that agreement, since, under the second paragraph of Article 1 thereof, express provision is made for possible derogations, so that the requirements of [Article 102 TFEU] could be met': ibid [86].

[80] Case T- 321/05 *AstraZeneca AB and AstraZeneca plc v Commission* [2010] ECR II-02805 [848].

[81] ibid [845]–[846]; this was the case in AstraZeneca's conduct in Sweden, and the General Court did not annul the Commission decision, as it did with regard to Denmark and Norway; ibid [862]–[863].

In that case, the roles of the public and private conduct are inverted and the public authorities' conduct simply gives effect to the abusive unilateral change of the regulatory situation exercised by the dominant undertaking. This is a relatively narrow point, as opposed to the shared responsibility between the undertaking and the authorities.[82] In addition, it could be said that, in *AstraZeneca*, the conduct by the undertaking did not qualify as an 'incitement to public authorities to act' (or 'petitioning' in the US antitrust dialect),[83] because the public authorities would exclusively rely upon unilateral representations of the dominant undertaking before deregistration and withdrawal of parallel import licences.

Nevertheless, the difficulty of actually proving that the dominant undertaking's conduct is an abuse of rights and thus the exceptional character of the corrupted form of the second route is also indicated by the fact that, in *AstraZeneca*, the General Court upheld the Commission decision in relation to only one of the three Member States in which the undertaking had exercised its right.

C. The Potential for Added Costs in Terms of Legal Analysis

It has been argued so far that, given the alternative routes open to dominant undertakings, conduct by dominant undertakings and genuine public policy justifications are 'more mythical than real', if not mutually exclusive, because of the potential for state involvement to occur. In addition, permitting in principle the marginal potential for 'abusive' conduct genuinely in the public interest—which has so far never appeared as an evidentiary matter—also has potential costs in terms of legal analysis.

Retention of the possibility of advancing public policy justifications under Article 102 TFEU has added costs in terms of legal analysis because it can potentially lead to a distorted application of competition law. In particular, the concern is the application of competition law with a regulatory mindset, not in the actual case in which the public policy justification has arisen, but in subsequent cases in which there is no interface between competition and regulation. These are the majority of cases, since the category of cases in which the dominant undertaking genuinely claims public policy justifications to its otherwise abusive conduct is marginal, as shown above.

[82] T Graf, 'The General Court's Judgment in AstraZeneca, Interacting with Regulatory Authorities' (6 September 2010) Kluwer Competition Law Blog, available at http://kluwercompetitionlawblog.com/2010/09/06/the-general-court's-judgment-in-astrazeneca-interacting-with-regulatory-authorities/.

[83] For an analysis of the case along these lines, see M Maggiolino and ML Montagnani, 'AstraZeneca's Abuse of IPR-Related Procedures: A Hypothesis of Anti-trust Offence, Abuse of Rights, and IPR Misuse' (2011) 34 *World Competition Law and Economics Review* 248–53.

The most telling example of the potential assimilation of regular competition law analysis has occurred when the abuse takes the form of 'margin squeeze'.[84] The test governing 'margin squeeze' was established at the EU level in *Deutsche Telekom*, a case involving allegedly shared responsibility between the state and the dominant undertaking, which involved the regulatory obligation of the dominant undertaking to provide access to its network.[85]

The same test was applied soon afterwards in *TeliaSonera*, a case of allegedly abusive margin squeeze, which did not involve the regulatory obligation imposed upon the dominant undertaking to supply the input, but the undertaking had chosen to do this, and the supply was to new customers.[86] There are good economic arguments that, for a margin squeeze to be abusive, there should be (either a regulatory or) a competition law obligation to supply an indispensable input.[87] However, the Court simply cited *Deutsche Telekom* and held that indispensability of the input is just one element taken into account for the purposes of assessing the potential anti-competitive effect; even under that test, its absence is not always conclusive.[88] In contrast, AG Mazak argued in favour of the indispensability of the input as a condition for establishing margin squeeze as an abuse. He pointed to the submissions that a number of alternative technologies were available to provide end-users with broadband services, as well as that, in the long term, TeliaSonera's competitors might have been capable of buying another form of access.[89] In addition, the test for margin squeeze under Article 102 TFEU, established with a regulatory mindset in *Deutsche Telekom*, was further applied in a Greek margin squeeze case under the national competition law provisions. However, there was no regulatory obligation to provide bit-stream access, and historical data show that Internet Service Providers were shifting over time from bit-stream to Unbundled Local Loop.[90] Therefore, the distorted application of

[84] A similar point is made by H Auf'mkolk, 'The "Feedback Effect" of Applying EU Competition Law to Regulated Industries: Doctrinal Contamination in the Case of Margin Squeeze' (2012) 3 *Journal of Competition Law and Practice* 149, from the perspective of the concurrent application of generic competition law and sector-specific regulation, by using the example of 'margin squeeze'.

[85] *Deutsche Telekom AG* Commission Decision 2003/707/EC [2003] OJ L263/9; Case T-271/03 *Deutsche Telekom v Commission* [2008] ECR II-477; Case C-280/08 P *Deutsche Telekom v Commission* [2010] ECR I-09555.

[86] Case C-52/09 *Konkurrensverket v TeliaSonera Sverige AB* [2011] ECR I-00527.

[87] There is considerable literature on the exceptional nature of the duty to supply under competition law and, in particular, its impact upon incentives to innovate. See the most well-known contribution by E Elhauge, 'The Scope of Antitrust Process' (1991) 104 *Harvard Law Review* 295.

[88] *Konkurrensverket v TeliaSonera Sverige AB* (n 86) [69]–[72].

[89] ibid, Opinion of AG Mazak [16]–[21]. See, in support, D Geradin, 'Refusal to Supply and Margin Squeeze: A Discussion of Why the "Telefonica Exceptions" are Wrong' (2011) TILEC Discussion Paper 009, http://papers.ssrn.com/sol3/papers.cfm?abstract_id=1762687; Auf'mkolk (n 84) 156.

[90] EETT No 447/01/26-07-2007 (in Greek). See V Brisimi and D Yannelis, 'The Price Squeeze Test as a "Wildcard" at the Hands of Competition Authorities: The Example of the Greek Broadband Internet Services Market' (2012) 35 *Competition and Regulation in Network Industries* 2–18 for a critical analysis.

competition law analysis spills over into national competition law, side by side with EU competition law.

D. Attribution as a Question Distinct from, and Prior to, the Substantive Legality Test

The research presented so far indicates that public policy justifications and market participation by dominant undertakings are, in practice, mutually exclusive. There is always the potential for state involvement when public policy considerations come into play, triggered in part by the lobbying efforts of the dominant undertakings. In this section it is suggested that the debate should move forward to explore the question of attribution of the anti-competitive effect to the undertaking or the state before assessment of the substantive legality of the conduct takes place. The somewhat more recent example of a market separation case under Article 102 TFEU, *Sotirios Lélos*, illustrates the importance of recognising the question of attribution as a step prior to applying a particular substantive legality test to the dominant undertaking's conduct.[91]

The argument advanced is exemplified by depicting a chain of conduct by both the undertaking and the state, such as approaching the public authorities and 'lobbying' by the dominant undertaking, state action in the public interest that facilitates or encourages abuse or even renders abuse superfluous, and allegedly abusive conduct by the dominant undertaking. The fact that the efforts by dominant undertakings preceded the state conduct in the chain of conduct does not render such efforts the source of the anti-competitive effect and of the exclusion of competitors. Therefore, it does not exert any effect upon the legality of the subsequent state action or of the private action, which is causally linked to state conduct. Otherwise, only the undertaking would be able to claim that its allegedly abusive conduct is justified by the same public interest considerations that underpin state regulation. The context of the litigation in *Sotirios Lélos* fits this paradigmatic sequence of conduct.

In *Sotirios Lélos*, the undertaking participated in price negotiations with the public authorities at the national level, state regulations set the selling prices for medicines and/or the scales of reimbursement for the cost of prescription medicines by the relevant social health insurance systems, and the undertaking refused to supply wholesalers in low-price Member States that engaged in parallel trade. The judicial proceedings were only launched in regard to the last form of conduct (refusal to supply). The undertaking advanced a justification based on the second form of conduct within Article 102 TFEU (state price regulation in the public interest alleged to be an obstacle to the undertaking's protection of its commercial

[91] *Sotirios Lélos* (n 64).

interests). The Court of Justice, on its own motion, pre-fixed the first conduct (the undertaking's participation in price negotiations) to state regulation in order to dismiss the undertaking's defence, while admitting that the defence ought to be operating at the applicability level.[92]

From the perspective of attribution, the Court could have had recourse to the undertaking's participation in price negotiations. However, it should have then dismissed the defence that the market distortion stems from state regulation, on the basis that the dominant undertaking took its turn in influencing public health expenditure and the amount of pharmaceutical research and development expenditure subsidised by the state. An alternative to this is that the Court should not have invoked the undertaking's participation in price negotiations, as this is neutral in regard to competition law assessment and is therefore immaterial in assessing the legality of the subsequent both state and private conducts. In that way, the Court would have been obliged to assess the legality of the state regulation.

Unfortunately, the Court of Justice, following the Opinion of AG Colomer,[93] held that:

> [T]he level at which the selling price or the amount of reimbursement of a given medicinal product is fixed reflects the relative strength of both the public authorities of the relevant Member State and the pharmaceuticals companies at the time of the price negotiations for that product.[94]

Based on the above, the Court further ruled, by reference to the Treaty clause on 'a system ensuring that competition in the Internal Market is not distorted',[95] that:

> [A]lthough the degree of price regulation in the pharmaceuticals sector *cannot preclude the Community rules on competition from applying* … it cannot be ignored that such State intervention is one of the factors liable to create opportunities for parallel trade. Furthermore … the Community rules on competition are also incapable of being interpreted in such a way that, *in order to defend its own commercial interests*, the only choice left for a pharmaceuticals company in a dominant position is not to place its medicines on the market at all in a Member State where the prices of those products are set at a relatively low level.[96]

Sotirios Lélos, viewed from the perspective of attribution of the market-distorting effect, indicates that whenever public policy justifications in proceedings under

[92] AG Mazak in his Opinion in Case C-280/08 P *Deutsche Telekom v Commission* (n 85) [13] hints at this interconnection between the use by the Court of the 'negotiations' criterion and the applicability of Article 102 TFEU, rather than the actual way that the Article is to be applied, by citing the Court's judgment in *Sotirios Lélos* when discussing the attribution of the alleged infringement in *Deutsche Telekom* and, therefore, the applicability of Article 102 TFEU.

[93] *Sotirios Lélos* (n 64) Opinion of AG Colomer [90]–[93].

[94] ibid [63].

[95] ibid [66].

[96] ibid [67]–[68], emphasis added.

Article 102 TFEU come into play,[97] there has been the potential for state involvement, triggered in part by the dominant undertaking's 'lobbying' efforts. Had the Court focused on a more principled examination of the causal link between the state and the undertaking's conducts, the test applied under Article 102 TFEU would probably have been different or, at least, have been explicitly allied with a concomitant assessment of the state conduct's legality, arguably under the free movement provisions.[98]

IV. CONCLUSIONS

This chapter has explored the interface between market separation as an abuse of the dominant position and non-economic justifications, as reflected in the notion of justified trade barriers. It has been argued that adding a trade barrier into the justification test initiates a dynamic and discursive process of competence distribution between the EU and the Member States for market regulation, rather than determining the substantive, non-economic content of such regulation in itself. The link between justified trade barriers and subsequent legislative action at either level is confirmed by the listing of the competence to build the Internal Market in the category of shared competences (Article 4(2)(a) TFEU).

An equivalent link is missing from the application of Article 102 TFEU and any (hypothetical) subsequent legislative intervention. Rather, the reverse link exists and this is confirmed by the listing of the competence to establish rules on competition in the category of exclusive competences of the EU (Article 3(1)(b) TFEU). Legislative action establishing the rules on competition precedes the implementation, centralised or decentralised, of these rules. Therefore, inasmuch as such legislative action integrating public policy considerations with competition law has not taken place, it cannot be assumed that non-market considerations, as reflected in the notion of justified trade barriers, are within the scope of Article 102 TFEU; otherwise, the competence distribution for market regulation would be 'pre-empted'.

Subsequently, this chapter examined the existing cases in which a dominant undertaking has advanced a claim that its very same, allegedly abusive, conduct is justified by public policy considerations. So far, such claims have never been shown, as an evidentiary issue, to be genuine, but, rather, have been used strategically in litigation. By contrast, alternative routes, such as genuine 'lobbying' efforts for the adoption and enforcement of 'anti-competitive' regulations, which have been pinpointed by the European courts as the other side of the coin, have

[97] *Sotirios Lélos* falls into that category, with the twist that the dominant undertaking did not allege public policy justifications for its own conduct, but, rather, invoked state regulation in the public interest as an impediment to protecting the undertaking's own commercial interests.

[98] See ch 5, text to nn 152–53 for the outcome of such potential assessment.

very rarely been found to constitute an abuse of rights. Therefore, whenever public policy considerations come into play, there is always the potential for state involvement. In addition, permitting these more mythical than real claims to be advanced may lead to spillover from cases in which a 'regulatory competition law' applies to cases appropriate for regular competition law analysis. The suggested way forward for the academic debate, as well as for better reasoned Court judgments, is to recognise that the question of the interface between a dominant undertaking's conduct and public policy justifications is a question of unclear attribution to the undertaking or the state. Subsequently, the focus should be on revising the state action defence, with an emphasis on clarifying the substantive test that governs the type, as well as the intensity, of the link between the state and the private conduct.

It is noteworthy that research in relation to both Treaty-based arguments presented in this chapter and the interpretation of the case law converge in regard to the reason why it is neither permitted nor desirable to introduce public policy considerations within the scope of Article 102 TFEU. This reason is the risk of a biased outcome against the Member State concerned and its non-market identity, and this conclusion will be applied in the subsequent chapters of this book in which the question of attribution is addressed.

5

Shared Responsibility for Market Separation by Dominant Undertakings and the State: The Question of Attribution Revisited

I. INTRODUCTION

Chapter four identified non-principled attribution as the analytical core of the interface between market separation, as an abuse of the dominant position, and non-economic values, as reflected in the notion of justified trade barriers under the free movement provisions. When public policy considerations come into play under Article 102 TFEU, there is always the potential for state involvement to occur, triggered in part by the incitement of dominant undertakings on public authorities to take action. Therefore, non-economic justifications to market separation cases raise de facto the question of attribution of the anti-competitive effect.

Chapters five and six build on these conclusions and seek to provide criteria for a principled attribution of the market-distorting effect to the dominant undertaking and/or the state, in these cases of shared responsibility for market separation. This chapter explores the so-called 'state action defence' as the closest concept for articulating attribution criteria used by the European courts. The fact that a state action defence has never succeeded so far lends support to the preliminary assumption that it does not provide adequate or operable attribution criteria. The analysis in this chapter fully confirms this assumption; hence, alternative solutions are introduced in chapter six.

The state action defence, as currently construed by case law, determines whether Article 102 TFEU is applicable and involves the claim that the conduct by the dominant undertaking is imposed by state regulation, at the national or the EU level, in the public interest. The essence of the claim is that, if it were not for such state action, the conduct of the dominant undertaking would not have occurred at all. Therefore, what is in the public interest or the substance of the non-market values promoted by the state regulation are not directly invoked.

From an analytical point of view, any academic discussion as to the normative value of the state action defence is linked to the question as to whether public policy justifications should also be available to undertakings under the competition provisions. The reason is that the state action defence, as a construction, seems to be aimed at counterbalancing principled objections to the legality of the undertaking's conduct, namely that there is a lack of democratic authorisation, rather than defending a specific public policy objective. The dominant undertaking is not claiming to have unilaterally defined a public policy objective, but, rather, that its conduct is authorised by the state as part of the pursuance of a public policy objective and therefore any restriction of competition should be attributed to the state.[1] The academic literature does not distinguish between the 'attribution' and 'legality' of the conduct by either the state or the undertaking, but attempts to incorporate considerations, based on both the democratic authorisation of the actor and the substantive values underpinning the measure, into one procedural test.[2] However, attribution should logically be determined first, since it leads to the identification of the entity that acts on each occasion.

In light of the above, this chapter analyses the state action defence as currently construed by case law. First, it examines the type of link as well as the intensity of the link required between the dominant undertaking's conduct and state regulation for a state action defence to succeed. Second, it examines the type of link and the intensity of the link between the undertaking's conduct and state regulation to assess the conformity of state regulation with Article 102 TFEU in conjunction with Article 4(3) TEU-L (the state action doctrine). In addition, whether the legality of the state action can be assessed against the free movement provisions, independently of any private conduct by undertakings, is explored.

The emphasis of this inquiry is on recent market separation cases, in particular *Deutsche Telekom* and *Sotirios Lélos*.[3] In these cases there were no procedural means by which the dominant undertaking was able to bring claims based on the alleged illegality of the state regulation before the EU courts. This assessment of the legality of state regulation cannot be accommodated under the state action defence as currently construed. In addition, it is the first time that the factual

[1] As pointed out by G Davies, 'Article 86 EC, the EC's Economic Approach to Competition Law, and the General Interest' (2009) 5 *European Competition Journal* 565, this is the case of the exceptions under Article 106(2) TFEU regarding undertakings entrusted with the operation of services of general economic interest or having the character of a revenue-producing monopoly.

[2] See, for example, J Baquero Cruz, 'The State Action Doctrine' in G Amato and C-D Ehlermann (eds), *EC Competition Law: A Critical Assessment* (Hart Publishing, 2007) 588–90; and H Schepel, 'Delegation of Regulatory Powers to Private Parties under EC Competition Law: Towards a Procedural Public Interest Test' (2002) 39 *Common Market Law Review* 33. The most complete articulation of the process view, in the context of the US antitrust distinction between state and private action, is by E Elhauge, 'The Scope of Antitrust Process' (1991) 104 *Harvard Law Review* 667, whose arguments stem from the view that financially interested actors cannot be trusted to decide which restrictions on competition advance the public interest, whereas financially disinterested and politically accountable actors are able to make such decisions.

[3] Case C-280/08 P *Deutsche Telekom v Commission* [2010] ECR I-09555; Joined Cases C-468/06–478/06 *Sotirios Lélos kai Sia EE and others v GlaxoSmithKline AEVE Farmakeftikon Proïonton, formerly Glaxowellcome AEVE* [2008] ECR I-7139.

scenarios in these market separation cases would need to be assessed under Article 102 TFEU in conjunction with Article 4(3) TEU-L, rather than in conjunction with Article 106(1) TFEU.

In the final section of the chapter, the interplay between private and state responsibility for breach of Article 102 TFEU is described, based on the above structural analysis of the state action defence and the state action doctrine in market separation cases. It is argued that the state action defence is not adequate as a threshold for determining the scope of application of Article 102 TFEU and this is why it has never succeeded. Whenever public policy considerations (and, hence, at least potential state action) come into play, the degree of legislative constraint upon the undertaking's autonomous conduct (relevant for the state action defence) necessarily leads to finding an abuse of dominance and establishing private responsibility for breach of Article 102 TFEU. This is depicted by the dual use of the clause on a 'system of undistorted competition in the Internal Market': first, to establish the state action doctrine and, second, to substantiate market separation as an abuse of the dominant position whenever a state action defence has not succeeded.

II. ABUSE AND THE STATE ACTION DEFENCE: ESTABLISHING PRIVATE RESPONSIBILITY

A state action defence in EU competition law is based upon the claim that the dominant undertaking's abusive conduct is required by state legislation, and for that reason, it should be outwith the scope of Article 102 TFEU. The defence relies on two main elements, namely the type of the link required between state legislation and the undertaking's conduct, and the intensity of that link. It is argued that the determinations by the European courts of these two elements are inadequate and involve major problems. First, the rejection of a legality-type of link bolsters the Commission's decision to address responsibility only against the undertaking from judicial review. Second, the requirement of compulsion, for ascertaining conduct which is not autonomous, means, in practice, that if compulsion were to exist, the activity would not be an economic function in the first place; hence, the inquiry about 'state compulsion' would not be a stand-alone one, but rather merged with the inquiry as to whether there is an 'undertaking'. On the other hand, where compulsion does not exist, this can only be asserted on the basis of a substantive competition law analysis of the market involved. In this case, the mismatch between the consequence, namely the inapplicability of the competition law provision, and the process of establishing the 'autonomous conduct', namely a substantive competition law analysis, indicates that the state action contributes, in part, to the market-distorting effect and highlights the problem of rejecting a legality-type of link between the private and state conduct.

A. The Type of Link between State Legislation and the Undertaking's Conduct: The Legality, Purpose and Margin of Autonomous Conduct

This section explores how a prior assessment of the legality of the state regulation or, more broadly, of the state action is excluded from the contours of proceedings against the dominant undertaking under Article 102 TFEU. The only material consideration, according to the case law, is whether the prior state action affects the autonomous conduct of the dominant undertaking. It is argued that this exclusion of a legality-type of link under the state action defence is problematic inasmuch as the Commission has unrestrained discretion as to whom and how to address market separation in situations of shared responsibility between the undertaking (in proceedings under Regulation 1/2003) and the state (in proceedings under Article 258 TFEU).

Indeed, the case law has, so far, considered that the legality or the purpose of the national legislation is immaterial in the context of a state action defence. The only criterion, as formulated in *Ladbroke Racing* by the Court of Justice, is whether the implicated undertaking is able to behave autonomously and engage in the conduct on its own initiative. In particular, competition rules may apply where 'the national legislation does not preclude the undertakings it governs from engaging in autonomous conduct that prevents, restricts or distorts competition'.[4] Conversely, a state compulsion defence (and thus the inapplicability of Article 102 TFEU) is only accepted if the anti-competitive conduct is 'required of undertakings by national legislation or if national legislation creates a legal framework which, itself, eliminates any possibility of competitive activity on the undertakings' part'.[5]

By contrast, in the judgment under appeal, the General Court ruled that the Commission could not decide on the part of the complaint concerning the undertakings without deciding on the substance of the complaint against the state, ie, on the compatibility of the national legislation with Article 106 TFEU. This is due to the fact that proceedings regarding the substance of the complaint against the state were still in progress at the time.[6] This led the Commission to challenge the judgment on the basis that the General Court established:

> [A]n order of priority as between the procedure provided for in [Regulation 1/2003] … and the procedure against a Member State for failure to fulfil its obligations, which is incompatible with the Commission's discretion to decide what aspect of a complaint should be considered first and against whom (the undertakings or the State) proceedings should be first initiated.[7]

[4] Joined Cases C-359/95 P and C-379/95 P *Commission and French Republic v Ladbroke Racing* [1997] ECR I-6265 [34].

[5] ibid [33].

[6] Case T-548/93 *Ladbroke Racing v Commission* [1995] ECR II-2565 [43]–[50].

[7] *Commission and French Republic v Ladbroke Racing* (n 4) [16].

It is noteworthy that, slightly earlier, the Commission itself decided to suspend the procedure it had initiated under (what is now) Regulation 1/2003 in *Rendo*, which concerned the prohibition on the importation of electricity in the field of public supply. The Commission suspended the procedure on the ground that this prohibition was covered by a new (national) law. It decided to 'defer consideration of that issue until the proceedings which are to be brought against the Kingdom of the Netherlands under [Article 258 TFEU]' (relating to public monopolies in the sector of trade in electricity)[8] yielded an outcome 'which will determine the assessment to be made, in the light of [Article 106(2) TFEU] of the corresponding restrictions'.[9] The General Court, once again, confirmed the Commission's decision. It curtailed the Commission's discretion by establishing a hierarchy between the two procedures against the undertakings under (what is now) Regulation 1/2003 and the Member State concerned under Article 258 TFEU, on the basis that examination of the legality of the national law under Article 258 TFEU proceedings involves questions of national public policy interests which are likely to be the subject of political and institutional debate.[10] According to the General Court, this would even justify the delay in the exercise of the procedural rights of the complainants, which would need to apply for the procedure under Regulation 1/2003 to be continued only once the procedure under Article 258 TFEU has come to an end.[11]

Rendo involved market separation considerations in the form of import prohibitions, albeit under Article 101 TFEU. At the same time, it raises the question of justified restrictions on the basis of national public policy interests in the field of energy, which are not embedded in competition law analysis. Indeed, the Court

[8] Case T-16/91 *Rendo NV, Centraal Overijsselse Nutsbedrijven NV and Regionaal Energiebedrijf Salland NV v Commission* [1992] ECR II-2417 [48].

[9] ibid [47]. The relevant case is one of the electricity monopoly cases in the mid-1990s, namely Case C-157/94 *Commission v Kingdom of the Netherlands* [1997] ECR I-5699.

[10] Case T-16/91 *Rendo NV, Centraal Overijsselse Nutsbedrijven NV and Regionaal Energiebedrijf Salland NV v Commission* [1992] ECR II-2417 [103]–[107]. In this case, it was only the complainants which challenged the General Court judgment, which was later confirmed by the European Court of Justice. However, the Court focused on the finding that the Commission was entitled to take the view that the Article 258 TFEU procedure was the most appropriate procedure for assessing the compatibility of the national law with the Treaty, rather than on the finding that ruling on the anti-competitive object or effect of the agreement could not have any practical effect so long as it had not been established that the national law in question is incompatible with the Treaty; Case C-19/93 P *Rendo NV, Centraal Overijsselse Nutsbedrijven NV and Regionaal Energiebedrijf Salland NV v Commission* [1995] ECR I-3319 [22]–[23].

[11] Case T-16/91 *Rendo NV, Centraal Overijsselse Nutsbedrijven NV* (n 10) [111]. However, the fact that the procedural rights of the complainants have been impaired is what renders the decision to suspend the administrative proceedings under Regulation 1/2003 actionable: ibid [53]–[57], confirmed in Joined Cases T-377/00, T-379/00, T-380/00, T-260/01 and T-272/01 *Philip Morris International, Inc and others v Commission* [2003] ECR II-1 [99]. *Cf* Case T-59/00 *Compagnia Portuale Pietro Chiesa Soc coop rl v Commission* [2001] ECR II-1019 [49]–[52], in which the Commission initiated, first, proceedings against the Member State and would only potentially initiate proceedings against the undertaking. This scenario does not render actionable any act by the Commission by which it informs the complainant of the progress of the first proceedings.

of Justice dismissed the Commission application against the Netherlands under Article 258 TFEU on the basis that the Commission had not adequately taken into account the justifications advanced by the Member State concerned under Article 106(2) TFEU for the exclusive import rights, which were, otherwise, incompatible with Article 37 TFEU.[12] The justifications in that case concerned the supply of electricity across the country in a socially responsible manner with costs that are as low as possible. Had the Commission not suspended proceedings against the undertaking under Regulation 1/2003, it would not have been possible for the Court to give due consideration to national public policy interests that were justified under Article 106(2) TFEU.[13]

The only case in which the Commission actually took 'double action' against both the undertaking and the Member State was the *CNSD* case, which involved the setting of compulsory tariffs by a public body, the representatives of customs agents, for their services. The Commission first issued a decision against the undertaking under Article 101 TFEU which was challenged before the General Court. Pending the appeal, the Commission initiated proceedings against Italy under Article 258 TFEU. The General Court stayed proceedings pending the judgment of the Court of Justice and rejected the appeal after the Court of Justice condemned Italy for failure to fulfil its obligations under Article 4(3) TEU-L (ex-Article 10 TEC) in conjunction with Article 101 TFEU.[14]

After the Court of Justice judgment in *Ladbroke Racing*, it is clear that substantive compatibility of national legislation with competition rules is not decisive as to the applicability and actual application of Article 102 TFEU (and Article 101 TFEU) to the conduct of undertakings which comply with that legislation. Therefore, whether the national legislation is justified on the basis of public interest or not is immaterial for the purposes of ascertaining the lawfulness, under Article 102 TFEU, of the undertaking's conduct in conformity with the legislation. The sole purpose of a prior evaluation of national legislation is to determine what effect that legislation may have on the existence of such conduct.[15]

Deutsche Telekom stands out from the subsequent cases in which the issue has arisen. It is a market separation case under Article 102 TFEU, which involved an allegedly abusive margin squeeze between regulated wholesale prices and approved retail tariffs regulated by a price cap in the markets for access to the Unbundled Local Loop (ULL). The European institutions equated the competitive harm with raising barriers to entry for out-of-state competitors.[16] Deutsche Telekom challenged, before the Court of Justice, the premise that the existence of

[12] *Commission v Kingdom of the Netherlands* (n 9).

[13] ibid [63]–[71].

[14] Case C-35/96 *Commission v Italian Republic* [1998] ECR I-3851; Case T-513/93 *Consiglio Nazionale degli Spedizionieri Doganali (CNSD) v Commission* [2000] ECR II-01807.

[15] See section II.B on the intensity of the required link.

[16] See ch 2, text to n 34.

scope of autonomous conduct, in this case the scope to adjust its retail prices for end-user access services to the ULL, is a necessary and sufficient requirement for the attribution of an infringement of Article 102 TFEU. It argued that both the legality and the purpose of the national regulatory intervention should also be taken into consideration.[17]

The Court of Justice insisted that the type of link between the national regulatory intervention and the dominant undertaking's conduct required for a state action defence to succeed is only related to the scope of autonomous conduct by the undertaking. The fact that the national regulatory intervention, in that case by the German Regulatory Authority for Telecommunications and Post (RegTP), is itself potentially incompatible with Article 102 TFEU in conjunction with Article 4(3) TEU-L (ex-Article 10 TEC) is immaterial. The reason is that Deutsche Telekom was able to make applications to the RegTP for authorisation to adjust its retail prices for end-user access services within the price cap.[18] Therefore, it could be argued that the content of autonomous conduct involves the exercise of the undertaking's right to approach the public authorities and incite them to change their conduct. This is consistent with the analysis in chapter four on subjecting to Article 102 TFEU the right of dominant undertakings to 'lobby'.[19] However, it should not have any normative implications in regard to the legality of the national authorities' conduct as such.

Similarly, the Court ruled that assessment of the purpose of the regulatory intervention is immaterial and could in no way deny the appellant the opportunity to engage in autonomous conduct. It ruled in this manner in relation to the prohibition of cross-subsidisation between retail access services or in relation to a weighted average retail price for a basket of broadband and narrowband access services.[20]

In addition, the Court refused to review the exercise of the Commission's discretion to initiate proceedings against the Member State concerned (Germany) in the context of litigation under Regulation 1/2003, as it considered this to be outside the remit of those proceedings.[21] Proceedings against Germany could have been initiated for failure to ensure the fulfilment by the RegTP of its obligations under EU law, including compliance with Article 102 TFEU and Article 4(3) TEU-L.[22] The

[17] *Deutsche Telekom v Commission* (n 3) [66]–[73].

[18] ibid [85]–[91]. The finding that Deutsche Telekom was able to make applications for retail price adjustments was not challenged. Also, the Court of Justice rejected as inadmissible claims in relation to wholesale prices made both by the Commission (that Deutsche Telekom had scope to adjust, in addition, its wholesale prices for access services by applying for a reduction of its wholesale prices if its costs decreased) and by the appellant (that the wholesale prices set by the RegTP were excessive and not cost-oriented); ibid [35]–[43].

[19] See ch 4, section III.A.ii.

[20] *Deutsche Telekom v Commission* (n 3) [92]–[95].

[21] ibid [44]–[47].

[22] The fact that the sector is governed by EU regulations aimed at gradually increasing competition and providing national authorities with discretion in that respect does not prejudge the application of Article 4(3) TEU-L and Article 106(1) TFEU. See, in relation to air transport services, Case 66/86 *Ahmed Saeed Flugreisen and Silver Line Reisebüro GmbH v Zentrale zur Bekämpfung unlauteren Wettbewerbs eV* [1989] ECR 803 [50]–[52]. In addition, contrary to some commentators, eg,

way the Commission has exercised its discretion, as well as the judicial control of such exercise, in this case only against the operator, Deutsche Telekom, is contrasted with the exercise of the same powers in the case of tariff imbalances in Spain. In the latter case, the Commission was led to, first, initiate proceedings against the Member State concerned in 2001[23] and, subsequently, to fine under Regulation 1/2003 and issue a decision against Telefónica, the Spanish traditional operator for alleged margin squeeze abuse of its dominant position (from September 2001 until December 2006).[24] However, only in the case brought by the Commission against Spain was there an opportunity for the Court to hold that Telefónica's commercial freedom, even to the maximum extent under the price cap system, was insufficient to achieve the tariff rebalancing and that the tariff imbalances were partly attributable to the Spanish authorities (at least for the period 2001–02).[25] It is noteworthy that Spain itself brought an action for annulment of the Commission decision against Telefónica, essentially suggesting that Spain, by acting through the Spanish regulator for telecommunications as an organ of the state, might have been a better target for the Commission than Telefónica.[26] However, the General Court repeated that even if the Spanish regulator had infringed a rule of EU law and the Commission could initiate proceedings against Spain based on Article 258 TFEU, such possibilities have no effect on the lawfulness of the Commission decision against Telefónica for breach of Article 102 TFEU.[27]

This confirms that there is in fact no judicial control over the exercise of the Commission's discretion to initiate proceedings under Article 258 TFEU in

M Hellwig, 'Competition Policy and Sector Specific Regulation for Network Industries' (2008) Preprints for the Max Planck Institute for Research on Collective Goods, Bonn 2008/29 6–7, the principle of supremacy of EU law vis-a-vis national law does not preclude a state action defence from applying where the undertakings have not contested the validity of national regulation. See Case C-198/01 *CIF v Autorità Garante della Concorrenza e del Mercato* [2003] ECR I-8055 [49]–[50], [52]–[55], in which the Court of Justice tried to resolve the tension by imposing on National Competition Authorities a duty to disapply the national legislation, while limiting the state compulsion defence to immunity from fines and damages for past conduct; see R Wainwright and R Bouquet, 'State Intervention and Action in EC Competition Law' [2003] *Fordham Corporate Law Institute* 552–57. However, in *Deutsche Telekom*, the Commission did not impose a symbolic fine on Deutsche Telekom, but simply reduced the basic amount of the fine by 10 per cent; *Deutsche Telekom AG*, Commission Decision 2003/707/EC [2003] OJ L 263/9 [212], confirmed in Case T-271/03 *Deutsche Telekom v Commission* [2008] ECR II-477 [310]–[313] and *Deutsche Telekom v Commission* (n 3) [277]–[279].

[23] Case C-500/01 *Commission v Kingdom of Spain* [2004] ECR I-583.

[24] *Wanadoo Espana v Telefónica* (Case COMP/38.784) [2008] OJ C 83/6 (Summary Commission Decision).

[25] See *Commission v Kingdom of Spain* (n 23) [37] in relation to the tariff imbalances recorded for the period after the introduction of the price cap system at the retail level. Whether such a pronouncement regarding state responsibility had any effect upon the level of the fine imposed on Telefónica cannot be asserted by comparison with *Deutsche Telekom*. This is because in *Telefónica*, the wholesale prices were not regulated and hence, according to the Commission, 'the room for manoeuvre left by regulation to Telefónica was much wider than that in *Deutsche Telekom*'; *Wanadoo Espana v Telefónica* (n 24) [748].

[26] Case T-398/07 *Kingdom of Spain v Commission*, Judgment of 29 March 2012 (NYR). Telefónica lodged a separate action for annulment of the same Commission Decision (Case T-336/07).

[27] ibid [115].

situations in which it decides to attribute the responsibility exclusively to the undertaking. Even though the Commission itself seems to accept, in *Deutsche Telekom*, that the RegTP was to some extent responsible for the margin squeeze,[28] it would be counter-productive for the Commission to initiate proceedings against Germany in order to discipline the National Regulatory Authorities (NRAs), because this would undermine the cooperative management of the decentralised enforcement of the sector-specific regulation.[29] Therefore, the Commission was shielded from judicial review as to its exercise of discretion not to initiate proceedings under Article 258 TFEU. Subsequent institutional reforms in the electronic communications sector, including the establishment of the Body of European Regulators for Electronic Communications (BEREC),[30] may suggest that the rationale for enforcing Article 102 TFEU against Deutsche Telekom lay within the Commission's own limited powers to regulate the NRAs.[31] In other words, if in the context of a state action defence in proceedings under Regulation 1/2003 the European courts do not adopt a legality criterion (of the national legislation or, more broadly, of the state action), the Commission's exercise of discretion as to whom, and how, the market distortion is attributed remains outside the scope of judicial review.

It is true that the Commission's exercise of discretion in regard to the instigation of proceedings against the Member State concerned is unconstrained. The Court has held that 'decisions whereby the Commission closes the case definitively on complaints of a State's conduct capable of giving rise to the initiation of infringement proceedings are not challengeable acts'.[32] Similarly, it is settled case law that:

> [I]ndividuals do not have standing to challenge a refusal by the Commission to initiate proceedings against a Member State for failure to fulfil its obligations. The Commission is not required to commence proceedings for failure to fulfil obligations, but enjoys a discretion, which precludes any right for individuals to require it to take a specific position and to bring an action against its refusal to take action.[33]

[28] '[The RegTP] made only a rough assessment to check that the applicable index figures were respected and that the proposed charges did not manifestly breach the requirements of the Telecommunications Act': *Deutsche Telekom AG* (n 22) [165]. C Veljanovski, 'Margin Squeezes in Telecoms' (2008) www.casecon.com/data/pdfs/MSIntermedia2008.pdf points to the inconsistency of the approach since, had the RegTP fixed rather than capped the retail tariffs, no competition law infringement by Deutsche Telekom would have been found, but, simply, an unfortunate regulatory error. G Monti, 'Managing the Intersection of Utilities Regulation and EC Competition Law' (2008) 4 *Competition Law Review* 129–31 associates the weakness of the RegTP with political interferences that undermine its independency.

[29] N Petit, 'The Proliferation of National Regulatory Authorities alongside Competition Authorities: A Source of Jurisdictional Confusion?' in D Geradin, R Muñoz and N Petit (eds), *Regulating through Agencies in the EU: A New Paradigm of European Governance* (Edward Elgar, 2005) 200.

[30] Council Regulation (EC) 1211/2009 establishing the Body of European Regulators for Electronic Communications (BEREC) and the Office [2009] OJ L 337/1 (Article 1).

[31] Similarly, see R O'Donoghue, 'Regulating the Regulated: DeutscheTelekom v European Commission' (2008) 1 *Global Competition Policy* 5.

[32] Eg, Case T-247/04 *Aseprofar and Edifa v Commission* [2005] ECR II-3449 [60].

[33] Eg, Case T-443/03 *Retecal and others v Commission* [2005] ECR II-1803 [44]; similarly, see *Aseprofar and Edifa v Commission* (n 32) [40].

The lack of transparency in Article 258 TFEU proceedings has been an issue of concern more generally in relation to its functions both as securing the rule of law and as a public policy instrument.[34] However, the legality of the Commission's decision is of paramount importance in 'mixed situations' of allegedly shared responsibility by the Member State and the individual undertaking under competition law, since the 'authorities of the Member States may in certain cases have a sufficient degree of latitude in regulating certain matters … in light of the specific social and cultural features of each Member State',[35] which the undertakings do not have. This is confirmed by the case law in which the Commission's broad-ranging powers not to take action against a Member State under Article 106(3) TFEU are upheld and actions by individual complainants against the Commission for failure to act are rejected as inadmissible.[36] By contrast, there is strict judicial review of the Commission's obligation to state the facts on the basis of which it finds no infringement of the competition rules by undertakings and rejects a complaint, even though the Commission is under no obligation to rule on whether there has been an infringement.[37] This indicates that there is a purportedly differentiated treatment in the way in which the Commission decides on attributing responsibility to the Member States and the undertakings, justified by the nature of the entity that acts on each occasion. The nature of the actor may reasonably support the inadmissibility of actions against the Commission's decision not to initiate proceedings under Article 258 TFEU against a Member State, but would equally justify a stricter judicial control of Commission decisions fining an undertaking under Regulation 1/2003. Therefore, in cases of alleged shared responsibility by the undertaking and the state for market distortions, there is a tension between the two standards that are needed to apply to judicial review of the Commission's discretion to address such a responsibility.

The Commission's decision not to attribute responsibility to the Member State involved cannot be assessed in the context of proceedings under Regulation 1/2003 on the basis of an alleged state action defence, nor can the responsibility of the Member State, as such, be taken into account. An alternative route for the fined undertaking to seek relief would be to go to national courts and seek damages on the basis of state responsibility. The national court would then be obliged to make a preliminary reference to the Court of Justice. This is certainly inefficient in terms of judicial economy. A more principled objection is that the undertaking does not have, in advance, an obligation to assess the legality of the

[34] See, eg, European Parliament, 'Report on the 25th annual report from the Commission on monitoring the application of Community law (2007)' (6 April 2009) A6-0245/2009 [13]. See also the decision by the European Ombudsmen on complaint 1288/99/OV concerning the failure of the Commission to initiate proceedings against Greece, as a high-ranking Commission official was also involved in a Greek political party. See M Smith, *Centralised Enforcement, Legitimacy and Governance in the EU* (Routledge, 2009) for a thorough analysis of the multiple functions of infringement proceedings under Article 258 TFEU.

[35] *Ladbroke Racing Ltd v Commission* (n 6) [37].

[36] Eg, ibid [34]–[46]; Case T-111/96 *ITT Promedia NV v Commission* [1998] ECR II-2937 [95]–[98].

[37] Eg, Case T-387/94 *Asia Motor France SA and others v Commission* [1996] ECR II-961 [46].

regulatory framework in its everyday business decisions.[38] In addition, it may be the case that the Commission may lack information concerning regulatory violations by the Member State involved, which come to its attention for the very first time when competition proceedings are initiated.

B. The Intensity of the Link between State Legislation and the Undertaking's Conduct: Encouragement and Compulsion

In light of the adoption by the European courts of the autonomous conduct criterion, the subsequent question is how close the association between state legislation and the undertaking's conduct should be. As early as *Suiker Unie*, the Court of Justice held that 'if a national law merely encourages or makes it easier for undertakings to engage in autonomous anti-competitive conduct, those undertakings remain subject to [Articles 101 and 102 TFEU]'.[39] This only means that the 'behaviour of the undertakings concerned could not be regarded with the usual severity'[40] and, therefore, the fines imposed by the Commission had to be reduced, 'in light of the legal framework which is a mitigating factor'.[41] Similarly, the Court of Justice in *CIF* and *Deutsche Telekom* has upheld these propositions.[42]

The autonomy of the undertaking's conduct is therefore affirmed whenever any exercise of competitive conduct is permitted, including other forms of competition than that required of the undertaking by national legislation.[43] Specifically, in *CIF*, the Court of Justice held that:

> [P]rice competition does not constitute the only effective form of competition or that to which absolute priority must in all circumstances be given. Consequently,

[38] In *Ladbroke Racing*, the Court of Justice did not accept the Commission's submission that the proper course of conduct for the undertaking would be to contest the validity of the national regulation, invoke the primacy of Articles 101 and 102 TFEU and refuse to comply with the national regulation. See Joined Cases C 359/95 P and C 379/95 P *Commission and French Republic v Ladbroke Racing* [1997] ECR I-6265 [20], later confirmed in *CIF v Autorità Garante della Concorrenza e del Mercato* (n 22) [49]–[50] [52]–[55].

[39] Joined Cases 40–48, 50, 54–56, 111, 113 and 114/73 *Coöperatieve Vereniging 'Suiker Unie' UA and others v Commission* [1975] ECR 1663 [63]–[73], as summarised and cited in *Deutsche Telekom v Commission* (n 3) [82].

[40] *Coöperatieve Vereniging 'Suiker Unie' UA and others v Commission* (n 39) [619]–[620].

[41] ibid, as cited in Case C-198/01 *CIF v Autorità Garante della Concorrenza e del Mercato* (n 22) [57].

[42] ibid; *Deutsche Telekom v Commission* (n 3) [82], [277]–[278].

[43] Similarly, in *GlaxoSmithKline* under Article 101 TFEU, the General Court held that this provision remains applicable if parameters of competition other than the price, which is regulated, and in particular innovation can be affected by the agreement. See Case T-168/01 *GlaxoSmithKline Services Unlimited v Commission* [2006] ECR II-2969 [104]–[108], confirmed in Joined Cases C 501/06 P, C-513/06 P, C-515/06 P and C 519/06 P *GlaxoSmithKline Services Unlimited v Commission* [2009] ECR I-9291 [74]–[75]. This analysis is also confirmed by Case T-87/05 *EDP—Energias de Portugal, SA v Commission* [2005] ECR II-3745 [116]–[119], [126]; the case law on the impossibility of wilful exercise of any form of competition is cited in support of precluding the application of Article 2(3) ECMR where competition in the market does not exist as a result of national and EU legislation (the Second Gas Directive in this case).

> pre-determination of the sales price of matches by the Italian State does not, on its own, rule out all scope for competitive conduct. Even if limited, competition may operate through other factors.[44]

However, it is difficult to see how the Commission, a National Competition Authority (NCA) or a national court can apply such a criterion without having undertaken a full market analysis in order to suggest that Article 102 TFEU is applicable. On a similar note, in *Deutsche Telekom*, the Court of Justice assessed the undertaking's fault (intent or negligence) in order to ascertain attribution to the undertaking of any infringement of Article 102 TFEU. It held that it is sufficient that:

> [T]he undertaking concerned cannot be unaware of the anti-competitive nature of its conduct, whether or not it is aware that it is infringing the competition rules of the Treaty … [Deutsche Telekom] could not have been unaware that, notwithstanding the authorisation decisions of RegTP, it had genuine scope to set its retail prices for end-user access services and, moreover, the margin squeeze entailed serious restrictions on competition.[45]

However, this condition cannot be fulfilled without a full market analysis for assessing the effects of the margin squeeze.[46]

Conversely, according to the Court of Justice in the same two judgments (*CIF* and *Deutsche Telekom*), the possibility of excluding particular anti-competitive conduct from the scope of Articles 101 and 102 TFEU can be upheld only if that conduct has been required of the undertakings in question by existing national legislation, or the legislation has precluded all scope for any competitive conduct on their part.[47] Thus, the degree of legislative constraint that is required for a state action defence to succeed is very high, close to compulsion and lacking in autonomy.[48] The Court, both in *CIF* and in *Deutsche Telekom*, cites *Italy v Commission* (telecommunications

[44] *CIF v Autorità Garante della Concorrenza e del Mercato* (n 22) [68]–[69].

[45] *Deutsche Telekom v Commission* (n 3) [124]–[125].

[46] To the extent that one accepts that the subjective element of the state action defence (intent or negligence) is symmetrical in scope to the objective element of the claim.

[47] *CIF v Autorità Garante della Concorrenza e del Mercato* (n 22) [67]; *Deutsche Telekom v Commission* (n 3) [81]. A similar claim was advanced in Case T-228/97 *Irish Sugar plc v Commission* [1999] ECR II-2969 [129]–[131] in relation to the system of 'sugar export rebates', but the Court rejected it, as the applicant had not cited any specific legislation or measure of the Irish government. Finally, in Joined Cases T-191/98, T-212–214/98 *Atlantic Container Line AB and others v Commission* [2003] ECR II-3275 [1128]–[1132], the Court examined claims that certain practices by the linear conference were required by US law.

[48] Alternatively, the General Court has held that: 'In the absence of any binding regulatory provision imposing the conduct at issue … the Commission is entitled to reject the complaints for want of autonomy on the part of the undertakings in question only if it appears on the basis of objective, relevant and consistent evidence that that conduct was unilaterally imposed upon them by the national authorities through the exercise of irresistible pressures, such as, for example, the threat to adopt State measures likely to cause them to sustain substantial losses.' Case T-387/94 *Asia Motor France SA and others v Commission* [1996] ECR II-961 [65]. Again, the language used by the General Court indicates the requirement of compulsion; similarly, in Case T-65/99 *Strintzis Lines Shipping SA v Commission* [2003] ECR II-5433 [119]–[122] and Case T-66/99 *Minoan Lines SA v Commission*

monopoly) and the Belgian and Dutch cases on tax legislation and price controls in the tobacco industry as examples of cases where a state compulsion defence has 'partially' or 'to a limited extent' been accepted.[49]

Italy v Commission places the question in the context of assessing whether there is an economic activity by an undertaking in relation to the autonomous exercise by British Telecom of rule-making powers strictly limited to the fixing of tariffs and the conditions of service provision of public telecommunications equipment for users.[50] In addition, any arguments by the applicants in relation to the substance of the Commission's finding were framed in terms of Article 106(2) TFEU.[51] Therefore, citing the case as an example in which a state compulsion defence was (even partially) accepted is misleading. Similarly, in a case involving the levy of surcharges on the price of electricity, the Court cited *Ladbroke Racing* on the autonomous conduct criterion, but dismissed the application of Articles 101 and 102 TFEU on the basis that the activity fell within the exclusive competence of the Member State concerned.[52] Therefore, it is not an economic activity, but the entity involved was, rather, acting as a tax collector on behalf of the state.[53]

In regard to tax cases in the tobacco sector, the Court's assessment is clearly part of its substantive analysis as to whether the undertakings' conduct restricts competition (under Article 101 TFEU) rather than on the applicability of the competition provisions in the first place. In neither case was compulsion found to exist. In fact, both cases produced similar assessments to that in *Suiker Unie*, since the Court held that the Belgian (and to a lesser extent the Dutch) legislation reduced the scope for retail price competition, but did leave tobacco manufacturers and importers with sufficient margin for effective competition.[54]

It is noteworthy that the Belgian tax case, *Van Landewyck*, resembles *Sotirios Lélos*. In the Belgian case, the Court held that the price control measures encouraged joint negotiations between the revenue authorities and the trade unions, during which 'great influence on the fixing of the retail price is exercised by the revenue authorities whose concern is above all to guarantee the revenue arising from the taxation of the products in question'.[55] However, this would not

[2003] ECR II-5515 [176]–[179]. The exercise of irresistible pressure was not demonstrated in any of the above-mentioned cases.

[49] Case 41/83 *Italian Republic v Commission* [1985] ECR 873; Joined Cases 209–215/78 and 218/78 *Van Landewyck v Commission* [1980] ECR 3125; Joined Cases 240–242/82, 261/82, 262/82, 268/82 and 269/82 *Stichting Sigarettenindustrie and others v Commission* [1985] ECR 3831.

[50] *Italian Republic v Commission* (n 49) [15]–[23].

[51] ibid [27]–[33].

[52] Case C-207/01 *Altair Chimica SpA v ENEL Distribuzione SpA* [2003] ECR I-8875 [30]–[35]: '[Articles 101 and 102 TFEU] are intended to apply only to the anti-competitive conduct of undertakings and are not intended to eliminate differences which may exist between the tax regimes of the different Member States.' ibid [36].

[53] ibid [35].

[54] *Van Landewyck v Commission* (n 49) [123]–[134]; *Stichting Sigarettenindustrie and others v Commission* (n 49) [23]–[29].

[55] *Van Landewyck v Commission* (n 49) [129].

prevent 'the manufacturer or importer from allowing particular wholesalers on an individual basis a larger profit margin out of the manufacturers' or importers' share of the retail price'.[56] This resembles *Sotirios Lélos*, in which the Court assessed the participation of the dominant pharmaceutical undertaking in the negotiations with the relevant public authorities.[57] However, in the tobacco case, there was an overlap between the nature of the tax authorities' conduct and the conduct of the association of undertakings under question, namely fixing the profit margins and the financial advantages that the manufacturers and importers permitted to the intermediary traders. By contrast, technically, there was no overlap between the form of the conduct of the authorities (fixing prices) and of the undertaking (restricting quantities) in *Sotirios Lélos*, even though both conducts had an effect on profit margins.

Overall, the intensity of the link required by the European court for a state compulsion defence is such that, in practice, it has never succeeded. The analysis indicates that assessment of the state compulsion defence has been part of the substantive analysis on restriction of competition within the scope of Articles 101 and 102 TFEU rather than of the conceptually distinct level of determining whether the competition law provisions are applicable. The reason for this is that autonomous conduct is defined by reference to any form of competition in the market. This definition of autonomous conduct under the state compulsion defence indicates that there is a market-distorting effect and that state responsibility also exists, in part, every time the state action defence is rejected. It also firmly indicates that, far from being concerned with the conduct of the undertaking as such, the link between the undertaking's conduct and the national legislation affects the causation between the conduct and the market-distorting effect. Furthermore, in cases in which it could be argued that a state action defence has, in part, succeeded, the Court actually classifies the issue as one of defining whether the function involved is an economic activity. Finally, the only case in which a state action defence was examined by the Court in the context of assessing attribution of the alleged violation was *Deutsche Telekom*, a market separation case under Article 102 TFEU. However, once again, compulsion was not found to exist.

III. ABUSE AND THE STATE ACTION DOCTRINE: ESTABLISHING STATE RESPONSIBILITY

The state action doctrine and the state action defence are two sides of the same coin, to the extent that the undertaking's allegation is that its conduct is authorised by the state, so any alleged restriction of competition should be attributed to the state. However, whether such an alleged restriction should be sanctioned

[56] ibid [131].

[57] See ch 4, section III.D.

and whether Article 102 TFEU should be the legal standard of assessment both depend on the nature and the intensity of the link between the national legislation and the dominant undertaking's conduct. This is because Article 102 TFEU is not addressed to Member States. An additional question that arises is whether state action can be found to be anti-competitive independently of any private conduct infringing Article 102 TFEU under a different set of provisions, such as the free movement provisions.

Before embarking on a structural analysis of the state action doctrine in relation to Article 102 TFEU, it should be noted that the recent market separation cases in which an issue of state involvement has arisen, namely *Deutsche Telekom* and *Sotirios Lélos*, bring to light instances of conduct by undertakings that are not covered by Article 106 TFEU. They can be viewed as a new category of cases inasmuch as it is the first time that indirect recourse to Article 4(3) TEU-L (ex-Article 10 TEC) in conjunction with Article 102 TFEU is, allegedly, required. *Deutsche Telekom* and *Sotirios Lélos* involved new factual scenarios that did not fit into the traditionally used formula of Article 106 TFEU in conjunction with Article 102 TFEU, because the dominant undertakings were not 'granted special or exclusive rights'. In *Deutsche Telekom*, the incumbent undertaking was a former state-owned monopoly, but at the material time the sector was fully liberalised. In *Sotorios Lélos*, the market power of Glaxo had not been granted by the state but achieved in the market.

Indeed, until now, the vast majority of Article 102 TFEU cases involving state action have been dealt with under the specific provision of Article 106 TFEU because they involved 'undertakings to which Member States grant special or exclusive rights'. The very limited use of Article 4(3) TEU-L in conjunction with Article 102 TFEU has only been in cases involving claims based on both Article 101 TFEU and Article 102 TFEU, in particular cases of setting prices/tariffs, from which the need for a judicial construction had arisen,[58] and in some rare instances, the association of undertakings setting the prices was also dominant.[59]

[58] Eg, Case 136/86 *Bureau National Interprofessionnel du Cognac v Yves Auber* [1987] ECR 4789; Case 229/83 *Association des Centres distributeurs Édouard Leclerc and others v SARL 'Au blé vert' and others* [1985] ECR 1; Case 231/83 *Henri Cullet and Chambre syndicale des réparateurs automobiles et détaillants de produits pétroliers v Centre Leclerc à Toulouse and Centre Leclerc à Saint-Orens-de-Gameville* [1985] ECR 305; Case 311/85 *ASBL Vereniging van Vlaamse Reisbureaus v ASBL Sociale Dienst van de Plaatselijke en Gewestelijke Overheidsdiensten* [1987] ECR 3801; Case 267/86 *Pascal Van Eycke v ASPA NV* [1988] ECR 4769.

[59] Case C-96/94 *Centro Servizi Spediporto Srl v Spedizioni Marittima del Golfo Srl* [1995] ECR I-2883 [20], [31], [34]; Case C-38/97 *Autotrasporti Librandi Snc di Librandi F & C v Cuttica spedizioni e servizi internationali Srl* [1998] ECR I-5955 [26], [27], [37]; Joined Cases C-140/94, C-141/94 and C-142/94 *DIP SpA v Comune di Bassano del Grappa, LIDL Italia Srl v Comune di Chioggia and Lingral Srl v Comune di Chiogga* [1995] ECR I-3257 [14], [15], [24], [27]; Case C-70/95 *Sodemare SA, Anni Azzurri Holding SpA and Anni Azzurri Rezzato Srl v Regione Lombardia* [1997] ECR I-3395 [44], [47]; C-250/03 *Giorgio Emanuele Mauri v Ministero della Giustizia and Commissione per gli esami di avvocato presso la Corte d'appello di Milano* [2005] ECR I-1267 [29], [37]; Joined Cases C-94/04 and C-202/04 *Federico Cipolla v Rosaria Fazari, née Portolese at al* [2006] ECR I-11421 [46], [53]–[54]. Yet again, the number of cases is negligible because in the vast majority of cases in which a joined question of Article

The sole exception to this, where Article 4(3) TEU-L was applied in conjunction with only Article 102 TFEU, was the very first case in which the Court addressed the issue of anti-competitive effects of national legislation: *INNO v ATAB*.[60]

Therefore, the following analysis of the state action doctrine is undertaken with a view to suggesting the optimal means of filling the gap that has recently emerged in market separation cases under Article 102 TFEU. As explained above, this gap cannot be filled by direct recourse to Article 106(1) TFEU in conjunction with Article 102 TFEU because the dominant undertakings are not 'granted special or exclusive rights', as is required by Article 106(1) TFEU. It seems that Article 106(1) TFEU, with its specific wording, could possibly follow the same path as Article 37 TFEU, which is used rarely, if at all, so long as 'State monopolies of a commercial character' no longer form part of the economic reality at the Member State level. That is, of course, until there is a new shift in politics at the Member State level, where the factual scenarios in market transactions are determined.

A. The Relationship between Article 4(3) TEU-L (ex-Article 10 TEC) and Article 106(1) TFEU in Conjunction with Article 102 TFEU

The starting point of the state action doctrine is to be found in the principle of *effet utile* of the competition provisions, which are expressly addressed to undertakings and not to Member States. Is the Member State responsible when it encourages and facilitates infringements of Article 102 TFEU by dominant undertakings? States cannot be held accountable directly under Article 102 TFEU alone when they assist an abuse of the dominant position by an undertaking. Commentators have perceived such inapplicability of Article 102 TFEU to state action as a constitutional gap under the scheme of the Treaty, which would not correspond to the reality of the 'mixed' economies of some Member States that have no clear division between private and public actors.[61] The Court of Justice

101 TFEU and Article 102 TFEU arose, there was an undertaking granted with a special or exclusive right, hence Article 102 TFEU was applied in conjunction with Article 106(1) TFEU.

[60] See Case 13/77 *SA GB-INNO-BM v Association des détaillants en tabac (ATAB)* [1977] ECR 2115 [31], [33] in relation to retail prices on tax labels of tobacco products. In this case, the Court has also expressly addressed the relationship between Article 4(3) TEU-L and Article 106(1) TFEU, which will be analysed below in section III.A.

[61] See, in particular the doctrinal debate originally between P Pescatore, 'Public and Private Aspects of European Community Competition Law' (1987) 10 *Fordham International Law Journal* 373 and G Marenco, 'Competition between National Economies and Competition between Businesses: A Response to Judge Pescatore' (1987) 10 *Fordham International Law Journal* 420 and, as further developed, between L Gyselen, 'State Action and the Effectiveness of the EEC Treaty's Competition Provisions' (1989) 26 *Common Market Law Review* 33; L Gyselen, 'Anti-competitive State Measures under the EC Treaty: Towards a Substantive Legality Standard' (1993) *European Law Review-Competition Checklist* 55; and R Joliet, 'National Anti-Competitive Legislation and Community Law' (1989) 12 *Fordham International Law Journal* 163.

soon filled in this perceived gap by using the clause on 'a system of undistorted competition within the common market' provided for in ex-Article 3(1)(g) TEC, which is the cornerstone of the state action doctrine. For the first time in *INNO v ATAB*, the Court held, by reference to ex-Article 3(1)(g) TEC and Article 4(3) TEU-L (ex-Article 10 TEC),[62] that:

> [W]hile it is true that [Article 102 TFEU] is directed at undertakings, nonetheless it is also true that the Treaty imposes a duty on Member States not to adopt or maintain in force any measure which could deprive [Article 102 TFEU] of its effectiveness.[63]

As explained above, state responsibility in relation to Article 102 TFEU has more frequently arisen in conjunction with Article 106(1) TFEU than with Article 4(3) TEU-L, while the latter is more commonly associated solely with Article 101 TFEU. Davies comments that this division is mainly the result of the wording of Article 106(1) TFEU ('undertakings to which Member States grant special or exclusive rights'), which makes it fit more comfortably with questions of dominance and abuse.[64]

However, in *INNO v ATAB*, the Court of Justice had already associated the principles of state responsibility under Article 106(1) TFEU and Article 4(3) TEU-L in conjunction with Article 102 TFEU, so that it makes little difference under which set of provisions the state action is addressed. In particular, directly after proclaiming the *effet utile* principle of the competition provisions in relation to state action under Article 4(3) TEU-L, the Court of Justice went on to state that:

> [Article 106 TFEU] provides that, in the case of public undertakings and undertakings to which Member States grant special or exclusive rights, Member States shall neither enact nor maintain in force any measure contrary to inter alia the rules provided for in [Articles 101 to 109 TFEU]. *Likewise* Member States may not enact measures enabling private undertakings to escape from the constraints imposed by [Articles 101–09 TFEU].[65]

Therefore, it seems that the Court itself construed the state action doctrine as a general rule, which finds specific application in Article 106(1) TFEU.[66]

The fact that Article 106(1) TFEU is perceived as a *lex specialis* whereas Article 4(3) TEU-L is a *lex generalis* would lead to the tentative conclusion that Article 106(1) TFEU cannot have a broader scope than Article 4(3) TEU-L, at least in the areas of overlap, namely when applied in conjunction with Article 102 TFEU. However,

[62] *SA GB-INNO-BM v ATAB* (n 60) [29]–[30].

[63] ibid [31].

[64] Davies (n 1) 552.

[65] *SA GB-INNO-BM v ATAB* (n 60) [32]–[33], emphasis added.

[66] Confirmed expressly in the same judgment (ibid [42]) in relation to the preliminary question on the application of Article 106(1) TFEU. The Court has also made the same pronouncement when it addressed the question from the perspective of Article 106(1) TFEU, eg, Case C-387/93 *Criminal Proceedings against Giorgio Domingo Banchero* [1995] ECR-I 4663 [46]: 'The obligations which Member States must perform in good faith under [Article 4(3) TEU-L] include the obligation, set out in [Article 106(1) TFEU], whereby they must not let public undertakings and undertakings to which they grant special or exclusive rights enact or maintain in force any measure contrary to the rules contained in the Treaty.'

this approach does not take into account the fact that the general principle was derived from a specific Treaty provision: Article 106(1) TFEU. Therefore, while it may be completely legitimate to restrict the scope of application of this judicially construed general principle, its restriction does not necessarily translate into a restriction of the scope of Article 106(1) TFEU. Before the construction and, equally, after any hypothetical abolition of the state action doctrine, the provision of Article 106(1) TFEU existed and will continue to exist in the Treaty.[67] At the same time, in light of cases such as *Deutsche Telekom* or *Sotirios Lélos*, in which the dominant undertaking does not fall under the personal scope of Article 106 TFEU, this provision can be used as an inspiration for a solution based on the free movement provisions, since Article 106(1) TFEU also applies in conjunction with the freedoms which are indisputably addressed to Member States. In other words, the very few existing cases applying Article 4(3) TEU-L in conjunction with Article 102 TFEU illustrate the structural defects of the state action doctrine, while the specific Treaty provision, Article 106(1) TFEU, can be used more extensively in relation to one of its aspects. This aspect is its combined application with the freedoms, which are already addressed to any state measure and not only to state measures granting special or exclusive rights to undertakings.

B. The Type of Link between State Legislation and the Undertaking's Conduct: Autonomous Conduct Prohibited under Article 102 TFEU

A Member State cannot be held responsible under either Article 4(3) TEU-L (ex-Article 10 TEC) or Article 106(1) TFEU in conjunction with Article 102 TFEU without an associated but autonomous infringement of Article 102 TFEU by the dominant undertaking. The reason is that the Treaty provisions on competition are expressly addressed to undertakings, and any other interpretation would risk being considered *contra legem*. Indeed, Article 4(3) TEU-L is not a substantive provision; it does not impose new obligations on Member States, nor, as highlighted by Temple Lang, can it make EU law rules broader by way of analogy.[68] Therefore, the need for a link with a dominant undertaking's independent conduct infringing Article 102 TFEU stems from the express wording of that Article, which is only addressed to undertakings.[69]

[67] See, forcefully on that opinion, J-L Buendia Sierra, *Exclusive Rights and State Monopolies under EC Law: Article 86 (former 90) of the EC Treaty* (A Read, translated from the Spanish) (Oxford University Press, 1999) 266–67; see also Davies (n 1) 551–52; Baquero Cruz (n 2) 556 for a more nuanced view.

[68] J Temple Lang, 'Article 10 EC—The Most Important "General Principle" of Community Law' in U Bernitz, J Nergelius, C Cardner and X Groussot (eds), *General Principles of EC Law in a Process of Development: Reports from a Conference in Stockholm, 23–24 March 2007, Organised by the Swedish Network for European Legal Studies* (Kluwer Law International, 2008) 80.

[69] ibid. Similarly, see D Gerard, 'EU Competition Policy after Lisbon: Time for a Review of the "State Action Doctrine"?' (2010) 1(3) *Journal of European Competition Law and Practice* 206; E Szyszczak, *The Regulation of the State in Competitive Markets in the EU* (Hart Publishing, 2007) 97;

In *INNO v ATAB*, the Court expressly stated that the obligation, which stems from the combined application of the two provisions, is not to permit Member States to enact measures enabling private undertakings to escape from the Treaty prohibitions.[70] Similarly, in the very few cases in which the issue of the combined application of Article 4(3) TEU-L and Article 102 TFEU arose,[71] the Court repeated the test first formulated in *Spediporto*:

> [Ex-]Article 3(g) TEC [Article 4(3) TEU-L and Article 102 TFEU] could only apply to legislation of the kind contained in the Italian Law if it were proved that the legislation concerned placed an undertaking in a position of economic strength enabling it to prevent effective competition from being maintained on the relevant market by placing it in a position to behave to an appreciable extent independently of its competitors, of its customers and ultimately of the consumers.[72]

However, in none of the cases in which the issue of the combined application of Article 4(3) TEU-L and Article 102 TFEU arose was the national legislation found to contravene those Articles, because the legislation was not even regarded as placing the undertakings in a dominant position. For this reason, these few cases mention nothing about the need for a link between national legislation and an independent abuse of dominance by an undertaking, inasmuch as dominance is not established in the first place. This is in contrast with the situation under Article 101 TFEU, in which the Court, after the so-called 'November Revolution',[73] has restrictively applied Article 4(3) TEU-L by, first, examining if an agreement exists contrary to Article 101 TFEU and, second, if the state has backed it up 'by requiring or favouring the adoption of such an agreement or by reinforcing its effects'.[74] In that sense, the Court of Justice has been quite explicit in requiring a link, since it had already stated in *Leclerc* that 'national legislation which renders corporate behaviour of the type prohibited under [Article 101(1) TFEU] *superfluous*'[75] does not contravene Article 4(3) TEU-L in conjunction with Article 101 TFEU.

State action has never been found in breach of Article 4(3) TEU-L combined with Article 102 TFEU because there was no link with a dominant position and,

for a more nuanced point of view, see Baquero Cruz (n 2) 586–87, who is in favour of a link, but not necessarily of an automatic link of lawfulness (or unlawfulness).

[70] *SA GB-INNO-BM v ATAB* (n 60) [33].

[71] See n 59.

[72] *Centro Servizi Spediporto Srl v Spedizioni Marittima del Golfo Srl* (n 59) [31].

[73] N Reich, 'The "November Revolution" of the European Court of Justice: *Keck*, *Meng* and *Audi* Revisited' (1994) 31 *Common Market Law Review* 459–92.

[74] The test has been applied restrictively by the Court of Justice in Case C-2/91 *Criminal Proceedings against Wolf W Meng* [1993] ECR I-5751; Case C-185/91 *Bundesanstalt für den Güterfernverkehr v Gebrüder Reiff GmbH & Co KG* [1993] ECR I-5801; Case C-245/91 *Criminal Proceedings against Ohra Schadeverzekeringen NV* [1993] ECR I-5851, all delivered during November 1993, just before the seminal Joined Cases C-267/91 and C-268/91 *Criminal Proceedings against Bernard Keck and Daniel Mithouard* [1993] ECR I-6097 in the field of free movement of goods.

[75] *Association des Centres distributeurs Édouard Leclerc and others v SARL 'Au blé vert' and others* (n 58) [15], emphasis added.

as a result, there could not possibly be an abuse, as explained above. When such a dominant position existed, the case was treated under Article 106(1) TFEU in conjunction with Article 102 TFEU. Under that provision, it was ambiguous whether national legislation granting special or exclusive rights is prohibited because it has the same exclusionary *effects* as an abuse of the dominant position, even when such an abuse has not *actually* or *potentially* taken place.[76] In other words, it was not clear, in the case law of the Court of Justice, whether a special or exclusive right granted by the state is, itself, contrary to the conjoint application of Articles 106(1) and 102 TFEU, despite the fact that the dominant position itself is not prohibited under Article 102 TFEU.[77] A relatively recent judgment by the General Court firmly confirms the view that a state measure cannot be in breach of Article 106(1) TFEU, in conjunction with Article 102 TFEU, without an abuse, even if only potential, of the dominant position by an undertaking being identified, that abuse having a link with the state measure.[78] The case concerned the granting and maintaining, by the Hellenic Republic, of quasi-monopolistic lignite exploration rights in favour of the former state-owned electricity monopoly, DEI. According to the Commission, this measure was, itself, in breach of Articles 106(1) and 102 TFEU because it distorted competition by creating inequality of opportunities between economic operators. The judgment of the General Court is on appeal before the Court of Justice, which is thereby given an excellent opportunity to clearly restate its so far floating case law on this issue.[79]

Indeed, the confusion was created during the process of liberalising former state-owned monopolies, because of the strategic use by the Commission of Directives based on Article 106(3) TFEU in the telecommunications sector and the threat of such use in other sectors, such as energy and postal sectors.[80] The proactive use of Article 106(3) TFEU is closely related to the shift in the interpretation of Article 106(1) TFEU in conjunction with Article 102 TFEU, advocated

[76] See J Maillo, 'Article 86 EC: Services of General Interest and EC Competition Law' in G Amato and C-D Ehlermann (eds), *EC Competition Law: A Critical Assessment* (Hart Publishing, 2007) 559–603 on the three categories of state measures that, first, lead to actual abuses; second, lead to potential abuses; and, third, merely have similar effects to an abuse.

[77] More generally, see D Edward and M Hoskins, 'Article 90: Deregulation and EC Law. Reflections Arising from the XVI FIDE Conference' (1995) 32 *Common Market Law Review* 157; A Gardner, 'The Velvet Revolution: Article 90 and the Triumph of the Free Market in Europe's Regulated Sectors' (1995) 16 *European Competition Law Review* 78; Buendia Sierra (n 67) 151–89; and J Temple Lang, 'Privatisation of Social Welfare: European Union Competition Law Rules' in E Spaventa and M Dougan (eds), *Social Welfare and EU Law* (Hart Publishing, 2005) 51–59 on the two opposing views regarding exclusive rights, namely the 'limited sovereignty approach' and the 'limited competition approach' under Article 106 TFEU.

[78] See Case T-169/08 *Dimosia Epicheirisi Ilektrismou AE (DEI) v Commission*, Judgment of 20 September 2012 (NYR) [86], [89], [105] in particular, and with extended analysis of the relevant cases of the Court of Justice.

[79] Case C-553/12 P *Commission v DEI* [2013] OJ C32/10.

[80] For a brief overview, see Szyszczak (n 69) 139–76; and the contributions in D Geradin (ed), *The Liberalization of State Monopolies in the European Union and Beyond* (Kluwer Law International, 2000).

first by the Commission[81] and endorsed by the Court in *RTT*.[82] The purpose of this was to suggest that some exclusive rights essentially have the same *effects* as abuses of dominant positions. Until then, exclusive rights were found to be incompatible with Article 106(1) TFEU in conjunction with Article 102 TFEU only in as far as separate abusive *behaviour* of the monopolist existed, which would, in principle, be contrary to Article 102 TFEU alone.[83] The suggestion that exclusive rights were illegal under Article 106(1) TFEU in conjunction with Article 102 TFEU, even without an associated abuse of a dominant position by the undertaking involved, was further strengthened by the Court of Justice judgment in *Corbeau*.[84] The Court of Justice directly examined whether the extension by law of a postal monopoly to specific services dissociable from the traditional postal service (such as collection from the sender's address) was justified, without first having considered whether the monopoly was prohibited in light of an independent breach of Article 102 TFEU by the undertaking concerned.[85]

However, *Corbeau* is no longer good law,[86] to the extent that the Court of Justice seems to have shifted back to its previous case law.[87] In the first case to overrule *Corbeau*, *la Crespelle*, it held that by granting an exclusive right, the Member State is in breach of Articles 106(1) and 102 TFEU only if 'in *merely*

[81] Eg, Commission Directive (EEC) 90/388 on Competition in the Markets for Telecommunications Services [1990] OJ L 192/10 (Recitals 13–17).

[82] Case C-18/88 *Régie des Télégraphes et des Téléphones (RTT) v GB-Inno-BM SA* [1991] ECR I-5973. The Court held that the extension by law of the monopoly in the operation of the telephone network to the market in telephone equipment infringes Article 106(1) in conjunction with Article 102 TFEU; ibid [24]. The law (state measure) granted to RTT the exclusive power to approve its competitors' telephone equipment, which was equated by the Court to an exclusive right to sell the equipment. This second exclusive right was prima facie illegal because it eliminated all competition in the market in telephone equipment; ibid [19]. The same interpretation was adopted in Joined Cases C-271/90, C-281/90 and C-289/90 *Kingdom of Spain, Kingdom of Belgium and Italian Republic v Commission* [1992] ECR I-5833 concerning the Telecommunications Service Directive 90/388 (n 81).

[83] See Case 155/73 *Sacchi* [1974] ECR 430 [14]–[18]; Case C-260/89 *Elliniki Radiophonia Tiléorassi AE (ERT) and Panellinia Omospondia Syllogon Prossopikou v Dimotiki Etairia Pliroforissis and Sotirios Kouvelas and Nicolaos Avdellas and others* [1991] ECR I-2925 [37]–[38]; Case C-41/90 *Klaus Höfner and Fritz Elser v Macrotron GmbH* [1991] ECR I-1979 [29]–[31]; Case C-179/90 *Merci convenzionali porto di Genova SpA v Siderurgica Gabrielli SpA* [1991] ECR I-5889 [16]–[19].

[84] Case C-320/91 *Criminal Proceedings against Paul Corbeau* [1993] ECR I-2533.

[85] ibid [11]–[14].

[86] *Corbeau* has been cited in subsequent judgments either alongside cases such as *la Crespelle* (eg, Case C-55/96 *Job Centre coop arl* [1997] ECR I-7119 [31]) or at the level of justification under Article 106(2) TFEU, once analysis under Article 106(1) TFEU based on the exercise of the right by the undertaking has been undertaken (eg, Joined Cases C-147/97 and C-148/97 *Deutsche Post AG v Gesellschaft für Zahlungssysteme mbH GZS and Citicorp Kartenservice GmbH* [2000] ECR I-825 [48]; Case C-340/99 *TNT Traco SpA v Poste Italiane SpA and others* [2001] ECR I-4109 [46]–[48]; Case C-49/07 *Motosykletistiki Omospondia Ellados NPID (MOTOE) v Elliniko Dimosio* [2008] ECR I-4863 [50]–[51]), or in support of other requirements under Article 106 TFEU irrelevant to the debate (eg, on the notion of undertakings entrusted with exclusive rights: Case C-209/98 *Entreprenørforeningens Affalds/Miljøsektion (FFAD) v Københavns Kommune* [2000] ECR I-3743 [54]).

[87] Case law prior to *Corbeau* is cited in n 83.

exercising the exclusive right, the undertaking in question *cannot avoid abusing* its dominant position'.[88] In *la Crespelle*, the national law:

> [M]erely allowed insemination centers to require breeders who requested the centers to provide them with semen from other production centers to pay the additional costs entailed by that choice. Although it left to the insemination centers the task of calculating those costs, such a provision did not lead the centers to charge disproportionate costs and thereby abuse their dominant position.[89]

Therefore, the Court of Justice seems to require a link between the right granted by the state and an actual or potential abuse of the dominant position acquired exactly because of the right that has been granted.[90] The pending appeal in *Commission v DEI* is a great opportunity for the Court of Justice to confirm its position.[91]

Based on the above, it is submitted that if the gap that has arisen in market separation cases, such as *Deutsche Telekom* and *Sotirios Lélos*, in relation to the state action involved (approval of tariffs and setting of prices, respectively) were to be covered by the conjoint application of Article 4(3) TEU-L and Article 102 TFEU, there should be a clear link with independent conduct by the dominant undertaking of the sort that is prohibited under Article 102 TFEU. Therefore, if compared with the type of link required for a state compulsion defence, an additional element is required here. Autonomous conduct by the dominant undertakings is not

[88] Case C-323/93 *Société Civile Agricole du Centre d'Insémination de la Crespelle v Coopérative d'Elevage et d'Insémination Artificielle du Département de la Mayenne* [1994] ECR I-5077 [18], emphasis added; further cited and followed by the Court in *Criminal Proceedings against Giorgio Domingo Banchero* (n 66) [51]–[56]; *Job Centre coop arl* (n 86) [31]–[38]; Case C-163/96 *Criminal Proceedings against Silvano Raso and others* [1998] ECR I-533 [27]–[32]; Case 67/96 *Albany International BV v Stichting Bedrijfspensioenfonds Textielindustrie* [1999] ECR I-5751 [93]–[97]; Case C-115/97 *Brentjens' Handelsonderneming BV v Stichting Bedrijfspensioenfonds voor de Handel in Bouwmaterialen* [1999] ECR I-6025 [93]–[97]; Case C-219/97 *Maatschappij Drijvende Bokken BV v Stichting Pensioenfonds voor de Vervoer- en Havenbedrijven* [1999] ECR I-6121 [83]–[87]; Case C-180/98 *Pavel Pavlov and others v Stichting Pensioenfonds Medische Specialisten* [2000] ECR I-6451 [127]–[128]; Case C-340/99 *TNT Traco SpA v Poste Italiane SpA and others* [2001] ECR I-4109 [44]–[47]; *MOTOE v Elliniko Dimosio* (n 86) [48]–[53]. The link between the granting of an exclusive right and a separate abuse is retained as a distinct step of assessment prior to justification, even in subsequent cases in which *la Crespelle* is not cited, such as *Deutsche Post AG* (n 86) [48].

[89] *Société Civile Agricole du Centre d'Insémination de la Crespelle* (n 88) [20]–[21].

[90] For the case of a potential abuse, the issue arises mainly in relation to conflict of interests scenarios in which the undertaking is active in the market for which it has been granted, eg, the power to give authorisations (*MOTOE v Elliniko Dimosio* (n 86) [51]–[52]) or, eg, the right to supply temporary labour (*Criminal Proceedings against Silvano Raso and others* (n 88) [28], [31]).

[91] *Commission v DEI* (n 79). AG Wathelet, in his Opinion of 5 December 2013 (in French) [40], [58], [64], suggested that the General Court has erred in law and, essentially, argued that there is no need, in principle, for the Commission to prove separate abusive behaviour of the monopolist, insofar as it can show that the exclusive rights have the same effects as an abuse of the dominant position. In case the Court of Justice accepts the need to prove separate abusive behaviour of the monopolists, AG Wathelet suggested that the General Court judgment was vitiated by inadequate reasoning, or misconstruction of evidence, inasmuch as the Commission has proved that DEI, by merely exercising its lignite exploitation rights, was led to commit an abuse of dominance in the secondary market of wholesale electricity supply; ibid [87]–[91].

sufficient, but the autonomous conduct should also be in breach of Article 102 TFEU for the state action doctrine not to end up being a *contra legem* interpretation of the Treaty.

C. The Intensity of the Link between State Legislation and the Undertaking's Conduct: An Issue of Indeterminacy

The intensity of the required link between state action and the undertaking's conduct raises the most significant doubts as to the usefulness of the state action doctrine itself (Article 4(3) TEU-L in conjunction with Article 102 TFEU). There must be a link between the national legislation and an independent breach of Article 102 TFEU by the undertaking involved, as argued in section III.B above. However, the degree of causation between the national legislation and independent breach of Article 102 TFEU by the undertaking cannot be determined ('indeterminacy question'). The reason is that, on the one hand, compulsion would counteract any autonomy of the conduct by the dominant undertaking, which is a precondition for finding the required independent breach of Article 102 TFEU (see section II.B above). On the other hand, encouragement by creating, or by strengthening, the dominant position of an undertaking would not be sufficient, because any high market power granted, rather than achieved in the market, facilitates abuse.

In what follows, the tension between the autonomous abusive conduct by the undertaking and state compulsion, as it is reflected in the application of Article 106(1) TFEU, is explored. It is argued that such tension does exist but that it is not easily discernible, because state action takes the form of granting market power (amounting to a monopoly), which is also the distinguishing element of Article 102 TFEU itself and a condition for the anti-competitive effect of certain abuses to occur.[92] This is contrasted with the state action cases in relation to Article 101 TFEU, under which the autonomous conduct of the type prohibited should take a specific form, namely it should take the form of an agreement (or concerted practice). Therefore, the difficulty of determining with precision the intensity of the link between this conduct and state compulsion is noticeable in relation to cases under Article 101 TFEU. It is argued that the gap cases of market separation under Article 102 TFEU are more comparable to state action cases under Article 101 TFEU[93] and, for that reason, they bring the indeterminacy question in relation to state action under Article 102 TFEU to the surface. Subsequently, guidance on

[92] See ch 2, text to nn 99–114 and ch 3, section II.B.

[93] Than to Article 106(1), read together with Article 102 TFEU; see also section III above on the new factual scenarios introduced by these gap cases, which do not fit into the personal scope of Article 106(1) TFEU.

answering the indeterminacy question in relation to Article 102 TFEU is sought by looking into the case law under Article 37(1) TFEU (see section III.C.i below).

The tension between autonomous abusive conduct and state compulsion is the essence of the indeterminacy question. This tension exists under Article 106(1) TFEU in conjunction with Article 102 TFEU and is reflected in the test followed by the Court of Justice after *la Crespelle*: 'in merely exercising the granted right, the undertaking is led to abuse [or cannot avoid abusing] its dominant position'. The autonomous abusive conduct is reflected in the 'mere exercise' of the right, whereas the inducement by the state is reflected in the use of words indicating coercion, such as 'cannot avoid' or 'led to'.[94]

However, the tentative outcome is to tip the balance between the two sides in favour of paying additional attention to the 'coercion' side in relation to 'special or exclusive rights' under Article 106(1) TFEU. This is because dominance (which regularly comes together with exclusivity) is a condition for the anti-competitive effect to occur.[95] Therefore, the issue of whether the dominant position has been achieved by the undertaking alone in the market or granted to it by someone else (such as the state) influences the attribution of the anti-competitive effect to the undertaking (or to the state).[96] This is also recognised by the Commission in its Guidance Paper on Enforcement Priorities under Article 102 TFEU in relation to refusals to supply, where it is stated that:

> [A]n obligation to supply is manifestly not capable of having negative effects on the incentives to invest and innovate upstream ... where the upstream market position of the dominant undertaking has been developed under the protection of special or exclusive rights or has been financed by State resources.[97]

This part of the Guidance Paper has received fierce criticism from academics, given that the Commission and the Court have already made use of it in margin squeeze abuses.[98] However, from the point of view of the attribution of the

94 See Davies (n 1) 559–60 for a thoughtful analysis of the language of the Court of Justice in Article 106(1) TFEU cases.

95 At least in market separation cases; see ch 2, text to nn 99–114.

96 In Case C-209/10 *Post Danmark A/S v Konkurrencerådet*, Judgment of 27 March 2012 (NYR) [23], the Court of Justice seems to imply that the existence of a dominant position which has its origins in a former legal monopoly affects the scope of its special responsibility not to allow its conduct to impair undistorted competition.

97 Commission (EC), 'Guidance on Commission's enforcement priorities in applying Article 82 of the EC Treaty to abusive exclusionary conduct by dominant undertaking' (Communication) [2009] OJ C 45/7 [82].

98 In *Telefonica*, a margin squeeze case, this line of reasoning provided the basis for the Commission to reject Telefonica's argument that there was no competition law duty, on the basis of *Oscar Bronner*, to supply the upstream input: *Wanadoo Espana v Telefónica* (n 24) [302]–[309], particularly [304]. This is confirmed by the General Court in *Kingdom of Spain v Commission* (n 26) [73]–[76]. For a criticism, see EG Diaz and J Padilla, 'The *linkLine* Judgement—A European Perspective' (2009) 1 *Global Competition Policy* 7: 'it is far from being the case that where the investor is a government, it will spend money without considering the impact of an ex post obligation to supply on its future finances'. See also D Geradin, 'Refusal to Supply and Margin Squeeze: A Discussion of Why the "Telefonica Exceptions" are Wrong' (2011) TILEC Discussion Paper 009, 10: 'whether or not the "firm's

market-distorting effect, it reflects the reason why it seems natural to assume inducement by the state, at least in cases of 'special or exclusive rights' granted by the state.

By contrast, under Article 101 TFEU applied to state action, in conjunction with Article 4(3) TEU-L, the state action can be distinguished from the undertaking's autonomous conduct of the type prohibited under Article 101 TFEU. The reason for this is, precisely, that the market power needed for the anti-competitive effect to occur under Article 101 TFEU has to originate in a specific form of conduct, namely an agreement between undertakings.[99] For example, in *Albany*, the same state measure involving the granting of an exclusive right, notably making affiliation to a specific pension fund compulsory at the request of organisations representing employers and workers in a given sector, received different treatment under Articles 101 and 102 TFEU.[100] Under Article 101 TFEU, in conjunction with Article 4(3) TEU-L, the Court famously held that:

> [On the basis of] an interpretation of the provisions of the Treaty as a whole which is both effective and consistent, agreements concluded in the context of collective negotiations between management and labour in pursuit of such objectives must, by virtue of their nature and purpose, be regarded as falling outside the scope of [Article 101(1) TFEU].[101]

By contrast, when it came to the assessment of the same state measure under Article 106(1) TFEU in conjunction with Article 102 TFEU, the Court, first, held that:

> [T]he decision of the public authorities to make affiliation to a sectoral pension fund compulsory necessarily implies granting to that fund an exclusive right to collect and administer the contributions paid with a view to accruing pension rights.[102]

And, second, that:

> [D]oubtless, some undertakings in the sector might wish to provide their workers with a pension scheme superior to the one offered by the Fund. However, the fact that such undertakings are unable to entrust the management of such a pension scheme to a single insurer, and the resulting restriction of competition, derive directly from the exclusive right conferred on the sectoral pension fund.[103]

upstream market position has been developed under the protection of special or exclusive rights or has been financed by state resources" may not be clear-cut'. See also R Downing and A Jones, 'Margin Squeeze in Telecommunications Markets' in S Anderman and A Ezrachi (eds) *Intellectual Property and Competition Law: New Frontiers* (Oxford University Press, 2011) 233–234.

[99] See ch 3, section II.B on the distinction between unilateral conduct and agreements.

[100] *Albany International BV* (n 88); similarly, Case C-115/97 *Brentjens' Handelsonderneming BV* (n 88); and Case C-219/97 *Maatschappij Drijvende Bokken BV* (n 88).

[101] *Albany International BV* (n 88) [60].

[102] ibid [90].

[103] ibid [97]. However, the exclusive right granted to the fund was found to be justified under Article 106(2) TFEU for the same reasons why the Court of Justice excluded collective labour agreements from the scope of Article 101 TFEU.

The difference in treatment is arguably justified on the basis of the different distinguishing elements of Articles 101 and 102 TFEU—the form of the conduct and the degree of market power, respectively. When the state measure in question grants exclusivity and therefore market power to the required degree, it is much more difficult to deny the risk of potential abuse. Therefore, in the case of 'special and exclusive rights', the intensity of the link between the state measure and the undertaking's conduct can, as an issue subject to proof, be affirmed without the need to be determined with further precision. Any type of exercise of an exclusive right qualifies as both a voluntary act and, at least, a potential abuse. By contrast, in relation to Article 101 TFEU, which is distinguished because it applies to a specific form of conduct rather than to a certain degree of market power, the difficulty of defining the intensity of the link with precision is evident. The specific type of conduct required by the undertaking either exists or does not exist, while it is distinct from the state action.[104] However, the fact that the indeterminacy of the intensity of the link is not noticeable under Article 106(1) TFEU, in conjunction with Article 102 TFEU, does not mean that the question does not arise.[105]

The indeterminacy question with regard to Article 102 TFEU comes to the surface in the gap cases identified above, such as *Deutsche Telekom* and *Sotirios Lélos*. These cases cannot be addressed under Article 106(1) TFEU as there is no undertaking granted a special or exclusive right. If they were to be treated under Article 4(3) TEU-L, in conjunction with Article 102 TFEU, it is hard to determine the intensity of the link required between the state action and the undertaking's autonomous abuse of the dominant position. The market power of the undertaking has not been granted by the state, but rather achieved in the market, as in the case of Glaxo. Even in the case of Deutsche Telekom, which is a former state-owned monopoly, 'it will not always be easy to say that the source of funds is unambiguously public in nature. Much of the infrastructure of former State monopolies has been the subject of significant improvements following privatization with the result that sources of funding are now substantially mixed'.[106]

[104] Critiques of the state action doctrine in relation to Article 101 TFEU on the basis of the incapability to precisely identify the intensity of the link between the state conduct and the undertaking's conduct are voiced in the Opinion of AG Jacobs in *Pavel Pavlov and others v Stichting Pensioenfonds Medische Specialisten* (n 88) [161]; Opinion of AG Léger in Case C-35/99 *Criminal Proceedings against Manuele Arduino* [2002] ECR I-1529 [87]; and Opinion of AG Maduro in *Federico Cipolla v Rosaria Fazari, née Portolese et al* (n 59) [32]–[35]. In particular, AG Maduro focuses the critique on the inconsistencies in applying the 'active supervision by the state' (or 'the delegation') criterion.

[105] In addition, state action cases in which both an Article 101 TFEU question and an Article 102 TFEU (in conjunction with Article 106(1) TFEU) question arise, like *Albany*, demonstrate that the issue of attribution extends beyond the classification of the entity that acts as an undertaking. For example, in *Albany*, the Court could not have addressed one question altogether under the notion of undertaking, which is common under both Articles 101 and 102 TFEU. The reason is that Article 106 TFEU would then be deprived of any scope of application, since it requires that an undertaking exists.

[106] Case C-52/09 *Konkurrensverket v TeliaSonera Sverige* [2011] ECR I-00527, Opinion of AG Mazak [27].

Therefore, it becomes more difficult to strike a balance between autonomous abusive conduct by the dominant undertaking on the one hand and inducement to such a degree as to implicate the state on the other hand, precisely because the state involvement does not take the form of granting market power.

The two gap cases mentioned above are similar to Article 101 TFEU state action cases, in which it could be said that voluntarism, as an indication or a result of the link between the undertaking's conduct and the state's conduct, is reflected in the type of conduct required, namely, an agreement. For example, had *Deutsche Telekom* been an Article 101 TFEU case and had the undertaking set the tariffs not unilaterally but via an agreement with another undertaking, it could have been argued that there is an independent conduct by the undertaking, possibly of the type prohibited under the relevant competition law provision. In *Sotirios Lélos*, the autonomous conduct by Glaxo can be distinguished from the public authorities' conduct inasmuch as, technically, the former's conduct was of a different form (restriction of quantities) in comparison with the latter's conduct (setting prices). However, in both cases, the market-distorting effect of the undertaking's conduct was induced by the state: in *Deutsche Telekom*, the RegTP had set a price cap, whereas in *Sotirios Lélos*, the public authorities had set the profit margins in the relevant markets. This is the reason why the subsequent question of the intensity of the link arises in a discernible manner in these cases.

It is doubtful whether there is merit in setting a legal test across the lines of a distinction that cannot be described a priori with precision. It follows from the analysis above that the indeterminacy question of the intensity of the link between the state conduct and the undertaking's conduct is visible in the recent market separation cases, in which there were no special or exclusive rights granted by the state to the undertakings. Section III.C.i below examines whether one could draw guidance from the jurisprudence under the second sub-paragraph of Article 37(1) TFEU for the purposes of articulating a test to determine with precision the intensity of the link required. If no such conclusion can be reached, that would confirm and reinforce the inappropriateness of the state action doctrine itself in setting the standard of assessment for the legality of the state action.

i. De Facto Discrimination under Article 37(1) TFEU

Article 37 TFEU regulates state monopolies of a commercial character and, in particular, imposes upon the Member States an obligation to adjust such monopolies so as to ensure that 'no discrimination regarding the conditions under which goods are procured and marketed exists between nationals of Member States'. The second sub-paragraph of Article 37(1) TFEU stipulates that the obligation also applies to 'situations in which the national authorities are in a position to control, direct or appreciably influence trade between Member States through a body established for that purpose or a delegated monopoly'. This test confirms that Article 37 TFEU aims to eliminate obstacles to the free movement arising not from a state measure but from the *conduct* of state monopolies.[107] According to AG Cosmas, the situations governed by the second sub-paragraph of Article 37(1) TFEU must consist of two elements: both an organic element and a functional element. They comprise:

> [T]he capacity of the national authorities to influence intra-Community trade by means of the abovementioned 'bodies' or entities, where such influence may, in accordance with the second sub-paragraph of Article 37(1), consist in controlling or supervising, in law or in fact, imports or exports between Member States, or any other type of direct or indirect influence, provided that it is appreciable.[108]

It is important to look at what the alternative is according to the case law, when the aforementioned test is not fulfilled, in order to assess whether this test can be of any help in determining with precision the intensity of the link required between the state conduct and the undertaking's abusive conduct under the state action doctrine. On the one hand, there are cases in which the Court of Justice applied Article 101 or 102 TFEU in conjunction with Article 106(1) TFEU as an alternative.[109] On the other hand, there are cases in which the Court of Justice applied the free movement provisions as another alternative measure.[110] Only the first category of cases is relevant for the question of attribution, because the Court, in those cases, decides whether or not to hold the state responsible for an autonomous breach of Treaty provisions by the undertakings. By contrast, in the second category of cases, the Court makes decisions already within the state's sphere of exclusive responsibility and it determines the specific content of such responsibility. In other words, this second category of cases raises the question as to whether the obligations stemming from Articles 37 and 34 TFEU have the same content and, hence, whether the Articles apply jointly in a complementary or alternative way. However, this reasoning has nothing to do with attribution, since it is already the state conduct that is being exclusively assessed.[111]

[107] See Case C-438/02 *Criminal Proceedings against Krister Hanner* [2005] ECR I-4551, Opinion of AG Léger [27]–[28], who cites the Spaak Report: 'A particular problem arises when imports are directly regulated, not by means of quotas, but by the institution of a purchasing monopoly … The authority which determines the import ceiling and the purchaser itself are one and the same.'

[108] Joined Opinion of AG Cosmas in *Commission v Kingdom of the Netherlands* (n 9), *Commission v Italian Republic* (n 14), Case C-159/94 *Commission v French Republic* [1997] ECR I-5815 and Case C-160/94 *Commission v Kingdom of Spain* [1997] ECR I-5851 [28].

[109] See the cases analysed below in the present section.

[110] See, eg, Case C-170/04 *Klas Rosengren and others v Riksåklagaren* [2007] ECR I-4071 [17]–[18], in which the case law on national rules which are separable from the operation of the monopoly, although they have a bearing upon it, and which must be examined with reference to Article 34 TFEU, is summarised. Most recently, this ruling was applied in Case C-456/10 *ANETT v Administración del Estado*, Judgment of 26 April 2012 (NYR) [21]–[31]. See also *Commission v Kingdom of the Netherlands* (n 9) [24]: 'Since SEP's exclusive import rights are thus contrary to [Article 37 TFEU], it is unnecessary to consider whether they are contrary to [Article 34 TFEU] or, consequently, whether they might possibly be justified under [Article 36 TFEU].'

[111] One limitation to this distinction of the cases could be that the case law on the reach of Article 37 TFEU and its interaction with either Article 34 TFEU or Article 106 TFEU is not consistent. To

The research presented here examines cases in which the Court has reasoned on the basis of whether Article 37 TFEU regulates the behaviour of state monopolies of a commercial character and whether such regulation is to the exclusion of the application of Articles 101 and 102 TFEU in conjunction with Article 106(1) TFEU. If Article 37 TFEU, on the one hand, and Articles 106(1) and 102 TFEU, on the other hand, apply concomitantly, it can be assumed that the intensity of the link between the state conduct and the undertaking's conduct is the same as the test provided for in the second sub-paragraph of Article 37(1) TFEU for the state to be held responsible. Otherwise, it could be argued that the delegation test under Article 37(1) TFEU is, in terms of intensity, more stringent than the link required for state responsibility under Article 106(1) TFEU.

In *Hansen*, the Court of Justice held that Article 37 TFEU was breached in light of the marketing of a product with the aid of public funds at an abnormally low resale price compared with the price, before tax, of a product of comparable quantity imported from another Member State.[112] This was so, despite the fact that:

> [T]here is no causal connection between the amount of the aid ... and the selling price ... the selling price being determined independently by the monopoly for reasons inherent in its sales policy, without reference to the destination and the amount of aid.[113]

This case may indicate that Member States may indeed be held responsible under Article 37 TFEU for the apparently independent behaviour of state monopolies of a commercial character.[114] However, the judgment says nothing in regard to the question of attribution, since Article 37 TFEU is not *expressis verbis* a reference rule in regard to the competition law provisions, equivalent to Article 106(1) TFEU. Therefore, no conclusion can be drawn from a case in which arguments based on Article 101 or 102 TFEU were not litigated, regarding state responsibility for behaviour potentially caught by Articles 101 and 102 TFEU.

By contrast, in *Bodson*, the Court of Justice explicitly reasoned along the lines of a mutually exclusive distinction between Article 37 TFEU and Treaty provisions applicable to undertakings, in particular Articles 101, 102 and 106 TFEU. The measure in question was national legislation that entrusted the 'external services' for funerals to the communes, which are at liberty to grant private undertakings

some extent, this is natural because of the different factual setting of the cases as well as the arguments raised by the parties and the questions referred by the national courts. However, Article 37 TFEU itself has established a reputation of 'obscure clarity' precisely because of the uncertainty as to the normative content of the obligation it contains; see Buendia Sierra (n 67) 110. The Court of Justice itself has referred to the 'complexity of its wording' in Case 6/64 *Flaminio Costa v ENEL* [1964] ECR 585 (English Special Edition) [598].

112 Case 91/78 *Hansen GmbH & Co v Hauptzollamt Flensburg* [1979] ECR 935.

113 ibid [13].

114 See Buendia Sierra (n 67) 107.

the concession to provide the service, to leave it entirely unregulated or to operate it themselves.[115] The Court ruled that:

> [T]he fact that the holders of concessions in a number of communes covering a large part of the national territory belong to a single group of undertakings and can thus influence patterns of trade is the result of the conduct of the undertakings in question and not of the national or municipal authorities.[116]

On that basis, it rejected the applicability of Article 37 TFEU in favour of Articles 106(1) and 102 TFEU. On the issue of combined applicability of those two Articles, the Court ruled that:

> [T]he grant of the concession for the 'external services' for funerals is regarded in France as a contract concluded between the commune and the concession holder ... It follows from that finding that the level of prices is indeed attributable to the undertaking, since the latter assumes full responsibility for the contracts which it has concluded.[117]

From that case, it seems that the intensity of the link under Article 106(1) TFEU between the undertaking's conduct and the state conduct is more lax than the delegation test under the second sub-paragraph of Article 37(1) TFEU. This observation does not necessarily provide any useful guidance as to the precise degree of state involvement under Article 106(1) TFEU.[118]

Similarly, in *Almelo*, the Court rejected the application of Article 37 TFEU to prohibitions, by means of an exclusive purchasing clause, of electricity importation, imposed by a regional electricity distributor (holding a non-exclusive concession for the distribution of electricity in the territory covered by the concession) on local electricity distributors. It held that:

> [T]he contracts determine the conditions under which the [regional undertaking] supplies electric power to the local distributors, and do not have the effect of transferring to those distributors the public service concession granted to the regional undertaking. The conditions of supply, in particular the exclusive purchasing clause, stem from the agreement between the parties and are not inherent in the territorial concession granted to [the regional undertaking] by the public authorities.[119]

However, in this case, the prohibition on imports imposed by the regional distributors on the local distributors was simply subjected to Articles 101, 102 and 106(2) TFEU, without any concomitant assessment of the state involvement under Article 106(1) TFEU. The reason may be that the Commission addressed the legality of the state's earlier intervention in the form of conferring exclusive import

[115] Case 30/87 *Corinne Bodson v SA Pompes funèbres des régions libérées* [1988] ECR 2479.

[116] ibid [14].

[117] ibid [32].

[118] Equally, it could be argued that the very same observation supports the view that the delegation test under Article 37(1) TFEU is empty of content when juxtaposed with the test under Article 106(1) TFEU. Indeed, this interpretation seems to be more often assumed, precisely because of the reduction over time of the use of Article 37 TFEU, as state monopolies are 'adjusted'.

[119] Case C-393/92 *Municipality of Almelo and others v NV Energiebedrijf Ijsselmij* [1994] ECR I-1477 [31].

rights to the undertakings responsible for production ('generators') under Article 37 TFEU.[120] In any case, the genuinely independent behaviour of the undertakings, namely the regional distributors, could not be attributed to state action, either under Article 37 TFEU or under Article 106(1) TFEU. Therefore, no conclusions can be drawn from the case with regard to the required intensity of the link between the undertaking's conduct and the state conduct because it seems that the Court of Justice did not confirm the existence of such a link in the first place.[121]

Overall, the case law under the second sub-paragraph of Article 37(1) TFEU does not clarify the intensity of the link between the undertaking's conduct and the state conduct required for the state to be held responsible under the state action doctrine. *Bodson* is the only relevant case. However, its relevance with regard to the question of attribution is limited to the observation that the intensity of the link under the state action doctrine is less stringent than the functional element under the second sub-paragraph of Article 37(1) TFEU. Therefore, it is suggested from the case law that there is a spectrum of links between the state conduct and the undertaking's conduct, under which the state may be held responsible for a breach of different Treaty provisions. In the case of the free movement provisions, there is no need for such a link in the first place, since it is the state conduct which is exclusively assessed. In the case of the second sub-paragraph of Article 37(1) TFEU, there should be a link so intense that the state monopoly's conduct is attributed, exclusively, to the state. Finally, in the case of the state action doctrine, there should be a link which is less intense than the link under Article 37(1) TFEU but which, at the same time, does not preclude an autonomous undertaking's conduct of the type prohibited under the competition law provisions. How this last link can be described with precision has yet to be identified, if, indeed, it is even possible.

D. The Relationship between the State Action Doctrine and the Free Movement Provisions

The above-described spectrum leads to the question whether state action allegedly falling under the state action doctrine could be assessed, instead, only under the free movement provisions.[122] Is there an added-value of the state action

[120] This was the case in one of the monopoly cases in the electricity sector against the Netherlands; *Commission v Kingdom of the Netherlands* (n 9).

[121] Similarly, in *Criminal Proceedings against Giorgio Domingo Banchero* (n 66) [26], [30]–[31], the Court of Justice held that Article 37 TFEU does not apply to national legislation which reserves the retail sale of manufactured tobacco products to distributors authorised by the state, provided that the procurement choices were a matter entirely for retailers to determine on the basis of market demands. In addition, the Court rejected the applicability of Article 106(1) TFEU in conjunction with Article 102 TFEU because there was no link between the national legislation and the producer's conduct; ibid [43], [52].

[122] See U Ehricke, 'State Intervention and EEC Competition Law: Opportunities and Limits of the European Court of Justice's Approach—A Critical Analysis of Four Key-Cases' (1990) 14 *World Competition Law and Economics Review* 101–02; and Gerard (n 69) 207–10, who are in favour of

doctrine, in light of the requirement for a link between the state conduct and the undertaking's conduct? Historically, the European courts have shown a preference for the free movement provisions because the state action doctrine is a narrower rule. In other words, if there is no violation of Article 4(3) TEU-L read together with Article 101 or 102 TFEU because, for example, there is no independent breach of the competition provisions by the undertakings, this does not necessarily mean that the state measure cannot be in breach of the free movement provisions, irrespective of the undertaking's conduct. Therefore, there is no automatic link of lawfulness between the undertaking's conduct and the state measure.

This is supported by the case law under Article 4(3) TEU-L in conjunction with Article 101 TFEU, particularly the French cases on book (*Leclerc*) and fuel (*Cullet*) retail minimum price fixing. The Court of Justice first declared that 'national legislation which renders corporate behaviour of the kind prohibited by [Article 101 TFEU] superfluous' is compatible with Article 4(3) TEU-L in conjunction with Article 101 TFEU 'as [EU] law stands'.[123] Subsequently, it assessed the same national law under the free movement of goods even though the national court had not raised the relevant question. In *Leclerc*, it held two specific provisions of the national legislation relating to imports and reimports to be measures equivalent to quantitative restrictions, to the extent that the minimum fixed price did not allow the lower cost price of imports to be reflected and it was therefore indirectly discriminatory (or else distinctly applicable).[124]

Similarly, under Article 106(1) TFEU, the granting of 'special or exclusive rights' will normally be in breach of the free movement provisions independently of any 'exercise of such rights' by the undertakings involved. The reason is that it favours the domestic incumbent and, hence, the market foreclosing effect is indirectly discriminatory, or it could be said to substantially impede market access for imported goods.[125] For example, in *la Crespelle* discussed above,[126] the Court upheld, under Articles 106(1) and 102 TFEU, the exclusive right granted to the insemination centres to require breeders who requested the centres to provide

subjecting state intervention to the free movement provisions only. Davies (n 1) 556, 562, writing in relation to measures contrary to Article 106(1) TFEU, adopts the view that 'such measures will invariably be restrictions on free movement'. *Cf* K Li, 'The Dormant Commerce Clause, Anticompetitive State Regulation, Competition and Consumers' (2013) American Antitrust Institute Working Paper No 13-01, and the very interesting, similar, submission in the context of US law, namely that anticompetitive state regulation, which is the basis for a successful 'state action immunity' defence under antitrust law, could be subject to the dormant Commerce Clause.

[123] *Association des Centres distributeurs Édouard Leclerc and others v SARL 'Au blé vert' and others* (n 58) [15], [20]; similarly, *Henri Cullet and Chambre syndicale des réparateurs automobiles et détaillants de produits pétroliers* (n 58) [17].

[124] *Association des Centres distributeurs Édouard Leclerc and others v SARL 'Au blé vert' and others* (n 58) [25]–[27]; similarly, *Henri Cullet and Chambre syndicale des réparateurs automobiles et détaillants de produits pétroliers* (n 58) [23], [25]–[27].

[125] According to Buendia Sierra (n 67) 192–202, one function of Article 106(1) TFEU is to *remind* Member States that they should respect the free movement provisions even when the beneficiary of the measure is a public undertaking or one granted special or exclusive rights.

[126] See text to nn 86–91.

them with semen from other production centres to pay the additional costs entailed by that choice because there was no independent abuse of dominance by the undertakings. However, it found that:

> Rules of a Member State which require private economic operators importing into its territory quantities of bovine semen from another Member State to store it, subject to a charge, in an authorized center which enjoys an exclusive concession with regard to storage of the semen and insemination constitute such a barrier to imports. Since that requirement applies at the stage immediately following importation and imposes an economic burden on importers, it is liable to restrict the volume of imports.[127]

Similarly, in the case concerning Greek lignite exploration rights, the Commission could have addressed the market distortion exclusively against the Hellenic Republic[128] under the free movement provisions (in conjunction with Article 106(1) TFEU). Indeed, the exclusion of third-party access to the lignite deposits in favour of the former state-owned monopoly impedes market access inasmuch as it distorts competition by creating inequality of opportunities between the market participants. It seems that the Commission got it wrong and did not pick up the appropriate legal provision to address the market distortion, which is misleadingly attributed, as has been pointed out by the General Court, since there is no abuse of the dominant position by the undertaking involved.[129]

In the sphere of Article 102 TFEU in conjunction with Article 4(3) TEU-L, the Court of Justice in *INNO v ATAB* had already implied the link between the state action doctrine and the free movement provisions. After upholding the national scheme under Article 4(3) TEU-L in conjunction with Article 102 TFEU, the Court stated, in addition, that:

> In any case, a national measure which has the effect of facilitating the abuse of a dominant position capable of affecting trade between Member States will generally be incompatible with [Articles 34 and 35 TFEU], which prohibit quantitative restrictions on imports and exports and all measures having equivalent effect.[130]

Trying to further pinpoint the specific areas of overlap between the two sets of provisions, it becomes clear that in *INNO v ATAB*, the additional application of the free movement of goods is arguably unrelated to the substantive assessment of the private conduct under competition provisions, which is conclusive in regard to the state action doctrine. In particular, the Court of Justice stated that 'the national court must also determine, taking into account the obstacles to trade in manufactured tobacco between States which may result from the nature of the fiscal arrangements in question, whether that measure as such is capable of affecting trade between Member States' (in paragraph [38]) and this is the

[127] *Société Civile Agricole du Centre d'Insémination de la Crespelle* (n 88) [29].

[128] *DEI v Commission* (n 78).

[129] ibid [89]: 'the impossibility, for other economic operators, of having access to the lignite deposits still available cannot be imputed to the applicant ... The non-granting of lignite exploitation licenses depends exclusively on the will of the Hellenic Republic'.

[130] *SA GB-INNO-BM v ATAB* (n 60) [35].

case, 'apart from any abuse of a dominant position which such arrangements might encourage' (Operative Part, point 2). Further, the inquiry that the national court was asked to undertake to establish 'effect on trade', as described in paragraph [38], is the same as the one that was required to be undertaken in order to establish whether the national measure is compatible with the free movement of goods, as described in the judgment in paragraphs [52]–[56].[131] This arguably indicates that the statement found in paragraph [35], namely that national measures compelling anti-competitive practices would generally be incompatible with the free movement provisions, is based on the fact that such a national measure 'affects trade' within the meaning of Article 102 TFEU even before an abuse of dominance is established.[132] Indeed, on the facts of the case, the national scheme that sets retail prices at the level fixed freely upstream by the manufacturer or the importer would most probably also escape the prohibition of Article 34 TFEU to the extent that 'no distinction is made between domestic products and imported products, because it generally has exclusively internal effects'.[133]

It could be said that state measures that fall outside the scope of the freedoms are the alleged added-value of the state action doctrine vis-a-vis the free movement provisions. The conjoint application of Article 4(3) TEU-L and Article 102 TFEU would then cover these excluded state measures, such as purely internal situations or cases that impact upon market access in a too indirect and uncertain manner. In chapter one, section IV.B, it was shown that 'effect on trade' is, arguably, a broader concept than the 'purely internal situations' test, as the latter test is reflected in the MEQR under Article 34 TFEU, but there is no conclusive case law. If 'effect on trade' is established in otherwise 'purely internal situations' (eg, when the conduct covers only a single Member State), then it should be possible to assume that the Internal Market is established and competition law is just a tool for the proper functioning of the Internal Market.[134] Therefore, it is expected that state action cases would not arise then.

For example, in a relatively recent case, the Court of Justice rejected as inadmissible a preliminary reference as regards the interpretation of Articles 56 and 49 TFEU, since all aspects of the main proceedings were confined within one Member State.[135] In the same case, the Court also rejected as inadmissible the question with regard to Article 4(3) TEU-L and Article 101 or 102 TFEU, on the basis that 'it is quite obvious that the national legislation at issue in the main proceedings … cannot, in itself or by its application, affect trade between Member States'.[136]

[131] The similarity in the language used by the Court is striking, particularly in paras [38] and [56].

[132] See also ch 1, section IV.B on the comparison between MEQR under Article 34 TFEU and 'effect on trade'.

[133] *SA GB-INNO-BM v ATAB* (n 60) [53].

[134] However, in practice, this is not always the case, since the geographic market is defined across national lines whenever there are divergent regulatory interventions. See ch 6, section II.B on the suggested revision of the geographic market in these cases.

[135] Case C-393/08 *Emanuela Sbarigia v Azienda USL RM/A and others* [2010] ECR I-6337 [23]–[25], [28].

[136] ibid [31]–[33].

Furthermore, to the extent that Article 102 TFEU is expressly addressed to undertakings, the extension of the reach of EU law to cover such cases should be done explicitly under the freedoms, not indirectly through the back door of Article 4(3) TEU-L and Article 102 TFEU, if it is desirable at all in the first place. Indeed, the relatively recent cases on citizenship confirm the heated debate as to the extension of EU residence and movement rights when there is no link to cross-border movement.[137] Academics have voiced arguments that pushing for more inclusion under the free movement provisions (or the EU citizenship provisions) could present challenges from the perspective of EU competence and legitimacy.[138] It should be recalled that the Court of Justice seems to require an explicit 'renvoi' technique employed by the national law, which should actually prohibit reverse discrimination, when a preliminary question is admitted in purely internal situations.[139] By contrast, it is arguable that there would not be so many 'competence creep'-based objections to the expansion of the application in purely internal situations of the competition law provisions when enforced against undertakings.[140]

A fortiori, the same critique could be voiced in cases of justified trade barriers under Article 36 TFEU or the mandatory requirements doctrine. By keeping both legal routes open, namely the state action doctrine and the free movement provisions, the Commission and the courts can decide whether to assume competence for market regulation. The reason is that market regulation under the competition law provisions would, necessarily, take place at the EU level.[141] Therefore, when non-economic values come into play, which would merit protection even

[137] See Case C-34/09 *Gerardo Ruiz Zambrano v Office national de l'emploi (ONEm)* [2011] ECR I-01177; Case C-434/09 *Shirley McCarthy v Secretary of State for the Home Department* [2011] ECR I-03375; Case C-256/11 *Murat Dereci and others v Bundesministerium für Inneres* [2011] ECR I-11315; and Joined Cases C-356/11 and C-357/11 *O and S v Maahanmuuttovirasto and Maahanmuuttovirasto v L*, Judgment of 6 December 2012 (NYR). See P Van Elsuwege, 'Shifting the Boundaries? European Union Citizenship and the Scope of Application of EU Law—Case No. C-34/09, *Gerardo Ruiz Zambrano v Office National de l'Emploi*' (2011) 38(3) *Legal Issues of Economic Integration* 271–76; and H van Eijken and S de Vries, 'A New Route into the Promised Land? Being a European Citizen after Ruiz Zambrano' (2011) 36(5) *European Law Review* 709–13. For two opposing views as to the reach of the 'market citizenship', see N Nic Shuibne, 'The Resilience of EU Market Citizenship' (2010) 47 *Common Market Law Review* 1612–19; and F Wollenschläger, 'A New Fundamental Freedom beyond Market Integration: Union Citizenship and its Dynamics for Shifting the Economic Paradigm of European Integration' (2011) 17 *European Law Journal* 1.

[138] In particular, see D Hanf, '"Reverse Discrimination" in EU Law: Constitutional Aberration, Constitutional Necessity or Judicial Choice?' (2011) 18 *Maastricht Journal* 55–58: 'Despite its inherent inconsistencies, and the existence of alternative approaches, the internal situation doctrine is a suitable instrument to meet the constitutional necessity of respecting the division of powers between the Union and its Member States' (ibid 57). See C Ritter, 'Purely Internal Situations, Reverse Discrimination, *Guimont*, *Dzodzi* and Article 234' (2006) 31 *European Law Review* 696–703, 709–10 for a similar competence-based argument.

[139] See ch 1, text to nn 133–35.

[140] See text to n 134.

[141] This is why public policy considerations cannot be taken into consideration under the competition law provisions when enforced against undertakings; see ch 4, section II.B.

by anti-competitive national regulations, those non-economic values have been exempted from the scope of the competition law provisions applied to state action. The reason is precisely that a balancing exercise similar to the one under the free movement provisions cannot be undertaken under the competition provisions. The outcome is characterised by inconsistency without any persuasive justification. In that respect, the typical example is the treatment of collective labour agreements which were exempted from the scope of the state action doctrine in *Albany*,[142] but, as expected, were subjected to the free movement provisions in *Viking* and *Commission v Germany* (in the field of public procurement) on the basis that 'those two sets of provisions are to be applied in different circumstances'.[143] It is noteworthy that AG Trstenjak in her Opinion in *Commission v Germany* seems to suggest that, instead of applying the *Albany* exclusion from the scope of the competition rules to the scope of the freedoms, the principles established in *Albany* in relation to competition law would need to be re-examined.[144]

If, however, the EU institutions seek to assume competence for market regulation without putting non-economic values to the test, the easiest way to address the market-distorting effect is against the undertaking involved via competition law infringement proceedings. This could lead to leverage against the non-economic identity of the Member State concerned, under certain conditions, namely if the question of the legality of the state action does not reach the EU courts. This is arguably the situation of the gap in the state action doctrine with regard to Article 102 TFEU, as revealed in *Deutsche Telekom* and *Sotirios Lélos*, which is analysed in section IV below.[145]

IV. THE INTERPLAY BETWEEN PRIVATE AND STATE RESPONSIBILITY UNDER THE COMPETITION LAW PROVISIONS

This section critically describes the interplay between the state action defence and the state action doctrine, with the hindsight of the preceding structural analysis of the two mechanisms. In so doing, the focus is on the recent market separation cases. In those cases, the Commission and/or the courts have only addressed one

[142] The state action doctrine in relation to Article 101 TFEU; on the difference between that and the conjoint application of Article 102 TFEU and 106 TFEU in *Albany*, see text to nn 99–105.

[143] Case C-271/08 *Commission v Federal Republic of Germany* [2010] ECR I-7091 [48]; Case C-438/05 *International Transport Workers' Federation and Finnish Seamen's Union v Viking Line ABP and OÜ Viking Line Eesti* [2007] ECR I-10779 [53], in which *Meca-Medina* is also cited in support (see ch 2, text to 64 on this point).

[144] *Commission v Federal Republic of Germany* (n 143), Opinion of AG Trstenjak [68]. See also F Liberatore, 'UK Calls for Ban of Parallel Trade of Prescription Medicines—What are the EU Competition Law Implications?' (2013) 34 *European Competition Law Review* 196, who similarly sets the question as to the legality of national regulation banning parallel trade in pharmaceuticals, which would be justified under the free movement provisions, but not necessarily so under the state action doctrine.

[145] In particular, see the analysis presented in section IV.B.

side of the coin, namely private responsibility under the competition provisions, even though arguments in regard to state responsibility have been raised.

A. The Dual Role of ex-Article 3(1)(g) TEC

The interplay between the state action defence and the state action doctrine is an elusive one, and this is depicted in the dual use of ex-Article 3(1)(g) TEC on a 'system of undistorted competition within the Internal Market'. First, the clause is undeniably the cornerstone of the state action doctrine.[146] Second, the clause has played a preponderant role in substantiating an abuse of a dominant position in market separation cases in which a state action defence was raised unsuccessfully, thereby confirming that the state action defence cannot adequately fulfil its role as an applicability threshold.

In *Deutsche Telekom*, the Court of Justice had recourse to the regulatory obligation to provide wholesale access to the ULL by reference to a 'system ensuring that competition in the Common Market is not distorted'.[147] It did this for the purpose of establishing that the spread between the wholesale and retail prices charged by the dominant undertaking is abusive, because it makes market entry for potential equally efficient competitors very difficult and limits the choices available to consumers as to their sources of supply.[148] In addition, the Court upheld the finding that the EU regulatory principle of tariff rebalancing and the prohibition of cross-subsidisation require consideration of the revenues only from retail access services. Revenues from call services are not included, even though access services and call services can indeed constitute a whole from the point of view of the end-user.[149] This is because 'a system of undistorted competition can be guaranteed only if equality of opportunity is secured as between the various economic operators'.[150] Therefore, it seems that the Court's finding of an abusive margin squeeze is based on the prior regulatory intervention. This finding is made without, however, the Court having assessed the legality or the purpose of such regulatory intervention, but only after having rejected its impact upon the scope of autonomous conduct by the dominant undertaking.[151] This justifies the need to have recourse to the clause of ex-Article 3(1)(g) TEC for the purposes of informing the legal test, which governs market separation as an abuse of a dominant position.

[146] See section III.A, text to nn 61–63.

[147] *Deutsche Telekom AG v Commission* (n 3) [170], [180]. In addition, at [180], the Court cross-cites its judgment in *Sotirios Lélos* (n 3 [68]), in which the Court upheld the protection of price competition from restrictions on parallel trade by reference to 'the Treaty objectives to protect consumers by means of undistorted competition and the integration of national markets'.

[148] *Deutsche Telekom AG v Commission* (n 3) [169]–[184], [255].

[149] ibid [221], [227], [230]–[236].

[150] ibid [230], [234].

[151] ibid [91]–[92].

Similarly, in *Sotirios Lélos*, the Court of Justice, by reference to the Treaty objective 'of ensuring that competition in the Internal Market is not distorted', held that:

> [P]ractices of an undertaking in a dominant position which are aimed at avoiding all parallel exports from a Member State to other Member States [are prima facie abusive because] ... by partitioning the national markets, they neutralise the benefits of effective competition in terms of the supply and the prices that those exports would obtain for final consumers in the other Member States.[152]

However, as explained in chapter four, the Court subsequently asserted the participation of the dominant pharmaceutical undertaking in the negotiations for setting the price regulation. In that way, the Court seems to suggest that the effect of the regulation is actually attributed to the undertaking. Further, the Court seems to suggest that the undertaking's practices to avoid all parallel exports are, after all, abusive only to the extent that they are actually attributed to the dominant undertaking, since price regulation 'is one of the factors liable to create opportunities for parallel trade'.[153] However, the legality or the purpose of such price regulation at national level is not part of the Court's reasoning on substantiating why the prevention of the parallel exports is abusive.

B. The Structural Imbalance between Private and State Responsibility under the Competition Law Provisions

The ideal scenario of interaction between private and state responsibility under the competition law provisions could be depicted in the following chain of causation. Private responsibility under Article 102 TFEU is a precondition for state responsibility under Article 4(3) TEU-L (or Article 106(1) TFEU) in conjunction with Article 102 TFEU, which then feeds backs to private responsibility and forestalls the enforcement of Article 102 TFEU. However, this chain of causation is inherently paradoxical in EU law, because the causal link between private responsibility triggering state responsibility cannot be the same as the link that needs to exist for the state action defence to be successful.[154] In other words, on the one hand, a state action defence can only succeed if the state has forced the undertaking to abuse its dominant position ('compulsion'), but, on the other hand, so tight a link nullifies any willfulness and autonomy of the undertaking's conduct, which is a precondition for finding an abuse from which state responsibility is derived. Similarly, the link between private conduct and state conduct only affects the existence of the private conduct, whereas, from the perspective of

[152] *Sotirios Lélos* (n 3) [66].

[153] ibid [67]; see also ch 4, section III.D.

[154] See also F Castillo de la Torre, 'State Action Defence in EC Competition Law' (2005) 28 *World Competition Law and Economics Review* 412, who, however, uses this paradox in order to argue that the state action defence is too 'lenient' for the dominant undertakings affected and should be abolished altogether: ibid 421–22.

state responsibility, private responsibility is a cause for the anti-competitive effect of the national legislation.

The case law has construed the state action defence in such a way that it is conceptually impossible to find state responsibility for a breach of competition law and immunity for the undertaking's conduct as the two sides of the same coin, ie, to attribute the violation either to the state or to the undertaking.[155] This is also evidenced in the only case in which the Commission took double action against both the undertaking and the Member State involved; the Italian custom agents case (*CNSD*).[156] It is striking that the Court of Justice judgment against Italy pre-empted the outcome of the General Court judgment on the responsibility of the undertaking, precisely because, for the purposes of substantiating state responsibility, the Court of Justice first had to substantiate that the undertaking's autonomous conduct was restrictive of competition.[157]

The following table depicts the structural imbalance between the conditions required for the state action defence and the state action doctrine to succeed:

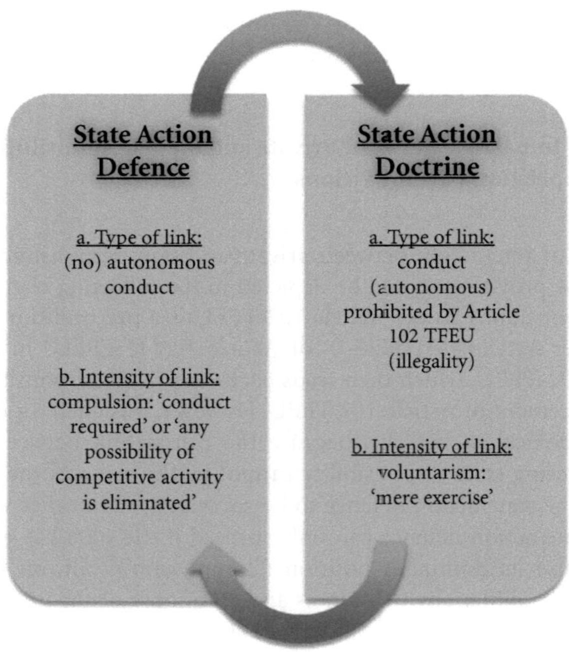

Figure 5.1: Structural Imbalance between the State Action Defence and the State Action Doctrine

[155] *Cf* Baquero Cruz (n 2) 552 and 590, who seems to assume that the state action doctrine (both as it stands and in his revised version) and the state action defence are symmetrical.

[156] See text to n 14.

[157] *Commission v Italian Republic* (n 14) [45]–[51].

At the same time, there are no compulsory procedural (enforcement) mechanisms that would permit the state involved to be brought before the Court of Justice, as the Commission's exercise of discretion to initiate proceedings under Article 258 TFEU is not subject to judicial review.[158] Once the Commission has decided that it will not address the market distortion against the Member State involved, private responsibility is established, since a state action defence cannot succeed. Therefore, the problem is not an evidentiary one in a grey zone of shared state and private responsibility, but it turns out to be a problem of principle. The state responsibility under the EU competition law provisions remains unaddressed precisely because of the way that the state action doctrine and the state action defence interact according to case law. *Deutsche Telekom* and *Sotirios Lélos*, in which, allegedly, there was shared responsibility between the dominant undertaking and state regulation for the anti-competitive market separation, have recently brought that issue to the surface. The reason is that in neither case was the dominant undertaking procedurally able to bring before the European courts the question of the legality of state action.

In particular, the problem in this situation is, first, that the market-distorting effect is attributed exclusively to the undertaking. This leads to a biased outcome in cases in which both state and private conduct are alleged to have contributed to the anti-competitive effect (alleged illegality), but state conduct is not the only cause of the private responsibility (namely that there is 'autonomous conduct'). Second, if the question of the legality of the market-distorting state regulation does not reach the EU courts, it does not matter whether such market-distorting regulation is justified or not for the purposes of attributing the conduct to the undertaking under a state action defence. This can, in addition, involve a biased outcome against the Member State concerned, to the extent that the national non-economic values involved are not taken into consideration when enforcing Article 102 TFEU.

One typical example of this is *Sotirios Lélos*. Public health is a largely unharmonised sector because the organisation and delivery of health services and medical care have been expressly excluded from the scope of EU action.[159] The non-economic values underpinning price and distribution regulation at the national level in the pharmaceutical sector are related to each Member State's healthcare expenditure objectives, and the degree of price regulation is dependent upon the aim to protect the budgets of the social health insurance funds in each

[158] See section II.A.

[159] Under Article 152(5) TEC: 'Community action in the field of public health shall fully respect the responsibilities of the Member States for the organisation and delivery of health services and medical care.' Article 152(5) TEC has been replaced by Article 168(7) TFEU: 'Union action shall respect the responsibilities of the Member States for the definition of their health policy and for the organisation and delivery of health services and medical care.'

Member State, as well as the extent to which each Member State is willing to subsidise pharmaceutical research and development (R&D).[160]

Therefore, obliging a dominant undertaking to charge a uniform price across Member States, with varying degrees of price regulation, would reduce access for consumers in countries where prices are currently lower, because economic and social conditions mean that consumers cannot afford higher prices. Price uniformity would also provoke a steady diminution of Europe's contribution to pharmaceutical R&D investment by reducing the profit margin allowed in countries where prices are currently high.[161] However, it is doubtful whether those uniform effects could be achieved by subjecting the national price and distribution regulations to the free movement provisions. As regards price controls, a recent opinion of AG Trstenjak in a case concerning the interpretation of Directive 89/105/EEC (transparency of measures regulating the prices of medicinal products for human use) summarises the relevant case law.[162] According to the case law, the relevant national regulations have consistently been held to be compatible with the free movement provisions. Even if price controls are caught by Article 34 TFEU, which would arguably be the case under a market access test, they would be justified on the basis of an economic evaluation (eg, financial balance of healthcare funds and pharmaceutical R&D) of a non-economic service (healthcare).[163] Under the free movement provisions, the non-economic values underpinning national pharmaceutical regulation would be, at least, extensively discussed in a structured and

[160] See T Nguyen, T Minssen and X Groussot, 'The Rule of Reason under Article 82 EC after Sot Lélos kai Sia' (2009) Working Paper, http://papers.ssrn.com/sol3/papers.cfm?abstract_id=1431010, 22–24 for a summary of the national regulation underpinning the pharmaceutical sector. See also G Tsouloufas, 'Limiting Pharmaceutical Parallel Trade in the European Union: Regulatory and Economic Justifications' (2011) 36 *European Law Review* 287–89 for a detailed survey of the regulatory practice of the Member States with regard to price controls of pharmaceutical products. See also Commission (EC), 'A Stronger European-based Pharmaceutical Industry for the Benefit of the Patient—A Call for Action' (Communication) COM(2003) 383 final [15]–[16]; and *Glaxo Wellcome* (Case IV/36.957/F3), *Aseprofar and Fedifar* (Case IV/36.997/F3), *Spain Pharma* (Case IV/37.121/F3), *BAI* (Case IV/37.138/F3), *EAEPC* (Case IV/37.380/F3) Commission Decision 2001/791/EC [2001] OJ L 302/1 [162], in which the Commission did not object to 'the grouping together of Germany, the United Kingdom, Denmark, Sweden, Finland, Ireland and Austria as high price countries and Belgium, Portugal, Italy, France, Greece and Spain as countries with relatively lower prices'.

[161] Case C-53/03 *Synaiterismos Farmakopoion Aitolias & Akarnanias and others (Syfait) v GlaxoSmithKline AEVE* [2005] ECR I-4609, Opinion of AG Jacobs [79]; Commission (EC), 'On the Single Market in Pharmaceuticals' (Communication) COM(1998) 558 final [10]–[11], [11]–[15]; Commission (EC), 'A Stronger European-based Pharmaceutical Industry for the Benefit of the Patient—A Call for Action' (Communication) COM(2003) 383 final [14]–[15], [21]–[22].

[162] Joined Cases C-352–356/07, C-365–367/07 and C-400/07 *Menarini Industrie Farmaceutiche Riunite Srl* [2009] ECR I-2495, Opinion of AG Trstenjak [60]–[65], with extensive citations. See also J Snell, 'Free Movement of Pharmaceutical Products: An Overdose of Cheap Drugs?' [2003] *European Business Law Review* 508–12; and L Hancher and W Sauter, *EU Competition and Internal Market Law in the Health Care Sector* (Oxford University Press, 2012) 168–73.

[163] For precedents, see, eg, Case C 120-/95 *Nicolas Decker v Caisse de maladie des employés privés* [1998] ECR I-1831 [39]; and Case C-158/96 *Raymond Kohll v Union des caisses de maladie* [1998] ECR I-1931 [41]. See also ch 3, text to n 59.

discursive manner under the proportionality test, as opposed to the 'all-or-nothing' approach under the competition law provisions.[164]

V. CONCLUSIONS

This chapter examines the operability of the state action defence in market separation cases as a test for attribution of responsibility for market separation under Article 102 TFEU. The argument advanced is that the degree of legislative constraint upon the undertaking's autonomous conduct is not only evidentially relevant in order to attribute an alleged competition law violation to the dominant undertaking, but also necessarily leads to the finding of a violation of Article 102 TFEU. Therefore, it becomes decisive in principle and renders the defence not operable as an applicability threshold.

The reason why the legislative constraint becomes decisive in principle under Article 102 TFEU is that there is a structural imbalance between the state action defence and the state action doctrine (state responsibility under Article 4(3) TEU-L (ex-Article 10 TEC) in conjunction with Article 102 TFEU). The state action defence does require compulsion by the undertaking, regardless of the legality of the state action, whereas the state action doctrine requires that private responsibility under Article 102 TFEU (autonomous conduct that constitutes an abuse of dominance) is already a reason for the anti-competitive effect of the national legislation.

Recent market separation cases such as *Deutsche Telekom* have brought to light such an imbalance between private and state responsibility under Article 102 TFEU because it is the first time when state action would need to be dealt with under Article 4(3) TEU-L (ex-Article 10 TEC) in conjunction with Article 102 TFEU rather than Article 106(1) TFEU. More importantly, these cases demonstrate the identified structural imbalance precisely because there was, procedurally, no other legal route for the dominant undertaking to bring the question of the state action legality before the EU courts. The imbalance between private and state responsibility under the competition law provisions leads to a biased outcome against the dominant undertaking and this is reflected in the use of the clause of ex-Article 3(1)(g) TEC for the purposes of substantiating private responsibility. In some instances, it also leads to a biased outcome against the non-economic values promoted by the Member State involved.

Finally, in analysing the state action doctrine, a spectrum has been constructed with regard to the varied intensity of links required under the different Treaty provisions between the state conduct and the undertaking's conduct, for the state

[164] See ch 4, sections II.A and II.B on the difference between the application of the proportionality principle under the free movement and the competition law provisions, at the justification stage, which is desirable and should be preserved.

to be held responsible for a breach of these Treaty provisions. The free movement provisions, the 'delegation test' under Article 37(1) TFEU on 'State monopolies of a commercial character' and the test under Article 106(1) TFEU on 'undertakings granted special or exclusive rights' are the Treaty provisions considered. It is submitted that the inability to identify with precision the intensity of such a link under the state action doctrine can be overcome by subjecting the state action to the free movement provisions. These provisions do not require any link with independent conduct by the undertaking involved. In chapter six, this proposition will be analysed and will form the basis of the suggested revision of the state action defence.

6

Principled Attribution of Market Separation to the Dominant Undertaking and the State: A Revised State Action Defence

I. INTRODUCTION

It has been argued in this book that the analytical core of the interface between market separation under Article 102 TFEU and non-economic justifications is the question of attributing the market-distorting effect to the dominant undertaking or the state. The alternative of incorporating non-economic justifications into the assessment under Article 102 TFEU exposes the risk of a biased outcome against the Member State concerned and its non-market identity (chapter four). Furthermore, it has been shown that the existing attribution mechanism, the so-called state compulsion defence, is not adequate as an applicability threshold, as construed by the case law. The principal reason is that it leads to a biased outcome against the dominant undertaking, since it cannot accommodate an assessment of the state's responsibility (chapter five).

This chapter identifies a solution to the question of the principled attribution of market separation in proceedings under Article 102 TFEU by combining the two findings mentioned above. The conclusions of chapter four only permit distinct substantive legality tests for the dominant undertaking and the state. However, the conclusions of chapter five indicate that the state compulsion defence excludes assessment of state responsibility, whereas it necessarily leads to establishment of private responsibility under Article 102 TFEU, rather than simply ascertaining that there is autonomous conduct by the undertaking. This is the reason for the structural imbalance between private and state responsibility under the competition law provisions. The proposed solution is to incorporate an assessment of the legality of the state action under the free movement provisions in the context of Article 102 TFEU enforcement proceedings against the dominant undertaking.

This is addressed in section II of this chapter, which is structured as follows. First, the substantive legality test for state action is analysed in section II.A. Building on the spectrum of links required under the different Treaty provisions between the state conduct and the undertaking's conduct, it is argued that the state conduct should be subjected to the free movement provisions only rather than to Article 102 TFEU read together with Article 4(3) TEU (or Article 106(1) TFEU).

Second, section II.B explores how the assessment of the dominant undertaking's conduct and the state conduct could be linked in the context of enforcement proceedings against the dominant undertaking. The geographic market definition is proposed as an adequate filter for introducing the control of state responsibility as a subordinate issue in the context of Article 102 TFEU enforcement proceedings. The implications of such a measure for the applicability and actual application of Article 102 TFEU against the dominant undertaking are further analysed.

The institutional capacity of competition enforcement authorities (namely the Commission, the National Competition Authorities (NCAs) and the national courts) to undertake control of state responsibility under the free movement provisions is explored in section II.C. The implications of the Court of Justice judgment in *SYFAIT*, in which a preliminary reference from a NCA was held to be inadmissible, are emphasised.

Section III tests the proposed defence of contributory responsibility for market separation in proceedings against the dominant undertaking, through the example of regulation of intellectual property rights (IPRs) in the context of private litigation. The 'non-exhaustion' of specific IPRs under the free movement provisions fits in the proposed interaction between the competition law and the free movement provisions when they are applied concomitantly in the context of private litigation. By contrast, the 'exhaustion' of IPRs under the free movement provisions does not fit in the proposed, principled application of the two sets of provisions and, for this reason, it illustrates the risk of added costs in terms of legal analysis and doctrinal assimilation.

II. FROM ARTICLE 3(1)(G) TEC TO PROTOCOL NO 27 TFEU: DISTINCT SUBSTANTIVE LEGALITY TESTS AND ASSOCIATED ENFORCEMENT MECHANISMS

The starting point of the analysis is the structural paradox identified in chapters four and five. There needs to be independent conduct by the undertaking of the type prohibited under Article 102 TFEU for state responsibility to be established under the state action doctrine, while at the same time the causal link between the state conduct and the undertaking's conduct requires compulsion under a state action defence.

A. Demise of the State Action Doctrine in Favour of the Free Movement Provisions

Davies, writing in the context of Article 106(1) TFEU, suggests that one principled solution to the paradox of the causal link between the undertaking's conduct of the type prohibited under Article 102 TFEU and state responsibility under Article 106(1) TFEU is to include state responsibility under the free movement provisions at the very beginning of the chain of causation.[1] Then, the dominant undertaking, by 'merely exercising' rights granted in violation of the free movement provisions, would itself violate Article 102 TFEU.

The problem with this proposal is that it encompasses an automatic link between state illegality and illegality of the undertaking's conduct. However, the proposition is a good starting point for further qualification in that it prefixes assessment of the state conduct under the free movement provisions to the assessment of the 'mere exercise' of the granted rights. In particular, assessment of the conformity of the state conduct with the free movement provisions cannot be part of the state action defence as presently construed by case law, but does require the revision of the doctrine. Similarly, this suggestion may have further implications as regards the actual application of Article 102 TFEU against the undertaking in cases in which the right granted is not illegal under the free movement provisions.

The suggested solution in this chapter is inspired by the General Court ruling in *Ladbroke Racing*, in which the Commission could not decide on the part of the complaint concerning the undertakings without deciding on the substance of the complaint against the state.[2] In *Ladbroke Racing*, the substance of the complaint against the state was based on the competition provisions through Article 4(3) TEU-L. By contrast, it is here advanced that the vehicle through which applicability of Article 102 TFEU would be asserted is dependent upon the substance of a complaint against the state based on the free movement provisions. Figure 6.1 depicts the proposed interaction between state and private responsibility for competition law violations, in particular for market separation, within the current context of the state action defence. This involves the following three steps (under A, B and C in figure 6.1, below).

However, the introduction of the assessment of state responsibility under the free movement provisions, namely Step A in Figure 6.1, leads, first, to a replacement of the standard of legality as regards the state action; ie, the use of the free movement provisions instead of the state action doctrine. Second, the replacement necessarily leads to a reversal of the order of assessment of legality between the undertaking's conduct and the state conduct and hence to a revision of the state action defence. Therefore, Step C in Figure 6.1 is redundant and its added value is lost, whereas the assessment under Step B is dependent upon the outcome of the assessment under Step A. Figure 6.2 depicts this simplified version

[1] G Davies, 'Article 86EC, the EC's Economic Approach to Competition Law, and the General Interest' (2009) 5 *European Competition Journal* 556–58, 562, who hence rejects any added value of Article 106(1) TFEU (or Article 4(3) TEU-L) read together with Article 102 TFEU over the free movement provisions.

[2] See Case T-548/93 *Ladbroke Racing v Commission* [1995] ECR II-2565 [47]–[51], reversed on appeal by the Court of Justice in Joined Cases C-359/95 P and C-379/95 P *Commission and French Republic v Ladbroke Racing* [1997] ECR I-6265 [30]–[32].

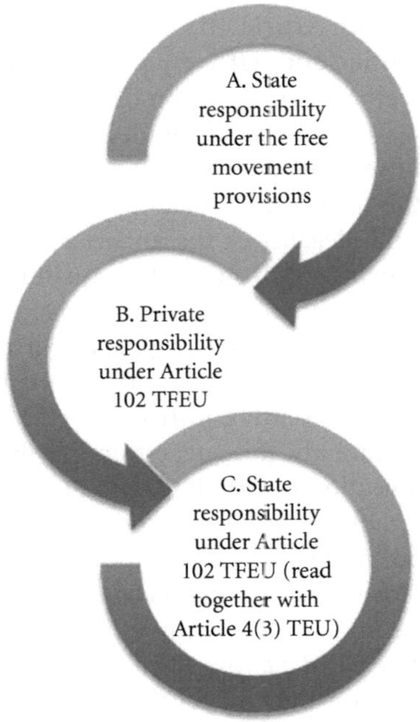

Figure 6.1: State responsibility under the free movement provisions as a supplement within the remits of the state action defence

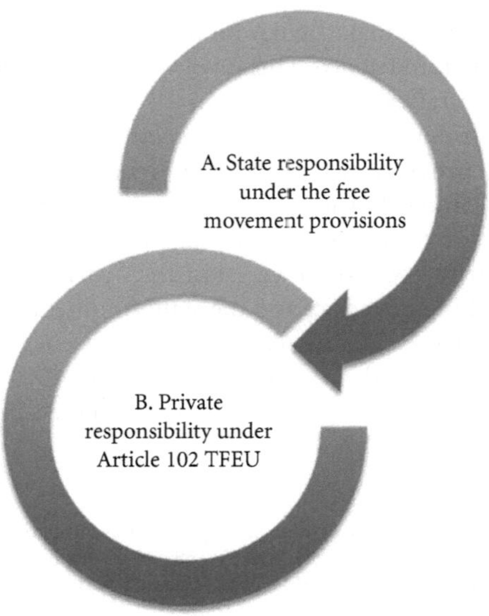

Figure 6.2: Replacement of the standard of legality for state action and the concomitant revision of the state action defence

of the interaction between the responsibility of the state and of the undertaking for competition law violations.

The proposed interpretation could be considered as fuelled by the relocation of the clause provided for in ex-Article 3(1)(g) TEC to Protocol No 27 TFEU on the Internal Market and competition, which states that the Internal Market 'includes a system ensuring that competition is not distorted'. The link between competition and free trade, as identified in chapter one,[3] is reflected in the analysis for finding trade barriers against Member States. At the same time, the policy integration necessary for backing up market integration is achieved at the national level by finding justified trade barriers, which can further trigger EU initiatives to harmonise such policy areas.

The link between competition and free trade, as well as the important role played by policy integration in the realm of Member State action, was recently confirmed in *FIFA v Commission*.[4] In that case, the General Court confirmed the Commission's approval of measures taken by the UK in accordance with Article 3(a) of Directive 89/552/EEC concerning broadcasting rights on an exclusive basis for events of major importance to the UK population, including the Football World Cup. The measures involved restrictions on the freedom to provide services on an exclusive basis for broadcasters which provide services that can be received by less than 95 per cent of the population. FIFA challenged the decision claiming, inter alia, that this was contrary to the freedom to provide services, the freedom of establishment, the rules on competition and Article 106(1) TFEU in conjunction with Article 102 TFEU. The General Court explicitly merged the competition law considerations with the restrictions on the freedom to provide services in relation to the reduction in the number of broadcasters competing for the exclusive right to broadcast World Cup matches live. However, precisely because those restrictions were held to be justified under the free movement provisions, the General Court held that the measures were also not contrary to the rules on competition.[5] However, neither the complainant nor the General Court identified what was actually meant by 'rules on competition', which indicates that a single set of rules applies, namely the free movement provisions. These rules also cover 'a system ensuring that competition in the Internal Market is not distorted', as per ex-Article 3(1)(g) TEC, which can only be side-stepped in cases of overriding reasons of public interest.

Similarly, for secondary legislation under Article 114 TFEU, the Court of Justice has confirmed, since the adoption of the Single European Act, that measures having as their object the establishment and the functioning of the Internal Market include measures which directly affect the establishment and functioning of the

[3] See ch 1, section III.B.

[4] Case T-68/08 *Fédération internationale de football association (FIFA) v Commission* [2011] ECR II-00349. An appeal is pending before the Court of Justice: Case C-205/11P *FIFA v Commission* [2011] OJ C 232/13.

[5] *FIFA v Commission* (n 4) [173].

then Common Market provided for in Article 115 TFEU.[6] This overlap primarily concerns appreciable distortions of the competition conditions, as was first analysed by AG Tesauro in *Titanium Dioxide*.[7] AG Tesauro held that harmonisation of the conditions of competition 'should be functionally linked with the establishment and the functioning of the Internal Market' because they both relate to the same level of integration in terms of depth.[8] Relatively more recently, in *Laserdisken ApS*, the Court of Justice was called upon to rule on the validity of the EU-wide exhaustion principle established by Directive 2001/29/EC on harmonisation of certain aspects of copyright, in light of the Treaty rules relating to the establishment of a competition policy.[9] The Directive in question is based on Article 114 TFEU and the Court first upheld the legal basis of the Directive on the ground that 'it allows for the taking of measures necessary for the smooth functioning of the Internal Market as regards freedom of establishment and the freedom to provide services, through harmonisation of national laws pertaining to the content and exercise of copyright and related rights'.[10] Second, the Court ruled that 'the harmonisation achieved by that Directive is also intended to ensure undistorted competition in the Internal Market, in accordance with [ex-]Article 3(1)(g) TEC'.[11] Therefore, the Court of Justice reaffirmed the close link between free movement law and competition policy when it comes to EU legislation harmonising Member States' laws.[12]

The alleged added value of subjecting state measures to the state action doctrine rather than only to the free movement provisions is that the former covers national regulations which are anti-competitive but have purely internal effect or which concern cases of reverse discrimination. It could be argued that, with the demise of the state action doctrine in the suggested way, namely as part of the application of the free movement provisions, such an advantageous treatment of the 'undistorted competition' is lost. In other words, anti-competitive state measures are no longer prohibited when they concern purely internal situations; hence, they are no longer 'special' compared to all other state measures that may

[6] See Case C-300/89 *Commission v Council* [1991] ECR I-2867 [15]: 'In order to give effect to the fundamental freedoms mentioned in [Article 26(2) TFEU], harmonising measures are necessary to deal with disparities between the laws of the Member States in areas where such disparities are liable to create or maintain distorted conditions of competition. For that reason, [Article 114 TFEU] empowers the Community to adopt measures for the approximation of the provisions laid down by law, regulation or administrative action in Member States and lays down the procedure to be followed for that purpose.'

[7] Opinion of AG Tesauro in *Commission v Council* (n 6).

[8] ibid [10]. However, AG Tesauro recognised that, at that time, the breadth of harmonised conditions of competition was wider than the Internal Market, since it extended to areas which were not part of the Internal Market.

[9] Case C-479/04 *Laserdisken ApS v Kulturministeriet* [2006] ECR I-8089.

[10] ibid [31]–[32].

[11] ibid [49].

[12] At a policy level, the Commission also points out competition screening as an integral part of the impact assessment for EU legislation. See Commission (EC), '2005 Annual Report on Competition Policy' [27]–[29].

potentially constitute a trade barrier. However, there are principled arguments in favour of such an interpretation, based on the fact that Article 102 TFEU is expressly addressed to undertakings. Therefore, the abolition of the cross-border limitation upon the reach of EU law in relation to state action should be carried out, if appropriate, under the free movement provisions.[13] From this perspective, one could view the relocation of the clause of ex-Article 3(1)(g) TEC to Protocol No 27 TFEU as a downgrading of the status of competition policy in the scheme of the Treaty.

However, the structural paradox in the application of the state action defence is exemplified by the demise of the state action doctrine, because independent private conduct of the type prohibited under Article 102 TFEU is not required for finding a violation of the free movement provisions. This is a prerequisite for permitting a revision of the actual manner in which Article 102 TFEU is applied to the dominant undertaking's conduct (namely, step B in Figure 6.2). Therefore, once step C in Figure 6.1 becomes redundant, the analysis carried out as well as its outcome under Step B is dependent on the outcome of the assessment carried out under Step A (see Figure 6.2). This relationship is explored in section II.B below. The aim is to liberate competition law analysis from policy integration considerations and make it more self-contained in instances of shared responsibility between the dominant undertaking and the state for market separation.

The basis for the revision of the state action defence is the proposition that the order in which the legality of the state conduct and the undertaking's conduct are assessed is necessarily reversed by replacing the state action doctrine with the free movement provisions. This proposition finds, paradoxically, support in the cases in which the horizontal direct application of the free movement of goods provision is rejected. In both *Haug-Adrion* and *Sapod Audic*, the private conduct in question was a clause in a contract between undertakings.[14] However, what seems to be decisive in both cases is that there was a national law which merely permitted the undertakings to adopt the clauses and which was assessed under Article 34 TFEU and was found not to be in breach of that Article. This is noteworthy because, in light of the existence of private conduct linked to the prior state action, one would have expected the Court of Justice to simultaneously address both conducts under the state action doctrine. Instead, the Court asserted the compatibility of the state measures with the free movement provisions.

In *Haug-Adrion*, the Court of Justice held that the national rules did not fall within Article 34 TFEU because 'they merely authorize insurance companies to take into account in their tariff conditions particular circumstances in which vehicles are used which increase or diminish the insurance risk'.[15] Therefore, the

[13] See the analysis in ch 5, section III.D.

[14] This also fits into the research presented in ch 2, section V, according to which, in cases of horizontal application of the freedoms, the private actors involved, no matter how remote from some regulatory function, did not constitute undertakings; see also ch 2, n 83.

[15] Case 251/83 *Eberhard Haug-Adrion v Frankfurter Versicherungs-AG* [1984] ECR 4277 [21].

national rules merely permitted the motor insurance contract in question, which did not provide for a bonus to customers exporting their cars. Similarly, in *Sapod Audic*, there was a national law, which was interpreted by the Court of Justice as imposing only a general obligation to identify the packaging collected for disposal by an approved undertaking (in a system for waste disposal) and which was found to be a selling arrangement, outwith the scope of Article 34 TFEU.[16] In this case, the national rules also merely did not prohibit the undertakings involved from giving to this general obligation the specific form of an obligation to apply a mark or label on the packaging. Therefore, regardless of what the Court actually ruled with regard to the subsequent private conduct by the undertakings (namely the contractual clause),[17] it first subjected the prior national legislation, which permitted such private conduct, to the free movement provisions.

B. Geographic Market Definition

There is no need for a prior finding of independent conduct by the dominant undertaking of the type prohibited under Article 102 TFEU, under the free movement provisions. Therefore, subjecting state action to the free movement provisions, instead of the state action doctrine, also reverses the order of assessment of the legality as between the undertaking's conduct and the state conduct within the context of Article 102 TFEU enforcement proceedings. The subsequent questions are, first, at which stage of the analysis under Article 102 TFEU would an assessment of the legality of a state action be accommodated, and, second, whether such an assessment exerts influence on the applicability or actual application of Article 102 TFEU.

Geographic market definition is the most appropriate stage of the analysis under Article 102 TFEU under which to accommodate an assessment of the conformity of state action with the free movement provisions. The underlying proposition is that regulatory interventions influence competitive pressure which the dominant undertaking faces in a given geographic area and, for that reason, they isolate this area from other geographic areas.[18] This is why, in cases of the extreme example of regulatory intervention, namely statutory monopoly rights

[16] Case C-159/00 *Sapod Audic v Eco-Emballages SA* [2002] ECR I-5031[71]–[73].

[17] See *Eberhard Haug-Adrion v Frankfurter Versicherungs-AG* (n 15) [22]; and *Sapod Audic v Eco-Emballages SA* (n 16) [74].

[18] See, in particular, Commission (EC), 'Notice on the definition of relevant market for the purposes of Community competition law' [1997] OJ C 372/13 [30], in which the example of 'regulatory barriers arising from public procurement, price regulations, quotas and tariffs limiting trade or production, technical standards, monopolies, freedom of establishment, requirements for administrative authorizations, packaging regulations, etc' is mentioned.

which cover the whole of the territory of a Member State, the geographic market involved is defined across national lines.[19]

In chapter one, a paradox was highlighted as regards market separation cases. If a product market is not integrated, ie, is not already EU-wide because the regulatory framework is fragmented, but the undertaking concerned is active at an EU-wide level, the geographic market definition and the market coverage of the effect of the conduct do not coincide. This defeats the purpose of defining, in the first place, the market in the context of Article 102 TFEU enforcement, which is to identify the competitive constraints that the undertaking faces in order to assess the degree of its market power. [20] In addition, it has been pointed out in chapter two that legal entry barriers can be assessed against the free movement provisions.[21] Legal entry barriers are taken into consideration when determining the undertaking's market power, which feeds back to the geographic market definition.[22]

A revised application of Article 102 TFEU is needed in market separation cases in order to accommodate a prior assessment as to whether state action is in conformity with the free movement provisions. This could be achieved at the stage of geographic market definition, in particular under the notion of legal entry barriers. The geographic market definition is part of the assessment of the undertaking's market power.[23] Market power is the concept that associates the personal and material scope of Article 102 TFEU, since it is a condition *sine qua non* for the anti-competitive effect of market separation to occur.[24] As such, 'market power' is conceptually suitable to accommodate an enquiry into the question of contributory responsibility between the dominant undertaking and the state for market separation.

To incorporate the assessment of the legality of a state action into enforcement proceedings of Article 102 TFEU has implications for the applicability, or actual application, of Article 102 TFEU. The content of Step B in Figure 6.2 depends on the outcome of the assessment carried out under Step A in Figure 6.2, namely whether the state action is in conformity with, or in breach of, the free movement provisions. It is proposed that state action in conformity with the free movement provisions substantially alters the analysis under Article 102, in particular because

[19] See, for example, Case T-229/94 *Deutsche Bahn AG v Commission* [1997] ECR II-1689 [55].

[20] See ch 1, section IV.D.

[21] And see I Lianos, 'Shifting the Narratives in the European Internal Market: Efficient Restrictions of Trade and the Nature of "Economic" Integration' [2010] *European Business Law Review* 726–28, for example, who promotes an understanding of the case law under Article 34 TFEU by association with the Bainian or Stiglerian economic definition of an entry barrier.

[22] See ch 2, text to nn 115–19.

[23] See, for example, Case T-62/1998 *Volkswagen AG v Commission* [2000] ECR II-2707 [230]: 'For the purposes of [Article 102 TFEU], the proper definition of the relevant market is a necessary precondition for any judgment as to allegedly anti-competitive behaviour, since, before an abuse of a dominant position is ascertained, it is necessary to establish the existence of a dominant position in a given market, which presupposes that such a market has already been defined.'

[24] See ch 2, section V.A.

it leads to a wider, rather than just national, geographic market definition. By contrast, state action in breach of the free movement provisions rules out the subsequent enforcement of Article 102 TFEU against the dominant undertaking.

On the one hand, if the state conduct is in conformity with the free movement provisions, as was arguably the case for pharmaceutical price regulation in *Sotirios Lélos*,[25] then the geographic market should be exclusively defined on the basis of the economic activity of the undertaking involved and perception of the undertaking of the market in which it is active.[26] In the case of parallel trade in pharmaceuticals, the geographic market would be EU-wide rather than national.[27] Consequently, the geographic market involved and the geographic coverage of the effects of the conduct would coincide. In that sense, there is no interference of competition law with distributional effects, since all the benefits and costs of the conduct considered are within the same market but in relation to different categories of consumers, rather than across different markets.[28] This is also in line with the Commission's Notice on market definition and, in particular, with paragraph 32 as regards taking into account wider geographic markets, because of the continuing process of market integration, when defining the market concerned in the context of assessment of concentrations and structural Joint Ventures.[29] The effects of restricting or permitting parallel trade may lead to a structural change in the supply of a product in the future and, hence, it could be argued that it is similar to the assessment of concentrations.[30]

The application of Article 102 TFEU would change in two ways if the geographic market concerned is wide. First, it may be that the undertaking is no longer dominant. Second, it could be the case that different types of costs and benefits are aggregated across various categories of consumers in different countries.

If, on the other hand, the state conduct breaches the free movement provisions, the dominant undertaking's subsequent conduct should be shielded from the

[25] See ch 5, text to nn 159–64.

[26] See *Aberdeen Journals Ltd v Director General of Fair Trading* [2002] CAT 4; [2002] CompAR 167 [103]; *Genzyme Ltd v OFT* [2004] CAT 4; [2004] CompAR 358 [217] for precedents in regard to market definition in Article 102 TFEU cases, on the basis of the dominant undertaking's own perception of the market in which it is active.

[27] In *Sotirios Lélos*, this approach was advocated by the dissenting opinion in the decision by the Hellenic Competition Commission, from which *Syfait* originated; see ch 1, text to nn 151–52.

[28] The Commission seems to have taken a stand against aggregating effects across different markets under Article 101(3) TFEU; Commission (EC), 'Guidelines on the application of Article 81(3) of the Treaty' (Notice) [2004] OJ C 101/97 [43]. See also OFT, 'Article 101(3)—A Discussion of Narrow versus Broad Definition of Benefits' (Discussion Note for OFT Breakfast Roundtable) (2010), available at www.oft.gov.uk/shared_oft/events/Article101(3)-discussionnote.pdf [4.1]–[4.30] on a similar discussion under Article 101(3) TFEU and the arguments in favour, and against, of aggregating costs and benefits to consumers across separate geographic markets directly affected by an agreement. See [4.11], in particular, on the distributional effects.

[29] Commission (EC) (n 18) [32].

[30] See also ibid [12]: 'The different time horizon considered in each case might lead to the result that different geographic markets are defined for the same products depending on whether the Commission is examining a change in the structure of supply, such as a concentration or a cooperative joint venture, or examining issues relating to certain past behaviour.'

application of Article 102 TFEU, regardless of whether the undertaking's autonomous conduct was required or simply facilitated by the state. The Commission could then only, potentially, address the market distortion against the Member State by exercising its discretionary powers to initiate proceedings under Article 258 TFEU. However, once subordinate control of the conformity with the freedoms of the state action has been conducted either in the context of an appeal against a Commission decision under Regulation 1/2003 or against a decision by a NCA or in the context of private enforcement of competition law, the dominant undertaking would be protected from Article 102 TFEU enforcement. The Commission, the NCA or the national court would be under an obligation to abstain from applying Article 102 TFEU in the specific case, while at the same time disapplying the national legislation.

In effect, this is very close to the obligation imposed by the Court of Justice upon NCAs in *CIF* to control state intervention under the state action doctrine in the context of a state action defence raised in proceedings under Regulation 1/2003. Indeed, in *CIF*, the Court of Justice held that:

> [T]he primacy of [EU] law requires any provision of national law which contravenes an [EU] rule to be disapplied, regardless of whether it was adopted before or after that rule. The duty to disapply national legislation which contravenes [EU] law applies not only to national courts but also to all organs of the State, including administrative authorities.[31]
>
> ...
>
> As regards, by contrast, the penalties which may be imposed on the undertakings concerned, it is appropriate to draw a two-fold distinction ... by reference to whether the facts at issue pre-dated or post-dated the National Competition Authority's decision to disapply the relevant national legislation.
>
> ...
>
> If the general [EU]-law principle of legal certainty is not to be violated, the duty of National Competition Authorities to disapply such an anti-competitive law cannot expose the undertakings concerned to any penalties, either criminal or administrative, in respect of past conduct where the conduct was required by the law concerned.
>
> The decision to disapply the law concerned does not alter the fact that the law set the framework for the undertakings' past conduct. The law thus continues to constitute, for the period prior to the decision to disapply it, a justification which shields the undertakings concerned from all the consequences of an infringement of [Articles 101 and 102 TFEU] and does so vis-a-vis both public authorities and other economic operators.[32]

Therefore, Article 102 TFEU also remains inapplicable until a decision disapplying national law in breach of EU law has been made, that is, when arguably the dominant undertaking becomes aware of the illegality of the state action.

[31] Case C-198/01 *CIF v Autorità Garante della Concorrenza e del Mercato* [2003] ECR I-8055 [48]–[49].

[32] ibid [52]–[54].

In the UK, the *CIF* reasoning was directly applied in *VIP Communications Ltd v OFCOM*.[33] The Competition Appeal Tribunal held that the dominant undertaking, T-Mobile, was shielded from the application of Article 102 TFEU (and the equivalent provision of national competition law) for its refusal to provide services to a customer which enable that customer to carry on an activity contrary to domestic law, unless or until there is a definite decision by OFCOM to disapply the national law. The compatibility of that law with EU sectoral directives was questionable, even though OFCOM had not yet disapplied it.[34]

This is arguably the case in *Deutsche Telekom*. Assessment of the legality of the RegTP conduct under Article 102 TFEU could not be accommodated within the state action defence. Had the legality according to the freedoms been incidentally assessed when defining the geographic market which involved only Germany because of the existence of regulatory arrangements across national lines, the dominant undertaking would have been shielded from Article 102 TFEU inasmuch as, according to the Commission, the RegTP was also responsible for the margin squeeze.[35]

C. Procedural Limitations and Institutional Capacities of the Actors Involved

However, there are procedural limitations to addressing state responsibility for market separation under the free movement provisions in the context of Article 102 TFEU enforcement proceedings. These limitations arise only in the context of the public enforcement of Article 102 TFEU at either the national or the EU level, the latter of which is governed by Regulation 1/2003. The reason is that, in the context of the private enforcement of Article 102 TFEU, there is no divergence between the procedure and the institutional actors involved, in comparison with private enforcement of the free movement provisions which form the vast majority of cases. In both cases, it is the national courts that concurrently have the power and the obligation to apply both sets of directly applicable Treaty provisions on their own initiative or when invoked by individual applicants.

[33] *VIP Communications Ltd v OFCOM* [2009] CAT 28, [2010] CompAR 13.

[34] ibid [15]–[27] and in particular [24]: 'In the present case there has been no disapplication of the relevant UK domestic legislation—OFCOM does not accept that there is any need for any such disapplication. We accept … that if legislation is incompatible with [EU] rules, then OFCOM is under a duty to disapply that legislation. But whether or not OFCOM's failure to disapply the relevant UK provisions is right does not, in our judgment, concern us because it is clear from *CIF* that unless or until that issue is resolved and the decision to disapply the law becomes definitive, T-Mobile is shielded from all the consequences of an infringement of [Articles 101 and 102 TFEU] vis-a-vis both public authorities and other economic operators.'

[35] See ch 5, text to n 28.

The institutional actors involved in the public enforcement of Article 102 TFEU are either the Commission empowered under Regulation 1/2003 or NCAs. They could also be National Administrative Authorities, which are mainly responsible for the application of sector-specific regulations, which have the concurrent power to apply generic competition law in the sector.[36] The question is whether those enforcement authorities are empowered, at either level, to apply the free movement provisions in the context of Article 102 TFEU enforcement proceedings against a dominant undertaking or, in other words, if the free movement provisions are Treaty provisions that are directly applicable not only before a national court but also before an administrative authority.[37]

The question arises precisely because public enforcement of the competition law provisions is authorised under Regulation 1/2003, which is silent as regards the application of directly applicable Treaty provisions other than Articles 101 and 102 TFEU by the Commission or the NCAs.[38] An associated consequence is that the European courts, when reviewing applications for the annulment of Commission decisions under Regulation 1/2003 or in the course of appeals, have consistently held that their jurisdiction is necessarily limited to the competition provisions and cannot extend to other Treaty provisions. In *Piau* and *Meca-Medina*, those other Treaty provisions were the free movement provisions.[39] The outcome is the same when the Court of Justice rules upon preliminary references that originate in the public enforcement of competition law at the national level, even in cases in which the national court brings in questions on the basis of the free movement provisions. For example, in *OTOC*, the Court of Justice rejected as inadmissible questions referred by the national court as to the applicability of the freedom to provide services, conjunctively or alternatively to the competition law provisions, since they were not relevant to the resolution of the dispute at the

[36] For example, in the UK, the communications regulator, the Office of Communications, is entrusted with *ex post* competition enforcement powers, concurrently with the Office of Fair Trading, in relation to activities connected with communications matters; see Communications Act (2003), pt 5, ch 1, ss 369–72.

[37] For a similar inquiry as regards Article 106(2) TFEU in particular, see N Zevgolis, 'Anti-competitive Conduct from Public or Privileged Enterprises: Towards a Per Se Abuse of Dominant Position? Applicability of the Provision of TFEU Article 106(2) by National Competition Authorities' (2012) 33 *European Competition Law Review* 89–90.

[38] See Articles 4–6 of Regulation 1/2003, which deal with the powers of the Commission, National Competition Authorities and national courts respectively to apply Articles 101 and 102 TFEU. Similarly, in Case T-398/07 *Kingdom of Spain v Commission*, Judgment of 29 March 2012 (NYR) [47], the General Court stated that 'in the context of proceedings conducted by the Commission pursuant to [Articles 101 and 102 TFEU] ... Articles 11 to 16 of Regulation 1/2003, in Chapter IV headed "Cooperation", do not impose an obligation on the Commission to consult the National Regulatory Authorities, nor do they provide for the Commission being able ... to undertake "joint action" with them in proceedings conducted by the Commission pursuant to [Articles 101 and 102 TFEU]'.

[39] Case T-193/02 *Laurent Piau v Commission* [2005] ECR II-209 [79], confirmed in Case C-171/05 P *Laurent Piau v Commission* [2006] ECR I-37 (Summary Publication) [56]–[58]; Case C-519/04 P *David Meca-Medina and Igor Majcen v Commission* [2006] ECR I-6991 [58].

national level.[40] Similarly, under the national law which allocates competence to NCAs or to national courts to review decisions made by the NCAs, such competence expressly only refers to the application of Articles 101 and 102 TFEU, as well the equivalent provisions of national laws. For example, in *VIP Communications Ltd v OFCOM*, mentioned above, the UK Competition Appeal Tribunal held that it had no jurisdiction to review whether the administrative authority concerned, OFCOM, had a duty to revoke domestic legislation incompatible with EU law because the relevant class of appealable decisions concerned only infringements of Articles 101 and 102 TFEU as well as their equivalent national provisions.[41]

However, those procedural limitations do not, in themselves, prohibit the assessment of the legality of state action under the free movement provisions in Article 102 TFEU enforcement proceedings. On the contrary, the inadmissibility of the free movement provisions in public enforcement proceedings of competition law highlights the need to reformulate the state action defence in the proposed manner—that is, by making the assessment of state action legality under the freedoms an integral part of the application of the competition law provisions. The reason is that such an assessment influences the applicability or actual application of Article 102 TFEU, based on the proposed revision of the state action defence. The Commission, NCAs and the reviewing courts unequivocally have competence and jurisdiction for the application of Article 102 TFEU.[42]

Besides, in *Fratelli Costanzo*, the Court of Justice held that when the conditions under which individuals may rely on a provision of EU law before national courts are met, all organs of state administration are obliged to apply that provision.[43] Therefore, national authorities, including NCAs, are bound by EU free movement rules. In addition, *Fratelli Costanzo* was the basis for the Court of Justice to establish in *CIF* the obligation of NCAs to disapply national legislation that was incompatible with the competition law provisions read together with Article 4(3) TEU-L.[44] Therefore, it could be argued that the direct applicability of the competition law provisions before the NCAs in the case of state action is derived, according to *CIF*, from the Treaty itself on the basis of *Fratelli Costanzo*, rather than Regulation 1/2003, and the same direct applicability before the NCAs should

[40] See Case C-1/2012 *Ordem dos Técnicos Oficiais de Contas (OTOC) v Autoridade da Concorrência* Judgment of 28 February 2013 (NYR) [23]–[24], [29]–[31]. See also ch 2, text to n 65.

[41] According to s 46 of the Competition Act (1998). See *VIP Communications Ltd v OFCOM* (n 33) [12]–[14].

[42] See, in particular, Case T-193/02 *Laurent Piau v Commission* (n 39) [79]: 'This review can therefore extend to compliance with other provisions of the Treaty only in so far as any infringement of them reveals a concomitant *breach* of the rules on competition. Moreover, it can relate to a possible breach of fundamental principles only in the event that that breach resulted in an infringement of the rules on competition' (emphasis added). Similarly, see *VIP Communications Ltd v OFCOM* (n 33) [14]: 'In our judgment, the issue of the alleged inconsistency of our domestic legislation can only be relevant to this appeal if it is relevant to the question whether OFCOM's decision *to reject the complaint* of abusive behaviour was wrong' (emphasis added).

[43] Case 103/88 *Fratelli Costanzo SpA v Comune di Milano* [1989] ECR 1839 [28]–[33].

[44] *CIF v Autorità Garante della Concorrenza e del Mercato* (n 31) [49].

apply to the free movement Treaty provisions, which are Treaty provisions that are directly applicable before national courts.[45]

Aside from the procedural limitations sketched out above, a more important question is the institutional capacity and expertise of the NCAs to apply the free movement provisions. The public enforcement of the competition law provisions involves a great deal of discretion at the stage of selection of the cases. By contrast, in the context of private enforcement, the national courts could not possibly deny ruling on a claim or that would, indeed, be a denial of justice. This is the reason why, in a system relying almost exclusively on the private enforcement of competition law, it is very important to set restrictive substantive standards in light of the absence of self-controlling limitations to private applicants.[46] Given the consequence of a finding of incompatibility of the state action with the free movement provisions, namely non-applicability of the competition provisions, it could be argued that NCAs, as well as the Commission, have the discretion to select those cases of outright abuse that would be more likely to succeed rather than result in a finding of inapplicability. The discretion of the NCAs in regard to case selection is retained if a case involves state action in breach of the free movement provisions. However, NCAs have a duty to abstain from applying Article 102 TFEU once they pick up such a case, while at the same time they have a duty to diaspply the national regulation. Therefore, the proposed revision of the state action defence also eliminates artificial obstacles to the selection process of cases suitable for public enforcement, while it is left in the hands of private litigants to decide whether they are willing to bear the costs for testing borderline cases before the courts.

In the rather exceptional case in which there is an appeal either against a rejection by a NCA of a complaint or against a decision by a NCA rejecting a defence by the dominant undertaking that the state action is incompatible with EU law, the reviewing court should be fully capable of proclaiming on both issues of competition law and the free movement provisions. In that respect, the possibility of the NCAs to send preliminary references to the Court of Justice would operate

[45] *Fratelli Costanzo* is cited in Case C-429/09 *Günter Fuß v Stadt Halle* [2010] ECR I-12167 [40], [85] in support of the direct effect of specific provisions of Directive 2003/88 before a National Administrative Authority in its capacity as public employer. However, no question of the diasapplication of national law arose on the facts of this case. Similarly, see Joined Cases C-444/09 and C-456/09 *Rosa María Gavieiro Gavieiro and Ana María Iglesias Torres v Consellería de Educación e Ordenación Universitaria de la Xunta de Galicia* [2010] ECR I-14031 [73]; and Case C-341/08 *Domnica Petersen v Berufungsausschuss für Zahnärzte für den Bezirk Westfalen-Lippe* [2010] ECR I-00047 [80]–[81]. See also Case C-177/10 *Francisco Javier Rosado Santana v Consejería de Justicia y Administración Pública de la Junta de Andalucía* [2011] ECR I-07907 [53], [61], in which *Fratelli Costanzo* is cited, but, on the facts of the case, it was a national court and not a National Administrative Authority that was involved.

[46] This is well illustrated through the example of the reorientation of EU competition law to a more 'economics-based' approach at the same time as the modernisation initiative, based on a decentralised and private enforcement of the competition rules, was launched. See O Odudu, 'The Public/Private Distinction in EU Internal Market Law' (2010) 46 (4) *Revue Trimestrielle de Droit Européen* 839–40.

as a safety valve and it would also be consistent with considerations of judicial economy. However, this possibility is excluded by the Court of Justice judgment in *SYFAIT*.[47] *SYFAIT* was the predecessor of *Sotirios Lélos*, since the same preliminary questions that were raised in the latter case by the national court were first raised by the NCA and rejected as inadmissible. The reasoning in *SYFAIT* seems to suggest that no NCA can be considered a court or a tribunal for the purposes of sending a preliminary reference in proceedings intended to lead to a decision of a judicial nature. The reason is that, according to Article 11(6) of Regulation 1/2003, the NCAs are relieved of their competence where the Commission initiates its own proceedings, hence the proceedings initiated before that Authority will not lead to a decision of a judicial nature.[48] However, as clearly stated by AG Jacobs in his Opinion in *SYFAIT*, it would be preferable to send the preliminary question to the Court of Justice at the earliest possible stage before additional proceedings are initiated before a reviewing court, which would, in any case, be obliged to send the relevant questions.[49] This would also strengthen the safeguards of the uniform application of EU law, particularly after the Court of Justice judgment in *CIF*.[50] Therefore, the need for the possibility of an NCA to send a preliminary reference already exists as the case law stands, without the exclusion of such a possibility having affected the obligation of the NCAs to disapply national law that is incompatible with the competition law provisions. It would be preferable to allow that possibility, but in no way would its exclusion be a barrier to the suggested revision of the state action doctrine and defence.

III. PRINCIPLED ATTRIBUTION OF MARKET SEPARATION CONTROLLED: THE EXAMPLE OF THE 'EXHAUSTION' OF INTELLECTUAL PROPERTY RIGHTS

The exercise of IPRs is a very specific case in which the Court of Justice has been called upon to apply, or has applied on its own motion, both the free movement provisions and the competition law provisions, including Article 102 TFEU, in the context of private litigation. This potentially makes the regulation of IPRs either an example of how the proposed revision of the state action defence could be applied or an 'anti-example' showing the disadvantages associated with the non-principled interface between the free movement and the competition law provisions.

A historical overview of the early cases on the 'existence/exercise' dichotomy of IPRs is provided in section III.A as regards the interface between the free

[47] Case C-53/03 *Syfait and others v GlaxoSmithKline plc and GlaxoSmithKline AEVE* [2005] ECR I-4609.

[48] ibid [34]–[36].

[49] ibid, Opinion of AG Jacobs [45].

[50] ibid.

movement and the competition law provisions. In those early cases, intellectual property (IP) was regarded as an evil, because the relevant rights were national territorial rights. The purpose of this historical overview is to show that there has been a swift reversal of the initial proposition underpinning the interface between free movement and competition law, namely that conformity of the national IP law with the free movement of goods ('non-exhaustion') is a condition for the applicability of the competition law provisions, which is normally met. This proposition makes non-exhaustible IPRs a case study which fits into the main thesis underpinning the proposed revision of the interface between state and private responsibility for market separation. In section III.B, the EU principle of exhaustion of IPRs under the free movement of goods is considered, which, applied concomitantly with the competition law provisions, does not fit into the proposed principled interface of the two sets of provisions. For this reason, nevertheless, the case of exhaustible IPRs illustrates the risks for added costs in terms of unwarranted assimilations in the legal analysis under the free movement and the competition law provisions.

A. Side One of the Interface between the Free Movement and the Competition Law Provisions in Regard to IPRs: Non-exhaustion

Broadly speaking, IPRs confer upon the owners the right to prohibit third parties from carrying out certain activities, namely they confer exclusive rights inter alia to exports and imports. They do so for various reasons, depending on the type of IPR involved, such as encouraging and rewarding innovation and investments (patents), creativity and originality (copyright) or indicating the trade origin of a product (trademarks). A potential tension between those exclusive rights and market integration is easily discernible, in particular as regards parallel trade, and could lead to regulation of IPRs for the purposes of tackling barriers to inter-state trade. In that regard, the EU has adopted an EU-wide exhaustion regime, according to which the exclusive right of the holder of the IPRs to control the subsequent marketing of the protected goods is lost once the goods have been placed on the market within the EU by the rights holder or with his or her consent.[51] However, Article 36 TFEU provides for an exception to Article 34 TFEU (justification) based on the protection of 'industrial and commercial property'. In addition, according to Article 345 TFEU, 'the Treaties shall in no way prejudice the rules in Member States governing the system of property ownership'.

The way in which the EU-wide exhaustion regime was established by the Court of Justice raises questions in regard to the applicability of the free movement

[51] See ch 1, text to nn 76–79 for the efficiency arguments in favour of and against (international or regional) exhaustion of IPRs.

provisions to conduct by private undertakings; namely whether this application is a form of horizontal application of the freedoms. The reason is that, according to the case law, the free movement provisions govern the exercise of the IPRs by their holder even when the conditions for the application of the competition law provisions are not fulfilled, or cumulatively in the application of the competition law provisions. An analysis of the origins of the exhaustion principle under the free movement provisions explains why the subsequent application of the competition law provisions in recent IP cases involving market separation involves a distorted legal analysis (see section III.B). By contrast, the historical overview given below in this section of the evolution of the exhaustion regime reveals the initial proposition of the concomitant application of the two sets of provisions, which fits into the proposed paradigm of interface between the two. This initial proposition is composed of the conformity of the national IP law with the free movement provisions, and hence non-exhaustion, as a precondition for the subsequent application of the competition law, which is normally met.

From as early as 1966, the Court of Justice has dealt with the relationship between Article 345 TFEU and the regulation of IPRs in the context of the competition law provisions by establishing a dichotomy between the 'existence' (or grant) and the 'exercise' of IPRs. In *Consten and Grundig*, the Court upheld the Commission's decision that an exclusive distribution agreement conferring absolute territorial protection from parallel imports via trademark rights was subject to Article 101 TFEU. It rejected the appellant's arguments that the Commission decision not to permit the use of trademark rights to impede parallel trade was in breach of Article 345 TFEU by stating that the decision 'does not affect the grant of those rights but only limits their exercise to the extent necessary to give effect to the prohibition under [Article 101(1) TFEU]'.[52] The Court of Justice had already:

> [C]arried out a competitive analysis, abridged but real, during the course of which it held, in particular, that the agreement in question sought to eliminate any possibility of competition at the wholesale level in order to charge prices which were sheltered from all effective competition.[53]

Similarly, in regard to patent rights, the Court of Justice held in *Parke Davis*:

> [F]irst, that the existence of the rights granted by a Member State to the holder of a patent is not affected by the prohibitions contained in [Articles 101(1) and 102 TFEU]; secondly, that the exercise of such rights cannot of itself fall either under [Article 101(1) TFEU], in the absence of any agreement, decision or concerted practice prohibited by that provision, or under [Article 102 TFEU], in the absence of any abuse of a dominant position.[54]

[52] Joined Cases 56 and 58/64 *Établissements Consten SàRL and Grundig-Verkaufs-GmbH v Commission* [1966] ECR 299, 345.

[53] Case T-168/01 *GlaxoSmithKline Services Unlimited v Commission* [2006] ECR II-2969 [120], citing *Établissements Consten SàRL and Grundig-Verkaufs-GmbH v Commission* (n 52) 299, 342–43.

[54] Case 24/67 *Parke, Davis and Co v Probel, Reese, Beintema-Interpharm and Centrafarm* [1968] ECR 55, 72.

Most significantly, for the purposes of the discussion here, in *Parke Davis*, the Court of Justice began to reason by stating that the rules relating to the protection of IPRs are not harmonised within the EU and therefore the principles found in Article 36 TFEU are equally applicable to the sphere of the competition rules. As a consequence, the exercise of the rights does not, in itself, constitute an infringement of the competition provisions.[55] In regard to the finding of an abuse of dominance, the Court held that:

> [A] higher sale price for the patented product as compared with that of the unpatented product coming from another Member State does not necessarily constitute an abuse.[56]

The same reasoning appears in *Sirena v Eda*, in which case the Court further accepted, under Article 102 TFEU, an unqualified objective justification defence by stating that:

> [T]he price level of the product may not of itself necessarily suffice to disclose such an abuse, it may, however, if unjustified by any objective criteria, and if it is particularly high, be a determining factor.[57]

It seems from these early cases that the Court of Justice subjected the 'existence' of IPRs to the free movement provisions as opposed to the 'exercise' of the rights, which is subject to the competition provisions.[58] This makes great sense because Member States do not exercise IPRs, but, rather, determine their scope and, in particular, the legal requirements for granting IPRs through legislation or through judicial or administrative enforcement.[59] By contrast, private undertakings

[55] ibid [71].

[56] ibid [72].

[57] Case 40/70 *Sirena Srl v Eda Srl and others* [1971] ECR 69 [17].

[58] Later on, the distinction between the 'existence' and 'exercise' of IPRs was replaced by the notion of the 'specific subject matter' of the IPR. In Joined Cases C-241/91 P and C-242/91 P *RTE and ITP v Commission* [1995] ECR I-473, Opinion of AG Gulmann [31], AG Gulmann points out that: 'An exercise of rights that falls within the specific subject-matter of an intellectual property right will relate to its existence. In other words the distinction between the existence and the exercise of rights and the application of the concept of the specific subject-matter are basically expressions of the same conceptual approach.'

[59] C Stothers, *Parallel Trade in Europe: Intellectual Property, Competition and Regulatory Law* (Hart Publishing, 2007) 29; R Lane, 'The Internal Market and the Individual' in N Nic Shuibhne (ed), *Regulating the Internal Market* (Edward Elgar, 2006) 263–64; J Snell, 'Private Parties and the Free Movement of Goods and Services' in M Adenas and W-H Roth (eds), *Services and Free Movement in EU Law* (Oxford University Press, 2002) 214–15; similarly, see G Marenco and K Banks, 'Intellectual Property and the Community Rules on Free Movement: Discrimination Unearthed' (1990) 15 *European Law Review* 225–26 on the basis that the prohibitions contained in Articles 34 and 36 TFEU have a more incisive effect, they prohibit a national law to the extent that it empowers the rights holder to exercise his or her right in given circumstances and, as a result, they contemplate the possible existence of objectionable aspects of IP law. Contra D Keeling, *Intellectual Property Rights in EU Law: Volume I* (Oxford University Press, 2003) 53–54; A Heinemann, 'Intellectual Property Rights and Market Integration' in S Anderman and A Ezrachi (eds), *Intellectual Property and Competition Law—New Frontiers* (Oxford University Press, 2011) 320 backs up the application of the competition provisions to restrictions on parallel trade by reference to their role in complementing the rules on exhaustion under the free movement provisions.

exercise those rights through agreements or unilateral practices. Therefore, it is apparent from those early cases that subjecting the exercise of the IPRs to the competition law provisions implied that the grant of the right, in light of its exercise in the specific circumstances of the case, is already in conformity with the free movement provisions; otherwise there would be no right to be exercised, recognised at the EU level, and this exercise could not be subject to control under EU competition law.

This has been the general test governing the interface between Article 102 TFEU and the free movement provisions in relation to IPRs. The test was first expressly stated in *Hoffmann-La Roche v Centrafarm*, where the Court of Justice analysed the conditions under which a restriction of repackaging of goods under trademark rights could be in breach of Articles 34 and 36 TFEU. The Court held that:

> [T]he extent to which the exercise of a trademark right is lawful in accordance with the provisions of [Article 36 TFEU], such exercise is not contrary to [Article 102 TFEU] on the sole ground that it is the act of an undertaking occupying a dominant position on the market if the trademark right has not been used as an instrument for the abuse of such a position.[60]

Thus, the finding that the form of exercise of the IPR is typical of the category of IPR at stake and is hence justified under Article 36 TFEU is a necessary condition for the further enquiry as to whether such exercise constitutes an abuse of dominance.[61]

The distinction between 'existence' and 'exercise' may seem, on the face of it, artificial and formalistic.[62] However, it clearly connotes, as argued by Kallaugher, that there is an initial basis which does not reflect a policy judgment regarding the respective merits in fostering economic efficiency, but is, rather, a jurisdictional division of the EU competence to apply EU competition law and the Member

[60] Case 102/77 *Hoffmann-La Roche & Co AG v Centrafarm Vertriebsgesellschaft Pharmazeutischer Erzeugnisse mbH* [1978] ECR 1139 [14], [16]. AG Capotorti argued in his Opinion that Article 102 TFEU could be in breach only if the exercise of the trademark rights were outside the scope of Article 36 TFEU; see ibid 1180.

[61] This is more clearly shown by considering that competition law also applies to the exercise of IPRs, which are not national, but, rather, conferred by secondary EU legislation, such as the trademark rights under Directive 2008/95/EC. See, for example, Case C-385/07 P *Der Grüne Punkt—Duales System Deutschland GmbH v Commission* [2009] ECR I-6155, in which Article 102 TFEU was applied to the fee required by Duales System Deutschland (DSD) for the appearance of the 'Green Dot' logo on all products. Previously, the Court of Justice had rejected the argument according to which the Commission's finding under Article 102 TFEU infringes Article 5 of Directive 2008/95/EC, because the relationship between the proprietor and its contractual partners as regards the use of the trademark is outside the scope of Article 5 of Directive 2008/95/EC. See n 69 for more on that judgment.

[62] Indeed, the extent to which IP rights can be exercised also determines their economic value and existence. See, eg, V Korah, 'Notes of Cases: Dividing the Common Market through National Industrial Property Rights' (1972) 35 *Modern Law Review* 363 for a critique.

States' competence to create systems of IPRs.[63] According to the same author, the policy considerations, which inform the exercise of the specific type of IPR, may, exceptionally, become relevant at the stage of the initial competence allocation if such allocation is not clear in the specific case.[64] Otherwise they become relevant at the later stage of competition law application, namely once it is asserted that the competition law provisions are applicable.[65]

The same principles could be articulated via the prism of the suggested revision of state and private responsibility for market separation, which shows that non-exhaustible IPRs under the free movement provisions are a case study for the purposes of this book. If the form of exercise of the IPR is typical of the category of the IPR at stake and therefore, justified under Article 36 TFEU, this is a necessary condition for the applicability of Article 102 TFEU to the dominant undertaking's conduct which represents a specific use of that IPR. However, it does not necessarily lead either to finding a breach of Article 102 TFEU or, further, to shielding the conduct from the application of Article 102 TFEU. The Court of Justice, in those early cases, referred the case back to the national court, which was instructed to conduct an economic analysis for the purposes of substantiating an abuse of a dominant position. Therefore, it is noteworthy that assimilations in terms of outcome or reasoning under the free movement and the competition law provisions in cases in which the exercise of the IPR was not exhausted were avoided. There are no cases in which the Court of Justice says that the competition law provisions are not infringed for consistency purposes, once it has found that the IPRs at stake are not exhausted under Articles 34 and 36 TFEU. This type of assimilation would be very risky because it would cause a gap in the deterrent effect of competition law enforcement.

A typical example of this side of interaction between the free movement and competition law provisions is the case law governing non-exhaustible rights under the freedom to provide services. The application of Article 102 TFEU is principled, in particular as regards the practice of collecting societies, arguably

[63] J Kallaugher, 'Existence, Exercise and Exceptional Circumstances: The Limited Scope for a More Economic Approach to IP Issues under Article 102 TFEU' in S Anderman and A Ezrachi (eds), *Intellectual Property and Competition Law—New Frontiers* (Oxford University Press, 2011) 120–21; see also S Anderman and H Schmidt, *EU Competition Law and Intellectual Property Rights: The Regulation of Innovation* (Oxford University Press, 2011) 21, 23–25 against a generalised widening of the concept of the 'existence' of the IPRs beyond the conditions for granting the IPRs to extend to the legal prerogatives of the rights holder. Indeed, this is a specific example of the conceptual foundation of finding a justified trade barrier, which was identified in Ch 4, section II.A as the process of competence allocation for market regulation.

[64] Kallaugher (n 63) 120–29. According to Kallaugher, even in those cases, the examination by the Court of the economic purpose of the IPRs created by the national law through the concepts of 'essential function' and 'specific subject-matter' of the IPRs is not equivalent to the case-by-case analysis under competition law.

[65] See ibid 138–39 in favour of limiting Article 102 TFEU enforcement by excluding from its scope of application the exercise of 'core' IPRs, which determine in effect the 'existence' of the IPRs.

because no exhaustion doctrine is developed in relation to communication to the public, performance, rental and lending rights under Article 56 TFEU.

Coditel I, on the freedom to provide services, is the first case to establish that the exercise of the right to communicate a film to the public by performances assigned by copyright is not contrary to Article 56 TFEU. This is so when the right is exercised in such a way as to require fees for any exhibition and to prohibit the exhibition of that film by means of cable diffusion, after the film has been broadcasted in another Member State by a third party, even with the consent of the original owner of the copyright.[66] In addition, in *Coditel I*, the Court of Justice held that Article 56 TFEU did not, in principle, constitute an obstacle to the geographic limits upon which the parties to a contract of assignment of copyright have agreed in order to protect the author and his assigns in this regard.[67] Following that judgment, in *Coditel II* the Court of Justice had to determine whether the competition provisions were inapplicable because the exercise of communication to the public and performance rights were compatible with the free movement provisions. The Court, responding in the negative, stated that it is for the national court to make the enquiry as to whether the exercise of the right:

> [C]reates barriers which are artificial and unjustifiable in terms of the needs of the cinematographic industry, or the possibility of charging fees which exceed a fair return on investment, or an exclusivity the duration of which is disproportionate to those requirements, and whether or not, from a general point of view, such exercise within a given geographic area is such as to prevent, restrict or distort competition within the common market.[68]

The self-contained character of the application of the competition law provisions as regards the exercise of IPRs, after a finding that the freedom to provide services has not been infringed, is more evident in the cases which concern the exercise of IPRs by collecting societies on behalf of a number of rights holders.[69] In *Tournier*, the Court of Justice examined whether the royalties which a national

[66] Case 62/79 *SA Compagnie générale pour la diffusion de la télévision, Coditel and others v Ciné Vog Films and others* [1980] ECR 881 [12]–[14].

[67] ibid [16].

[68] ibid [19].

[69] The emphasis is on Article 102 TFEU; however, these cases also raised issues under Article 101 TFEU regarding reciprocal representation practices along national lines as a concerted practice between the national collecting societies. Recently, the Commission held that the territorial delineation of mandates based on national lines are not, in themselves, in breach of Article 101 TFEU, but only the coordination in a way which limits a licence to the territory of each collecting society constitutes 'concerted practice' and is in breach of Article 101 TFEU; see *CISAC* (Case COMP/C-2/38.698) [2008] OJ C 323/12. The decision is only limited to performing rights in relation to online, cable and satellite exploitation. Relatively recently, the General Court partially annulled the Commission's decision for lack of sufficient formal evidence of a 'concerted practice', because the alternative explanations adduced by the applicants—that is, that the parallel agreements and the geographic limitations were needed for effective monitoring in their domestic territory—could not be safely dismissed. See Case T-392/08 *AEPI Elliniki Etaireia pros Prostasian tis Pnevmatikis Idioktisias AE v Commission*, Judgment of 12 April 2013 (NYR) (in French and Greek) [125]–[166].

copyright management society charges for music played in public by means of sound recording constitute an abuse of a dominant position when the rates are appreciably higher than those charged in other Member States. The Court held that it is for the undertaking in question to justify the difference by reference to objective dissimilarities between the situation in the Member State concerned and the situation prevailing in all the other Member States, otherwise the comparison of the rates provides a useful indication of abuse.[70] In that context, it examined in detail, and rejected, the justifications produced by SACEM.[71] The Court had earlier classified the imposition of a performance royalty for music played by means of sound recordings as being governed by the services, rather than the goods, case law, thereby permitting the application of the *Coditel I* principles that excluded an exhaustion regime in relation to the exercise of communication and performance rights.[72]

B. Side Two of the Interface between the Free Movement and the Competition Law Provisions in Regard to IPRs: Exhaustion

Exhaustible IPRs under the free movement provisions and the subsequent application by the Court of Justice of the competition law provisions do not fit into the proposed concomitant application of the two sets of provisions, inasmuch as the

[70] In *Der Grüne Punkt—Duales System Deutschland GmbH v Commission* (n 61) [193]–[196], the General Court held that DSD was abusing its dominant position by requiring a fee for all packaging bearing the 'Green Dot' logo (registered as a trademark), even in cases in which it is proved that its customers are not using the DSD system for collection and recovery of all of that packaging (under Article 102 TFEU). However, that finding did not preclude the possibility for DSD to levy an adequate fee for merely using the mark, even if that packaging is not actually taken to the DSD system. The mark may have economic value as such, since it can inform the consumer that the packaging at issue may be taken to the DSD system. That finding was confirmed by the Court of Justice in Case C-385/07 P *Der Grüne Punkt—Duales System Deutschland GmbH v Commission* [2009] ECR I-6155 [72]–[78].

[71] Case 395/87 *Ministère Public v Jean-Louis Tournier* [1989] ECR 2521 [34]–[46], particularly that the difference between the rates is justified by the high prices charged by discotheques in France, the traditionally high level of protection provided by copyright in France and the peculiar features of French legislation whereby the playing of recorded musical works is subject not only to a performing right but also to a supplementary mechanical reproduction fee. Similarly, see Joined Cases 110/88, 241/88 and 242/88 *François Lucazeau and others v Société des Auteurs, Compositeurs et Editeurs de Musique (SACEM) and others* [1989] ECR 2811 [21]–[33]. More recently the *i-Tunes* case that was referred by the OFT to the European Commission on the basis that UK users had to pay more to download tracks than users in Germany or France was settled following Apple's announcement to equalise prices in Europe; see Press Release, IP/08/22 (9 January 2008) http://europa.eu/rapid/pressReleasesAction.do?reference=IP/08/22.

[72] Case 395/87 *Ministère Public v Jean-Louis Tournier* [1989] ECR 2521 [10]–[15]. Earlier in Case 402/85 *Basset, G v Société des auteurs, compositeurs et éditeurs de musique (SACEM)* [1987] ECR 1747, the Court had classified sound recordings as products to which the free movement of goods applies, but held that the 'supplementary reproduction fee' charged by the society is not in breach of Articles 34 and 36 TFEU on the basis that the fee is not charged on the importation or marketing of the sound recordings, but by reason of their public use. Therefore, it seems that the Court applies the right principles regardless of the formal classification of the case as a services—or goods—case.

competition law provisions are applied regardless of whether or not the IPR is in breach of the free movement of goods provisions. Recent cases under the freedom to provide services illustrate unwarranted assimilation in terms of legal analysis under the competition law provisions when those provisions are applied after a finding that the relevant free movement provision is infringed.

The exhaustion regime has been fully developed in the field of free movement of goods. In *Deutsche Grammophon*, the European Court transplanted the *Consten and Grundig* distinction between the existence and exercise of IPRs from the competition provisions to the application of Articles 34 and 36 TFEU in the field of copyright. The Court stated that:

> [I]f the exercise of the right does not exhibit those elements of contract or concerted practice referred to in [Article 101(1) TFEU], it is necessary, in order to answer the question referred, further to consider whether the exercise of the right in question is compatible with other provisions of the Treaty, in particular those relating to the free movement of goods.[73]

It is striking that the question referred by the national court was framed only in terms of the competition law provisions. Therefore, it was the Court, on its own motion, that subjected the exercise of IPRs to the free movement of goods provision.

In addition, it appears that the Court of Justice, by establishing the exhaustion regime in the first place, allowed a simultaneous application of the two sets of provisions.[74] For example, in *Deutsche Grammophon*, it held that the exercise of the exclusive right to distribute the products protected under copyright in a manner so as to prohibit the sale, in that Member State, of products placed on the market by the holder or with the holder's consent in another Member State would not be justified under Article 36 TFEU. However, it held that the difference between the controlled price and the price of the product reimported from another Member State does not necessarily suffice to disclose an abuse of dominant position and left it for the national court to determine whether the price was unjustified by any objective criteria and is particularly marked. In other words, it left the national court to carry out an economic analysis under Article 102 TFEU, which is not necessarily violated.[75]

[73] Case 78/70 *Deutsche Grammophon Gesellschaft mbH v Metro-SB-Großmärkte GmbH & Co KG* [1971] ECR 487 [7].

[74] See O-A Rognstad, 'The Exhaustion/Competition Interface in EC Law—Is There Room for a Holistic Approach?' in J Drexl (ed), *Research Handbook on Intellectual Property and Competition Law* (Edward Elgar, 2008) 429–32 for a summary of the academic literature. Rognstad is critical not so much of the simultaneous application of the two sets of provisions, but of the lack of interdependence in their application, in the sense that competition law does not determine exhaustion; *cf* S Enchelmaier, 'Intellectual Property, the Internal Market and Competition Law' in J Drexl (ed), *Research Handbook on Intellectual Property and Competition Law* (Edward Elgar, 2008) 417–23.

[75] Similarly, under Article 101 TFEU in relation to territorial import and export restrictions in licensing agreements; for example, in Case 258/78 *LC Nungesser KG and Kurt Eisele v Commission* [1982] ECR 2015 [62]–[63], the Court held that the application of Article 101 TFEU 'is not affected

This represents a double reversal of the initial proposition which underpinned the distinction between the existence and exercise of IPRs, namely that justification under Article 36 TFEU (and therefore non-exhaustion), is a condition for the application of the competition law provisions (see section III.A above). First, it appears that it does not matter for the purposes of ascertaining applicability of the competition law provisions whether or not the IPRs are exhausted. Second, it appears that non-exhaustion of the IPRs, in light of their specific exercise, is not the rule, but is rather an exceptional case, and this utterly precludes each specific exercise from being genuinely assessed under the competition law provisions. It is, instead, under the free movement provisions that the Court makes, by and large, a policy choice with regard to the breadth of territorial protection afforded, and the competition law provisions are applied cumulatively, regardless of the outcome of the assessment under the freedoms.

For example, in the early cases on exhaustion of patents, the Court of Justice held that a national patent right is exhausted if the product is marketed by or with the consent of the patent holder in another Member State, even though he or she may be unable to get a reward of monopoly profits in the Member State of export in which the product is not patentable.[76] The Court also held that the different national policies in relation to price controls on pharmaceutical products could not justify the exercise of the patent rights by putting the products into first circulation, unless the holder of the patent can prove that it is under a genuine, existing legal obligation to market the product in that Member State.[77] This ruling is, in effect, similar to the one in *Sotirios Lélos* in regard to a dominant undertaking's refusal to supply parallel traders.[78] In other words, the exhaustion of patent rights in pharmaceuticals under the free movement of goods restricts the ability of the pharmaceutical companies to discriminate geographically in Europe, regardless of the prevailing varying national regulations on pharmaceutical prices. In neither case were the national pricing regulations assessed under the free movement provisions. Korah notes that the incidental effect of the Court of Justice ruling on exhaustion of patent rights was to bring national laws on pharmaceutical pricing closer by pushing the French pharmaceutical companies to persuade the French government to raise the maximum allowed selling price for pharmaceuticals.[79] This effect is very similar to that identified in chapter four, section III.A in relation

by the fact that persons or undertakings subject to such restrictions are in a position to rely upon the provisions of the Treaty relating to the free movement of goods in order to escape such restrictions'.

[76] The principle was established in Case 187/80 *Merck & Co Inc v Stephar BV and Petrus Stephanus Exler* [1981] ECR 2063 [9]–[13] by extending the earlier ruling in Case 15/74 *Centrafarm BV and Adriaan de Peijper v Sterling Drug Inc* [1974] ECR 1147 [9], [11].

[77] See *Centrafarm BV and Adriaan de Peijper v Sterling Drug Inc* (n 76) [22]–[24]; *Merck & Co Inc v Stephar BV and Petrus Stephanus* Exler (n 76) [43]–[52].

[78] Joined Cases C-468–478/06 *Sotirios Lélos kai Sia EE and others v GlaxoSmithKline AEVE Farmakeftikon Proïonton, formerly Glaxowellcome AEVE* [2008] ECR I-7139.

[79] V Korah, *Intellectual Property Rights and the EC Competition Rules* (Hart Publishing, 2006) 9.

to the case law on rejecting public policy justifications under Article 102 TFEU. This similarity confirms that the question of the exhaustion of the patent rights should have been addressed under the competition law provisions, in light of the fact that public policy justifications for the varying price regulations constitute an integral part of the application of the free movement Treaty provisions.

It seems that the establishment by the Court of Justice of the exhaustion regime in the field of free movement of goods led the national courts to request further preliminary references framed in terms of both the free movement and the competition provisions. In that way, the Court was able to focus on the application of the free movement provisions that lacks enthusiasm concerning empiricism and economic analysis,[80] and to make the competition law analysis seem secondary and dependent, for consistency reasons, upon the outcome of applying the free movement provisions. Of course, any such reading of the Court's case law would be subject to the assumption that, in the preliminary reference procedure, the nature of the question plays a significant role.[81] Therefore, it is indeed valid to say that there are differences between the regulation of trademarks on the one hand and the regulation of copyrights and patents on the other hand, both in terms of how important a sophisticated economic analysis is for the parties involved and in terms of how far the EU has exercised its competence to harmonise the relevant divergent national laws.[82] However, it is also fair to say that competition law provisions provide a more structured and appropriate forum for the analysis of the territorial breadth of the geographic protection afforded to the rights holder, even in the case of trademark rights. This is especially the case in the context of preliminary references, which originate in litigation before national courts, because the Court of Justice has jurisdiction to interpret the law, but not to apply it on the facts of the actual case, and the distinction between interpretation and application is far from easy to draw.[83] The application of the proportionality principle under the free movement provisions is the epitome of such difficulty and is one that distinguishes the legal reasoning under the free movement provisions from the legal reasoning under the competition law provisions, as is explained in chapter four.[84] Therefore, the framework within which a question is asked also feeds back

[80] See ch 3, section V.A.

[81] See M Broberg and N Fenger, *Preliminary References to the European Court of Justice* (Oxford University Press, 2010) 421–23.

[82] The stakes and money involved in infringement of copyright and patent rights are extraordinary compared with trademark infringement. This may be precisely the reason why the trademark protection is almost fully Europeanised, whereas the former remain national-based.

[83] See, eg, J Snell, 'EU Courts and Intellectual Property: A Tale of Hercules, Zeus and Cyclops' (2004) 29 *European Law Review* 187–93, who argues that the distinction is not dependent upon how detailed the analysis is, but upon how abstract or concrete is the language used in the ruling. *Cf* G Davies, 'Abstractness and Correctness in the Preliminary Reference Procedure: Implications for the Division of Powers and Effective Market Regulation' in Nic Shuibhne (n 59) 225–33.

[84] See ch 4, sections II.A and II.B.

to the reasoning and the outcome of the case, in particular as regards the choice of the applicable legal provisions and their intersections.

This has been illustrated in a case involving the reception and viewing of Greek broadcasts of Premier League football matches in the UK.[85] The Court appears to assume that satellite transmission services over protected works in one Member State involve the reception of those services by persons resident outside the Member State of broadcast. In other words, accessing and watching the broadcasts in a Member State other than the Member State of origin is not a separate act of exploitation of the IPRs.[86] Based on this, the Court restricted its analysis in assessing compatibility with the freedom to provide services of the first broadcasting in Greece only, as Article 1(2)(b) of the Satellite Broadcasting Directive provides that 'the act of communication to the public by satellite occurs solely in the Member State where, under the control and responsibility of the broadcasting organisation, the programme-carrying signals are introduced into an uninterrupted chain of communication'.[87] This permitted the Court to rule out from the specific subject matter of that right the payment of a premium for UK exclusivity, since remuneration had already been paid to the rights holder by the Greek broadcaster. The latter could calculate the number of actual and potential viewers because reception of the broadcast requires possession of a decoding device card, and consequently, could pay the appropriate remuneration to the rights holder.[88] On that basis, the Court also distinguished the case from *Coditel I* and the question of exhaustion.[89]

However, the reasoning of the Court led it to assess the one and the same alleged obstacle to cross-border reception of broadcasting services under, first, the provisions of free movement and, second, the competition law provisions. The Court did so even though it conceded that 'the actual origin of the obstacle to the reception of such services is to be found in the contracts concluded between the broadcasters and their customers', on the basis that 'as the legislation confers legal protection on those restrictions and requires them to be complied with on pain of civil-law and pecuniary sanctions, it itself restricts the freedom to provide services'.[90]

[85] Joined Cases C-403/08 and C-429/08 *Football Association Premier League and others* [2011] ECR I-09083.

[86] ibid [153]–[182].

[87] ibid [111].

[88] ibid [106]–[116].

[89] ibid [118]–[120].

[90] ibid [88]. However, *cf* Case T-321/05 *AstraZeneca AB and AstraZeneca plc v Commission* [2010] ECR II-02805 [362], with a very distinct factual background (namely misleading representations made to the public authorities for the purposes of improperly obtaining exclusive rights). The General Court rejected the applicants' argument that a finding of an abuse of a dominant position requires that the exclusive right has been enforced, on the basis that such an argument would tend to make the application of Article 102 TFEU conditional on the contravention by competitors of the public regulations by their infringing the exclusive right of an undertaking.

Once the Court had found both provisions to be applicable, it is very interesting to highlight the assimilation in its reasoning under the two sets of provisions. The Court first established a violation of the freedom to provide services, which is not well informed in terms of economic analysis, by using language reminiscent of Article 102 TFEU case law on excessive pricing. It held the restriction not to be justified by the specific subject matter of the IPRs for the following reasons:

> [T]he specific subject-matter of the intellectual property does not guarantee the rights holders concerned the opportunity to demand the highest possible remuneration … only appropriate remuneration for each use of the protected subject-matter. In order to be appropriate, such remuneration must be reasonable in relation to the economic value of the service provided …[91]

> [The] premium is paid to the rights holders concerned in order to guarantee absolute territorial exclusivity which is such as to result in artificial price differences between the partitioned national markets. Such partitioning and such an artificial price difference to which it gives rise are irreconcilable with the fundamental aim of the Treaty, which is completion of the Internal Market.[92]

Subsequently, the Court of Justice did not engage in a full economic analysis under the competition law provisions by making a cross-reference to the above-mentioned finding under the freedom to provide services, arguably for consistency reasons.[93] Had the Court first (or only) addressed the obstacle under the competition law provisions, it would have been harder to substantiate a violation.[94] Therefore, it seems that the double framework of one and the same question provides the Court of Justice with a flexible mechanism by which to influence the outcome of the question at its discretion.

Another example of the distorted concomitant application of the free movement provisions and the competition law provisions as regards the exercise of IPRs is provided, from the perspective of the referring national courts, by the judgment of the UK Court of Appeal in *Oracle America (Formerly Sun Microsystems).*[95]

[91] *Football Association Premier League and others* (n 85) [108]–[109].

[92] ibid [115].

[93] ibid [145]. The Court of Justice ruling is narrower than the solution suggested by AG Kokott because it based its findings on the provisions of both free movement and competition law when considering the interpretation of 'communication to the public' under the Satellite Broadcasting Directive. AG Kokott had developed a much broader theory that services, like goods, are subject to exhaustion; see *Football Association Premier League and others* (n 85), Opinion of AG Kokott.

[94] For the consequences of the ruling in terms of the options now available to the Football Association Premier League for organising its licensing policy, see A Wood, 'Case Comment: The CJEU's Ruling in the Premier League Pub TV Cases—The Final Whistle Beckons: Joined Cases *Football Association Premier League Ltd v QC Leisure* (C-403/08) *and Murphy v Media Protection Services Ltd* (C-429/08)' (2012) 34 *European Intellectual Property Review* 207; and E Szyszczak, 'Karen Murphy: Decoding Licences and Territorial Exclusivity' (2012) 3 *Journal of European Competition Law and Practice* 173–74.

[95] *Oracle America Inc (formerly Sun Microsystems Inc) v M-Tech Data Ltd* [2010] EWCA Civ 997; [2011] 1 CMLR 43. The judgment was reversed on appeal by the Supreme Court in *Oracle America Inc (Formerly Sun Microsystems Inc) v M-Tech Data Ltd* [2012] UKSC 27 essentially by applying the general rule that EU (maximum) harmonisation legislation supersedes the application of Articles 34

Lady Justice Arden allowed an appeal against a summary judgment and ordered the case to be remitted to the Chancery Division for trial, with a view to the judge making a reference to the Court of Justice. The summary judgment had ruled that, because Oracle's rights to sue for trademark infringement were not exhausted according to Articles 5 and 7 of the Trademark Directive 2008/95/EC, a defence based on the alleged violation of Articles 34 and 36 TFEU did not have a realistic prospect of success.[96]

Lady Justice Arden argued that, in principle, the complete harmonisation regime of EU-wide exhaustion of trademarks established by Articles 5 and 7 of the Trademark Directive did not exclude the defences based on Articles 34 and 36 TFEU when it is shown that the proprietor of a trademark has adopted practices which distort trade within the single market. In the case of *Oracle America*, such practices comprise the conduct of the trademark holder in failing to make publicly available a serial mark tracker for the purposes of identifying whether the goods are produced under the licences granted by it, in aggressively pursuing infringement proceedings against non-licensed resellers of goods using its mark and in agreeing terms it contends are designed to reduce a grey market in its goods.

A reasoned means of understanding the ruling is as a claim of abuse of rights conferred by the Trademark Directive based on Article 114 TFEU, which would a fortiori violate the primary Treaty provisions on the free movement of goods.[97] Lady Justice Arden hinted at this analytical interpretation by making a reference to the defendants' arguments on the basis of *Halifax*.[98] She contended that Oracle's refusal to provide access for independent resellers to its internal database had 'more to do with restricting imports with the object of preventing price competition within the EEA and thereby protecting Oracle's profit margins than with the proper exercise of the right to control the first marketing of Oracle equipment within the EEA'.[99]

and 36 TFEU. The analysis advanced here complements the analysis advanced in the Supreme Court judgment.

96 *Sun Microsystems Inc v M-Tech Data Ltd, Stephen Lawrence Lichtenstein* [2009] EWHC 2992 (Pat).

97 See, in other areas of law, the example of AG Mengozzi in Case C-341/05 *Laval un Partneri Ltd v Svenska Byggnadsarbetareförbundet and others* [2007] ECR I-11767 [149]: 'A measure that is incompatible with Directive 96/71 [which is based on Articles 53(1) and 62 TFEU] will, a fortiori, be contrary to [ex-]Article 49 TEC, because that Directive is intended, within its specific scope, to implement the terms of that article.' In *Oracle America*, the Supreme Court seems, implicitly, to adhere to the reading of the Court of Appeal ruling as an 'abuse of rights' claim; see *Oracle America Inc (Formerly Sun Microsystems Inc) v M-Tech Data Ltd* (n 95) [26]: 'the only economically intelligible way in which M-Tech's case may be understood ... is in principle an *ordinary exercise* of the essential right conferred on him by Articles 5 and 7(1) of the Trademark Directive' (emphasis added). See also V Brisimi, 'On the Interface between the "Exhaustion" of IP Rights under Internal Market Law and Competition Law: *Oracle America Inc v M-Tech Data Limited*' [2012] *Competition Law Journal* 312–21.

98 Case C-255/02 *Halifax plc, Leeds Permanent Development Services Ltd and County Wide Property Investments Ltd v Commissioners of Customs & Excise* [2006] ECR I-1609. See R de la Feria, 'Prohibition of Abuse of (Community) Law: The Creation of a New General Principle of EC Law through Tax' (2008) 45 *Common Market Law Review* 395–441 for a first theorisation of 'abuse of rights' after *Halifax*.

99 *Oracle America Inc (formerly Sun Microsystems Inc) v M-Tech Data Ltd* (n 95) [33].

It is submitted that it is illogical to bring competition law considerations, such as price competition, into the equation of controlling, under the cloudy doctrine of abuse of rights by reference to the free movement provisions, the exercise of IP rights conferred by secondary Internal Market legislation. The application of Article 102 TFEU to private conduct, such as the refusal of Oracle to provide access to the serial track marker, could, indeed, inform the value judgment as to whether such conduct constitutes an abusive exercise of the rights conferred by the Trademark Directive, since these rights were not exhausted under Internal Market law.[100] This proposition of the interface between the free movement and the competition law provisions is identified in section III.A above, namely that the application of the competition law provisions to the exercise of IPRs presupposes that the IPRs are in conformity with EU Internal Market law.

However, the application of Article 102 TFEU in the case of Oracle also presupposes that its own substantive conditions are fulfilled, as well as that, procedurally, the relevant claim has been advanced within the prescribed limitations. Lady Justice Arden herself submitted that 'the judge may ultimately be right in saying that these complaints sound in competition law rather than trade mark law, but the space between the two sets of rights is not necessarily exclusively populated by the one or the other set of provisions of European Union law and, thus, the points are in my judgment reasonably arguable under the Trademark Directive'.[101] The doctrine of abuse of rights by reference to the free movement provisions, in this case trademark rights conferred by secondary harmonisation legislation, should not be used as a means by which to sidestep the substantive and procedural requirements for applying Article 102 TFEU.[102] Recourse in *Oracle America* to the free movement provisions, in order to define what constitutes an abuse of rights as conferred by the Trademark Directive, indicates a misunderstanding of the initial proposition that Article 102 TFEU is applicable to the exercise of IPRs only once the rights are justified under the free movement provisions.

IV. CONCLUSIONS

This chapter has provided a principled answer to the question of shared responsibility for market separation by the dominant undertaking and the state. The guiding

[100] Had Article 102 TFEU applied in this case, it could be argued that the prohibition of an abuse of a dominant position functions as a 'European anti-abuse clause' to the exercise of European-based rights.

[101] *Oracle America Inc (formerly Sun Microsystems Inc) v M-Tech Data Ltd* (n 95) [33].

[102] See J Snell, 'The Notion of and a General Test for Abuse of Rights' in R de la Feria and S Vogenauer (eds), *Prohibition of Abuse of Law: A New General Principle of EU Law?* (Hart Publishing, 2011) 219–31 for normative arguments as regards the very exceptional use of the doctrine of abuse of rights.

principle for attribution of the market-distorting effect is that competition law enforcement takes the regulatory structure of the (Internal) Market as given. This means that the legality of state intervention is a necessary condition for Article 102 TFEU applicability. State compulsion defence, therefore, is not adequate as an applicability threshold because it cannot accommodate an assessment of the legality of the state action and, hence, may lead to a biased outcome against the undertaking involved. It has also been argued that the substantive legality test for state conduct should be different from the test governing the undertaking's conduct under Article 102 TFEU in order to avoid biased outcomes against the state involved and its non-market identity. The free movement provisions already provide a structured test for the assessment of the legality of the state action, since a 'system of undistorted competition' is an integral part of the Internal Market sought by the latter provisions. Therefore, the fact that the clause of ex-Article 3(1)(g) TEC has moved to Protocol No 27 TFEU might lead to a revision of the state action doctrine by applying the free movement provisions to state conduct instead. In practice, a defence based on shared responsibility for market separation in the context of Article 102 TFEU enforcement proceedings would lead to an assessment of the state action under the free movement provisions as a subordinate issue at the stage of geographic market definition and, in particular, of regulatory entry barriers. If the regulatory framework is not in conformity with the free movement provisions, then the undertaking's conduct is further shielded from the application of Article 102 TFEU. The additional application of the competition law provisions ensured, in the past, that the free movement rules are, indeed, enforced against market distortions stemming from the national regulations in light of the undertaking's conduct. However, this purpose is now obsolete since the question of the state action legality under the free movement provisions is procedurally associated with Article 102 TFEU enforcement proceedings and is therefore addressed before a court. By contrast, if the regulatory framework is in conformity with the free movement provisions, then market integration should be taken into account in the analysis under Article 102 TFEU, leading to a wide geographic market definition rather than to a geographic market defined across national lines.

If Article 102 TFEU is enforced by public authorities at the national level, it would be better, in terms of judicial economy, to allow an NCA to make preliminary references to the Court of Justice. This is currently precluded by the Court of Justice judgment in *SYFAIT*. The distinction between assessment of the undertaking's conduct in light of the regulatory framework and assessment of the regulatory framework in light of the undertaking's conduct is difficult to draw when Article 102 TFEU is enforced by national courts. This is exemplified by the regulation of IPRs and, in particular, the historical evolution of the interface between the exhaustion of IPRs under the free movement provisions and the application of Article 102 TFEU. The framework in which a question is asked feeds back to the outcome of the case. Therefore, non-exhaustible IPRs under the free movement provisions and the concomitant application of the competition law provisions constitute a case study of the principled interface between the two sets of provisions, inasmuch as the relevant case law reveals that 'non-exhaustion' is a precondition for the application of competition law. By contrast, the reversal of this relationship in the case of exhaustible IPRs does not fit into the proposed interface, but, for this reason, illustrates the risks of assimilation in the legal reasoning under the two sets of provisions.

Conclusions

This book argues that there is nothing special about the interface between competition and market integration that would justify a distinctive treatment of market separation cases under Article 102 TFEU, other than a principled understanding of the Treaty as a whole. Indeed, deconstruction of the elements for establishing market separation in the Internal Market as an abuse of the dominant position emphasises that clinging to tensions between competition and market integration presents, in the vast majority of cases, imaginary rather than actual conflicts.

The inherent economic limits of market integration should also be respected under Article 102 TFEU enforcement; otherwise, it may be difficult, if not impossible, to justify these outcomes from an economic perspective. These economic limits are reflected in the conceptual foundation for finding a trade barrier, based on a market access test, which defines the very core of what is considered 'internal' in the Internal Market, regardless of whether or not such a trade barrier is found to be justified.

Tensions between competition and the Internal Market may, nevertheless, arise when non-economic values, which are reflected in the finding of justified trade barriers, come into play. It is a cornerstone of this book that the interface between market separation by dominant undertakings and non-economic values is best understood as a question of shared responsibility for the market distorting effect between the undertaking and the state. The existing tensions are conceptualised as stemming from an unclear attribution of the anti-competitive effect of market separation in regard to the dominant undertaking and the state. Therefore, these tensions are expected to be relieved if the question of principled attribution to the undertaking or the state is addressed before the assessment of the substantive legality of the undertaking's conduct takes place.

A widening of the objectives of EU competition law to embrace non-economic values is desirable, in accordance with the Lisbon Treaty reforms which are predicated on the objective of a 'social market economy', as well as in accordance with the new reality that alleges a growth of business self-regulation. However, the widening of the objectives of EU competition law cannot oppose or ignore basic principles, in particular the normative distinction between market participation and market regulation. A strict distinction between the undertaking's conduct in the market and the state is not possible, nor is absolute convergence between the substantive tests under the legal rules applied to market participation and to state regulation. The aim should therefore be to manage the overlap of private and state responsibility rather than either separate them or model one on the other. Grey areas will always exist and this book advances what is considered to be, first, the most appropriate 'label' for such grey areas and, second, the most appropriate place under Article 102 TFEU to unravel the threads behind this 'label'.

The proposed 'label' is a defence based on shared responsibility between the dominant undertaking and the state for the alleged market-distorting effect. It is suggested that the defence should operate at the earliest possible stage of the application of Article 102 TFEU. The earliest possible stage is that of geographic market definition and, in particular, the notion of regulatory trade barriers, which are in themselves subject to the free movement provisions, while the geographic market definition also feeds back to the substantive test for establishing an abuse of a dominant position.

Front-loading the issue of state responsibility under the free movement position means that applicability and the actual application of Article 102 TFEU takes into account in a consistent and transparent manner the legality, including non-economic objectives, of regulatory interventions in the Internal Market. This is all the more important in a framework of private and decentralised enforcement of Article 102 TFEU once private litigants have decided to bear the costs of litigating borderline competition law cases. In addition, analytical clarity as to the conditions for the non-applicability of Article 102 TFEU removes artificial obstacles to case selection suitable for public enforcement of competition law. Hence, it could be said that, from an enforcement policy viewpoint, the revised state action defence might lead to a reversal of the Commission enforcement priorities at the EU level in accordance with the progressive evolution of the Internal Market.

Bibliography

BOOKS

Akman, P, *The Concept of Abuse in EU Competition Law: Law and Economic Approaches* (Hart Publishing, 2012)

Amato, J, *Antitrust and the Bounds of Power: the Dilemma of Liberal Democracy in the History of the Market* (Hart Publishing, 1997)

Anderman, S and Schmidt, H, *EU Competition Law and Intellectual Property Rights: The Regulation of Innovation* (Oxford University Press, 2011)

Balassa B, *The Theory of Economic Integration* (Allen & Unwin, 1962)

Baquero Cruz, J, *Between Competition and Free Movement: The Economic Constitutional Law of the European Community* (Hart Publishing, 2002)

Barak, A, *Purposive Interpretation in Law* (Princeton University Press, 2005)

Barnard, C, *The Substantive Law of the EU: The Four Freedoms* (Oxford University Press, 2010)

Beck, G, *The Legal Reasoning of the Court of Justice of the EU* (Hart Publishing, 2013)

Bishop, S and Walker, M, *The Economics of EC Competition Law: Concepts, Application and Measurement* (3rd edn, Sweet & Maxwell, 2010)

Black, O, *Conceptual Foundations of Antitrust* (Cambridge University Press, 2005)

Bork, R, *The Antitrust Paradox: A Policy at War with Itself* (Free Press, 1993)

Bouterse, R, *Competition and Integration: What Goals Count?: EEC Competition Law and Goals of Industrial, Monetary, and Cultural Policy* (Kluwer Law and Taxation, 1994)

Bredimas, A, *Methods of Interpretation and Community Law* (Elsevier, 1978)

Broberg, M and Fenger, N, *Preliminary References to the European Court of Justice* (Oxford University Press, 2010)

Buendia Sierra, J-L, *Exclusive Rights and State Monopolies under EC Law: Article 86 (Former 90) of the EC Treaty* (trans A Read from the Spanish) (Oxford University Press, 1999)

Buttigieg, E, *Competition Law: Safeguarding the Consumer Interest-A Comparative Analysis of US Antitrust Law and EC Competition Law* (Kluwer Law International, 2009)

Carrier, M, *Innovation for the 21st Century. Harnessing the Power of Intellectual Property and Antitrust Law* (Oxford University Press, 2009)

Cecchini, P, *The European Challenge 1992: The Benefits of a Single Market* (Wildwood House, 1988)

Cini, M and McGowan, L, *Competition Policy in the European Union* (Palgrave Macmillan, 2009)

Conway, G, *The Limits of Legal Reasoning and the European Court of Justice* (Cambridge University Press, 2012)

Craig, P, *The Lisbon Treaty: Law, Politics, and Treaty Reform* (Oxford University Press, 2010)
Dale, G, *Karl Polanyi: The Limits of the Market* (Polity Press, 2010)
Davies, G, *Nationality Discrimination in the European Internal Market* (Kluwer Law International, 2003)
Davies, J, *The European Consumer Citizen in Law and Policy* (Palgrave Macmillan, 2011)
De la Feria, R and Vogenauer, S (eds), *Prohibition of Abuse of Law: A New General Principle of EU Law?* (Hart Publishing, 2011)
De Vries, S, *Tensions within the Internal Market: The Functioning of the Internal Market and the Development of Horizontal and Flanking Policies* (Europa Law, 2006)
Dougan, M, *National Remedies before the Court of Justice: Issues of Harmonisation and Differentiation* (Hart Publishing, 2004)
Egan, M, *Constructing a European Market: Standards, Regulations, and Governance* (Oxford University Press, 2001)
Fatur, A, *EU Competition Law and the Information and Communication Technology Network Industries. Economic versus Legal Concepts in Pursuit of (Consumer) Welfare* (Hart Publishing, 2012)
Geradin, D (ed), *The Liberalization of State Monopolies in the European Union and Beyond* (Kluwer Law International, 2000)
Gerber, D, *Law and Competition in the Twentieth Century Europe: Protecting Prometheus* (Oxford University Press, 2001)
Gillingham, J, *Coal, Steel and the Rebirth of Europe, 1945–1955: The Germans and French from Ruhr Conflict to Economic Community* (Cambridge University Press, 1991)
Gormley, L, *EU Law of Free Movement of Goods and Customs Union* (Oxford University Press, 2009)
Gormsen, L, *A Principled Approach to Abuse of Dominance in European Competition Law* (Cambridge University Press, 2010)
Hancher, L and Sauter, W, *EU Competition and Internal Market Law in the Health Care Sector* (Oxford University Press, 2012)
Horner, S, *Parallel Imports* (Collins Professional Books, 1987)
Hovenkamp, H, *The Antitrust Enterprise: Principle and Execution* (Harvard University Press, 2005)
Jans, J-H, de Lange, R, Prechal, S and Widdershoven, R, *Europeanisation of Public Law* (Europa Law, 2007)
Jarvis, M, *The Application of EC Law by National Courts: The Free Movement of Goods* (Clarendon Press, 1998)
Joliet, R, *Monopolization and Abuse of Dominant Position: A Comparative Study of the American and European Approaches to the Control of Economic Power* (Nijhoff, 1970)
Jones, A and Sufrin, B, *EU Competition Law: Texts, Cases and Materials* (4th edn, Oxford University Press, 2011)
Keeling, D, *Intellectual Property Rights in EU Law, Volume I: Free Movement and Competition Law* (Oxford University Press, 2003)
Kingston, S, *Greening EU Competition Law and Policy* (Cambridge University Press, 2012)
Korah, V, *Intellectual Property Rights and the EC Competition Rules* (Hart Publishing, 2006)
Lindberg, L, *The Political Dynamics of European Economic Integration* (Oxford University Press, 1963)
Maduro, M, *We the Court: The European Court of Justice and the European Economic Constitution: A Critical Reading of Article 30 of the EC Treaty* (Hart Publishing, 1998)

Mantzavinos, C, *Individuals, Institutions, and Markets* (Cambridge University Press, 2001)
Molle, W, *The Economics of European Integration: Theory, Practice, Policy* (Ashgate, 2006)
Motta, M, *Competition Policy: Theory and Practice* (Cambridge University Press, 2004)
Nazzini, R, *The Foundations of European Union Competition Law: The Objective and Principle of Article 102* (Oxford University Press, 2011)
O'Donoghue, R and Padilla, J, *The Law and Economics of Article 82 EC* (Hart Publishing, 2006)
Odudu, O, *The Boundaries of EC Competition Law: The Scope of Article 81* (Oxford University Press, 2006)
Oliver, P (ed), *Oliver on Free Movement of Goods in the European Union* (Hart Publishing, 2010)
Ortiz-Blanco, L, *Market Power in EU Antitrust Law* (Hart Publishing, 2012)
Østerud, E, *Identifying Exclusionary Abuses by Dominant Undertakings under EU Competition Law: The Spectrum of Tests* (Kluwer Law International, 2010)
Polanyi, K, *The Great Transformation* (Beacon Press, 1957)
Posner, R, *Antitrust Law* (2nd edn, University of Chicago Press, 2001)
Prosser, T, *The Limits of Competition Law: Markets and Public Services* (Oxford University Press, 2005)
Rousseva, E, *Rethinking Exclusionary Abuses in EU Competition Law: Rethinking Article 82 of the EC Treaty* (Hart Publishing, 2010)
Sally, R, *Classical Liberalism and International Economic Order: Studies in Theory and Intellectual History* (Routledge, 1998)
Sauter, S and Schepel, H, *State and Market in European Union Law: The Public and Private Spheres of the Internal Market before the EU Courts* (Cambridge University Press, 2009)
Scharpf, F, *Governing in Europe: Effective and Democratic?* (Oxford University Press, 1999)
Schumpeter, J, *Capitalism, Socialism and Democracy* (6th edn, Unwin Paperbacks 1987)
Schutze, R, *From Dual to Cooperative Federalism: The Changing Structure of European Law* (Oxford University Press, 2009)
Shipman, A, *The Market Revolution and its Limits: A Price for Everything* (Routledge, 1999)
Smith, M, *Centralised Enforcement, Legitimacy and Governance in the EU* (Routledge, 2009)
Snell, J, *Goods and Services in EC Law: A Study of the Relationship Between the Freedoms* (Oxford University Press, 2002)
Stothers, C, *Parallel Trade in Europe: Intellectual Property, Competition and Regulatory Law* (Hart Publishing, 2007)
Szyszczak, E, *The Regulation of the State in Competitive Markets in the EU* (Hart Publishing, 2007)
Thaler, R and Sunstein, C, *Nudge: Improving Decisions about Health, Wealth, and Happiness* (Yale University Press, 2008)
Tinbergen, J, *International Economic Integration* (Elsevier, 1965)
Townley, C, *Article 81 EC and Public Policy* (Hart Publishing, 2009)
Tridimas, T, *The General Principles of EU Law* (2nd edn, Oxford University Press, 2006)
Tryfonidou, A, *Reverse Discrimination in EC Law* (Kluwer Law International, 2009)
Veljanovski, C, *The Economics of Law* (2nd edn, Institute of Economic Affairs, 2006)
Wesseling, R, *The Modernisation of EC Antitrust Law* (Hart Publishing, 2000)
Whish, R, *Competition Law* (6th edn, Oxford University Press, 2009)

ARTICLES AND CHAPTERS

Ahdar, R, 'Consumers, Redistribution of Income and the Purpose of Competition Law' (2002) 23 *European Competition Law Review* 341

Ahlborn, C and Padilla, J, 'From Fairness to Welfare: Implications for the Assessment of Unilateral Conduct under EC Competition Law' in C-D Ehlermann and M Marquis (eds), *European Competition Law Annual 2007: A Reformed Approach to Article 82 TEC* (Hart Publishing, 2008) 55–101

Akman, P, '"Consumer" v "Customer": The Devil in the Detail' (2008) Centre for Competition Policy Working Paper 08-34, http://papers.ssrn.com/sol3/papers.cfm?abstract_id=1313802

Albors-Llorens, A, 'Competition Policy and the Shaping of the Single Market' in C Barnard and J Scott (eds), *The Law of the Single European Market: Unpacking the Premises* (Hart Publishing, 2002) 311–31

—— 'The Role of Objective Justification and Efficiencies in the Application of Article 82 EC' (2007) 44 *Common Market Law Review* 1727

Allendesalazar, R, 'Can We Finally Say Farewell to the "Special Responsibility" of Dominant Companies?' in C-D Ehlermann and M Marquis (eds), *European Competition Law Annual 2007: A Reformed Approach to Article 82 EC* (Hart Publishing, 2008) 319–25

Andrews, P, 'Is Meeting Competition a Defence to Predatory Pricing? The Irish Sugar Decision Suggests a New Approach' (1998) 19 *European Competition Law Review* 49

Ardy, B and El-Agraa, A, 'The Economics of the Single Market' in A El-Agraa (ed), *The European Union: Economics and Policies* (Cambridge University Press, 2007) 130–43

Auf'mkolk, H, 'The "Feedback Effect" of Applying EU Competition Law to Regulated Industries: Doctrinal Contamination in the Case of Margin Squeeze' (2012) 3 *Journal of Competition Law and Practice* 149

Averitt, N and Lande R, 'Consumer Sovereignty: A Unified Theory of Antitrust and Consumer Protection Law' (1997) 65 *Antitrust Law Journal* 713

—— 'Using the "Consumer Choice" Approach to Antitrust Law' (2007) 74 *Antitrust Law Journal* 176

Avgoustis, I, 'Parallel Imports and Exhaustion of Trade Mark Rights: Should Steps Be Taken Towards an International Exhaustion Regime?' (2012) 34 *European Intellectual Property Review* 108

Azoulai, L, 'The Court of Justice and the Social Market Economy: The Emergence of an Ideal and the Conditions for its Realisation' (2008) 45 *Common Market Law Review* 1335

Bailey, D, 'Presumptions in EU Competition Law' (2010) 31(9) *European Competition Law Review* 362

Baquero Cruz, J, 'The State Action Doctrine' in G Amato and C-D Ehlermann (eds), *EC Competition Law: A Critical Assessment* (Hart Publishing, 2007) 551–90

Barents, R, 'Constitutional Horse Riding: Some Comments on the Protocol on the Internal Market and Competition' in M Bulterman, L Hancher, A McDonnell and H Sevenster (eds), *Views of European Law from the Mountain: Liber Amicorum Piet Jan Slot* (Kluwer Law International, 2009) 123–32

Barnard, C, 'Fitting the Remaining Pieces into the Goods and Services Jigsaw' (2001) 26 *European Law Review* 35

Barnard, C and Deakin, S, 'Market Access and Regulatory Competition' in C Barnard and J Scott (eds), *The Law of the Single European Market: Unpacking the Premises* (Hart Publishing, 2002) 197–224

Bavasso, A, 'The Role of Intent under Article 82 EC: From "Flushing the Turkeys" to "Spotting Lionesses in Regent's Park"' (2005) 26 *European Competition Law Review* 616

Bellis, J-F and Kasten, T, 'Will Efficiencies Play an Increasingly Important Role in the Assessment of Conduct under Article 102 TFEU?' in F Etro and I Kokkoris (eds), *Competition Law and the Enforcement of Article 102 TFEU* (Oxford University Press, 2010) 129–37

Bengoetxea, J, MacCormick, N and Moral Soriano, L, 'Integration and Integrity in the Legal Reasoning of the Court of Justice' in G de Búrca and H Weiler (eds), The European Court of Justice (Oxford University Press, 2001) 43–85

Bernard, N, 'Discrimination and Free Movement in EC Law' (1996) 45 *International and Comparative Law Quarterly* 82

Bishop, W, 'Price Discrimination under Article 86: Political Economy in the European Court' (1981) 44 *Modern Law Review* 282

Blomme, E, 'State Action as a Defence against 81 and 82 EC' (2007) 30 *World Competition Law and Economics Review* 243

Bonadio, E, 'Parallel Imports in a Global Market: Should a Generalised International Exhaustion Be the Next Step?' (2011) 33 *European Intellectual Property Review* 153

Bowles, S and Gintis, H, 'The Revenge of Homo Economicus: Contested Exchange and the Revival of Political Economy' (1993) 7(1) *Journal of Economic Perspectives* 83

Brisimi, V, 'On the Interface between the "Exhaustion" of IP Rights under Internal Market Law and Competition Law: Oracle America Inc v M-Tech Data Limited' [2012] *Competition Law Journal* 312

Brisimi, V and Yannelis, D, 'The Price Squeeze Test as a "Wildcard" at the Hands of Competition Authorities: The Example of the Greek Broadband Internet Services Market' (2012) 35 *Competition and Regulation in Network Industries* 2

Busschaert, G, 'Revisiting the Fundamentals of Internal Market Law: Civil Society as a Third Sector between the State and the Market' [2011] *European Business Law Review* 725

Camesasca, P and van den Bergh, R, 'Irreconcilable Principles? The Court of Justice Exempts Collective Labour Agreements from the Wrath of Antitrust' (2000) 25 *European Law Review* 492

Caporaso, J and Tarrow, S, 'Polanyi in Brussels: European Institutions and the Embedding of Markets in Society' (2008) RECON Online Working Paper 2008/01, www.reconproject.eu/main.php/RECON_wp_0801.pdf?fileitem=5456241

Carlton, D, 'Why Barriers to Entry are Barriers to Understanding' [2004] *American Economic Review* 466–70

Carrier, M, 'Two Puzzles Resolved: Of the Schumpeter-Arrow Stalemate and Pharmaceutical Innovation Markets' (2007–08) 93 *Iowa Law Review* 393

Cass, R and Hylton, K, 'Antitrust Intent' (2010) Boston University School of Law, Working Paper Series-Public Law and Legal Theory-WP No 00-02, http://papers.ssrn.com/sol3/papers.cfm?abstract_id=239324

Castillo de la Torre, F, 'State Action Defence in EC Competition Law' (2005) 28 *World Competition Law and Economics Review* 407

Chard, J and Mellor, C, 'Intellectual Property Rights and Parallel Imports' (1989) 12 *The World Economy* 69

Cseres, K, 'The Controversies of the Consumer Welfare Standard' (2007) 3 *Competition Law Review* 121

—— 'Comparing Laws in the Enforcement of EU and National Competition Law' (2010) 3 *European Journal of Legal Studies* 7

Dashwood, A, 'Viking and Laval: Issues of Horizontal Direct Effect' [2007–08] *Cambridge Yearbook of European Legal Studies* 525

Davies, G, 'Abstractness and Correctness in the Preliminary Reference Procedure: Implications for the Division of Powers and Effective Market Regulation' in N Nic Shuibhne (ed), *Regulating the Internal Market* (Edward Elgar, 2006) 210–45

—— 'Article 86 EC, the EC's Economic Approach to Competition Law, and the General Interest' (2009) 5 *European Competition Journal* 549

—— 'Understanding Market Access: Exploring the Economic Rationality of Different Conceptions of Free Movement Law' (2010) 11 *German Law Journal* 671

—— 'Freedom of Movement, Horizontal Effect, and Freedom of Contract' (2012) 3 *European Review of Private Law* 805

—— 'The Court's Jurisprudence on Free Movement of Goods: Pragmatic Presumptions, Not Philosophical Principles' (2012) 2 *European Journal of Consumer Law* 25

De Búrca, G, 'Unpacking the Concept of Discrimination in the EC and International Trade Law' in C Barnard and J Scott (eds), *The Law of the Single European Market: Unpacking the Premises* (Hart Publishing, 2002) 181–95

De Búrca and de Witte, B, 'The Delimitation of Powers between the EU and the Member States' in A Arnull and D Wincott (eds), *Accountability and Legitimacy in the European Union* (Oxford University Press, 2002) 201–22

De la Feria, R, 'Prohibition of Abuse of (Community) Law: The Creation of a New General Principle of EC Law through Tax' (2008) 45 *Common Market law Review* 395

De Witte, B, 'Non-market Values in Internal Market Legislation' in N Nic Shuibhne (ed), *Regulating the Internal Market* (Edward Elgar, 2006) 61–86

Diaz, E-G and Padilla, J, 'The *linkLine* Judgement: A European Perspective' (2009) 1 *Global Competition Policy*, www.globalcompetitionpolicy.org

Dougan, M, 'Minimum Harmonisation and the Internal Market' (2000) 37 *Common Market Law Review* 853

Downing, R and Jones, A, 'Margin Squeeze in Telecommunications Markets' in S Anderman and A Ezrachi (eds), *Intellectual Property and Competition Law: New Frontiers* (Oxford University Press, 2011) 209–37

Drexl, J, 'Competition Law as Part of the European Constitution' in A von Bogdandy and J Bast (eds), *Principles of European Constitutional Law* (2nd revised edn, Hart Publishing, 2010) 659–98

Dworkin, R, 'Is Wealth a Value?' (1980) 9 *Journal of Legal Studies* 191

Economides, N, 'The Economics of Networks' (1996) 14 *International Journal of Industrial Organization* 673

Edward, D and Hoskins, M, 'Article 90: Deregulation and EC Law. Reflections Arising from the XVI FIDE Conference' (1995) 32 *Common Market Law Review* 157

Ehricke, U, 'State Intervention and EEC Competition Law: Opportunities and Limits of the European Court of Justice's Approach—A Critical Analysis of Four Key-Cases' (1990) 14 *World Competition Law and Economics Review* 79

Eilmansberger T, 'Dominance—The Lost Child: How Effects-Based Rules Could and Should Change the Dominance Analysis' (2006) 2 *European Competition Journal* 15

—— 'Restrictive Agreements and Unilateral Restraints: Merging Regimes on Market Power and Exclusion' in J Drexl, L Idot and J Moneger (eds), *Economic Theory and Competition Law* (Edward Elgar, 2009) 153–75

El-Agraa, A, 'General Introduction: The EU within the Global Context of Regional Integration' in A El-Agraa (ed), *The European Union: Economics and Policies* (Cambridge University Press, 2007) 1–20

—— 'The Theory of Economic Integration' in A El-Agraa (ed), *The European Union: Economics and Policies* (Cambridge University Press, 2007) 109–28

Elhauge, E, 'The Scope of Antitrust Process' (1991) 104 *Harvard Law Review* 667

—— 'Defining Better Monopolization Standards' (2003) 56 *Stanford Law Review* 253

Enchelmaier, S, 'Intellectual Property, the Internal Market and Competition Law' in J Drexl (ed), *Research Handbook on Intellectual Property and Competition Law* (Edward Elgar, 2008) 405–26

—— 'Mandatory Requirements under Art 101(3) TFEU? The Complementary Relationship between EU Competition and Free Movement Law' [2012] *Competition Law Journal* 182

Evans, P, 'Assessing Consumer Detriment' (2007) 28 *European Competition Law Review* 26

Farrell, J and Katz, M, 'The Economics of Welfare Standards in Antitrust' (2006) 2 *Competition Policy International*, www.competitionpolicyinternational.com

Faull, J, 'Effect on Trade between Member State and Community: Member State Jurisdiction' [1989] *Fordham Corporate Law Institute* 486

Feros, A, 'Free Movement of Pharmaceuticals within the EU: Should Rights Be Exhausted Regionally? (2010) 32 *European Intellectual Property Review* 486

Fisher, F, 'The Social Costs of Monopoly and Regulation: Posner Revisited' (1985) 93 *Journal of Political Economy* 410

Fox, E, 'The Modernization of Antitrust: A New Equilibrium', (1981) 66 *Cornell Law Review* 1140

Fox, E and Sullivan, L, 'Antitrust—Retrospective and Prospective: Where are We Coming from? Where are We Going?' (1987) 62 *New York University Law Review* 936

Freedland, M, 'Law, Public Services, and Citizenship: New Domains, New Regimes?' in M Freedland and S Sciarra (eds), *Public Services and Citizenship in European Law* (Clarendon Press, 1998) 1–35

Frerichs, S, 'Re-embedding Neo-Liberal Constitutionalism: A Polanyian Case for the Economic Sociology of Law' in C Joerges and J Falke (eds), *Karl Polanyi, Globalisation and the Potential of Law in Transnational Markets* (Hart Publishing, 2011) 64–84

Friederiszick, H, 'Economic Analysis in EU Competition Cases' in J Drexl, L Idot and J Moneger (eds), *Economic Theory and Competition Law* (Edward Elgar, 2009) 3–19

Friederiszick, H and Gratz, L, 'Dominant and Efficient: On the Relevance of Efficiencies in Abuse of Dominance Cases' ESMT White Paper No WP–12–01

Gal, M and Faibish, I, 'Six Principles for Limiting Government-Facilitated Restraints on Competition' (2007) 44 *Common Market Law Review* 69

Gardner, A, 'The Velvet Revolution: Article 90 and the Triumph of the Free Market in Europe's Regulated Sectors' (1995) 16 *European Competition Law Review* 78

Gavil, A, 'Secondary Line Price Discrimination and the Fate of Morton Salt: To Save it, Let it Go' (1999) 4 *Emory Law Journal* 1058

Geradin, D, 'Refusal to Supply and Margin Squeeze: A Discussion of Why the "Telefonica Exceptions" are Wrong' (2011) TILEC Discussion Paper 009, http://papers.ssrn.com/sol3/papers.cfm?abstract_id=1762687

Geradin, D and Petit, N, 'Price Discrimination under EC Competition Law' in Swedish Competition Authority (ed), *The Pros and Cons of Price Discrimination* (Elanders Gotab, 2005)

Gerard, D, 'Price Discrimination under Article 82(2)(c) EC: Clearing Up the Ambiguities' (2005) Global Competition Law Centre: Research Paper on the Modernisation of Article 82 EC, www.coleurop.be/content/gclc/documents/GCLC%20Research%20Papers%20on%20Article%2082%20EC.pdf

—— 'EU Competition Policy after Lisbon: Time for a Review of the "State Action Doctrine"?' (2010) 1(3) *Journal of European Competition Law and Practice* 202

Gerber, D, 'Constitutionalizing the Economy: German Neo-Liberalism, Competition Law and the "New" Europe' (1994) 42 *American Journal of Comparative Law* 25

—— 'The Future of Article 82: Dissecting the Conflict' in C-D Ehlermann and M Marquis (eds), *European Competition Law Annual 2007: A Reformed Approach to Article 82 TEC* (Hart Publishing, 2008) 37–54

—— 'Competition Law and Institutional Embeddedness of Economics' in J Drexl, L Idot and J Moneger (eds), *Economic Theory and Competition Law* (Edward Elgar, 2009) 20–44

Gormley, L, 'Free Movement of Goods and their Use: What is the Use of it?' (2009–10) 33 *Fordham International Law Journal* 1589

Gormsen, L, 'The Conflict between Economic Freedom and Consumer Welfare in the Modernisation of Article 82 EC' (2007) 3 *European Competition Journal* 329

—— 'The Parallels between the Harvard Structural School and Article 82 EC and the Divergences between the Chicago and the Post-Chicago Schools and Article 82 EC' (2008) 4 *European Competition Journal* 221

Graf, T, 'The General Court's Judgment in AstraZeneca, Interacting with Regulatory Authorities', Kluwer Competition Law Blog, 6 September 2010, http://kluwercompetitionlawblog.com/2010/09/06/the-general-court's-judgment-in-astrazeneca-interacting-with-regulatory-authorities/

Grossman, G and Lai, E, 'Parallel Imports and Price Controls' (2008) 39 *RAND Journal of Economics* 378

Gyselen, L, 'State Action and the Effectiveness of the EEC Treaty's Competition Provisions' (1989) 26 *Common Market Law Review* 33

—— 'Anti-competitive State Measures under the EC Treaty: Towards a Substantive Legality Standard' (1993) *European Law Review: Competition Checklist* 55

Hanf, D, '"Reverse Discrimination" in EU Law: Constitutional Aberration, Constitutional Necessity or Judicial Choice?' (2011) 18 *Maastricht Journal* 29

Hatzopoulos, V, 'The Economic Constitution of the EU Treaty and the Limits between Economic and Non-economic Activities' [2012] *European Business Law Review* 973

Hawk, B, 'Antitrust in the EEC: The First Decade' [1972–73] *Fordham Law Review* 229

Heinemann, A, 'Intellectual Property Rights and Market Integration' in S Anderman and A Ezrachi (eds), *Intellectual Property and Competition Law: New Frontiers* (Oxford University Press, 2011) 303–22

Hellwig, M, 'Competition Policy and Sector Specific Regulation for Network Industries' (2008) Preprints for the Max Planck Institute for Research on Collective Goods, Bonn 2008/29, www.coll.mpg.de/pdf_dat/2008_29online.pdf

Hildebrand, D, 'Using Conjoint Analysis for Market Definition: Application of Modern Market Research Tools to Implement the Hypothetical Monopolist Test' (2006) 29 *World Competition Law and Economics Review* 315

Horsley, T, 'Anyone for *Keck*?' (2009) 46 *Common Market Law Review* 2001

Ibáñez-Colomo, P, 'The Application of EC Treaty Rules to Sport: The Approach of the European Court of First Instance in the *Meca Medina* and *Piau* Cases' (2006) *Entertainment and Sports Law Journal*, www2.warwick.ac.uk/fac/soc/law/elj/eslj/issues/volume3/number2/colomo

Immordino, G and Polo, M, 'Optimal Legal Standards in Antitrust: Traditional v Innovative Industries' (2011) Innocenzo Gasparini Institute for Economic Research Working Paper No 420, www.igier.unibocconi.it/files/420.pdf

Joerges, C, 'What is Left of the European Economic Constitution?' (2004) EUI Working Paper LAW No 2004/13

—— 'Democracy and European Integration: A Legacy of Tensions, a Re-conceptualisation and Recent True Conflicts' (2007) European University Institute Working Papers Law 2007/25, http://cadmus.eui.eu/dspace/handle/1814/7081

Joerges, C and Rödl, F, 'Informal Politics, Formalised Law and the "Social Deficit" of European Integration: Reflections after the Judgments of the ECJ in Viking and Laval' (2009) 15 *European Law Journal* 1

Johnston, A, '"Spillovers" from EU Law into National Law: (Un)intended Consequences for Private Law Relationships' in D Leczykiewicz and S Weatherill (eds), *The Involvement of EU Law in Private Law Relationships* (Hart Publishing, 2013) 357–94

Joliet, R, 'National Anti-competitive Legislation and Community Law' (1989) 12 *Fordham International Law Journal* 163

Joliet, R (in collaboration with Keeling, D), 'Trade Mark Law and the Free Movement of Goods: The Overruling of the Judgment in Hag I' (1991) *International Review of Industrial Property and Copyright Law* 303

Kallaugher, J, 'Existence, Exercise and Exceptional Circumstances: The Limited Scope for a More Economic Approach to IP Issues under Article 102 TFEU' in S Anderman and A Ezrachi (eds), *Intellectual Property and Competition Law: New Frontiers* (Oxford University Press, 2011) 113–39

Karayigit, M, 'The Horizontal Effect of the Free Movement Provisions' (2011) 18 *Maastricht Journal* 303

Karsten, S, 'Eucken's "Social Market Economy" and its Test in Post-War West Germany: The Economist as Social Philosopher Developed Ideas that Paralleled Progressive Thought in America' (1985) 44 *American Journal of Economics and Sociology* 169

Kerber, W, 'Should Competition Law Promote Efficiency? Some Reflections of an Economist on the Normative Foundations of Competition Law' in J Drexl, L Idot and J Moneger (eds), *Economic Theory and Competition Law* (Edward Elgar, 2009)

Kerber, W and van den Bergh, R, 'Mutual Recognition Revisited: Misunderstandings, Inconsistencies, and a Suggested Reinterpretation' (2008) 61 *Kyklos* 447

—— 'Mutual Recognition in the Global Trade Regime: Lessons from the EU Experience' in I Lianos and O Odudu (eds), *Regulating Trade in Services in the EU and the WTO: Trust, Distrust and Economic Integration* (Cambridge University Press, 2012) 121–46

Kingston, S, 'Joined Cases C-468/06 to C-478/06 Sot Lélos kai Sia EE and Others v GlaxoSmithKline AEVE Farmakeftikon Proïonton, formerly Glaxowellcome AEVE (Case Comment)' (2009) 46 *Common Market Law Review* 683

Kirkwood, J and Lande, R, 'The Fundamental Goal of Antitrust: Protecting Consumers, Not Efficiency' (2008) 84 *Notre Dame Law Review* 191

Kokkoris, I, 'Are We Underenforcing Article 102 TFEU?' in F Etro and I Kokkoris (eds), *Competition Law and the Enforcement of Article 102 TFEU* (Oxford University Press, 2010) 139–63

Komnimos, A, 'Continuity and Change in EU Competition Policy' (2010) 1 *Competition Policy International*, www.competitionpolicyinternational.com/journal

Korah, V, 'Notes of Cases: Dividing the Common Market through National Industrial Property Rights' (1972) 35 *Modern Law Review* 634

Krenn, C, 'A Missing Piece in the Horizontal Effect "Jigsaw": Horizontal Direct Effect and the Free Movement of Goods' (2012) 49 *Common Market Law Review* 177

Krzeminska-Vamvaka, J, 'Horizontal Effect of Fundamental Rights and Freedoms: Much Ado About Nothing? German, Polish and EU Theories Compared after *Viking Line*' (2009) Jean Monnet Working Paper 11/09, http://centers.law.nyu.edu/jeanmonnet/papers/09/091101.html

Lane, R, 'The Internal Market and the Individual' in N Nic Shuibhne (ed), Regulating the Internal Market (Edward Elgar, 2006) 245–76

—— 'EC Competition Law Post-Lisbon: A Matter of Protocol' in M Bulterman, L Hancher, A McDonnell and H Sevenster (eds), *Views of European Law from the Mountain: Liber Amicorum Piet Jan Slot* (Kluwer Law International, 2009) 167–78

Leibstein, H, 'Allocative Efficiency vs "X-Efficiency"' [1966] *American Economic Review* 392

Lemley, M, 'Industry-Specific Antitrust Policy for Innovation' [2011] *Columbia Business Law Review* 637

Levenstein, M, Sivadasan, J and Suslow, V, 'The Effect of Competition on Trade Patterns: Evidence from the Collapse of International Cartels' (2010) Research Seminar in International Economics Discussion Paper No 603, University of Michigan, www.fordschool.umich.edu/rsie/workingpapers/Papers601-625/r603.pdf

Lewinsohn-Zamir, D, 'Consumer Preferences, Citizen Preferences, and the Provision of Public Goods (1998–99) 108 *Yale Law Journal* 377

Li, K, 'The Dormant Commerce Clause, Anticompetitive State Regulation, Competition and Consumers' (2013) American Antitrust Institute Working Paper No 13-01

Lianos, I, 'Shifting the Narratives in the European Internal Market: Efficient Restrictions of Trade and the Nature of "Economic" Integration' [2010] *European Business Law Review* 705

—— 'Competition Law in the European Union after the Treaty of Lisbon' in D Ashiagbor, N Countouris and I Lianos (eds), *The European Union after the Treaty of Lisbon* (Cambridge University Press, 2012) 252–83

Lianos, I and Gerard, D, 'Shifting Narratives in European Economic Integration: Trade in Services, Pluralism and Trust' in I Lianos and O Odudu (eds), *Regulating Trade in Services in the EU and the WTO: Trust, Distrust and Economic Integration* (Cambridge University Press, 2012) 173–261

Lianos, I and Matteus, A, 'Antitrust in the New US Administration: A Transatlantic View' (2009) 2 *Global Competition Policy*, http://papers.ssrn.com/sol3/papers.cfm?abstract_id=1399693

Liberatore, F, 'UK Calls for Ban of Parallel Trade of Prescription Medicines: What are the EU Competition Law Implications?' (2013) 34 *European Competition Law Review* 189

Lindh, P, 'The Influence of Competition Law on Free Movement Rules' in H Kanninen, N Korjus and A Rosas (eds), *EU Competition Law in Context: Essays in Honour of Virpi Tiili* (Hart Publishing, 2009) 17–25

Lindstrom, N, 'Constitutionalism between Normative Frameworks and the Socio-legal Frameworks of Societies' in D Schiek, U Liebert and H Schneider (eds), *European Economic and Social Constitutionalism after the Treaty of Lisbon* (Cambridge University Press, 2011) 74–94

Lodge, M, 'Regulatory Accountability: Towards a Single Citizen-Consumer Model?' in K Dowding, J Hughes and H Margetts (eds), *Challenges to Democracy: Ideas, Involvement and Institutions: The PSA Yearbook 2000* (Palgrave, 2001) 205–219

Loewenthal, P-J, 'The Defence of "Objective Justification" in the Application of Article 82 EC' (2005) 28 *World Competition Law and Economics Review* 455

Maggiolino, M and Montagnani, M, 'AstraZeneca's Abuse of IPR-Related Procedures: A Hypothesis of Anti-Trust Offence, Abuse of Rights, and IPR Misuse' (2011) 34 *World Competition Law and Economics Review* 245

Maher, I, 'Competition Law Modernization: An Evolutionary Tale?' in P Craig and G de Búrca (eds), *The Evolution of EU Law* (2nd edn, Oxford University Press, 2011) 717–41

Maillo, J, 'Article 86 EC: Services of General Interest and EC Competition Law' in G Amato and C-D Ehlermann (eds), *EC Competition Law: A Critical Assessment* (Hart Publishing, 2007) 591–625

Majumdar, A, 'Whither Dominance?' (2006) 27 *European Competition Law Review* 161

Manne, G and Wright, J, 'Innovation and the Limits of Antitrust' (2010) 6 *Journal of Competition Law and Economics* 153

Marenco, G, 'Competition between National Economies and Competition between Businesses: A Response to Judge Pescatore' (1987) 10 *Fordham International Law Journal* 420

Marenco, G and Banks, K, 'Intellectual Property and the Community Rules on Free Movement: Discrimination Unearthed' (1990) 15 *European Law Review* 224

Martino, M, 'Effectiveness of Traffic Direction Techniques in Mobile International Roaming and Implications for Market Definition' (2007) 66 *Communications and Strategies* 137

Maskus, K, 'Parallel Imports' in P Lloyd and C Milner (eds), *The World Economy: Global Trade Policy 2000* (Blackwell, 1998) 1269–84

McAfee, P, Mialon, H and Williams, M, 'What is a Trade Barrier?' [2004] *American Economic Review* 461

McDonald, F, 'Market Integration in the European Union' in F McDonald and S Dearden (eds), *European Economic Integration* (3rd edn, Longman, 1999)

Melamed, D, 'Exclusionary Conduct under the Antitrust Laws: Balancing Sacrifice, and Refusals to Deal' (2005) 20 *Berkeley Technology Law Journal* 1249

Mestmäcker, E-J, 'Concentration and Competition in the EEC (Part I)' (1972) 6 *Journal of World Trade Law* 615

—— 'On the Legitimacy of European Law' (1994) *Rabels Zeitschrift für ausländisches und internationales Privatrecht* 615

Mitchell, G, 'Taking Behavioralism Too Seriously? The Unwarranted Pessimism of the New Behavioral Analysis of Law' (2002) 43 *William and Mary Law Review* 1907

Moisejevas, R, 'The Importance of Intent in Predatory Pricing Cases' (2010) 4 (122) *Jurisprudencija* 319

Monti, G, 'Article 81 EC and Public Policy' (2002) 39 *Common Market Law Review* 1057

—— 'Managing the Intersection of Utilities Regulation and EC Competition Law' (2008) 4 *Competition Law Review* 123

Mortelmans, K, 'Towards Convergence in the Application of the Rules on Free Movement and on Competition?' (2001) 38 *Common Market Law Review* 613

—— 'The Relationship between the Treaty Rules and Community Measures for the Establishment and Functioning of the Internal Market: Towards a Concordance Rule' (2002) 39 *Common Market Law Review* 1303

Möschel, W, 'Competition Policy from an Ordo Point of View' in H Willgerodt and A Peacock (eds), *German Neo-Liberals and the Social Market Economy* (Macmillan for the Trade Policy Research Centre, 1989) 142–59

—— 'The Proper Scope of Government Viewed from an Ordoliberal Perspective: The Example of Competition Policy (2001) 157 *Journal of Institutional and Theoretical Economics* 3

Nazzini, R, 'The Wood Began to Move: An Essay on Consumer Welfare, Evidence and Burden of Proof in Article 82 EC Cases' (2006) 31 *European Law Review* 518

Nguyen, T, Minssen, T and Groussot, X, 'The Rule of Reason under Article 82 EC after Sot Lelos kai Sia' (2009) Working Paper, http://papers.ssrn.com/sol3/papers.cfm?abstract_id=1431010

Nicolaidis, K, 'Kir Forever? The Journey of a Political Scientist in the Landscape of Mutual Recognition' in M Maduro and L Azoulai (eds), *The Past and Future of EU Law: The Classics of EU Law Revisited on the 50th Anniversary of the Rome Treaty* (Hart Publishing, 2010) 447–64

Nic Shuibhne, N, 'Margins of Appreciation: National Values, Fundamental Rights and EC Free Movement Law' (2009) 34 *European Law Review* 230–56

—— 'The Outer Limits of EU Citizenship: Displacing Economic Free Movement Rights?' in C Barnard and O Odudu (eds), *The Outer Limits of European Union Law* (Hart Publishing, 2009) 167–95

—— 'The Resilience of EU Market Citizenship' (2010) 47 *Common Market Law Review* 1597

Nic Shuibhne, N and Maci, M, 'Proving Public Interest: The Growing Importance of Evidence in Free Movement Case Law' (2013) 50 *Common Market Law Review* 965

Niels, G and Jenkins, H, 'Reform of Article 82: Where the Link between Dominance and Effects Breaks Down' (2005) 26 *European Competition Law Review* 605

O'Donoghue, R, 'Regulating the Regulated: DeutscheTelekom v European Commission' (May 2008) 1 *Global Competition Policy*, www.globalcompetitionpolicy.org

O'Donoghue, R and Macnab, L, 'Dominant Firms' Duties to Deal with Pharmaceutical Parallel Traders Following Glaxo Greece' (2009) 1 *Competition Policy International* 153

Odudu, O, 'Interpreting Article 81(1): Object as Subjective Intention' (2001) 26 *European Law Review* 60

—— 'Interpreting Article 81(1): The Object Requirement Revisited' (2001) 26 *European Law Review* 379–90

—— 'Restrictions of Competition by Object: What's the Beef?' [2009] *Competition Law Journal* 11

—— 'The Public/Private Distinction in EU Internal Market Law' (2010) 46(4) *Revue Trimestrielle de Droit Européen* 826

—— 'The Wider Concerns of EU Competition Law' [2010] *Oxford Journal of Legal Studies* 1

O'Leary, S, 'The Past, Present and Future of the Purely Internal Rule in EU Law' in M Dougan, N Nic Shuibhne and E Spaventa (eds), *Empowerment and Disempowerment of the European Citizen* (Hart Publishing, 2012) 37–71

Oliver, P, 'Of Trailers and Jet Skis: Is the Case Law on Article 34 TFEU Hurtling in a New Direction? (2009–10) 33 *Fordham International Law Journal* 1423

O'Loughlin, R, 'EC Competition Rules and Free Movement Rules: An Examination of the Parallels and their Furtherance by the ECJ Wouters Decision' (2003) 24 *European Competition Law Review* 62

Orbach, B, 'The Antitrust Consumer Welfare Paradox' (2010) Arizona Legal Studies Discussion Paper No 10-07, http://papers.ssrn.com/sol3/papers.cfm?abstract_id=1553226

Parret, L, 'The Multiple Personalities of EU Competition Law: Time for a Comprehensive Debate on its Objectives' in D Zimmer (ed), *The Goals of Competition Law* (Edward Elgar, 2010) 61–84

Pecho, P, 'Good-Bye Keck? A Comment on the Remarkable Judgment in Commission v Italy, C-110/05' (2009) 36 *Legal Issues of Economic Integration* 257

Pelkmans J, 'Economic Theories of Integration Revisited' (1980) 18 *Journal of Common Market Studies* 333

—— 'Mutual Recognition in Goods and Services: An Economic Perspective' in F Padoa-Schioppa (ed), *The Principle of Mutual Recognition in the European Integration Process* (Palgrave Macmillan, 2005) 85–128

Persky, J, 'Retrospectives: The Ethology of Homo Economicus' (1995) 9(2) *Journal of Economic Perspectives* 221

Pescatore, P, 'Public and Private Aspects of European Community Competition Law' (1987) 10 *Fordham International Law Journal* 373

Petersmann, E-U, 'National Constitutions, Foreign Trade Policy and European Community Law' (1992) 3 *European Journal of International Law* 1

—— 'Proposals for a New Constitution for the European Union: Building-Blocks for a Constitutional Theory and Constitutional Law of the EU' (1995) 32 *Common Market Law Review* 1123

Petit, N, 'The Proliferation of National Regulatory Authorities Alongside Competition Authorities: A Source of Jurisdictional Confusion?' in D Geradin, R Muňoz and N Petit (eds), *Regulating Through Agencies in the EU: A New Paradigm of European Governance* (Edward Elgar, 2005) 180–212

—— 'The Economics of Parallel Trade: Iconoclast Views on a Dogma of EU Competition Law' (2010) http://papers.ssrn.com/sol3/papers.cfm?abstract_id=1661884

Pinder, J, 'Problems of European Integration' in G Denton (ed), *Economic Integration in Europe* (Weidenfeld & Nicolson, 1969) 143–70

Posner, R, 'The Social Costs of Monopoly and Regulation' (1975) 83 *Journal of Political Economy* 807

—— 'The Value on Wealth: A Comment on Dworkin and Kronman' (1980) 9 *Journal of Legal Studies* 243

—— 'Antitrust in the New Economy' (2001) 68 *Antitrust Law Journal* 925

Regibeau, P and Rockett, K, 'The Relationship between Intellectual Property Law and Competition Law: An Economic Appraoch' in S Anderman (ed), *The Interface between Intellectual Property Rights and Competition Policy* (Cambridge University Press, 2007) 505–52

Reich, N, 'The "November Revolution" of the European Court of Justice: *Keck*, *Meng* and *Audi* Revisited' (1994) 31 *Common Market Law Review* 459

Riley, A, 'The EU Reform Treaty and the Competition Protocol: Undermining EC Competition Law' [2007] *European Competition Law Review* 703

Ritter, C, 'Purely Internal Situations, Reverse Discrimination, *Guimont*, *Dzodzi* and Article 234' (2006) 31 *European Law Review* 690

Rognstad, O-A, 'The Exhaustion/Competition Interface in EC Law: Is there Room for a Holistic Approach?' in J Drexl (ed), *Research Handbook on Intellectual Property and Competition Law* (Edward Elgar, 2008) 427–50

Roth, W-H, 'Economic Justifications and the Internal Market' in M Bulterman, L Hancher, A McDonnell and H Sevenster (eds), *Views of European Law from the Mountain: Liber Amicorum Piet Jan Slot* (Kluwer Law International, 2009) 71–90

Rousseva, E, 'Modernizing by Eradicating: How the Commission's New Approach to Article 81 EC Dispenses with the Need to Apply Article 82 EC to Vertical Restraints' (2005) 42 *Common Market Law Review* 587

Sadowska, M and Willems, B, 'Market Integration and Economic Efficiency at Conflict? Commitments at the Swedish Interconnectors Case' (2013) 36 *World Competition* 99

Schammo, P, 'Arbitrage and Abuse of Rights in the EC Legal System' (2008) 14 *European Law Journal* 351

Scharpf, F, 'The European Social Model: Coping with the Challenges of Diversity' (2002) 40 *Journal of Common Market Studies* 645

Schepel, H, 'Delegation of Regulatory Powers to Private Parties under EC Competition Law: Towards a Procedural Public Interest Test' (2002) 39 *Common Market Law Review* 31

—— 'Constitutionalising the Market, Marketising the Constitution, and to Tell the Difference: On the Horizontal Application of the Free Movement Provisions in EU Law' (2012) 18 *European Law Journal* 177

Schiek, D, 'Re-embedding Economic and Social Constitutionalism: Normative Perspectives for the EU' in D Schiek, U Liebert and H Schneider (eds), *European Economic and Social Constitutionalism after the Treaty of Lisbon* (Cambridge University Press, 2011) 17–46

Schmalensee, R, 'Antitrust Issues in Schumpeterian Industries' [2000] *American Economic Review* 192

Schmid, C, 'Diagonal Competence Conflicts between European Competition Law and National Regulation: A Conflict of Laws Reconstruction of the Dispute on Book Price Fixing' (2000) 1 *European Review of Private Law* 153

Schmutzler, A, 'The Relation between Competition and Innovation: Why is it Such a Mess?' (2010) Centre for Economic Policy Research Discussion Paper No 7640, http://papers.ssrn.com/sol3/papers.cfm?abstract_id=1539312

Schweitzer, H, 'Competition Law and Public Policy: Reconsidering an Uneasy Relationship. The Example of Art 81' (2007) EUI Working Papers-Law 2007/30

—— 'The History, Interpretation and Underlying Principles of Section 2 Sherman Act and Article 82 EC' in C-D Ehlermann and M Marquis (eds), *European Competition Law Annual 2007: A Reformed Approach to Article 82 TEC* (Hart Publishing, 2008) 119–64

Scitovsky, T, 'Economies of Scale, Competition and European Integration' [1956] *American Economic Review* 71

Scotford, E, 'Mapping the Article 174(2) Case Law: A First Step to Analysis Community Environmental Principles' (2008) 8 *Yearbook of European Environmental Law* 1

Scott, C, 'Governing without Law or Governing without Government? New-ish Governance and the Legitimacy of the EU' (2009) 15 *European Law Journal* 160

Semmelmann, C, 'The European Union's Economic Constitution under the Lisbon Treaty: Soul-Searching among Lawyers Shifts the Focus to Procedure' (2010) 35 *European Law Review* 516

Shaw, J, 'Citizenship: Contrasting Dynamics at the Interface of Integration and Constitutionalism' in P Craig and G de Búrca (eds), *The Evolution of EU Law* (2nd edn, Oxford University Press, 2011) 575–609

Shelanski, H and Sidak, G, 'Antitrust Divestiture in Network Industries' (2001) 68 *University of Chicago Law Review* 1

Sidak, G and Teece, D, 'Dynamic Competition in Antitrust Law' (2009) 5 *Journal of Competition Law and Economics* 581

Singham, S, 'Competition and Innovation: A Non-zero Sum Approach to Economic Growth' (2010) 2 *Competition Policy International Antitrust Journal*, www.competition-policyinternational.com

Siragusa, M, 'The Application of Article 86 to the Pricing Policy of Dominant Companies: Discriminatory and Unfair Prices' (1979) 16 *Common Market Law Review* 179

Slot, P-J, 'Harmonisation' (1996) 21 *European Law Review* 378

—— 'The Past, Present and Future of Competition Law in the European Union' in A Arnul, C Barnard, M Dougan and E Spaventa (eds), *A Constitutional Order of States? Essays in EU Law in Honour of Alan Dashwood* (Hart Publishing, 2011) 375–97

Snell, J, 'Private Parties and the Free Movement of Goods and Services' in M Adenas and W-H Roth, *Services and Free Movement in EU Law* (Oxford University Press, 2002) 211–43

—— 'Free Movement of Pharmaceutical Products: An Overdose of Cheap Drugs?' (2003) *European Business Law Review* 507

—— 'Who's Got the Power? Free Movement and Allocation of Competences in EC Law' (2003) 22 *Yearbook of European Law* 323

—— 'EU Courts and Intellectual Property: A Tale of Hercules, Zeus and Cyclops' (2004) 29 *European Law Review* 178

—— 'Economic Aims as Justification for Restrictions on Free Movement' in A Schrauwen (eds), *Rule of Reason: Rethinking Another Classic of European Legal Doctrine* (Europa Law, 2005) 35–56

—— '"European Constitutional Settlement", an Ever Closer Union, and the Treaty of Lisbon: Democracy or Relevance?' (2008) 33 *European Law Review* 619

—— 'The Notion of Market Access: A Concept or a Slogan?' (2010) 47 *Common Market Law Review* 437

—— 'The Notion of and a General Test for Abuse of Rights' in R de la Feria and S Vogenauer (eds), *Prohibition of Abuse of Law: A New General Principle of EU Law?* (Hart Publishing, 2011) 219

Sorensen, E, 'Abuse of Rights in Community Law: A Principle of Substance or Merely Rethoric?' (2006) 43 *Common Market Law Review* 423

Spaventa, E, 'Leaving Keck Behind? The Free Movement of Goods after the Rulings in *Commission v Italy* and *Mickelsson and Roos*' (2009) 34 *European Law Review* 914

Steenbergen, J, 'Proportionality in Competition Law and Policy' (2008) 35 *Legal Issues of Economic Integration* 259

Stevenson, C, 'Exhausting All the Arguments: A Short Guide to the Economics of Trademark Exhaustion' in J Grayston (ed), *European Economics and Law-Competition, Single Market, Trade* (Palladian Law, 1999) 88–94

Straetmans, G, 'Market Access, The Outer Limits of the Free Movement of Goods and … the Law?' in M Bulterman, L Hancher, A McDonnell and H Sevenster (eds), *Views of European Law from the Mountain: Liber Amicorum Piet Jan Slot* (Kluwer Law International, 2009) 91–105

Streit, M and Mussler, W, 'The Economic Constitution of the European Community: From "Rome" to "Maastricht"' (1995) 1 *European Law Journal* 5

Sunstein, C, 'Willingness to Pay vs Welfare' [2007] *Harvard Law and Policy Review* 303

Szyszczak, E, 'Karen Murphy: Decoding Licences and Territorial Exclusivity' (2012) 3 *Journal of European Competition Law and Practice* 169

Temple Lang, J, 'Privatisation of Social Welfare: European Union Competition Law Rules' in E Spaventa and M Dougan (eds), *Social Welfare and EU Law* (Hart Publishing, 2005) 45–77

—— 'Article 10 EC: The Most Important "General Principle" of Community Law' in U Bernitz, J Nergelius, C Cardner and X Groussot (eds), *General Principles of EC Law in a Process of Development: Reports from a Conference in Stockholm, 23–24 March 2007, Organised by the Swedish Network for European Legal Studies* (Kluwer Law International, 2008) 75–114

Thorelli, H, 'Antitrust in Europe: National Policies after 1945' (1958–59) 26 *University of Chicago Law Review* 222

Townley, C, 'Which Goals Count in Article 101 TFEU? Public Policy and its Discontents: The OFT's Roundtable Discussion on Article 101(3) of the Treaty on the Functioning of the European Union' (2011) 32(9) *European Competition Law Review* 441

Tridimas, T, 'Proportionality in Community Law: Searching for the Appropriate Standard of Scrutiny' in E Ellis (ed), *The Principle of Proportionality in the Laws of Europe* (Hart Publishing, 1999) 65–84

—— 'Competence after Lisbon: The Elusive Search for Bright Lines' in D Ashiagbor, N Countouris and I Lianos (eds), *The European Union after the Treaty of Lisbon* (Cambridge University Press, 2012) 47–77

Tryfonidou, A, 'The Outer Limits of Article 28 EC: Purely Internal Situations and the Development of the Court's Approach through the Years' in C Barnard and O Odudu (eds), *The Outer Limits of European Union Law* (Hart Publishing, 2009) 197–223

Tsouloufas, G, 'Limiting Pharmaceutical Parallel Trade in the European Union: Regulatory and Economic Justifications' (2011) 36 *European Law Review* 385

Ullrich, H, 'Anti-Unfair Competition Law and Anti-Trust Law: A Continental Conundrum?' (2005) EUI Working Paper LAW No 2005/01

Valletti, T, 'Differential Pricing, Parallel Trade, and the Incentive to Invest' (2006) 70 *Journal of International Economics* 314

Van de Gronden, J, 'Rule of Reason and Convergence in Internal Market Law and Competition Law' in A Schrauwen (ed), *Rule of Reason: Rethinking Another Classic of European Legal Doctrine* (Europa Law, 2005) 77–94

—— 'The Internal Market, the State and Private Initiative' (2006) 33 *Legal Issues of Economic Integration* 105

Van der Esch, B, 'The Principles of Interpretation Applied by the Court of Justice of the European Communities and their Relevance for the Scope of the EEC Competition Rules' (1991–92) 15 *Fordham International Law Journal* 366

Van der Vijver, T, 'Article 102 TFEU: How to Claim the Application of Objective Justifications in the Case of *Prima Facie* Dominance Abuses' (2013) 4(2) *Journal of European Competition Law and Practice* 121

Van Eijken, H and de Vries, S, 'A New Route into the Promised Land? Being a European Citizen after Ruiz Zambrano' (2011) 36(5) *European Law Review* 704

Van Elsuwege, P, 'Shifting the Boundaries? European Union Citizenship and the Scope of Application of EU Law: Case No. C-34/09, *Gerardo Ruiz Zambrano v Office National de l'Emploi*' (2011) 38(3) *Legal Issues of Economic Integration* 263

Van Gerven, W, 'Twelve Years of EEC Competition Law (1962–1973) Revisited' (1974) 11 *Common Market Law Review* 38

Van Gestel, R and Micklitz, H-W, 'European Integration through Standardization: How Judicial Review is Breaking Down the Club House of Private Standardization Bodies' (2013) 50 *Common Market Law Review* 145

Vedder, H, 'Of Jurisdiction and Justification. Why Competition is Good for "Non- economic" Goals, But May Need to be Restricted' (2009) 6 *Competition Law Review* 51

Veljanovski, C, 'Margin Squeezes in Telecoms' (2008) www.casecon.com/data/pdfs/MSIntermedia2008.pdf

Velu, C and Iyer, S, 'Dominance and Innovation' (2010) Cambridge Working Papers in Economics 1009 www.econ.cam.ac.uk/dae/repec/cam/pdf/cwpe1009.pdf

Vickers, J, 'Abuse of Market Power' (speech to the 31st Conference of the European Association for Research in Industrial Economics, Berlin, 3 September 2004) www.oft.gov.uk/shared_oft/speeches/spe0304.pdf

Vogelenzang, P, 'Abuse of Dominant Position in Article 86. The Problem of Causality and Some Applications' (1976) 13 *Common Market Law Review* 61

Vossesstein, A, 'Corporate Efforts to Influence Public Authorities, and the EC Rules on Competition' (2000) 37 *Common Market Law Review* 1383

Waelbroeck, D, 'The Assessment of Efficiencies under Article 102 and the Commission's Guidance Paper' in F Etro and I Kokkoris (eds), *Competition Law and the Enforcement of Article 102 TFEU* (Oxford University Press, 2010) 115–27

Wainwright, R and Bouquet A, 'State Intervention and Action in EC Competition Law' [2003] *Fordham Corporate Law Institute* 539–79

Wartin, C, 'Germany's Social Market Economy' in A Kilmarnock (ed), *The Social Market and the State* (Social Market Foundation, 1999) 89–104

Wasmeier, M, 'The Integration of Environmental Protection as a General Rule for Interpreting Community Law' (2001) 38 *Common Market Law Review* 159–77

Weatherill, S, 'Beyond Pre-emption? Shared Competence and Constitutional Change in the European Community' in D O'Keeffee and P Twomey (eds), *Legal Issues of the Maastricht Treaty* (Chancery Law, 1994)

—— 'After *Keck*: Some Thoughts on How to Clarify the Clarification' (1996) 33 Common Market Law Review 885–906

—— 'Case C-415/93 *Union Royale Belge des Sociétés de Football Association and others v Bosman and others.* Article 177 Reference by the Cour d'Appel, Liège, on the Interpretation of Articles 48, 85 and 86 EC. Judgement of the European Court of Justice of 15 December 1995 (Case Comment)' (1996) 33 *Common Market Law Review* 991

—— 'Pre-emption, Harmonisation and the Distribution of Competence to Regulate the Internal Market' in C Barnard and J Scott (eds), *The Law of the Single European Market: Unpacking the Premises* (Hart Publishing, 2002)

—— 'Supply and Demand for Internal Market Regulation: Strategies, Preferences and Interpretation' in N Nic Shuibhne (ed), *Regulating the Internal Market* (Edward Elgar, 2006) 29–60

—— 'I. Free Movement of Goods' in J McMahon (ed), *Current Developments: European Union Law* (2009) 58 *International and Comparative Law Quarterly* 985–93

—— 'Eugene Buttigieg: Competition Law: Safeguarding the Consumer Interest. A Comparative Analysis of US Antitrust Law and EC Competition Law (Book Review)' (2010) 33 *Journal of Consumer Policy* 287

—— 'The Road to Ruin: "Restrictions on Use" and the Circular Lifecycle of Article 34 TFEU' (2012) Oxford University Legal Research Paper Series, Paper No 58/2012

Weiler, J, 'The Transformation of Europe' (1990–91) 100 *Yale Law Journal* 2403

—— 'Mutual Recognition, Functional Equivalence and Harmonization in the Evolution of the European Common Market and the WTO' in F Padoa-Schioppa (ed), *The Principle of Mutual Recognition in the European Integration Process* (Palgrave Macmillan, 2005) 25–59

Wenneras, P and Boe-Moen, K, 'Selling Arrangements, Keeping *Keck*' (2010) 35 *European Law Review* 387

Williamson, O, 'Economies as an Antitrust Defense: The Welfare Tradeoffs' [1968] *American Economic Review* 18

—— 'Economies as an Antitrust Defence Revisited' (1977) 125 *University of Pennsylvania Law Review* 699

Wils, W, 'Discretion and Prioritisation in Public Antitrust Enforcement, in Particular EU Antitrust Enforcement' (2011) 34 *World Competition Law and Economics Review* 353

Wilsher, D, 'Does Keck Discrimination Make Any Sense? An Assessment of the Non-discrimination Principle within the European Single Market' (2008) 33 *European Law Review* 3

Wollenschläger, F, 'A New Fundamental Freedom beyond Market Integration: Union Citizenship and its Dynamics for Shifting the Economic Paradigm of European Integration' (2011) 17 *European Law Journal* 1

Wood, A, 'Case Comment: The CJEU's Ruling in the Premier League Pub TV Cases: The Final Whistle Beckons: Joined Cases *Football Association Premier League Ltd v QC Leisure* (C-403/08) *and Murphy v Media Protection Services Ltd* (C-429/08)' (2012) 34 *European Intellectual Property Review* 203

Wyatt, D, 'Horizontal Effect of Fundamental Freedoms and the Right to Equality after Viking and Mangold, and the Implications for Community Competence' [2008] *Croatian Yearbook of European Law and Policy* 1

Zanon di Valgiurata, L, 'Primary Discrimination under Article 86 of the EEC Treaty: The *United Brands* Case' (1982) 31 *International and Comparative Law Quarterly* 36

Zevgolis, N, 'Anti-competitive Conduct from Public or Privileged Enterprises: Towards a Per Se Abuse of Dominant Position? Applicability of the Provision of TFEU Article 106(2) by National Competition Authorities' (2012) 33 *European Competition Law Review* 84

Zimmer, D, 'Competition Law *De Lege Ferenda*' in R Zach, A Heinemann and A Kallerhals (eds), *The Development of Competition Law: Global Perspectives* (Edward Elgar, 2010) 320–30

Index

9 781509 909278

Printed by Libri Plureos GmbH in Hamburg,
Germany